HOLMAN
Old Testament Commentary

HOLMAN
Old Testament
Commentary

I & II *Chronicles*

GENERAL EDITOR
Max Anders

AUTHOR
Winfried Corduan

HOLMAN
REFERENCE

Nashville, Tennessee

Holman Old Testament Commentary
© 2004 Broadman & Holman Publishers
Nashville, Tennessee

ISBN 0-8054-9468-5
Dewey Decimal Classification:
Subject Heading: BIBLE. O.T. Chronicles

Chronicles / Winfried Corduan
p.   cm. — (Holman Old Testament commentary)
Includes bibliographical references. (p.).
ISBN
  1. Bible. Chronicles—Commentaries.   I. Title.   II. Series.

—dc21

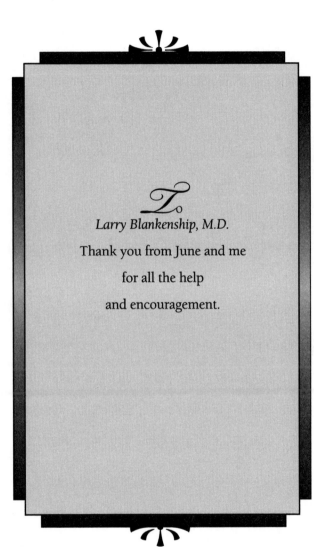

To

Larry Blankenship, M.D.

Thank you from June and me

for all the help

and encouragement.

Contents

Contents

Editorial Preface

Today's church hungers for Bible teaching, and Bible teachers hunger for resources to guide them in teaching God's Word. The Holman Old Testament Commentary provides the church with the food to feed the spiritually hungry in an easily digestible format. The result: new spiritual vitality that the church can readily use.

Bible teaching should result in new interest in the Scriptures, expanded Bible knowledge, discovery of specific scriptural principles, relevant applications, and exciting living. The unique format of the Holman Old Testament Commentary includes sections to achieve these results for every Old Testament book.

Opening quotations stimulate thinking and lead to an introductory illustration and discussion that draw individuals and study groups into the Word of God. Verse-by-verse commentary interprets the passage with the aim of equipping them to understand and live God's Word in a contemporary setting. A conclusion draws together the themes identified in the passage under discussion and suggests application for it. Bible teachers and pastors will find the teaching outline helpful as they develop lessons and sermons.

Some of the major psalms are given additional treatment. A "Life Application" section provides additional illustrative material. "Deeper Discoveries" gives the reader a closer look at some of the words, phrases, and background material that illuminate the passage. "Issues for Discussion" is a tool to enhance learning within the group. Finally, a closing prayer is suggested.

It is the editors' prayer that this new resource for local church Bible teaching will enrich the ministry of group, as well as individual, Bible study and that it will lead God's people truly to be people of the Book, living out what God calls us to be.

Acknowledgments

When I was a college student, I worked in a Christian bookstore, and I remember looking over the commentary section and musing that some day I would like to write a commentary on a book of the Bible. I further recollect thinking that I wanted it to be on a book for which relatively few commentaries were being written. I believe that I got my wish.

Thanks must go to Steve Bond of Broadman & Holman for extending to me the opportunity to make this wish come true. Anyone who has ever worked with Steve has learned to appreciate his patience and kindness.

Max Anders, general editor of this series and pastor of Castleview Baptist Church, is the consummate Bible teacher. When this project came along, before June and I were called to another ministry, we took a few Sundays to hear Max's preaching. Every sermon is a banquet of Bible exposition. This commentary series could not be in better hands.

I wonder how many books written over the last fifteen years mention Paul House of Wheaton College in their acknowledgments. From the moment Paul came out of graduate school and started to work on publishing his dissertation, he has encouraged his colleagues to write books with words, deeds, and examples. Specifically, Paul was the one who mentioned to Steve Bond, first in connection with Shepherd's Notes, that he knew someone who would be interested in writing on 1 and 2 Chronicles.

Except for some sample chapters, almost all this commentary was written from February to April 2003, thanks to a sabbatical from teaching at Taylor University. Let me mention by name those who specifically advocated or facilitated my receiving this time for writing: David Guyertson, Dwight Jessup, Steve Bedi, Faye Chechowich, Mike Harbin, and Ted Dorman.

June has, as always, been an incredible support for me during this intensive time of writing. The proofreading she did and invaluable suggestions she made do not even begin to scratch the surface of how much help she provides constantly to me in my writing efforts.

First and Second Chronicles are not among the most widely studied books of the Bible. It is my fervent hope that I may have contributed to making this section of God's Word more accessible. If I have been successful in this at all, I need to give credit to two writers, both now deceased, who have had a deep impact on my love for the Old Testament. First I need to remember J. Barton Payne, a former professor, who combined the highest standards of fidelity to the Bible with a willingness to try some fresh approaches. And second, I am indebted to a man I never met: John Hercus, the Australian eye surgeon who helped us to see the people of the Old Testament as true human beings. Dr. Hercus confronted us with the reality of God's work by holding up the people with whom he worked as a mirror for ourselves.

Finally, I dedicate this book to Dr. Larry Blankenship. He has not only looked after the physical health of June and me for a number of years now, but he has become a wonderful friend in the process. Thank you for all you have done for us!

Winfried Corduan

Holman Old Testament Commentary Contributors

Vol. 1, Genesis
ISBN 0-8054-9461-8
Kenneth O. Gangel and
Stephen J. Bramer

Vol. 2, Exodus, Leviticus, Numbers
ISBN 0-8054-9462-6
Glen Martin

Vol. 3, Deuteronomy
ISBN 0-8054-9463-4
Doug McIntosh

Vol. 4, Joshua
ISBN 0-8054-9464-2
Kenneth O. Gangel

Vol. 5, Judges, Ruth
ISBN 0-8054-9465-0
W. Gary Phillips

Vol. 6, 1 & 2 Samuel
ISBN 0-8054-9466-9
Stephen Andrews

Vol. 7, 1 & 2 Kings
ISBN 0-8054-9467-7
Gary Inrig

Vol. 8, 1 & 2 Chronicles
ISBN 0-8054-9468-5
Winfried Corduan

Vol. 9, Ezra, Nehemiah, Esther
ISBN 0-8054-9469-3
Knute Larson and Kathy Dahlen

Vol. 10, Job
ISBN 0-8054-9470-7
Steven J. Lawson

Vol. 11, Psalms 1–75
ISBN 0-8054-9471-5
Steven J. Lawson

Vol. 12, Psalms 76–150
ISBN 0-8054-9481-2
Steven J. Lawson

Vol. 13, Proverbs
ISBN 0-8054-9472-3
Max Anders

Vol. 14, Ecclesiastes, Song of Songs
ISBN 0-8054-9482-0
David George Moore and Daniel L. Akin

Vol. 15, Isaiah
ISBN 0-8054-9473-1
Trent C. Butler

Vol. 16, Jeremiah, Lamentations
ISBN 0-8054-9474-X
Fred M. Wood and Ross McLaren

Vol. 17, Ezekiel
ISBN 0-8054-9475-8
Mark F. Rooker

Vol. 18, Daniel
ISBN 0-8054-9476-6
Kenneth O. Gangel

**Vol. 19, Hosea, Joel, Amos,
Obadiah, Jonah, Micah**
ISBN 0-8054-9477-4
Trent C. Butler

**Vol. 20, Nahum, Habakkuk,
Zephaniah, Haggai, Zechariah, Malachi**
ISBN 0-8054-9478-2
Stephen R. Miller

Holman New Testament Commentary Contributors

Vol. 1, Matthew
ISBN 0-8054-0201-2
Stuart K. Weber

Vol. 2, Mark
ISBN 0-8054-0202-0
Rodney L. Cooper

Vol. 3, Luke
ISBN 0-8054-0203-9
Trent C. Butler

Vol. 4, John
ISBN 0-8054-0204-7
Kenneth O. Gangel

Vol. 5, Acts
ISBN 0-8054-0205-5
Kenneth O. Gangel

Vol. 6, Romans
ISBN 0-8054-0206-3
Kenneth Boa and William Kruidenier

Vol. 7, 1 & 2 Corinthians
ISBN 0-8054-0207-1
Richard L. Pratt Jr.

Vol. 8, Galatians, Ephesians, Philippians, Colossians
ISBN 0-8054-0208-X
Max Anders

Vol. 9, 1 & 2 Thessalonians, 1 & 2 Timothy, Titus, Philemon
ISBN 0-8054-0209-8
Knute Larson

Vol. 10, Hebrews, James
ISBN 0-8054-0211-X
Thomas D. Lea

Vol. 11, 1 & 2 Peter, 1, 2, 3 John, Jude
ISBN 0-8054-0210-1
David Walls and Max Anders

Vol. 12, Revelation
ISBN 0-8054-0212-8
Kendell H. Easley

Holman Old Testament Commentary

Twenty volumes designed for Bible study and teaching to enrich the local church and God's people.

Series Editor	Max Anders
Managing Editor	Steve Bond
Project Editor	Dean Richardson
Product Development Manager	Ricky D. King
Marketing Manager	Stephanie Huffman
Executive Editor	David Shepherd
Page Composition	TF Designs, Greenbrier, TN

Introduction to

1 & 2 Chronicles

THE GOSPEL ACCORDING TO EZRA

The book of Chronicles epitomizes God's message of good news to the people of the Old Testament. It was a book of hope for a nation that was looking for a way to reconnect with God's will. After a lengthy period of spiritual apathy, the book burst on the scene to inject a floundering nation with a new sense of spiritual excitement.

This may sound like an extravagant description for a book that has the reputation of creating a soothing stupor in people trying to read through the first nine chapters. First and Second Chronicles tax our patience with their seemingly interminable lists of names. You may start to read Chronicles and decide quickly that you don't see the least spark of excitement in it, spiritual or otherwise.

But you do not live in Jerusalem in the fifth century B.C. Chronicles will not speak to you in the same way it spoke to its original readers. But this does not mean that you cannot come to understand why Chronicles was a book of hope for its time. As we get to know the content of the book, we will even come to see what is universal in God's message, surpassing the framework of the times in which and for which it was written.

We will call the message of 1 and 2 Chronicles the "gospel according to Ezra." The term *gospel* does not refer to the identical teaching as the Christian gospel in important respects. First, it is not primarily a message of personal salvation. Even though the salvation of individuals was always an important part of the Old Testament, and it is in Chronicles as well, the primary focus was often on the corporate people of God, the nation of Israel. A person's relationship to God came in a package with his or her relationship to the people of God. So the gospel at which we are looking in Chronicles is a word to the nation. Second, the "gospel according to Ezra" is not about the coming of Christ into the world, his death, and his resurrection. These events were still far in the future. Chronicles is about how God selected a line of kings, how he provided a temple, and how he called priests and Levites to administer the rites of the temple.

Still, there are fundamental truths that the Christian gospel and the "gospel according to Ezra" share. The gospel begins with the basic truth of human sinfulness, that the natural condition of human beings is alienation from God. We will find the descriptions of depraved behavior by various people in Chronicles to be sufficiently explicit to make this point. But we also see in Chronicles how God extended his hand and provided his people with a way to be reconciled to him. This way centers on the temple in Jerusalem, the king as custodian of this temple, and the priests and Levites, whose job it was to lead the people to obey the Lord. But we also will see many failures on the part of king and people to live up to God's calling.

Another component of this gospel is divine judgment. The divine offer of mercy makes little sense if there is no difference between obedience and disobedience; disobedience will garner severe punishment. But still God's offer of redemption is always there. It is expressed primarily in terms of the nation returning to proper worship in the temple, but it is not just a mechanical performance of rituals that makes everything OK. God wants his people to return to him with hearts that are committed to seeking his will.

Chronicles is a road map. By providing information about the people's heritage, their kings, their priests, and their temple, the book pulls together all the Old Testament teachings about what it means to be God's chosen people.

We will see how this culmination of the Old Testament gospel message works itself out as we look at the content of 1 and 2 Chronicles more closely.

TIME AND CIRCUMSTANCES OF WRITING

Chronicles was one of the last books of the Old Testament to be written. In our Bibles it is placed right after 1 and 2 Samuel and 1 and 2 Kings as a part of the historical books. But in the traditional Hebrew compilation of the canon, it was placed dead last. The content of the book gives us information about when it must have been written. Its last verse refers to the decree from Cyrus for the restoration of the people from the Babylonian exile, but in an earlier passage we find the genealogy of several generations after the restoration (1 Chr. 3:17–21). From what we know about the history of Israel, the book was written some time after the Jews had returned to Jerusalem. They had rebuilt the temple; there was weak local government; and devotion to the Lord was perfunctory.

Chronicles was written at a time when the people needed to be reminded of who they were. They needed to be told once again that they were special in God's eyes and that they could plug into a long heritage of blessings if they would concentrate on living up to their identity. All these attributes fit with the time of Ezra and Nehemiah in the fifth century B.C. When these two men came to Jerusalem, they found a group of people who had a superficial awareness of God. These people maintained a shallow observance of the temple rituals, but they had lost their zeal and sense of identity as God's special people. The book of Chronicles was what they needed.

AUTHORSHIP

The book does not claim the authorship of a specific person, so we have to rely on tradition, inference, and speculation. There was a strong ancient tradition that the priest Ezra wrote the books of Chronicles—not a bad start, though not definitive. Nevertheless, there are some further good reasons to believe that Ezra was the author of Chronicles.

1. The last two verses of Chronicles (2 Chr. 36:22–23) are identical to Ezra 1:2b–3a. Furthermore, Ezra 1:36 then actually completes the thought begun in the sentence they have in common.

2. In style and subject matter, Chronicles and Ezra are identical. Both show the same love for lists, genealogies, the purity of temple worship, and the privileges and obligations of the Levites. If one were simply to add Ezra to Chronicles, someone reading all the way through these books would not notice any difference—other than the fact that Ezra starts to speak in the first person when the story gets to his own time.

3. Given the profound focus of Chronicles on the temple and the priesthood, one might expect the author to have been a priest. This holds true for Ezra (Ezra 7:1–6).

4. The nature of the project demanded that the person who wrote Chronicles was knowledgeable and that he had access to written sources. The person who wrote 1 and 2 Chronicles reminds us that he had access to official royal records. One might expect a man of Ezra's stature to have this background, but there is more to go on. Ezra and Nehemiah became friends and coworkers in the restoration of Judah, and there is some strong data to support the idea that Nehemiah assembled a sizable library (in the "apocryphal" book of 2 Maccabees 2:13–15). Whether Ezra actually checked out scrolls from Nehemiah's collection is not as important as the fact that there were scrolls available which contained the information that Ezra would have needed for the task of writing Chronicles. Two of these scrolls were of the books of Samuel and Kings, but the author used other sources as well.

5. The author of 1 and 2 Chronicles must have been in a prominent position of leadership. There would have been no point in someone compiling all this information if it was not to serve as an important tool in the national revival. Again, Ezra fits the bill nicely.

Thus there is good reason to believe that Ezra was the author of 1 and 2 Chronicles. I will generally refer to the author with the traditional term, "the chronicler," but from time to time, I will speak of the author as Ezra.

THE SOURCES USED FOR CHRONICLES

Throughout the book, particularly at the conclusion of describing each king's reign, Ezra refers us to certain sources for more information. In addition, it is clear that he used numerous other Bible passages to compile his lists—for example the genealogical material, much of which is found in the first five books of the Old Testament. Among the sources that Ezra cites, we find the following:

- 1 and 2 Samuel (e.g., 1 Chr. 29:29);
- 1 and 2 Kings (e.g., 2 Chr. 27:7);
- prophets, such as Isaiah, whose writings are a part of the Bible (e.g., 2 Chr. 32:32);
- prophets, such as Nathan, from whom we do not have any writings, but who are familiar to us because of their role in the narratives (e.g., 1 Chr. 29:29);
- prophets, such as Iddo, of whom we know nothing beyond specific allusions (e.g., 2 Chr. 9:29).

On the whole, the identification of sources for the chronicler can be overrated. For some liberal critics, the fact that the chronicler refers to specific historical sources in order to validate his account suggests that he made them up as deliberate deceptions. Assuming that the references to various sources indicate historical reliability, not deception, it is not Ezra's sources but what he did with the information that is important.

THE STRUCTURE OF CHRONICLES

There is reason to believe that 1 and 2 Chronicles were bound together at some point as one scroll, although this does not rule out the possibility that it originated in two scrolls. In either case there can be no question of the bond between the two halves; clearly 2 Chronicles is a continuation of 1 Chronicles. The major divisions of these two books are as follows:

Chapters	Content	Significance
1 Chr. 1–9	Genealogies, with emphasis on the tribes of Judah and Levi	Preparing the stage for the kingdom of Judah and the priestly tribe
1 Chr. 10	Death of Saul	Transition to David's kingdom; declaration that the throne belonged to the tribe of Judah, not Benjamin
1 Chr. 11–29	Reign of David	The ideal kingdom phase 1; detailed preparations for the temple
2 Chr. 1–9	Reign of Solomon	The ideal kingdom phase 2; installation of the temple
2 Chr. 10–36	Kings of Judah	Succession of kings, all of whom were descended from David, who implemented the standards of David and Solomon to varying degrees

Let us see what God teaches us about his work in the world as he taught his own people long ago through Ezra and the book of Chronicles.

1 Chronicles 1:1–54

The Roots of God's People: From Adam to Jacob

I. **INTRODUCTION**
The Power of Discovering Your Roots

II. **COMMENTARY**
A verse-by-verse explanation of the chapter.

III. **CONCLUSION**
How to Fix Shoes

An overview of the principles and applications from the chapter.

IV. **LIFE APPLICATION**
A Reluctant Evangelist

Melding the chapter to life.

V. **PRAYER**
Tying the chapter to life with God.

VI. **DEEPER DISCOVERIES**
Historical, geographical, and grammatical enrichment of the commentary.

VII. **TEACHING OUTLINE**
Suggested step-by-step group study of the chapter.

VIII. **ISSUES FOR DISCUSSION**
Zeroing the chapter in on daily life.

"*A*re you the Sons of Adam and the Daughters of Eve?" the Beaver said. "We're some of them," said Peter.

C . S . L e w i s

1 Chronicles 1:1–54

IN A NUTSHELL

*T*he Israelites could trace their descent from Adam to Jacob, the father of the twelve tribes, by way of Seth, Noah, and Abraham. Just as they could look back on a great heritage, so we can look back on a heritage of God's grace in the lives of people who came before us. Just as they needed to live up to God's calling, so we need to pass the treasure of God's gospel on to the next generation.

The Roots of God's People: From Adam to Jacob

I. INTRODUCTION

The Power of Discovering Your Roots

*I*n 1977 large television audiences watched a miniseries based on the book *Roots* by Alex Haley. This noted African-American author had traced back his ancestry and was now telling the story of his own family background. He began this family history with an African man named Kunta Kinte, who was enslaved and transported to the United States. Haley then followed the fortune of Kunta Kinte's descendants, his own forebears, up to the time of emancipation. It was a story of personal strength as well as human weakness, and it exposed much of the cruelty to which Africans were subjected as slaves in America.

Many analysts were surprised by the intensity with which people reacted to this program. African-Americans all over the country, reminded of how their ancestors had been abused, restated their grievances. Many white Americans once again confessed their guilt and sorrow over the events of the past.

People identify not only with their personal past but also with the past of their ancestors. If their forefathers were treated badly, they still feel the offense, and if an earlier generation accomplished great things, they take pride in those deeds. How we think of ourselves is often influenced by how we think of our ancestors.

Genealogies can help us uncover the history of our people, and thus our own history. The first nine chapters of 1 Chronicles are primarily genealogies, and no one would deny that these are difficult passages to plow through. We read lengthy lists of names that appear as meaningless to us as they are hard to pronounce. But the purpose of these lists was obvious to the original readers of the book. When the people of God were trying to reestablish their identity as a nation during Ezra's time, they were hungry for information about who they were and what they had been through. What did it mean to be a Jew? The genealogies provided important knowledge to help cement their identity.

II. COMMENTARY

The Roots of God's People: From Adam to Jacob

MAIN IDEA: *The origin of the people of God begins with Adam and leads to Jacob (Israel). All human beings, including the Ishmaelites and Edomites who are more closely related to the Hebrews, branched off the same line.*

A Adam to Abraham (1:1–27)

SUPPORTING IDEA: *As many nations developed from Adam, one line of descent would lead to Abraham, the father of God's chosen people.*

1:1–3. We begin with **Adam**. Of course. But is this a fact worth noting? It certainly is a fact to anyone who knows anything about biblical history. The original readers of 1 Chronicles would have been aware of the fact that all humanity began with Adam. Even contemporary skeptics who give little credence to the Bible would recognize "Adam" as a figurative reference to the first human being. Everyone has heard that the human race started with Adam, so why state the obvious?

Nevertheless, in terms of the larger point that the chronicler was possibly making, there is significance in this first verse. All humanity had its start in Adam. It follows as a result that all human beings are united in their common origin. There is only one human race—that which began with Adam—and we are all equal in our descent from him. If this statement seems too obvious to need mentioning, let us focus on one contrasting account, just as an example of how people could believe something to the contrary.

Hinduism has a number of creation myths. In one of these myths, the human race is considered to be descended from the disintegrating body of Purusha, the ancient ancestor. But different people were produced from different parts of Purusha, with the highest caste of Hinduism, the Brahmins, stemming from his head and the lowest caste, the Shudras, arising from his feet. Thus in the very beginnings of the human race, the Indian mythology creates a distinction among people. But the biblical narrative never teaches anything other than that human beings have one common origin in Adam; the later divisions of people had other causes.

The people of God are united in their humanity with all others. Not even the Jews, God's chosen people, are anything but the descendants of Adam in their origin. Their subsequent "chosenness" is based on a call from God, not on a separate creation.

The list continues through the ancient ancestors, pursuing the line of **Seth** up to **Noah**. Abel, because of his unfortunate death, had no descendants, and the chronicler is not interested in the fallen race of Cain. But note that Cain's line in the biblical account of Genesis is just as much descended from Adam as Seth's was, and that the separation of Cain's line occurred because of Cain's sinful act. As this genealogy in Chronicles is basically a list of people and not events, we find here no mention of the stories that Genesis tells of these people.

1:4–7. The chronicler now gives us the line of descent from **Noah**. At this point the list branches out in three directions, one for each of the three sons of Noah. The writer starts with the branches that he will not pursue further—**Japheth** and **Ham**—and then picks up the thread of the line that continues toward his end goal—**Shem**.

This account parallels closely Genesis 10; however, Chronicles does not mention the geographic distribution of the various groups, so we do not get the same information of the repopulation of the world after the flood into three basic areas. In Genesis we see that the descendants of Japheth migrated primarily into what is now southeastern Europe and Turkey; the offspring of Ham located in northern Africa and in the land of Canaan; and the Semites became established in Mesopotamia. The latter are the group from whom the line continues to Abraham.

Japheth had seven sons, but we are given information about only two of them—**Gomer** and **Javan**—and then only the names of their sons. On the whole, we know that the Japhethites did not figure as prominently in the history of Israel as the Hamites or other Semites. The one nation in the Japhethite line that eventually had a serious impact on Israel was Persia.

1:8–16. A Bible student reading the list of the sons of **Ham** will run across a few familiar names. It is safe to say that the list emphasizes those descendants whose offspring turned into larger groups, sometimes even identified with geographic locations, many of which are important to the story of the Israelites. Among the names we might recognize are **Cush**, usually identified with Ethiopia; **Canaan**, whose name came to be synonymous with Israel's promised land; the Philistines, Israel's future enemy; and the ancient inhabitants of the land of Canaan, such as the Hittites, Jebusites, and Amorites.

A name we might not recognize is **Mizraim**. This is another name for Egypt, and Israel had a long and eventful relationship with this nation. The stage is set for future encounters with these people in history. The chronicler makes a special reference to the mighty **Nimrod**, whose prowess had become proverbial a long time before (Gen. 10:9).

1:17–27. Finally, the line of **Shem** leads us to **Abraham**, but not without a little exploration of a further side branch. Actually we get some of the same information twice. The direct line is stated in verses 24–27, while the lengthier account in verses 17–23 also includes the extraneous line of Joktan. Two individuals stand out in this passage: **Eber** and his son **Peleg**.

Eber is important because his name may be responsible for what became the usual name for the entire nation, the "Hebrews," who would thus be the "descendants of Eber." Thus, one of the original readers of the book might have taken special note as Eber's name came up.

For Eber's son **Peleg** we have a reference to the **time the earth was divided**. One would probably not be going too far out on a limb in inferring that this expression applies to the chaos resulting from the tower of Babel (Gen. 11). So we have just a tidbit, only a teaser, to connect the list of names with a well-known event.

Peleg's brother **Joktan** did not have the honor of being in the line of promise. But he was the father of thirteen sons, so he left his own heritage.

Verses 24–27 restate the list up to Peleg, leave out Joktan and his descendants, and continue on to Abraham, here called by his original name Abram (traditionally translated as "exalted father"), which in the next verse is transformed to his covenant name Abraham ("father of many").

Ⓑ Abraham to Jacob (1:28–34)

> **SUPPORTING IDEA:** Abraham's son Ishmael became the father of a nation, and Keturah gave Abraham many sons. But it is through Jacob (Israel) that the promised line continues.

1:28. This verse contains a surprise. The chronicler introduces us to the **sons of Abraham** by mentioning **Isaac and Ishmael**. Anyone who has already caught on to the chronicler's methods would anticipate that he would discuss Ishmael's offspring before Isaac's, and that is exactly what happens. However, before actually getting to Isaac, the author mentions yet another set of sons descended from Abraham—those whom he fathered by his later wife, Keturah.

1:29–31. First we read about **Ishmael**, Abraham's son by Sarah's handmaid, Hagar (Gen. 16:1–15). The chronicler does not give us any information beyond a list of Ishmael's twelve sons. But let us not forget how important the Ishmaelites became in Old Testament times as well as today. Although Abraham had to expel Ishmael from his home, thereby excluding him from God's covenant line, God also had a special blessing for Ishmael. He promised that

Ishmael would become fruitful and the father of a great nation (Gen. 17:20), and he is considered the ancestor of the Arabian tribes.

In the Qur'an, the holy book of Islam, Ishmael and not Isaac takes up the place of prominence among Abraham's sons. It is legitimate to see the beginnings of the conflict between present-day Israel and her Arab neighbors as yet another chapter in the ongoing opposition that began with Isaac and Ishmael. As a matter of fact, Genesis concludes its account of Ishmael's descendants with the statement, "And they lived in hostility toward all their brothers" (Gen. 25:18).

1:32–33. Now the chronicler inserts an overview of the sons whom Abraham had by **Keturah**, the woman whom he married after Sarah's death (Gen. 25:1). There are six of them, and we learn that at least two of them had grandsons for Abraham.

1:34. Still, the important thread continues on through **Isaac** and his two sons, **Esau** and **Israel**. The chronicler frequently uses Jacob's covenant name "Israel" when referring to him. This was the name that Jacob was given after he had wrestled with the angel of the Lord (Gen. 32:28).

C Esau and Edom (1:35–54)

SUPPORTING IDEA: *We receive information about the Edomites, an important group of people in the history of Israel.*

1:35–42. The chronicler focuses on **Esau** before concentrating on Jacob, his main interest. The key to understanding this section is Genesis 36:9, which mentions "Esau the father of the Edomites in the hill country of Seir." Here we have all three elements that make up the rest of this chapter: Esau, the fact that he was the father of the Edomites (because he was also called "Edom"), and the fact that his people lived in the hill country of Seir. These three concepts—the man Esau, the people of Edom, and the hill country of Seir—are the tie-ins for this section.

Esau had five sons, not as many as the twelve or thirteen we encountered with other prominent men earlier and will again with Jacob. But again, just as with Ishmael, we do well to keep in mind that Esau also was within the plan of God, although God's promise to him through Isaac was skimpy (Gen. 27:39–40). Essentially he was promised a hard life, servitude, and hostility toward Jacob—but eventual liberation. Nevertheless, Esau was also embraced by God's providence.

Of the various names listed here, **Amalek**, a grandson of Esau, stands out because the Amalekites eventually became one of Israel's most bitter enemies. They were the first nation Israel had to fight upon fleeing Egypt—not long after the parting of the Red Sea (Exod. 17:8–16). Not until the time of King Saul was this conflict resolved (1 Sam. 15:1–2). Without any other side remarks, we read the names of Esau's and Seir's descendants.

1:43–54. As we focus on Edom, the chronicler takes the opportunity to give us a list of the great kings of Edom. This is an ancient compilation. The text states that these kings ruled before there were kings in Israel. This would take the original list back at least to the time of the judges. But this list must be older than that, since Moses had already included it in Genesis 36.

In this list, special note is made of two men named *Hadad*. The first of the two, **Hadad son of Bedad**, fought a decisive battle against the Midianites, another of Israel's enemies. These were the same people against whom Gideon won his miraculous victory centuries later. The reference to the other **Hadad** in verse 50 stands out because the chronicler specifies who his wife was, along with his wife's mother and grandmother. Evidently **Mehetabel** was a prominent person in her day, but we know nothing else about her.

The chapter closes with a quick roll call of **the chiefs of Edom**. "Chiefs" are not the same thing as "kings." There is not enough information to specify exactly what a chief's duties might have been, perhaps those of a general in war.

MAIN IDEA REVIEW: *The origin of the people of God begins with Adam and leads to Jacob (Israel). All human beings, including the Ishmaelites and Edomites who are more closely related to the Hebrews, branch off the same line.*

III. CONCLUSION

How to Fix Shoes

From as far back as I can remember my childhood in Germany, my father mended our shoes. Usually on Saturday afternoons, he would put on an old sweater and get busy with pliers, knife, glue, and hammer. I will always picture him bent over the tripod, several tacks protruding from his lips, his eyes focused on the work before him, swinging the hammer in short, powerful strokes as he drove the nails into the new soles.

Then one Saturday afternoon, when I was about twelve years old, my father said, "I'm going to show you how to fix shoes." He walked me through all the steps involved in putting new soles on a pair of shoes, even taking a chance on having me do some of the work.

A part of my family heritage is the practice of the trade of shoemaker. Even though this craft had not been pursued by anyone in my family for several generations, everyone knew about it. Thus, passing on the skill from one generation to the next signified a certain family continuity. My father and I knew that my picking up that hammer and nailing the tacks into the sole contributed to my being a "Corduan." I had established continuity with the generations of Corduans who went before me.

But there is another heritage that outstrips the repair of shoes in significance. This is the heritage of being a part of the people of God. This is the heritage that the chronicler presents for the people of Israel. Through the long and confusing list of names, the message is loud and clear: "You have inherited a legacy of being God's chosen people. Look how the Lord has led up to this time with generation after generation of those who became his nation, and you are a part of it."

But inheriting such a legacy also brings a great responsibility. To reckon with one's past may also lead to reckoning with one's future and the obligation to extend the heritage. We must continue to pass on the knowledge of God's grace to the next generation. The chronicler saw it this way, and we should too.

PRINCIPLES

- God directs all events in human history, including the lines of descent as they are reported to us in biblical genealogies.
- All human beings are descended from Adam.
- God has a chosen line of those who are specifically his people, the Israelites.
- God also cares about those who are not among the direct line of his chosen people.
- As Christians we partake of a heritage of faith.
- As those who partake of a heritage of faith, we have the obligation to do our best to pass this heritage on to the next generation.

APPLICATIONS

- Take time to discover your heritage as a believer in Christ.
- Do all you can to understand the faith that has become your legacy.
- Evaluate your life to see if you are living as someone whose identity is by God's grace as God's child.
- Take some actions to make sure that the next generation will have the opportunity to become children of God.

IV. LIFE APPLICATION

A Reluctant Evangelist

Who is Franklin Graham? Many people don't recognize his name, but they know that of his father, the evangelist Billy Graham. When Franklin was young, it was difficult for him to be known as "Billy Graham's son," so he resorted to rebellion to assert his own identity. It was not until he was twenty-two years old, sparked by a confrontation with his dad, that Franklin finally accepted Christ as his Savior. It was still many years later that he finally agreed to become involved in the Billy Graham Evangelistic Association, for which he is now the designated successor to Billy.

The story of Franklin Graham, as he tells it himself in his book *Rebel with a Cause,* illustrates the lessons we can learn from this chapter in Chronicles.

Franklin came from a godly family. Many of us can look back, as the Israelites could, on a long line of those who walked with God.

Nevertheless, as Franklin Graham realized, being a Christian is not something we can inherit. We can rejoice over our Christian ancestors and savor our Christian homes. But our salvation depends on our personal response to Jesus Christ. We must never confuse our Christian upbringing and the Christian culture in which we live with actually being a Christian.

Billy Graham approached his son and told him he needed to make a decision for Christ. The world's most famous evangelist did not take it for granted that his son would be a Christian. Neither did he rationalize away his son's non-Christian behavior.

As we look at the transmission of faith from generation to generation, we need to keep in mind that this is not automatic. Just as we have received the gospel from the preceding generation, so God wants us to pass the gospel on.

V. PRAYER

Lord Jesus, we are overwhelmed by your grace, not only in giving us salvation, but also in allowing us to be a part of a long line of those who are your people. Help us to be faithful in continuing to pass the gospel of salvation on with the same soundness with which it has been entrusted to us. Amen.

VI. DEEPER DISCOVERIES

A. Genealogies: Guarding the Deposit

It is clear that the genealogies of 1 Chronicles are not idle pieces of infor-mation the writer decided to record. These genealogies express the legacy of being the people of God. The people in these genealogies represent not just themselves as a part of the sequence but also a heritage that they pass down to others.

Many families have objects that get passed from generation to generation. These may be valuable (such as a piece of jewelry), but they also may be of little monetary value (perhaps a tablecloth). Christians often cherish a Bible that was owned by one's grandparents or even great-grandparents. I recently heard about a Jewish family that passes along a prayer shawl (*talit*) to be used at each successive generation's bar mitzvah. The value of the old piece of cloth is not very high, but to the family it is priceless.

In the genealogy of chapter 1 of 1 Chronicles, the item that is passed on is God's calling to become his people. As the chapter progresses, it comes more clearly into focus. At first, with Adam, it is the calling to be human beings as people come into the world, but as the line narrows so does the specificity of the call. At the end we have a clear delineation between Abraham and his descendants, the clear bearers of the great promise, and the other lines, par-ticularly exemplified by Ishmael and Esau, who have lesser promises.

As believers in Christ, we stand in a genealogy of faith. Our standing with God is not based on our genetic composition, but on our relationship with him as we respond to the gospel. Nevertheless, there is a genealogy in the sense that we are a part of the continuity of God's people over the centuries. We have been given the gospel and are expected to pass it on.

Paul wrote to Timothy, "Guard the good deposit that was entrusted to you" (2 Tim. 1:14). The word *deposit* refers to something that has been given to us for safekeeping, an item for which we are responsible. This deposit is the gospel, the message of divine salvation. Since we have received a "deposit" from God, we need to treat it conscientiously and make sure it is passed on safely.

B. To Adam and Back: Chronicles and Luke (1:1)

We have another genealogy in the Bible that closely follows the first few chapters of 1 Chronicles. It is the genealogy of Jesus Christ as reported in Luke 3:23–38. If you will look closely at verses 34–38 in this passage, you will see our present chapter in a nutshell. There you see Jacob, the son of

Isaac, the son of Abraham, the son of Terah, and so forth. This time, though, the process moves backward, beginning with Jesus in verse 23 and then going back through all the generations until it stops with Adam, "the son of God."

What the chronicler started, Luke completes. There is no further need to continue a genealogy of the human race because with Christ a new race has come into existence. He brought the race of Adam to fulfillment and began a new race—those who are reborn through him (2 Cor. 5:17; Rom. 5:12–20).

C. One Sheba Too Many? (1:9,32)

Someone reading along in chapter 1 of 1 Chronicles might come to verse 9 and see the name of "Sheba" (along with his brother "Dedan") and conclude that this must be an ancestor of the queen of Sheba who eventually made her famous visit to King Solomon (2 Chr. 9:1–12). But as we continue to read on, in verse 32 of the first chapter of 1 Chronicles, we find another "Sheba and Dedan" among the sons of Keturah. Thus, we are left in doubt about the identity of this Sheba.

Names and even pairs of names do get repeated a lot in all cultures. As we continue to study Chronicles, we need to be careful not to read too much (if anything) into the recurrence of a name. In most cases, the simple answer is that the chronicler repeated the name because two persons had the same name.

D. Eber the Hebrew (1:25)

Eber, fourth in the line of Shem, may have given his name to the nation of the Hebrews. But there is another term associated with the name of the Hebrews as well. In Middle Eastern writings from about 2000 B.C. to 1200 B.C., there are occasional references to the "Habiru." Apparently, these were wandering people who moved in and out of certain territories and caused mischief from time to time. There is a collection of tablets sent from various kings of Canaan to the king of Egypt, appealing to him to help them deal with the marauding Habiru, who seemed to be in the process of taking over their land. These ancient letters date from about the time of Joshua's invasion of Canaan. Many scholars believe that here we have a firsthand look into the Canaanite side of the conflict. If so, then we would also have good reason to believe that the terms *Habiru* and *Hebrew* are related.

D. The Edomites (1:43)

According to the Old Testament, the Edomites were the descendants of Esau, brother of Jacob. The word *Edom* has the root meaning of "Red," Esau's nickname because of his ruddy complexion. As we see in our passage, the distinction between the regions of Edom and Seir is not clear. Perhaps Seir was the older name of the geographical region in which the Edomites established themselves—a barren piece of land extending from south of the Dead Sea to the Gulf of Aqabah. Although the land itself was not particularly productive, it held great strategic importance because a major thoroughfare, leading from Egypt into the Jordan Valley and on to Syria, ran through Edom. To control Edom was to control an important transportation route.

The Edomite language was close to Hebrew. But just as the relationship between Jacob and Esau was uneasy, so Israel and the Edomites did not get along. At the time of the exodus, Moses asked the Edomites for permission to pass through their territory, but they refused (Num. 20:14–22). When Edom made sure Israel would not trespass by deploying a large army, Israel turned away.

King David subdued the Edomites in a decisive battle (1 Chr. 18:13–14), and for a while Edom was a vassal state to Judah. But for most of the period covered by Chronicles, Edom and Judah went back and forth on who would have the upper hand over the other. At stake, more than anything else, was the port on the Red Sea at the Gulf of Aqabah.

When the major Mesopotamian empires—Assyria, Babylonia, Persia— took over Palestine, the Edomites stood on the sidelines at first, jeering at Israel's fate. This attitude was condemned by Israel's prophets (see, e.g., Jer. 49:7–22; Obad. 1–21). The Edomites themselves were eventually conquered and left greatly diminished. By the time of the New Testament, the Romans had rehabilitated Edom, now known as Idumea, to a certain extent, but most of their territory then belonged to the kingdom of Nabatea.

Idumea made one other significant contribution to the history of Israel. When the Romans took over, they installed an Idumean, Antipater by name, over the entire area, including Judea. This Antipater turned out to be the father of a dynasty of kings and princes of Judea known as the Herod family. So as we read later on in Chronicles about the subjugation of the Edomites, it is interesting that the Edomites would have another moment of power. Many years later, when the Messiah was born, an Idumean was in charge of the land.

VII. TEACHING OUTLINE

A. INTRODUCTION

1. Lead Story: The Power of Discovering Your Roots
2. Context: Chronicles was written at a time when the people of God needed assurance of their continued relationship to him. In order to

help the people recognize that they still were in God's plan, the chronicler provides teaching on the continuity of the present people with the historic times of old. The first part of displaying this connectedness consists of the genealogy from Adam to Jacob, the father of the twelve tribes.

3. Transition: In this passage we see the basic line of descent from Adam to Jacob by way of well-known people, such as Seth, Noah, and Abraham, as well as many connecting links of otherwise unknown people. The chronicler also gives us information about a number of branches not in the direct line of the promise, including the descendants of Ishmael and Keturah and the sons of Esau.

B. COMMENTARY

1. Adam to Abraham (1:1–27)
2. Abraham to Jacob (1:28–34)
3. Esau and Edom (1:35–54)

C. CONCLUSION: HOW TO FIX SHOES

VIII. ISSUES FOR DISCUSSION

1. Is it necessary for people to know about their ethnic and family history in order to function well in society? Why was it important for the Jews of Ezra's day to have this knowledge?
2. How does it benefit believers if they know the history of their denomination and their own church?
3. Can you trace back your own spiritual descent by those who brought you to Christ, who in turn brought them to Christ, and so forth? Have you thanked God for this blessing?
4. What are you doing to make sure the next generation will have a clear opportunity to hear and respond to the gospel?

1 Chronicles 2:1–4:23

From Judah to David: The Royal Line

I. **INTRODUCTION**
How to Make Linen

II. **COMMENTARY**
A verse-by-verse explanation of these chapters.

III. **CONCLUSION**
Safari to Timbuktu

An overview of the principles and applications from these chapters.

IV. **LIFE APPLICATION**
The Delayed Medical Missionary

Melding these chapters to life.

V. **PRAYER**
Tying these chapters to life with God.

VI. **DEEPER DISCOVERIES**
Historical, geographical, and grammatical enrichment of the commentary.

VII. **TEACHING OUTLINE**
Suggested step-by-step group study of these chapters.

VIII. **ISSUES FOR DISCUSSION**
Zeroing these chapters in on daily life.

"The Jews are, as it were,

the first-born in the family of God."

John Calvin

1 Chronicles 2:1–4:23

IN A NUTSHELL

These chapters present genealogical material from the tribe of Judah beginning with the son of Jacob, highlighting King David and then up to the time when Chronicles was written. In addition to the royal line, we see a diverse group of human beings, some of whom walked with God while others showed character flaws. In the "gospel according to Ezra," we see how God often graciously works through flawed people who are not worthy of his love but who become the instruments of his plan.

From Judah to David: The Royal Line

I. INTRODUCTION

How to Make Linen

*L*inen is a cloth that is much sturdier than cotton. Its origins go back to ancient Egypt, and there seems to be consensus among scholars that the Romans were responsible for its distribution throughout their empire. During the Middle Ages there was a stiff rivalry between the producers of linen and the wool industry, and, of course, linen has continued in use to this day.

But linen is a complicated fabric to create. It begins with the flax plant. When the plants are mature, they must be pulled out of the ground by hand in order to get the longest possible stems. The plants are first aged in water or left to be moistened by dew and rain. After the seeds have been removed and the flax plants are dried, they can be useful by themselves as a strong waxy fiber that is softer and more flexible than straw.

Next, the flax must be processed. The fibers are combed, rolled out, and sorted so the cellulose is removed from the fiber and only the smooth cell material remains. In order for it to become thread, it must be spun, just like cotton or wool. Finally, dying and weaving will create the fabric that can be made into clothes, tablecloths, or other articles.

As God worked in human history, he has often used lengthy, complicated processes. Just as we cannot get linen without the right process, so God in his infinite wisdom knows what route is best in order to achieve his goal. We may not know why he chooses a particular method, but we can be sure that he knows that the straightest path may not always produce the best result.

A case in point is the genealogy of the tribe of Judah. Reuben, Jacob's firstborn, the natural inheritor of the covenant promise, was set aside. Then we are introduced to a colorful line of people. Some of the people in this line inspire us with their devotion to the Lord; others leave us breathless with their brazen ungodliness. But the entire picture shows how God is in charge of the process that brings us King David and then eventually the Messiah.

II. COMMENTARY

From Judah to David: The Royal Line

> **MAIN IDEA:** *The tribe of Judah became the tribe of kings, but in its genealogy we see many different kinds of people, some of whom are distinguished by their godliness and some by their less-than-righteous lives. They show how God works in different ways to bring about his purpose.*

A Jacob to Hezron's Sons (2:1–9)

> **SUPPORTING IDEA:** *The line of Judah gets off to a shaky start. Judah and some of his offspring are disreputable in their behavior, but God's grace manifests itself in continuing the line of promise through them.*

2:1–2. In 1 Chronicles 1:34 the chronicler left off with the sons of Isaac, Jacob (or Israel) and Esau. Having finished his discussion of Esau, he now turns to Jacob and his offspring. These first two verses are really the heading for the next eight chapters. Right through chapter 9 we read the genealogies of the various tribes, and we have a preliminary listing here.

As the chronicler develops the genealogies of the tribes over the next chapters, he skips over Dan and Zebulun. Any explanation of why he does so is pure speculation. It is possible that he had no information on them. If he did, it could be that Dan and Zebulun's descendants were of no interest to him, although a lot of the material he does include does not seem to have significance either. There does remain the possibility, for Dan at least, that the chronicler (under the guidance of the Holy Spirit) deliberately avoided including some material because he did not consider it beneficial. One purpose of Chronicles was to reunify the nation around the worship of God at the temple. But Dan had been a major center of pagan worship, complete with golden calf, competing with Jerusalem (1 Kgs. 12:29). So the chronicler may have avoided giving Dan any recognition.

Note that in this listing Joseph is mentioned as one of the sons of Jacob. But when we get to the actual tribes, there is no tribe of Joseph. Instead, Joseph's two sons, Ephraim and Manasseh, each have a tribe named after them.

2:3–9. The first tribe to be treated at length is **Judah**. After visiting the other tribes, most of Chronicles will be occupied with Judah, the royal tribe, and Levi, the priestly tribe.

Judah had no intrinsic right to be first among his brothers. The firstborn son was Reuben, although he forfeited that position because of his incestuous actions (which we will discuss further in connection with 1 Chr. 5:1–2). The official rights of the firstborn actually went to Joseph, born to Jacob's favorite wife Rachel. Judah was not even the second or third son born; he came fourth in strict birth order. Nevertheless, it was he who received God's assurance that the line of the promise would come through him (Gen. 49:8–12).

If we think that the line of Judah distinguished itself by its purity and righteousness, we are in for a sad surprise. Right from the beginning, there was defilement, and Judah himself was guilty of it (see Gen. 38). Of the five sons of Judah mentioned, three were born to a Canaanite wife, and the other two were born through his own daughter-in-law, another Canaanite woman, posing as a prostitute. The first two (**Er** and **Onan**) were killed by the Lord because of their wickedness. The third (**Shelah**) received some mention later on as a fringe descendant (1 Chr. 4:21). It was **Perez**, son of the scheming **Tamar**, who actually became the one through whom the promised line continued. While our chronicler is busy making reference to the scandal in the eventual royal line, he also reminds his readers of another link in this chain—**Achar** (Achan) in the time of Joshua, who cost the lives of many Israelites through his disobedience (Josh. 7).

Did the chronicler have a nasty streak that caused him to mention all the reprobates of the line of Judah out of malice? Or did he have a deeper purpose? The latter option seems to be the more plausible. He was reminding his readers of the obstacles of the past, including the character of their earliest progenitors. God had worked through the line of Judah, but neither Judah nor his sons were worthy of this honor. The reader comes away with a distinct awareness of the reality of God's grace, even in his choice of ancestry for the line of David.

There are also some outstanding people in this lineup: **the sons of Zerah: Zimri, Ethan, Heman, Calcol and Darda**. These men come up at several other places in the Old Testament. In 1 Kings 4:31 they are mentioned as extremely wise (though not as wise as Solomon), and this **Heman** is also credited with the writing of Psalms 88 and 89.

The focus now moves to Judah's grandson, **Hezron**, and his offspring. At first three of his sons are mentioned—**Ram, Caleb**, and **Jerahmeel**—but later on we learn of even more offspring of Judah.

B The Descendants of Ram and Caleb and More Sons of Hezron (2:10–24)

> **SUPPORTING IDEA:** *Ram and Caleb, two sons of Hezron, counted among their descendants King David as well as Bezalel, the builder of the tabernacle in the wilderness. Hezron had more children later.*

2:10–12. The chronicler gives us a straightforward line of descent with no excursion. He does not even mention that the line included Ruth, the Moabitess, as the wife of Boaz and mother of Obed.

These passages do not mention historical situations. Judah and his clan moved to Egypt along with his other brothers after Joseph had established a safe haven for them during the famine (Gen. 46:8–27). So although the list skips some generations, some of these people would have lived in Egypt. Nor does the chronicler take notice of the time of wandering and the exodus; we just get bare lines of genealogy, and shortened ones at that. What applies here also applies to some of the other lists below.

2:13–17. The roster of the seven sons of **Jesse** is not all-inclusive. It is ironic how **David** is mentioned in passing here when we know that he will be one of the main personalities later on. The sisters mentioned here were actually half sisters. Their father was a man named Nahash (2 Sam. 17:25). One way of making sense of the situation is that Jesse married Nahash's widow as his second wife. The sons of **Abigail** and **Zeruiah** became distinguished soldiers in David's army, particularly **Joab** who became his chief general. **Amasa** eventually led Absalom's army against David.

2:18–20. The **Caleb** mentioned here is not Caleb the godly spy who, along with Joshua, trusted God to help them conquer the promised land. We will actually not meet this Caleb until 1 Chronicles 4:15. The Caleb in this passage lived three hundred years before the Caleb of Joshua's time.

The chronicler ignores the historical circumstances of the sojourn in Egypt, the exodus, and the conquest, but he includes people who lived during those times. One such important individual was **Bezalel** because he was the person in charge of producing all the various furnishings of the tabernacle in the wilderness. Chronicles does not put much emphasis on the tabernacle since it focuses on the temple built by Solomon, so Belazel does not get any further identification here. Nevertheless, many of Ezra's readers would probably have recognized the name.

2:21–24. **Hezron** had two more sons after Ram, Caleb, and Jerahmeel. **Segub** was the son of a late marriage into a family located in Gilead on the east bank of the Jordan River. Hezron's grandson, **Jair**, was in charge of twenty-three towns in that region. And just before Hezron died, his last wife, **Abijah**, had become pregnant. So after Hezron's death one more person was added to his progeny. This man, named **Ashhur**, will receive further treatment from the chronicler in 1 Chronicles 4.

Hezron died in **Caleb Ephrathah**. The identification of this place is not without debate, but Ephrathah is usually synonymous with Bethlehem. This indicates that at some time Hezron had left Egypt and moved back into the land of Canaan.

C The Line of Jerahmeel (2:25–41)

> **SUPPORTING IDEA:** *The line of Hezron's firstborn son does not seem important for subsequent history, but it reveals some important beliefs about children in the Old Testament.*

2:25–41. Of the three key sons of Hezron, the chronicler leaves the oldest, **Jerahmeel**, for last in his discussion. Unfortunately, compared to the heroic heritage of Caleb's line, let alone the splendor of Ram's royal bequest, no greatness is associated with Jerahmeel's descendants. They pop up as dwellers in the desert a few times in later history (1 Sam. 27:10; 30:29). Nevertheless, a few points of interest are buried in this list.

All this emphasis on genealogy shows how much people cherished having offspring. When it is said of people that they had no children—namely **Seled** and **Jether**—this is more than a report; it is a lament for them. **Sheshan** did have a daughter but not a son to carry on the family heritage. He gave his daughter **Ahlai** to his **Egyptian servant Jarha** in marriage, and they continued the family line. Thus, we see again non-Israelite blood in the line as variety in the genealogies continues.

Verses 33 and 34 mark the turning point in the arrangement of this section on the tribe of Judah. Verse 33 looks like the end of the discussion of Jerahmeel's descendants, but then it picks up again in verses 34–41. Now we will again have sections on Caleb's line, then Ram's line, then Hezron's son Ashhur, and then finally back to Judah's son Shelah.

D The Villages Descended from Caleb (2:42–55)

> **SUPPORTING IDEA:** *In a second listing of the descendants of Caleb, son of Hezron, the focus is on the villages whose inhabitants trace their ancestry back to him.*

2:42–55. We return to the sons of Caleb. This list differs from the earlier one, so some scholars suggest that this is a different list that contradicts the earlier list. But an informed Bible student will recognize the names listed here as including those of towns and villages. There is a different intent with this list. In the first genealogy we read of the descendants of Caleb as individuals; now we encounter the towns and villages with inhabitants that can trace their ancestry back to either Caleb or one of his offspring.

Remember that this is not the Caleb who spied out the promised land and remained true to God in Numbers 13:30. This is Caleb, the son of Hezron, one of the three people from whom much of the tribe of Judah was derived. In this section the chronicler clarifies for us how much of Judah actually came from this Caleb's line. When we examine the list of towns, we see that they touched on most of the territory of Judah.

Hebron was an important town because it was the place from which King David reigned for seven years before establishing himself in Jerusalem. Hebron had, in a sense, been the capital of Judah, and the line of Caleb had populated this town.

When we move down to verse 51, we see **Bethlehem** mentioned. This was David's hometown. In the latter part of this section, the chronicler also tells us of particular clans, such as the **Zorites** or the **Sucathites**. There is an interesting little teaser about a clan of scribes known as the **Kenites**, who lived at **Jabez**, at the end of the section.

E The Descendants of David (3:1–24)

> **SUPPORTING IDEA:** *The line of David, beginning with his many sons, led from Solomon through all the kings of Judah, continuing through the exile and right into Ezra's day.*

3:1–9. The chronicler gives us a list of **the sons of David**, arranged by their places of birth and including the names of their mothers. There are two places involved: **Hebron**, where David reigned for about seven years, and **Jerusalem**, where he was king for thirty-three years. Several points stand out from even a cursory look at this list. Aside from the fact that David had a lot of sons, he also had a lot of wives. Among the first six sons listed, each one born in Hebron, there is a different wife each time. Only when we get to Jerusalem do we encounter a wife of David who bore four sons—Bathsheba. There are nine names of David's sons in verses 6–8 for whom we are not given a mother's name.

Furthermore, we see that Michal, David's first wife, is not represented at all. David did not have any offspring by her; in fact, the relationship between the two was strained (see 1 Chr. 15:29). On the other hand, there are still many more sons—those born of David's concubines—who are not officially considered his sons. Nonetheless, they presumably lived in the same household and were part of the larger "David clan." Finally, the chronicler also mentions **Tamar**. It would be hard to imagine that she was David's only daughter. She comes to our attention in the power struggle between her brothers that is recounted in 2 Samuel 13.

Sometimes when we read an account in the Bible, it is easy for us to lose track of the fact that these were real people. Just as modern patchwork "families" consisting of the offspring of various spouses, brought together for the convenience of the adults and not the children, is a recipe for disaster, so David's "family" was an unhealthy situation. The chronicler does not go into two of the biggest negative events of David's life—his affair with Bathsheba and the rebellion by Absalom—but we can sense that family disaster was bound to strike.

In 2 Samuel 13 we read how Amnon, David's oldest son, raped Tamar, his own half sister and Absalom's full sister. When David heard about this, he was furious but did nothing. Absalom killed Amnon in revenge and fled. But at the instigation of Joab, David's commander, David eventually allowed Absalom back at his court (2 Sam. 14:33). Later on Absalom set out to kill and replace his own father (2 Sam. 15–18). People seem to believe that human beings can be shuffled around like furniture with no regard for the laws of psychology or the ordinances of God without suffering serious long-term consequences.

3:10–16. Now follows a list of the descendants of David, or more specifically, of Solomon. It is a roster of the kings of Judah. This list will be the outline for the latter part of Chronicles, where the lives of the various kings are discussed more fully. For now we simply get a quick preview in genealogical form.

But even this simple list tells us something that will become important later on. We know how messed-up David's own home life was, and Solomon's marriage indiscretions have become as legendary as his wisdom. Furthermore, these kings were frequently either unintelligent or evil or both. Yet the line of inheritance moves from generation to generation, not quite as a straight arrow, but not around a lot of curves either, staying all the while in the family.

Contrast this with the kings of Israel, the Northern Kingdom, whose longest dynasty lasted five generations, and who frequently switched between families from king to king. The Southern Kingdom (Judah), as full of corruption as it may have been at times, had one great advantage—God's promise that David's throne would remain in David's family forever. In spite of all the problems, God's work continued to move along.

3:17–24. The lineage continued onward from the kings right into and back out of the Babylonian exile. **Zerubbabel**, though no longer styled as king, was the leader of the Jews when they first returned from the exile in order to rebuild the temple and resettle the city of Jerusalem (Ezra 3:2; Neh. 12:1; Hag. 2:20–23). Zerubbabel is usually called the son of **Shealtiel**. But verse 19 associates him with his uncle, Pedaiah, who may have been his substitute father in keeping with Old Testament law (Deut. 25:5–10).

F Descendants of Hur and Ashhur (4:1–10)

SUPPORTING IDEA: *The descendants of Hur, son of Caleb and founder of Bethlehem, receives more attention, and then we learn of the sons of Ashhur, including Jabez.*

4:1–4. Once more we get more information about **Hur**, the great-great-grandson of Judah, although he has come up twice before in 1 Chronicles 2:19 and 2:50. After all, he was directly associated with the founding **of Bethlehem**, also known by his mother's name, **Ephrathah**. So his name was important to the post-exilic Jews for whom this was written.

4:5–8. As the chronicler continues on his wide-sweeping arc, he returns to **Ashhur**, briefly mentioned in 1 Chronicles 2:24 as Hezron's posthumous son. Now we learn of Ashhur's own two sons and some of their offspring.

4:9–10. Presumably **Jabez** fits in here as one of the descendants of Ashhur, though this is not exactly specified, and there are some other unconnected lists coming up. Jabez had a big problem: his name. His mother, going through extraordinary labor pains, named her poor baby "Pain." This is what "Jabez" sounds like in Hebrew, and the child was stuck with this label. In our own culture we treat names as irrelevant and disposable. We generally do not believe that a person's name is important or significant. But not so in Jabez's day. Names were thought of as summing up a person's central character.

So Jabez came into the world as the "man of pain." According to ancient beliefs, pain should have been his destiny. But Jabez did not resign himself to the fate inflicted on him by his name. We do not know how pious Jabez was, but we do read that he was **more honorable than his brothers** and that he knew to turn to God as the solution to his problem. He **cried out** to God and pleaded with God to turn aside the life foreshadowed by his name. He asked boldly for God's blessing and entreated the Lord to turn aside any harm that could result in pain. And **God granted his request**.

Jabez's prayer was not particularly profound; he asked for land and to be kept from the pain that he believed his name would bring him. What makes this little episode so important is not so much *what* he prayed as *that* he prayed. He was not afraid to turn to God with his most deeply felt longings and to state them in a straightforward way. One does not get the feeling that Jabez checked whether his prayer was proper; he went right to God's throne with what was on his mind. This is prayer in its truest, fullest sense—the unscripted and spontaneous cry of the child of God before the heavenly father.

Ⓖ Further Members of the Tribe of Judah (4:11–23)

SUPPORTING IDEA: *The circle of genealogies associated with the tribe of Judah closes. First, there are the people who were associated with the tribe without a direct connection. Then, finally, there are the descendants of Judah's third son, Shelah.*

4:11–20. In this section the chronicler includes a number of family groups without giving us their specific link to the preceding genealogies. We do not know which, if any, of the sons of Hezron these groups might be related to. A number of scholars even go so far as to suggest that the people mentioned here were not actually descended from Judah but were adopted into the tribe of Judah.

The two pivotal verses in this section are verses 13 and 15. Here we have two people whom we know quite a bit about from the rest of the Old Testament. Here, finally, is the **Caleb** with whom we are familiar—the faithful spy who, along with Joshua, was rewarded by God for his obedience (Num. 13:31). Although this is not indicated in our passage, Caleb and **Othniel** were brothers (see Judg. 1:13). Othniel became the first judge, who ruled over Israel forty years after Joshua's death (Judg. 3:7–11). Thus we see two important people of the tribe of Judah in this passage. If the genealogies were supposed to encourage the people by reminding them of their great heritage, Othniel and Caleb definitely needed to be listed.

The chronicler continues his policy of pointing out some of the unusual angles in the various genealogies by mentioning **Mered** in 1 Chronicles 4:17–18. This Mered had two wives, one Jewish and one Egyptian. Furthermore, the Egyptian wife was Pharaoh's daughter, **Bithiah**. Once again we see how God worked inclusively to form his chosen people, even in the Old Testament, by making room for Gentiles.

4:21–23. A listing of Shelah's descendants has a bit of poignancy to it. It was **Shelah** who was the occasion for Judah's own sin, although Shelah did not actually cause it. After his two sons Er and Onan died, Judah was supposed to have given his third son Shelah to Tamar, his daughter-in-law, to have children by her (in keeping with Deut. 25:5). But Judah refused to do so. He himself fathered Perez and Zerah by Tamar. So when we read about Shelah's sons, we naturally think that one of them must have had Tamar for his mother. But none did.

One interesting feature of the line of Shelah is the reference to the guilds of crafts. We meet the linen workers at **Beth Ashbea**. These people presumably went through the complicated process of making linen. There was also a family of potters who were under special contract to the king.

And so the circle is complete. We began with the sons of Judah, traced his offspring particularly through the sons of Hezron, paid special attention to the line of David, and have finally finished with another of Judah's sons. This is the tribe of the royal line, the tribe most heavily represented among those who returned from the exile, and the tribe from which the Messiah sprang.

> **MAIN IDEA REVIEW:** *The tribe of Judah became the tribe of kings, but in its genealogy we see many different kinds of people, some of whom are distinguished by their godliness and some by their less-than-righteous lives. They show how God works in different ways to bring about his purpose.*

III. CONCLUSION

Safari to Timbuktu

One of the most famous early European explorers of Africa was Heinrich Barth, a German. He led an extensive expedition from 1850 to 1855, crossing the Sahara Desert and traveling around the lands south of the desert. One of the goals of this expedition was the gathering of information about the cruelty of the slave trade. In brief, Barth and his companions set out from Tripoli (modern Libya), traveled south to Lake Chad, slid west to Timbuktu (modern Mali), and then retraced their steps home. But what an incredible understatement this is!

Barth's journey took about five years. Along the way they had to battle the elements as well as marauders. They were attacked numerous times, held for ransom, and Barth himself almost died of thirst. The party split up several times in order to cover more area. Each time, one of Barth's companions did not make it back to the rendezvous point. By the time Barth arrived back in Tripoli, all by himself, his health had been destroyed by intestinal ailments, and he lived for only a short while after that. Nevertheless, his safari was a great success, and Heinrich Barth became the role model for many subsequent explorers.

When we read the genealogies in 1 Chronicles, we are reminded of Heinrich Barth and his safari. There was a goal, a clear end point, but the trip was not easy. Eventually where we want to wind up is with the royal line of David (which will, in time, lead to the Messiah). But like Barth's safari through the Sahara Desert, we must crisscross again and again. The lines split, seem to come together again, only to distance themselves again. There are many dead-ends in these genealogies. Many of the people listed do not seem to make any contribution to the story other than just being a part of the tribe of Judah. Others are significant in their own way, though not as a part of the coming royal line.

Is there a spiritual lesson in all this confusion? There is, and we can see it in our own lives. When I look at my own life, I find myself crossing the desert, pursuing dead-ends, losing my way, picking up and dropping threads. It can be a confusing muddle at times. But then I can remind myself through the genealogies of how God has worked. He knows where everything fits, and he is guiding the whole process to his ordained end. For God, my life (just as the genealogies) is his workshop to turn me into who he wants me to be.

PRINCIPLES

- God was directing the development of his people so it would bring about the royal/messianic line of David.
- God had important roles for those people who were not directly in the royal/messianic line.
- As God works in our lives, he may take us on many side trips whose purpose may not be immediately apparent to us.
- God works not only in the good things that happen in our lives, but sometimes through the actions of evil people.
- God's goals for us may not be clear, but we know he is relentlessly moving us toward them, molding and shaping our lives.

APPLICATIONS

- Reflect on the truth that God is sovereign and in charge of the events of history. In what ways can you see God's sovereign activity in your life and in the life of your family?
- Let the next problem that comes up in your life be an occasion for asking God to show you that problem as a thread in the fabric of your life.
- Ask God to give you a profound knowledge of how apparent dead ends can actually be opportunities for greater service to him and others. Recall people in the Bible whose seemingly dead ends became open doors for greater service.

IV. LIFE APPLICATION

The Delayed Medical Missionary

Albert Schweitzer initially studied theology. By age twenty-five he had doctorates in philosophy and theology. Then he began a successful career teaching theology and writing books. However, he was not satisfied with his life; he felt he needed to do more for the welfare of his fellow human beings. So Schweitzer began to take courses in medicine. He earned a third doctorate, this time as a physician, at age thirty-seven. Then he set out for Africa to establish what would become a world-famous jungle hospital. Throughout the latter part of his life, Albert Schweitzer became famous for his call to "reverence for life." He received the Nobel Peace Prize and influenced the lives of millions who sought to emulate his attitude of service.

Albert Schweitzer's teachings were sometimes controversial. Not everything he said should be accepted by evangelical Christians uncritically (e.g., he did not always treat the Gospels as trustworthy records). Nevertheless, he illustrates the principles of the genealogies in 1 Chronicles. Schweitzer first pursued his career as a theologian, sensing God's call to the mission field much later in life. And even then he prepared himself thoroughly so that when he arrived he was equipped to do competent work and to speak with authority.

The Lord may take a long time to bring us to the point where he wants us. In the meantime, he expects us to prepare ourselves to do the particular work he has called us to.

V. PRAYER

Lord Jesus, we are people who want everything to go in straight lines. We want to know what is going to happen; we want results; and we want them now. But Lord, we realize that you do not work that way. You may take us around curves and corners; you may lead us up the mountain and through the valley. Help us to trust you, even when we do not see your plan clearly. Amen.

VI. DEEPER DISCOVERIES

The Prayer of Jabez (4:9–10)

We have already mentioned the main features of the prayer of Jabez. But I want to add a few further observations.

1. Jabez's prayer should be an example to us. The simple story of Jabez shows us a man who felt in distress and turned directly to God. What is most striking about his prayer is its directness. Jabez had certain desires, and he put them before the Lord exactly as he felt them.

Christians should never be afraid to go directly to God with their requests exactly as they need them. God is our Heavenly Father, and we have a direct relationship with him as his sons and daughters. We should always feel free to express ourselves to him even if we think our requests are silly, self-centered, or even wrong. God knows what we are thinking. We will not shock him by coming to him with our innermost feelings.

How tragic it is that a Christian is afraid to pray because he or she worries that the prayer will not meet the correct standards for prayer! There is nothing intrinsically wrong with a prayer following a certain form, but there should never be a mandatory form that a prayer has to follow in order to be answered by God. Jabez is our example of a person who expressed his needs to God right from the heart.

2. Just as Jabez prayed from within his own life and situation, so should we. Each person is accountable to the Lord for the specific role in life to which God has called him. This is the Christian doctrine of vocation. Each person, regardless of what station in life he occupies, has a calling from God. We should never make another person's experience or calling the standard by which we measure ourselves, no matter how appealing the other person's life may look. Our measuring stick is God's call for us, not other people.

This doctrine of vocation applies to Jabez as well. God responded to his prayer and increased his land. Many of us are not called to be land developers, either in a literal or figurative sense; we may be called to plow the land we have and no more. Not everyone is called to a ministry of expansion; some people's vocation is to occupy the corner in which God has placed them. Sometimes God wants us simply to be dependable within the boundary lines he has established for us.

3. God blessed Jabez in response to his prayer. God does, indeed, answer our prayers, and there are many passages in the Bible that describe how God responds to people who pray. For example, Moses (Exod. 32:11–14) and Hezekiah (2 Chr. 32:20,24) can be counted among the numerous Bible figures to whom the Lord gave exactly what they asked for.

But we should not think of prayer as a requirement without which we will never obtain God's blessings. The fact that God blesses us when we pray should not lead us to think that God blesses us *only* when we pray. God is free to bless and not bless. God will not withhold a good thing from us because we do not pray a certain prayer. Jabez illustrates for us how richly God blesses, but we should not look to him for a technique on how to get more blessings. We are free to come to him with confidence that he does hear and respond to our prayers.

VII. TEACHING OUTLINE

A. INTRODUCTION

1. Lead Story: How to Make Linen
2. Context: Just as making linen is a long and complicated process with many steps, so the derivation of God's people provided some complex genealogies. In chapter 1 we saw the beginnings of all human beings with Adam and how this line eventually led to Jacob. Now the writer focuses on the tribe of Judah.
3. Transition: There are many lines of descent within the tribe of Judah, the three main ones coming from three brothers: Ram, Caleb, and Jerahmeel. These lines include many diverse people ranging from kings to peasants as well as from flagrant sinners to faithful saints.

B. COMMENTARY

1. Jacob to Hezron's Sons (2:1–9)
2. The Descendants of Ram and Caleb and More Sons of Hezron (2:10–24)
3. The Line of Jerahmeel (2:25–41)
4. The Villages Descended from Caleb (2:42–55)
5. The Descendants of David (3:1–24)
6. Descendants of Hur and Ashhur (4:1–10)
7. Further Members of the Tribe of Judah (4:11–23)

C. CONCLUSION: SAFARI TO TIMBUKTU

VIII. ISSUES FOR DISCUSSION

1. Why was it important that there be records of genealogies specifically for the tribe of Judah? Why might people in Ezra's day have wanted to know exactly who belonged to this tribe?
2. What can we learn from the people in these genealogies who seemed to be failures?
3. The lines of some of the people in these lists do not seem to make much difference for the future of the tribe (e.g., those of Jerahmeel, Ashhur, or Shelah). How do we see God at work in these lines?
4. Relate some of your own experiences in which you have seen God move in a lengthy process rather than bringing about an end result instantaneously.

1 Chronicles 4:24–5:26

The Tribes That Vanished

I. INTRODUCTION
A Team Sport with Unknown Teams

II. COMMENTARY
A verse-by-verse explanation of these chapters.

III. CONCLUSION
"But I Wanted to Be a Missionary!"

An overview of the principles and applications from these chapters.

IV. LIFE APPLICATION
You Are Not an Ant!

Melding these chapters to life.

V. PRAYER
Tying these chapters to life with God.

VI. DEEPER DISCOVERIES
Historical, geographical, and grammatical enrichment of the commentary.

VII. TEACHING OUTLINE
Suggested step-by-step group study of these chapters.

VIII. ISSUES FOR DISCUSSION
Zeroing these chapters in on daily life.

1 Chronicles 4:24–5:26

| Q u o t e |

"*N*obody wants to play rhythm guitar behind Jesus;

everybody wants to be the lead singer of the band."

T . A . H i l l

IN A NUTSHELL

*T*hese passages present us with further genealogical material, this time from the four (actually three and one-half) tribes that lived on the fringes of Israel and were the first to disappear. The tribe of Simeon was presumably absorbed into the tribe of Judah, but only after establishing themselves as valiant men of God. On the eastern side of the Jordan River lived the tribes of Reuben, Gad, and half of Manasseh. These were the first tribes to be conquered by the Assyrians and carried off into exile. Just as these four tribes were geographically on the sidelines of Israel, ultimately they were not very significant in the history of God's people either. Still, we can learn from their experience: faithful Simeon received a commendation, while the other three, because of their lack of faithfulness, were vanquished.

The Tribes That Vanished

I. INTRODUCTION

A Team Sport with Unknown Teams

*O*ver the last twenty years the sport of auto racing has increased dramatically in popularity in the United States. People are attracted to the color, noise, speed, and drama of close calls. Skilled drivers put their lives on the line to seek out yet one more victory. And when the winner pulls into the victory lane, he thanks his car owner, his sponsors, and his team. Yes, even though the driver circles around the track all by himself, he will insist afterwards that his victory was due to a great team effort. From time to time someone may even proclaim that auto racing is a team sport.

But then, as a team sport, auto racing is in a somewhat peculiar position. When a baseball team plays, one of the first pieces of information that is conveyed to the spectators in the stadium or on television is the lineup; people want to know who is playing. Similarly in basketball, hockey, volleyball, water polo—or whatever the team sport—the audience will be provided with the names of those who comprise the team. Even in football, the announcer will at least report on who made a particular play. But in auto racing, the team is rarely presented to the audience. Spectators may see them perform their tasks during a pit stop, but they tend to be clad in anonymity.

The tribes that constitute the subject matter of this section are—or could have been—a part of such an anonymous team. They were among God's chosen people. As with all God's people, they were expected to live according to his covenant and to represent him on earth. There is no question that they were a part of the "pit stop team," with Judah taking on the role of the driver. They were geographically remote; they did not supply priests; there would never be a legitimate king from their line; and the Messiah would come from another tribe. But they were still under obligation to be faithful members of God's "team" on earth. Three of the four tribes mentioned did not live up to their calling, and they lost their place on the team.

II. COMMENTARY

The Tribes That Vanished

> **MAIN IDEA:** *The tribes of Simeon, Reuben, Gad, and the half tribe of Manasseh were on the fringe of Israel, but that should not have kept them from living as God's covenant people. Simeon is an example of a small tribe that made only a minor contribution to the history of Israel; the other three forsook God and as a consequence wound up defeated, with only a memory as their legacy.*

A The Tribe of Simeon (4:24–43)

> **SUPPORTING IDEA:** *The tribe of Simeon had little significance in the larger history of Israel. It had to share its territory with Judah and eventually was absorbed into the larger tribe. But they carried out some positive military ventures.*

4:24–27. As we have come to expect, the chronicler gives us a genealogy, but a somewhat patchy one. The basic line of descent is: Simeon to Shaul, to Shallum, to Mibsam and Mishma, to Shimei, and finally to Shimei's sixteen sons and six daughters. But then we are told, almost apologetically, that these sixteen sons—potentially the ancestors of a great clan—did not produce many offspring, so the line remained small in number.

4:28–33. This is a list of the towns that were officially allocated to the tribe of Simeon. Most of these fell into the territory of Judah; in fact, many of the same towns were also given to Judah. In the last part of verse 29, we learn that these places retained their designation as Simeonite towns until at least the reign of David.

The list enumerating these towns and "their villages" seems to conjure up images of urban sprawl in our Western, industrialized minds. In terms of their actual size by contemporary standards, we need to think of small villages and tiny villages. The people living in a typical "town" would all be jammed behind walls surrounding an area no larger than a football stadium. The "villages" would be clusters of shacks on the far side of the parking lot.

The Simeonites kept a genealogical record. Obviously, this would have been something far more extensive than the skimpy information in verses 24–27, which hardly deserves such a grandiose label. The people of this tribe, dispersed as they were throughout the more powerful tribe of Judah, kept track of their ancestry so that, for a time at least, they could retain their identity. Eventually, however, the trail would give out, the tribe of Simeon would be absorbed into the tribe of Judah, and Simeon would be no more.

4:34–43. The chronicler concludes his discussion of Simeon by mentioning two military successes of this tribe. A number of Simeonite leaders decided that they needed more land, so they took it away from some of the indigenous population. These two stories are decorated with lists of otherwise unknown people who distinguished themselves in their capacity as leaders of their clans.

However, there is more to these stories than just a grab for land by some obscure warriors belonging to an increasingly obscure tribe. Taking possession of the land was a religious matter for the tribes of Israel. Even though no religious motive is expressly stated, the very act of taking on new land and in the process further eliminating pagan competition was an act of faith in God.

The first event concerns some families who needed more land. They came across a suitable area, which they appropriated to their use. This episode, at first stated almost perfunctorily, occurred in the days of King Hezekiah of Judah. But the chronological setting of this story makes it extremely interesting. As we shall see later on in Chronicles, even though Hezekiah's reign was characterized by obedience to God and, consequently, a certain amount of success in the immediate territory of Judah, things were quite different in the outlying countryside.

Earlier the Assyrian king Shalmanezer had destroyed Samaria, the capital of Israel, which was composed of the ten northern tribes. This theoretically included Simeon, even though Simeon was geographically far from the north. During Hezekiah's reign, another Assyrian king, Sennacherib, swept through the southern area, Judah, rampaging and pillaging as he went. According to his own reports, he captured forty-six fortified towns and deported more than two hundred thousand people (see 2 Chr. 32:1–21 for a biblical account of the same events).

This would not seem to be the best time for a tribe to look toward expanding its territory. Then, again, perhaps everyone was so preoccupied with defending themselves against the Assyrians that they let down their defenses against some local marauders from the tribe of Simeon. Regardless of how these events may have happened, these Simeonites were establishing themselves on a more secure footing during a tough time in Israel. (The **Meunites** were a tribal group who had descended from Ishmael and had apparently been assimilated by Canaanite society.)

We also receive brief notice of a second campaign, this one waged by certain Simeonites into the mountainous region of Seir, an area that was traditionally counted with the land of Edom. This area was located on the eastern side of the Jordan River, definitely not a part of the land originally deeded over to Simeon. In the process of setting themselves up here, these men also put an end to the Amalekites.

By now there was not much left of these ancient enemies of Israel. They had been defeated by King Saul (1 Sam. 15:1–35) and trounced by David (1 Sam. 30:17), but a few escaped. The Simeonites finally finished the task for good, thereby acquiring further land, eliminating a vicious enemy (Judg. 6:4–6), and fulfilling an obligation that God had placed on Saul several centuries earlier.

B The Eastern Tribes: Early Faithfulness (5:1–24)

SUPPORTING IDEA: *At first the eastern tribes—Reuben, Gad, and half of Manasseh—were faithful members of God's people, and God blessed them with success.*

5:1–2. The first of the three tribes on the eastern side of the Jordan River to be discussed is **Reuben**. The chronicler gives us an explanation for why this tribe found itself on the fringe of Israel rather than in a more central role. After all, Reuben was Jacob's **firstborn**, so his descendants should have had a superior position over the other tribes. But Reuben had lost his birthright when he committed incest by having intercourse with Bilhah, one of Jacob's concubines, the mother of Dan and Naphtali (Gen. 35:22). Because Rachel, Jacob's favorite wife, was unable to bear children, she had designated Bilhah as her surrogate, and Bilhah gave birth to two sons (Gen. 30:4–8). Reuben's own mother was Leah, but of course that made no difference for the severity of the infraction.

Because Reuben had slept with the mother of two of his brothers, he was not allowed to occupy the position of firstborn (Gen. 49:4). But neither did that honor go to the second oldest of his brothers, which would have been Simeon, nor to the next in line, Levi, but to Joseph, who was much younger.

Joseph was designated as the official firstborn among his brothers (e.g., by wearing "the coat of many colours," KJV), a position that they resented (Gen. 37). But no tribe was called "Joseph." Joseph's sons, Manasseh and Ephraim, each became the ancestors of a tribe that was named after them (Gen. 48:5). In yet another reversal of the role of the firstborn, Jacob endowed Ephraim, the younger of the two, with the greater standing, so that Ephraim, and not Manasseh, would be the leader among all the tribes. In fact, Ephraim did hold dominance among the tribes of the North. Nevertheless, the chronicler notes, Judah was the tribe that achieved the highest status.

5:3–8a. Now follows a list of the descendants of Reuben. Once again this list only highlights some of the people whose names had persevered into the time of Ezra. Our text mentions Reuben's four sons—Hanoch, Pellu, Hezru, and Carmi—and then skips to a certain Joel. We have no further information about this Joel. Presumably he was the son of one of Reuben's sons (thus a grandson of Reuben), but this is only a guess. Again, we need to realize that not every generation is represented in this list. After only seven links we have already moved from Reuben, who would have lived around 1900 B.C., to **Beerah**, a leader at the time of **Tiglath-Pileser**, the **king of Assyria**, who carried the Reubenites into exile in 733 B.C.

This Beerah was considered the leader of the tribe, though we must remember that, theoretically at least, by this point Reuben would have been a part of the ten tribes that comprised the Northern Kingdom of Israel. Beerah had the dubious distinction of presiding over the conquest and forced exile of his people. This list concludes with a few more of the people who were related to Reuben's offspring.

5:8b–10. The information on Reuben concludes by describing the tribe's territory. The Reubenites lived on the eastern side of the Jordan River along the Dead Sea. At their time of greatest prosperity, their territory extended all the way **to the Euphrates River**. This was part of the original dimensions of the promised land that God had disclosed through Moses (Deut. 1:7). The chronicler also tells us that the tribe of Reuben defeated the Hagrites and took over their area. Apparently these **Hagrites** or Hagarites were a division of the tribes descended from Ishmael, naming themselves after Ishmael's mother, Hagar. Reuben thus came to occupy the formerly Hagrite areas **throughout the entire region east of Gilead**.

Like a number of other biblical place-names, *Gilead* had a flexible meaning. It could refer to the more northern area of the eastern side of the Jordan River, touching on the Sea of Galilee, in which case that was the area where half the tribe of Manasseh and the tribe of Gad lived. But it could also refer to the entire eastern bank, and that is the meaning it has here. Thus Reuben at one point had control over the entire territory east of the Jordan River.

5:11–17. Next we receive information about the tribe of **Gad**. Gad was Jacob's seventh son; his mother was Zilpah, Leah's handmaid and surrogate, when she competed for offspring with Rachel and Bilhah (Gen. 30:11–13). Jacob's deathbed statements about this tribe predicted an existence marked by strife: "Gad will be attacked by a band of raiders, but he will attack them at their heels" (Gen. 49:19).

Gad lived in Bashan, the area closest to the Jordan River between the Dead Sea and the Sea of Galilee, a fertile and hospitable country, also at times referred to as a section of Gilead. The chronicler gives us a quick overview of some of the important people in this tribe. He makes a point of documenting his sources by telling us specifically when these genealogical records were compiled—during the time of King **Jeroboam** of Israel and King **Jotham** of **Judah**. The Jeroboam mentioned here was Jeroboam II, who ruled during the Northern Kingdom's last period of stability before the Assyrian invasion, when Gad was overrun.

5:18–22. Ezra now sets the reader up by painting a glorious picture of the exploits of Reuben and Gad. He also weaves the **half-tribe of Manasseh** into the story prior to a direct discussion of this tribe. We now see the people of God at their best. They assembled a large army and took possession of the entire area that God had granted to them, and they did so not in their own strength but by continually calling on the Lord. As a result God granted them some amazing victories. The chronicler gives us an accounting of how much booty they took: 50,000 camels, 250,000 sheep, and 2,000 donkeys. They did not achieve this on their own. God **answered their prayers, because they trusted in him**.

5:23–24. The tribe of **Manasseh** was large. It received sizable portions of land on both sides of the Jordan River. In this passage we are concerned with only the eastern half, which settled the area east of the Sea of Galilee. The chronicler treats this tribe perfunctorily, mentioning a few names and then providing them with what is a patronizing compliment: **They were brave warriors, famous men, and heads of their families**. No doubt they were heads of their families. Given the information in the previous section, there must have been some brave warriors among them. But the chronicler is more eager to talk about their failings than to share their exploits.

Ⓒ The Eastern Tribes: Faithlessness Punished (5:25–26)

> **SUPPORTING IDEA:** *When the eastern tribes broke faith with God, he sent the Assyrians to carry them into exile.*

5:25–26. Having bragged on the eastern tribes a moment ago, the narrator now changes his tune. Just a few verses ago we learned how the eastern tribes engaged in warfare and had success because of their reliance on the Lord. But then the tribes started to assimilate the religion of their pagan neighbors; in fact, having received victory at God's hands, they started to worship the gods of the people whom they had defeated. God would have none of that. In 733 B.C. he sent the king of Assyria to carry the people into captivity.

The text specifies that God **stirred up the spirit** of the king of Assyria. It was not just a matter of the Assyrians deciding to conquer the eastern tribes of Israel and God not preventing them from doing so. Nor was it just a matter of God not protecting these tribes from Assyria. God is in control of history, and the events of history do not occur by happenstance. And so we see that God caused King **Tiglath-Pileser** of **Assyria** to take over the eastern tribes to punish them for their sin of rejecting the Lord.

This is a crass scenario, one which will be repeated several more times in Chronicles. The chronicler does not mince any words. Just as he feels that God has rewarded the tribes when they trusted him, so God also punished them when they did not. In each case, God was ultimately the agent of their destiny. The tribes on the fringe could have had a happier future, but their idolatry caused their downfall. This would also happen with the northwestern tribes and the kingdom of Judah.

> **MAIN IDEA REVIEW:** *The tribes of Simeon, Reuben, Gad, and the half tribe of Manasseh were on the fringe of Israel, but that should not have kept them from living as God's covenant people. Simeon is an example of a small tribe that made only a minor contribution to the history of Israel; the other three forsook God and as a consequence wound up defeated, with only a memory as their legacy.*

III. CONCLUSION

"But I Wanted to Be a Missionary!"

Leota Ratcliffe taught school in Illinois for a while but then went to Taylor University in Indiana from 1906 to 1907 to further her education. While there, she experienced the call to become a missionary. Eventually she traveled to Liberia to the land of the Kru people. Her duty once she arrived on the mission field was to teach school.

Leota felt that she had not journeyed all the way to Africa just to do the same thing she had already done in Illinois. She wound up stepping out on her own, doing what she believed to be her true calling and apparently doing so effectively for a time. But she did not have the resources to maintain her independent work. After about a year in Africa, her days as a missionary were over (Rousselow and Winquist, *God's Ordinary People: No Ordinary Heritage*). Perhaps Leota should have been a little more cautious in identifying her calling and a lot more patient in establishing her ministry with her coworkers.

Most Christians will never have a direct, full-time ministry, let alone travel to faraway lands to be missionaries. Like the tribes of Simeon, Gad, Reuben, and Manasseh, we may always find ourselves on the fringe of the action. While famous evangelists thunder the Word of God from their pulpits to audiences of thousands, we work hard to present a Sunday school lesson to a small group.

Still, we have an important role in God's kingdom. The apostle Paul tells us that just as a body is composed of many parts, so the body of Christ, the church, has many members. Every one of these is of equal value, even though they may be very different from one another. In fact, he states that "those parts of the body that seem to be weaker are indispensable" (1 Cor. 12:22). Carrying out a supporting role in the church does not lessen our importance.

Although the tribes of Simeon, Reuben, Gad, and Manasseh were on the fringe of Israel, they were able to partake of God's blessings as much as any other tribe as long as they stayed true to the divine covenant. The ministry that any Christian performs, no matter how small, is significant in God's eyes—and he expects us to be faithful in carrying it out.

PRINCIPLES

- Sometimes God expects his servants to play what seems to be a small and insignificant role in his kingdom.
- What may seem like a small and insignificant ministry to us is just as important to God as superficially larger and more important tasks.
- God expects us to be faithful to his calling, whether we find ourselves at the center of his work or on the fringe.

APPLICATIONS

- Reflect on the fact that in team sports, the actions of a so-called minor player may cost the team a victory or secure the team a win.
- Consider your present ministry roles. Contrast what will happen if you carry this out wholeheartedly as unto the Lord as opposed to doing the work halfheartedly.
- Has your life been impacted positively by a person whom the world would consider to be playing a minor role? What was that like? Ask God to use your life in this way.

IV. LIFE APPLICATION

You Are Not an Ant!

Ants are amazing creatures. They have a queen, who constantly reproduces more residents for the ant colony. Every other ant pitches in to do the work necessary to keep their society thriving and growing. Some feed the queen, others guard the nest, and many others find food.

Everyone admires ants for their hard work and devotion to their community. But we are not ants. Ants carry out their tasks automatically. They act on instinct, not on the basis of fulfilling moral obligations. Their entire life is wrapped up in their colony, not like an individual who has joined an organization by choice. Even when ants seem to make decisions, such as whether to pick up a piece of food, they are really acting on the basis of instinct toward the group's welfare.

Ants probably have a group mind rather than an individual mind. The idea has been explored in fantasy and science fiction stories. For example, in Robert Heinlein's novel *Methuselah's Children,* on an alien planet there lives a race of beings that share one single mind among a group of 30-90 beings. What one thinks, the whole community thinks. What the group thinks, each being thinks. They have only one communal set of experiences, questions, or beliefs, so the entities that make up a unit do not have to undergo the unhappiness that normal human beings suffer. The lack of individual concerns leads the members to be suffused with a sense of happiness and contentment, which anyone can become a part of by giving up their own mind and letting it meld into the single mind of the community.

Ants illustrate one of the lessons we should learn from the tribes of Simeon, Reuben, Gad, and Manasseh. Just as an ant may be designated as the specific ant charged with moving one particular morsel of food, so the four tribes should have recognized their particular place in God's scheme of things, even if it meant not being one of the main tribes of the covenant people. In the same way, we should find out what particular job we should perform and carry it out faithfully, no matter how minor it may appear to us.

We are expected to carry out whatever tasks God has given us, but not mindlessly like an ant. We are responsible to our Lord to be faithful in whatever place God may put us. This places a greater burden on us than an ant would ever have to cope with. But it also gives us hope because we know that whatever we may do in God's kingdom is significant and meaningful.

V. PRAYER

Lord Jesus, we come to you as people who crave applause, rewards, and recognition for what we do. We want appreciation and pats on the back, and we like to think that what we do is important. But we realize that much of the time we wind up being asked to do small things, and even more often we may feel as though we are not getting the recognition we think we deserve. Lord, help us to be conscientious in all our tasks and not to give in to the temptation to become negligent in our duties because we think they are not important or to become resentful because we feel no one appreciates our efforts. Grant us the strength to be faithful servants in even the smallest details. Amen.

VI. DEEPER DISCOVERIES

A. Presenting Mibsam and Mishma (4:25)

We encountered the names "Mibsam" and "Mishma" before—as two sons of Ishmael listed in 1 Chronicles 1:29. Obviously these are not the same two men. Remember that Ishmael was Isaac's half brother, so the original Mibsam and Mishma would have been half cousins to Jacob, four generations ahead of these two people with the same names. What seems to be going on here is that Shallum, the father of the two, was acknowledging the importance to him of Ishmael's line of descent when he named these boys. Shallum's grandmother (Shaul's wife) was a Canaanite woman. So it is possible that by naming his two sons after two of Ishmael's two sons, Shallum intentionally paid respect to the presence of non-Hebrew blood in his ancestry.

B. The Amalekites (4:43)

We read in this passage that the tribe of Simeon finally put an end to the remaining Amalekites. The text makes clear that this was a mopping-up operation because it specifies that these were the Amalekites who had escaped earlier defeats.

The Amalekites were one of the many groups of people who lived in and around the land of Canaan and participated in constant hostility against the Israelites. They were a nomadic herding people, so we need to think of their territory more as the boundaries of their movements rather than as an area that they settled permanently with cities and villages. They considered their boundaries as flexible as they wanted them to be. Whenever they perceived the need, which was frequent, they carried out acts of aggression against Israel. Nevertheless, their basic home area was south of Judah toward the Red Sea. This land consisted mostly of desert ground on which to raise their livestock.

The Amalekites first appear in Genesis 14:7, where they get a brief mention as a group that was conquered by the alliance of Canaanite kings (who were later defeated by Abraham). Next they come up in Exodus 17, shortly after the Israelites' crossing of the Red Sea, when they attacked the Israelites as they were traveling through the desert toward Sinai. The Israelites were not able to defeat the Amalekites in their own power. But when Moses held up his hands in prayer, God granted Joshua and his army an advantage in the battle, which finally ended in victory for the Israelites.

Then, a generation later, when the Hebrews were making their way into the promised land marching north along the eastern side of the Jordan River, the Amalekites attacked them from behind (Num. 14:45). Finally, during the time of the judges, the Amalekites allied themselves first with the Moabites (Judg. 3:13) and then with the Midianites (Judg. 7:12) in oppressing Israel. Both times they were overcome by a judge, first Ehud and then Gideon.

It was up to Saul to put an end to the Amalekites once and for all (1 Sam. 15). Samuel the prophet gave him God's order to exterminate them, but Saul did not comply fully with God's command, thereby earning the Lord's judgment. David, Saul's successor, defeated the Amalekites (1 Sam. 27:8–9; 30:1–20). By the time the Simeonites launched their campaign, the Amalekites were no longer a strong force, and they do not come up in the Old Testament again.

C. Who's on First? (5:1)

Let's reflect a little further on the paradoxical way in which God used the notion of the "firstborn" in the life of Jacob. Jacob was the second twin to be born of his mother Rebekah (Gen. 25:26), but we also know that Jacob tricked the birthright away from his older brother Esau, first by buying it from Esau with a bowl of stew (Gen. 25:29–34) and then by deceiving their father Isaac into giving him the blessing (Gen. 27:1–29). So it was Jacob who inherited the Abrahamic covenant that his descendants would become a large and prosperous people (Gen. 12:1–3).

But then the reversals continued. Jacob's own firstborn son, Reuben, disqualified himself from the honors that went with the position, and that rank went to Joseph instead. It is generally agreed that the beautiful robe Jacob made for him was an insignia for being the leader among his brothers and the designated bearer of the divine promise (Gen. 37:3). Then, when the time came for Jacob to bless Joseph's children, he again put the younger, Ephraim, ahead of the older, Manasseh (Gen. 48:14).

But this is not where the reversals stop. Another set of Jacob's grandchildren also wound up being inverted in their birth order. Judah had a set of twins by Tamar, and when the first infant, who was named Zerah, started to emerge in the birthing process, the midwife tied a red ribbon to his wrist, immediately designating him as the firstborn. However, Zerah then withdrew, and Perez turned out to be the first one actually to be born (Gen. 38:27–30).

And, as we saw earlier in Chronicles, it turned out that Perez was the ancestor of the line of kings that eventually led to the Messiah (1 Chr. 2:5).

The lesson is clear: God does not follow the patterns we might expect. We can count on God to fulfill his promises, but we should never calculate the methods by which he will do so.

VII. TEACHING OUTLINE

A. INTRODUCTION

1. Lead Story: A Team Sport with Unknown Teams
2. Context: In the sport of auto racing, most people do not know the names of the people on the team other than the driver. Similarly, as God established his people and the line that would lead to the Messiah, some tribes would play a supporting role.
3. Transition: The tribes of Simeon, Reuben, Gad, and Eastern Manasseh were on the fringe of Israel, both geographically and in terms of importance. Nevertheless, God expected them to be faithful to his covenant. He blessed them when they obeyed him, and he punished them when they departed from his will.

B. COMMENTARY

1. The Tribe of Simeon (4:24–43)
2. The Eastern Tribes: Early Faithfulness (5:1–24)
3. The Eastern Tribes: Faithlessness Punished (5:25–26)

C. CONCLUSION: "BUT I WANTED TO BE A MISSIONARY!"

VIII. ISSUES FOR DISCUSSION

1. When do we feel as if we are on the fringe of God's work?
2. Are there times when we are justified in thinking that our work does not seem to matter much to God?
3. How can we encourage one another to be more faithful in carrying out small tasks without coming across as judgmental?

1 Chronicles 6:1–9:44

Priests, a King, and Many Soldiers: The Western Tribes

I. **INTRODUCTION**
The Privileges of Nobility

II. **COMMENTARY**
A verse-by-verse explanation of these chapters.

III. **CONCLUSION**
The Driver's License Is Only the Beginning
An overview of the principles and applications from these chapters.

IV. **LIFE APPLICATION**
A New Family Membership
Melding these chapters to life.

V. **PRAYER**
Tying these chapters to life with God.

VI. **DEEPER DISCOVERIES**
Historical, geographical, and grammatical enrichment of the commentary.

VII. **TEACHING OUTLINE**
Suggested step-by-step group study of these chapters.

VIII. **ISSUES FOR DISCUSSION**
Zeroing these chapters in on daily life.

Quote

"*A*ll true Christians are a chosen generation; they make one family, a people distinct from the world."

Matthew   Henry

1 Chronicles 6:1–9:44

I N   A   N U T S H E L L

*T*hese chapters in 1 Chronicles continue with genealogical and geographical information, touching on most of the remaining tribes, but they also address two crucial areas of concern. They give a detailed list of the priestly lineage because only those who were descended from Aaron could serve as priests. These chapters also focus on the heritage of the failed King Saul, who came from the tribe of Benjamin. This section reminds us that under the provisions of God's new covenant in Christ, we receive adoption into God's family by grace and not by birth.

Priests, a King, and Many Soldiers: The Western Tribes

I. INTRODUCTION

The Privileges of Nobility

In Europe during the later Middle Ages, many members of the nobility felt their rights were being encroached upon. In an earlier period, the lords lived in their castles enjoying every privilege, while the commoners lived in the surrounding area, depending on the nobility for protection. Peasants were expected to be subservient to their lords, and the lords were obligated to take care of their peasants. This system worked sometimes, and sometimes it did not. If the nobility wanted to exploit the peasantry, there was nobody to stop them. Even the noblest of the nobles thought of themselves as occupying a position of privilege and power.

Then a major change occurred in the social structure of Europe. Toward the end of the Middle Ages, locations that had once been only villages or market places turned into towns and cities. With the growth of cities, a new kind of person entered society: the independent craftsman or merchant. People living in cities no longer depended on the nobility to provide them with the essentials of life. They cobbled shoes, baked bread, or sold fabric without needing supervision from the nobility. They formed themselves into guilds or associations run by their own members. Some people without a background of privilege and status amassed riches to rival those of any duke or baron, and even moved up to the ranks of nobility.

Many members of the nobility resented this intrusion on their privilege. Working from their assumption that the only legitimate way to become noble was to be born noble, they felt that they had a position in the universe that should never be equaled by anyone who did not have a noble ancestry.

In the United States where equality is such a high priority, the idea that people could have special privileges just because they were born into a particular family seems out of order. We recognize that some people are born into wealth and others into poverty, but we chafe at the idea that a person's lineage should prevent him from improving his lot in life. Theoretically, "any child can grow up to be president."

First Chronicles 6–9 provides the genealogy of the tribe of Levi, a birthright that was essential for anyone who worked in the service of God associated with the temple. The "patents of priesthood" were an absolute requirement. We also see the genealogy of King Saul, situated within the tribe of Benjamin. But here the underlying message goes in the opposite direction: Royalty is not derived from descent alone. Saul had to earn the right to be king, a requirement at which he failed. Then there were the other tribes on the western bank of the Jordan River in the promised land. The chronicler gives us a certain amount of information to round out the picture, but he makes no further point about the significance of their derivation; in other words, these tribes were, just as the eastern tribes, playing primarily a supporting role.

II. COMMENTARY

Priests, a King, and Many Soldiers: The Western Tribes

MAIN IDEA: *The genealogy of the tribe of Levi is important because it delineates those who could officiate in the temple service. The genealogy of Benjamin leads to King Saul, whose reign was a failure, while the other tribes primarily provided military strength to the nation.*

A The Tribe of Levi (6:1–81)

SUPPORTING IDEA: *Because of its importance in the worship of God, the tribe of Levi receives a detailed genealogy.*

Levi had three sons: Gershon, Kohath, and Merari. We will refer to their descendants as "clans." Only the members of the clan of Kohath and the family of Aaron were allowed to be priests. All other Levites could assist with the temple worship, but they were not priests. By David's time, one descendant of each clan was a leader in temple music: Heman from the clan of Kohath, the main director, along with Asaph from the clan of Gershon and Ethan from the clan of Merari, who served as Heman's assistants. (See page 55 for a diagram of these basic relationships.)

6:1. Because the chronicler was so interested in the tribe of **Levi** and its functions in connection with the temple, the distinction between the three clans of **Gershon, Kohath,** and **Merari** was important to him. Even though it is correct to say that the tribe of Levi was the priestly tribe, only a small proportion of its descendants were actually eligible for the priesthood. One not

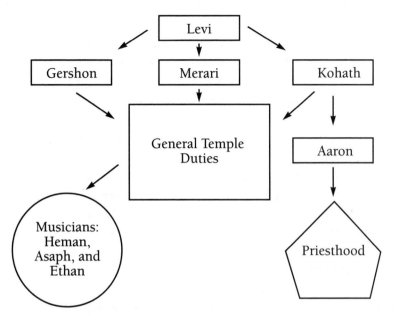

only needed to be a member of the clan of Kohath, but one had to fall under the category of descendants of Aaron. Even Moses was not allowed to fulfill the priestly functions that were assigned to Aaron, and the same thing applied to those who came after them.

6:2–3. The chronicler first zeroes in on the descendants of **Kohath** in order to provide us with the all-important line of high priests. There can be no question that in what follows being listed as a "son" should be understood as being a descendant from the previously mentioned person, but in some cases with several unmentioned generations intervening. For example, some figures familiar to Bible students, such as Eli who served in the temple when Samuel was a boy, are not named. The list covers the line of priests until the time of the exile, when the temple was destroyed.

Kohath had four sons, of whom Amram was the most significant because his children included the famous trio of Aaron, Moses, and Miriam. And of those three, Aaron was the particular object of the chronicler's interest.

Aaron, in turn, had four sons, all whom became priests (Exod. 28:1). The oldest son, Nadab, would have become the next high priest, but he and his brother Abihu violated the laws for burning incense in the tabernacle, and they were killed for defiling God's holiness (Lev. 10:1–3). As a result, Eleazar was the son of Aaron who continued the new priestly line.

6:4–15. The chronicler now gives us a list of priests that does not mention everyone who has held that office during the time period but does provide continuity from Aaron through Jehozadak, the priest at the time of the Babylonian exile. We have the priest when the tabernacle was first established (**Aaron**), the priest when the temple was first erected (**Zadok**), and the priest who saw the temple destroyed (**Jehozadak**). Also in the list are the names of certain priests who were particularly important to Ezra.

There is a note attached to **Azariah** to the effect that he served in the temple built by Solomon. This statement seems hardly worth making since that is what all the priests in this line did from the time of Zadok on. But when we take a closer look at Azariah, we see why the chronicler wanted to give him special mention. In 2 Chronicles 26:16–21 we will read how King Uzziah assumed the office of priest by attempting to burn incense in the temple. But a group of priests, led by the high priest, blocked his way and reproached him. When Uzziah continued to try to burn the incense, he came down with leprosy and was never allowed inside the temple again. The high priest who served as champion for the purity of the priesthood and the temple was Azariah. So it appears that the little side note about his service in the temple should be construed as Ezra's tip of the hat to someone who protected the laws of worship and holiness.

One more person stands out in this list. Later on in Chronicles (2 Chr. 34), we will get acquainted with **Hilkiah**. He was the priest who found the book of the law in the temple during the reign of Josiah and thereby brought about religious reform and temple renovation.

6:16–30. Now we receive information on some of the other branches of the tribe of Levi. These are the other two clans, Gershom and Merari, as well as some further descendants of the nonpriestly line of Kohath. The chronicler reminds us again of the three clans. In what follows, the genealogies are unwrapped like a package, first removing an outer layer and then delving into an inner, more specific core.

After the chronicler has reminded us of the names of the three clans, he quickly mentions the sons of each of the founders. Next we read of further descendants within each of the clans. Still the clan of Kohath receives the most attention, this time bringing up people who were not in the high priestly succession.

Amminadab is not listed in verses 2 and 18 as one of the four sons of Kohath, but this name is clearly an alternative name for Izhar, since he is listed in this place in Exodus 6:21. His son Korah is not exactly a bright spot in this list, but again, he was an important person to mention in the light of Ezra's labors to restore the integrity of the priesthood. In Numbers 16 we read how Korah with a gang of supporters attempted to usurp the office of priest for himself and any other Israelite who wanted to work at the tabernacle. There is no reason other than Moses' arrogance, he claimed, why the priesthood should be limited to Aaron and his sons.

In response Moses presented Korah with a challenge: He and 250 other men could present incense to the Lord and see if God would accept their worship. When they did so, God caused the earth to open up and swallow them. Anyone reading this account who recognized the name of Korah would have been reminded of the strict limitation of the priesthood to the Aaronic line.

The name **Elkanah** appears several times in this list. The Elkanah who is familiar to us from previous Bible passages is Elkanah, the son of Jeroham, mentioned in verse 27 and again in verse 34. This Elkanah was the father of Samuel, the great prophet. In his day the office of high priest was held by Eli, who does not appear in Chronicles. Samuel spent his youth in the tabernacle as assistant to Eli (1 Sam. 2:11), but Samuel was not a priest either. It is true that he officiated at sacrifices as he went on his annual circuit of Israel (1 Sam. 9:13), but he did not hold office as priest at the tabernacle (as Korah had sought to do). The restrictions of sacrifices to the temple alone (Deut. 12:13) would not go into effect until some time after Samuel's death, when the temple was built.

The chronicler reminds us in verse 28 of **Joel** and **Abijah**, the sons of Samuel. They had been unfaithful to the Lord with graft, corruption, and bribery (1 Sam. 8:2–3), so they could no longer fulfill the special calling of prophet and judge that Samuel had held. The people installed a king instead. Nevertheless, Joel did become the father of one more important Levite, the chief musician Heman.

6:31–47. It has become apparent by now that it is difficult to get the chronicler to sit still for one particular historical time period as his frame of reference. Sometimes he assumes the standpoint of his own day a hundred years after the exile, while at other times he seems to speak from the vantage point of one of the earlier eras to which he makes reference. For the rest of 1 Chronicles, he will eventually settle in and maintain the perspective of the reign of King David (though still not consistently, with chapters 9 and 10 as important interludes). Thus, in this section, the focus is on the leading musicians of the tabernacle after David had moved the ark of the covenant to Jerusalem. David had a deep commitment to music, as evidenced by his writing of so many psalms as well as the institution of regular music in worship.

Each of the three persons mentioned here made significant contributions. **Heman** was the leader, and he also performed the task of seer or prophet to the king (1 Chr. 25:5). **Asaph** wrote twelve psalms (Pss. 50; 73–83). **Ethan** is also called Jeduthun (e.g., in 1 Chr. 25:1) and under that name wrote a number of psalms (Pss. 39; 62; 77) specifically for use in worship. Obviously the genealogies presented for these singers differ from the genealogies for their cousins, the priests.

6:48–53. Here follows a recapitulation of the duties of the Levites. In addition to the tasks of offering incense and sacrifices—limited to the Aaronic priesthood—and the performing of music—assigned to the three musicians—there were many other regular tasks that needed to be done. Running a major religious complex geared to animal sacrifices required a huge payroll for cleaning, animal inspection, crowd management, security, information services, food breaks, and so forth.

Think of the sanctuary as a large corporation whose lifeblood depended on hundreds of employees performing their jobs. And if you are thinking of the time of David, you need to multiply this picture by two. Even though David brought the ark of the covenant to Jerusalem and created a new sanctuary to go with it, the original tabernacle still existed as well and demanded attention until Solomon built the temple in Jerusalem. All these supporting chores were performed by those Levites who were neither in the direct priestly line nor singled out for musical service.

In verses 50–53 the chronicler again cites a short list of high priests. This time, because he is slowly zeroing in on the time of David, he stops with Zadok and Ahimaaz, who were priests in David's time.

6:54–81. As the chronicler had done with the tribes he mentioned earlier, he also details the cities allocated to the tribe of Levi. There is a catch here: Levi did not actually have a territory of its own. When Jacob pronounced his formal blessings on his sons (Gen. 49:1–27), he prophesied that both Levi and Simeon would be dispersed throughout the land (Gen. 49:7), and that prediction came about. For Simeon it meant that his lineage would eventually vanish as it became intermingled with the tribe of Judah, but for Levi the prophecy was fulfilled by the fact that the Levites would live in many different towns throughout the promised land.

The distribution of towns for Levites was carried out by strictly observing clan membership. In general, the Kohathites received cities in the south (among Judah, Benjamin, Simeon, and Ephraim), the Gershonites were told to live in the north (among Issachar, Asher, and Naphthali), and the Merarites were allocated home cities on the eastern bank of the Jordan River (within Reuben, Gad, and Manasseh).

Remember that sacrificial worship throughout the time of the judges and the reign of King David was not yet confined to one specific place (even though the tabernacle was the headquarters), so the Levites would have been responsible to make sure that all God's laws were obeyed in their areas. We also learn later on in Chronicles that some Levites had a distinct teaching ministry among the common people (2 Chr. 17:7–9).

B The Northern Tribes (7:1–40)

SUPPORTING IDEA: *In this listing for the so-called "northern tribes," the emphasis is on their provision of military might.*

7:1–5. **Issachar** was Jacob's ninth son, the fifth son by Leah (Gen. 30:17–18). In the prophetic blessing from his father, Issachar received a rather tepid and unenthusiastic endorsement, likening him to a worn-out donkey who was content to rest between saddlebags and submit to forced labor (Gen. 49:14–15). His tribe settled south of the Sea of Galilee and led an undistinguished existence. Issachar provided one judge in the time prior to the monarchy—a man named Tola, the son of Puah and grandson of Dodo (Judg. 10:1). Also, during the divided kingdom, one of the numerous short-lived dynasties came from the tribe of Issachar—the quite forgettable Baasha and his son, the disastrous Elah (1 Kgs. 15:27–16:10).

Nevertheless, as the chronicler tells us about Issachar, none of these things seem to matter. What the chronicler was concerned with was the support that the tribe was able to provide for the kingdom of David. The central point of this short genealogy is the disclosure that the tribe of Issachar was able to muster a military force of 87,000 men.

7:6–12. This is only the first mention of Benjamin's genealogy. **Benjamin** was the twelfth son of Jacob, the second son by Rachel. Benjamin was born much later than Joseph, his older full brother. His mother died in childbirth with Benjamin (Gen. 35:16–18). Jacob's blessing for him was also not particularly flattering, designating him as a ravenous wolf who was always out to catch and devour his prey (Gen. 49:27).

The tribe of Benjamin tended to be the problem child among his peers. At one time, the evil behavior of some Benjamites and the tribe's refusal to turn the miscreants over to justice caused a civil war in which all but six hundred men of an army of approximately twenty-six thousand were obliterated, and the continued existence of the tribe of Benjamin was in serious doubt (Judg. 19–21). By the time of David, however, as we learn from this section, the tribe had recovered its forces and was able to contribute significantly to the pool of available men.

7:13. **Naphtali** is another tribe that did not spend much time in the limelight. Its founder was the sixth son of Jacob, the second by Rachel's handmaid Bilhah. Jacob's deathbed blessing describes him as a liberated and fertile doe

(Gen. 49:21). The tribe appears favorably whenever it is mentioned; the high-light of its contribution to the history of Israel was in the person of Barak, the judge who fought alongside Deborah (Judg. 4:6). In the brief reference to Naphtali by the chronicler, we learn the names of his four sons and are reminded that his mother was Bilhah, Rachel's handmaid.

7:14–19. Now we return to the tribe of **Manasseh**, this time the western half. The information about the eastern half, the group that had settled on the eastern side of the Jordan River, already came up in the previous chapter. Manasseh was the older of Joseph's two sons, but the place of prominence went to his younger brother, Ephraim (Gen. 48:5). There is no tribe of Joseph, *per se,* but only the two half tribes of Ephraim and Manasseh. There are occasions when the Bible speaks of the tribe of Joseph, but it has Ephraim in mind when it does so (e.g., 1 Chr. 7:29; Zech. 10:6).

A large portion of the tribe of Manasseh decided to establish homes on the eastern side of the Jordan River, but they fulfilled their duty in helping the other tribes conquer the land before returning to settle there. The other half of the tribe settled on the western side of the river in the main portion of the land. They are the ones in view in this chapter. Among Manasseh's various contributions to the history of Israel, it can boast of the heroic judge Gideon as coming from its ranks (Judg. 6:15).

Again we do not get any lengthy list, but what we have contains some interesting allusions. In verse 14 we read that at least a part of the line of Manasseh continued by way of an Aramean woman. This is one more example of how the genealogies often contain startling intrusions.

In verse 15 the chronicler mentions **Zelophehad** and the fact that he had only daughters. There is a story connected to this situation (Num. 27:1–6). Upon approaching the promised land, these five women went to see Moses and the other Israelite leaders with the request that, since they had no brothers, they should be provided with an inheritance. The request was approved, and the women received a share of the land (Josh. 17:3–6).

7:20–29. By the time of Ezra, **Ephraim**, though once the leader among all the northern tribes, was no longer a significant presence. The chronicler does not spend much time on this tribe either, compared to the lengthy treatments that Judah, Levi, and Benjamin rated. However, there are a few highlights in this list. Ephraim was the son of Joseph, who was the Pharaoh's grand vizier. It must have been while living in Egypt that his two sons, Ezer and Elead, were killed while going on a cattle raid to Gath, and Ephraim was inconsol-able for a long time. Eventually he had another son, to whom he gave the name **Beriah**, which is a play on the Hebrew word for "misfortune." One of

Beriah's children was a daughter named **Sheerah**, who distinguished herself by building several cities.

As the short genealogy of Ephraim unfolds, in verse 27 we come across one of the most important characters in the history of Israel—**Joshua**, the son of Nun. Joshua was the leader of the Israelites in the conquest and settlement of the land. But that's where the listing for Ephraim's descendants stops. Again, the Ephraimite line was not significant for the chronicler's purposes. Having shown how it led up to the great Joshua, he had no need to go further.

7:30–40. Once more we get some information on one of the less important tribes, the tribe of **Asher**. Asher was the second son whom Zilpah, Leah's servant, bore for Jacob. Asher's descendants also played a supportive role in the history of Israel, though, in keeping with Jacob's prophetic blessing (Gen. 49:20), they enjoyed prosperity. Just like the listings for Issachar and Benjamin, this listing concludes with a reference to Asher's military prowess.

ⓒ Benjamin and Saul (8:1–40)

> **SUPPORTING IDEA:** *Because the line of Saul out of the tribe of Benjamin provided the greatest rivalry to the house of David from Judah, the chronicler gives greater detail about Benjamin and Saul.*

8:1–28. This genealogy differs greatly from the one in chapter 7. However, there is no reason to assume this one is right and the other is wrong. We should think of this material as a supplement to or expansion of the information in 7:6–12. The reason we can do so lies in Genesis 46:21 and Numbers 26:38–41, which provide two further lists that differ from these two by different groupings of these names. It seems credible that both lists in this book are correct, but they give different angles on the subject.

We mentioned earlier that Benjamin caused a lot of trouble among the tribes of Israel. However, it also made some positive contributions. For example, in 1 Chronicles 8:6 we run across Ehud, the left-handed judge, who liberated Israel from Eglon, king of the Moabites (Judg. 3:12–30).

We have no further information about the events related in 1 Chronicles 8:7–11. Due to certain unknown circumstances, some Benjamites were deported to Moab. Among those exiles was a certain Shaharaim who had two wives, but he divorced them for no known reason. Infertility on the part of his first wives could not have been the problem since at least one of them, Hushim, had two sons: Abitub and Elpaal. And wouldn't you know it? It was through Elpaal, the second son of the rejected wife that the main line continued. Once again we see how, paradoxically, God chose the weak and insignificant to continue his work.

According to verse 28, the later leaders among Benjamin lived in Jerusalem, which at the time was a settlement at the foot of the Jebusite fortress (see "Deeper Discoveries" for more on this topic). Jerusalem became the capital of the kingdom of Judah, but it never lost its affinity for Benjamin. Consequently, at the time when the kingdom split, Benjamin was counted as affiliated with Judah as one of the two "southern" tribes.

8:29–40. Having provided us with a further genealogy for the tribe of Benjamin as a whole, the chronicler now takes a more specific look at the genealogy of King Saul and his descendants. Gibeon and Shimeah are names of places, not people. Both of these places are in the "greater Jerusalem metropolitan area."

The mention of Saul and his sons in verse 33 is brief. The line of descent is Ner, Kish, Saul, and Saul's sons. Of the four sons, Esh-Baal, also called Ish-Bosheth, was the only one who survived the slaughter by the Philistines, related in chapter 10. He ruled as king of the northern tribes for a short while after Saul's death (2 Sam. 2:10) before being killed himself as the kingdom was reunified under David.

The only other relative of Saul's to survive was a nephew, **Merib-Baal**, also called Mephibosheth, the son of Jonathan. In subsequent years David showed kindness to him out of love and respect for Jonathan. He gave Merib-Baal a permanent residence at the palace along with the privilege of dining at the king's table (2 Sam. 4:4). The entire lineage that follows is descended from Merib-Baal, and we can see that it replenished itself quickly, restoring the pride of Benjamin.

Ⓓ The Return from Exile (9:1–44)

SUPPORTING IDEA: *Having given us various historical roots, the chronicler now ties them into the list of those who returned from the Babylonian exile.*

9:1–2. The chronicler once again takes us through a time warp. He barely mentions the exile in Babylon, states that it happened because of Judah's unfaithfulness without explaining the charge at this time, and zips right on to the happier moment of the resettlement after the exile. To many of the first readers of this book, this chapter might have been the most important section. The chronicler was trying to explain to his audience the importance of understanding one's heritage among the people of God. This information, which took things right into their own day, would have been what everyone was looking for.

When we get a school yearbook, a new phone directory, or a group picture, one of the first things we look for is ourselves. So the readers of this book would have wanted to get to this chapter as quickly as possible. Are my grandparents listed here? Am I a recognized member of this group? Can I lay claim to an eminent place in society? Here was the all-important connection to their own time.

In 539 B.C. King Cyrus of Persia issued the decree that the Jews be allowed to return from Babylon to their own country. This order had one purpose: the rebuilding of the temple, which had been destroyed by King Nebuchadnezzar of Babylonia (2 Chr. 36:23). So when the people returned to Jerusalem, it was specifically for the purpose of rebuilding the temple and reestablishing worship. No wonder, then, that the majority of the initial resettlers of the land consisted of people associated with the temple: priests, Levites, and temple servants.

9:3. The tribal affiliations of those who returned to their homeland, other than Levi, were Judah, Benjamin, Ephraim, and Manasseh. Note that the latter two tribes were a part of the Northern Kingdom of Israel, which had been expatriated a long time earlier, as a part of the ten northern tribes. They are a part of what are referred to today as the "lost tribes," but everyone from the north disappeared completely. Nonetheless, even though Ephraim and Manasseh are mentioned here, that is as far as it went. The more detailed lists do not give us any information on these two groups.

9:4–6. A total of 690 families of Judah are counted by the chronicler in this enumeration, including that of Uthai, who could trace his lineage back to Perez, son of Judah. Thus, he could theoretically rank within the royal line.

9:7–9. Benjamin actually supplied a larger contingent than Judah with 956 families. The heads of families listed here by name were either representative or esteemed as particularly eminent.

9:10–13. There were more priestly families, with a total of 1,760, than the sum of lay families from Judah and Benjamin, which came to 1,646. This was due to the fact that the point of the return was the reestablishment of the temple. The chronicler compliments these men for their competence and reliability. Later on we will see how David had organized the priesthood into different shifts (1 Chr. 24:1–19), an arrangement that was revived after the exile (Luke 1:5). It is obvious that with that many priests, not everyone could perform sacrifices every day.

9:14–16. Here is a short listing of Levites with no actual count given. After a lengthy excursion about the gatekeepers, the tasks of the general Levites are resumed later in 9:28.

9:17–27. The gatekeepers were in charge of security for the tabernacle and later for the temple. Considering the sacredness of the objects stored there, not to mention some of their values in gold, precious fabrics, and other materials, it was only natural that there should be a group of devoted guards to keep the area safe. But even more importantly, someone needed to guard the sacredness of the grounds, lest a person should go into an area which was off-limits to the general population. Much later, during the time of Christ, a sign on the temple door announced that any uncircumcised person who proceeded any further would have only himself to blame for his death. A group of alert guards could prevent that kind of tragedy.

By alluding to Phinehas, the grandson of Aaron, the chronicler gives us an example of how important safeguarding the tabernacle was (Num. 25:1–18). During the latter years of Israel's sojourn in the desert, before the conquest of the promised land, some of the men began to worship Moabite gods in order to gain the favors of Moabite women. God sent a plague as punishment. Then, just as Moses was in the process of pronouncing judgment on the idolaters, in full view of everyone, a man from the tribe of Simeon showed up with a pagan Midianite woman at the entrance to the tabernacle, ready to stroll in and perform some worship ceremony. As soon as Phinehas caught sight of them, he grabbed a spear and killed both of them. With the death of Zimri from Simeon and Cozbi, his Midianite woman, God stopped the plague.

According to verses 22–27, there were at the time of Ezra only 212 of these gatekeepers. If one considers that there are 365 days in the year and 24 hours in a day, it becomes clear that this was an inadequate number. The guards had to be alert around the clock, and they had to be supplemented from time to time by other Levites who did not live in the city.

9:28–34. Here follows a list of tasks performed by Levites that went beyond the gatekeeping duties. Someone had to be in charge of the implements of worship: the bread on the altar, the wine and oil, the incense, and all the furniture. In a small aside we learn that some priests, probably trying to make sure everything they did conformed to divine law, took care of mixing their own spices. Special status went to the musicians; they were on call at all hours of the day and night, so they had no other obligations.

9:35–44. This section concludes with a second enumeration of the genealogy of Saul. Except for a few minor variations in the spelling of some names, this list is identical to the list in 1 Chronicles 8:29–40. We have no explanation for why the same passage is repeated, but it does serve a function at this location: to move from the genealogies to the first lengthy narrative passage, which tells the tragic story of Saul.

MAIN IDEA REVIEW: *The genealogy of the tribe of Levi is important because it delineates those who could be engaged in the temple service. The genealogy of Benjamin leads to King Saul, whose reign was a failure, while the other tribes primarily provided military strength to the nation.*

III. CONCLUSION

The Driver's License Is Only the Beginning

It is almost a routine expectation in the United States that when teenagers turn sixteen (or so), they will be able to earn their driver's licenses. Most schools have driver's education programs, and in most states a parent, older sibling, or even a friend are permitted to teach someone to drive. Consequently, "getting your license" is an important transition in a young person's life. Years of dreaming of what it would be like never to have to depend on anyone else for transportation and to be able to drive anywhere you want to go have finally come to fruition.

Of course, the illusion gives way quickly to the cold chill of reality. You can't go anywhere with your new driver's license if you don't have a car available. You need to pay for license plates and insurance. The car needs to be maintained. Even if you have a car, you can't just drive anywhere if you don't have time to do so—and life's obligations are probably becoming increasingly crowded right around that time.

Worst of all, the thrill of having entered the privileged circle of driver's license holders fades quickly. As a junior or senior in high school, you may feel pride in having the cherished card. A year or two later, everyone assumes that you have a license, and its main function may be to serve as identification for writing checks. For most of us adults, the only time the driver's license really occupies our attention is when we have to renew it every few years.

Being in the inner circle, like having a driver's license, was possible in ancient Israel by membership in a distinguished tribe. If you were in the tribe of Levi, for example, you held membership in a tribe of privilege—those who could be priests or temple attendants. If you were a member of the royal tribe, you were a part of the tribe that supplied the kings for Israel. But which tribe would that be?

Ephraim wanted to be the tribe of leadership and royalty for all Israel, but it never measured up. In our section we observe Benjamin as the royal tribe, looking for a moment as though it would be more privileged than all the others, but it also fell short. Ultimately, pride of place would go to Judah.

So in this context think of membership in a tribe as similar to holding a driver's license while many of your peers do not have one. You have privileges and opportunities that they can not experience. But just as someone can lose his driver's license for poor performance, so a tribe could lose its privileged standing for not being faithful to God. We see Benjamin as the leader among the tribes, but only temporarily because its favorite son, Saul, abused his privileges.

PRINCIPLES

- God has specific ministries in mind for each one of us, depending on our circumstances, talents, and—most importantly—his calling.
- God expects us to live faithfully in whatever calling he gives us.
- God judges us not by the standards of some other person's calling but by whether we are faithful to the work he has given us.

APPLICATIONS

- The Bible gives us many pictures of grace. Think about Paul's picture of grace in Ephesians 2:1,5. He says we were dead in sins and trespasses. What can a dead person do? Then God comes and makes us alive in Christ.
- Take some time just to think about the miracle of your own creation and God's sustaining your life second by second. Make a list of some of the strengths God has given you.
- Ask God to show you how you are to use the gifts he has planted in you.
- Ask God to show you any ways you have allowed envy of others' gifts to render you less effective in his service, then ask him to help you to put aside that envy.

IV. LIFE APPLICATION

A New Family Membership

In the time period reflected in this passage, we see how only those who were members of specific tribes could carry out particular functions. For example, only those who belonged to the tribe of Levi were eligible to serve in the tabernacle and temple. We encountered a long set of genealogies in order to clarify who might be a part of that circle of privilege.

However, those days are past. When God sent his Son, he turned things upside down. Rather than our status being derived from which family we were born into, our new spiritual state is based on one single fact: God has adopted us into his family. No one has an edge over anyone else. Galatians 3:26 reads: "You are all sons of God through faith in Christ Jesus." Anyone who comes to Christ through faith automatically becomes a member of God's "inner circle."

Our membership in the people of God is based on what God has done in Christ; birth or privilege have nothing to do with it. But God also has a specific calling for us as we live out our lives in Christ. He wants us to live up to that calling, whether it be as full-time ministers or as church members with various ministries on his behalf.

V. PRAYER

Lord Jesus, we are overwhelmed that you have called us to be your people, making it possible by your atoning death to be adopted into your family. We thank you for allowing each of us to have a relationship with you that doesn't have to be mediated by priests or sacrifices. Help us never to forget your love for us, and help us to live in such a way that your grace in our lives will be visible to everyone. Amen.

VI. DEEPER DISCOVERIES

A. Why Didn't the "Priesthood of All Believers" Apply to Korah (6:22)?

Even though the chronicler does not go into the story of Korah and simply mentions his name, there is significance to the fact that his name comes up in this context. Korah violated the strict divisions that God had instituted. Even though he was not from the line of Aaron, he tried to usurp the role of priest (Num. 16). When attempting to fulfill the priestly role of burning incense, he and his supporters were killed. God had declared through Moses that Aaron's descendants alone were allowed to be priests.

But this incident raises some questions. Is this fair? Doesn't God want a personal relationship with all human beings? Why should God care who burns incense to him? For that matter, since in the New Testament God did away with the priesthood (Heb. 10:11–12), why kill people for not observing such provisional rules at an earlier time?

These are difficult questions, and they will arise for the attentive reader at several places throughout Chronicles. The only way they can be answered is by first letting God be God and remembering that he is the only one in a position to fully understand his own actions. But second, from what we see about his plan throughout the Bible, God has allowed humanity to relate to him in many different ways. Each time he has demonstrated our inability to establish a relationship with him by our own means.

Whether it be through the simple sacrifices of the patriarchs or the complex system of the law, in each scenario two points become clear: our sinfulness and God's sovereignty in both punishment and grace. But this demonstration cannot be made in a particular context if God does not let the system play itself out rigorously and consistently.

Think of it this way: Humanity stands judged for its sinfulness in God's eyes. Given every possible opportunity, human beings failed to attain their own righteousness. Consequently, no person can say to God, "If only you would have let us relate to you in such and such a way, then we could have managed on our own." What if we could relate to God with sacrifices but without a priesthood? No, we tried that before Moses, and we failed. What if we could relate to God by means of a strict professional priesthood? Again, we tried that and we failed. And now you see that if the Aaronic priesthood could have been compromised right at the outset, there would have been no point to the demonstration. Once the demonstration was completed, God sent his Son to do for us what we could not do for ourselves under any other system (Heb. 9:11–12).

Furthermore, we need to be careful not to make God's grace a human right. The fact that as believers in Christ we may now know God personally without a priestly system does not mean that any human is entitled to this opportunity. It is only a gift from God, the exception to the rule, and not the rule itself.

So, even though we may not emotionally like the idea of a priesthood limited by heredity with severe sanctions for those who violate it, we need to recognize that it does fit into the plan of our holy and righteous God. To question it is ultimately to lessen the greatness of the grace that God has shown us in Christ.

B. Who Lived in Jerusalem? (8:28)

David finally conquered Jerusalem, as reported in 1 Chronicles 11:1–9. The problem is that Jerusalem comes up several times prior to this event. Joshua defeated the king of Jerusalem (Josh. 10:26). The sons of Judah transported a prisoner to Jerusalem and only subsequently attacked the city (Judg.

1:7–8). Even David carried the head of Goliath to Jerusalem long before he was king and conquered it (1 Sam. 17:54). In this verse we read about the Benjamites living in Jerusalem, apparently before David's time. There seems to be a glaring inconsistency here.

However, as is so often the case, the inconsistency vanishes as soon as we look at all the data. The key is in Judges 1:21, where it is pointed out that the Benjamites settled in Jerusalem but they did not dislodge the Jebusites from their fortress. Obviously, Jerusalem, was a cluster of several townships or "neighborhoods," with the other Jebusites right on top of the mountain, but other segments not as well defended were taken over by Israel in an erratic set of campaigns. Consequently, Jerusalem (the Jebusite fortress) was not conquered until David's kingship, but Jerusalem (the surrounding neighborhoods) was already under Israelite control.

C. Chapter 9—Before or After the Exile (9:2)

The NIV makes clear that the list in chapter 9 refers to those who returned to Jerusalem after the exile. But there is some debate among scholars about whether this is the correct translation. Some conservative, evangelical scholars (Payne, 374) believe that the reference to the exile in 9:1 should be thought of as the conclusion to chapter 8, and that 9:2 begins afresh with a listing of those who lived in Jerusalem prior to the exile. This would, of course, drastically change the understanding of the content of the chapter. Since this is not just a liberal criticism (since liberal scholars do not think these lists have much historical value anyway), the serious Bible student needs to be alerted to the fact that this opinion is also being published by people who are fully committed to the historic truth and the inerrancy of Scripture.

There is good reason to believe, however, that the NIV gets it right and that this chapter specifically mentions people who returned from the exile and resettled in Jerusalem. The list would be meager if it just referred to Jerusalem in its days of glory prior to the exile. The fact that the majority of families were priestly only makes sense in a post-exilic setting, when they would have been the ones to come back to restore temple worship. And why would anyone care that Uthai was descended from the line of Judah through Perez before the exile when Jerusalem was crowded with members of the royal family? This commentary is not about settling disputes among scholars, but it is nice to be able to use this occasion to point out that we can feel safe that the Bible translation we are using is reliable.

VII. TEACHING OUTLINE

A. INTRODUCTION

1. Lead Story: The Privileges of Nobility
2. Context: Just as in the Middle Ages the status of nobility was a cherished and exclusive privilege, so in this passage we see how God established certain tribes to carry out specific duties. In particular, we see how the priesthood is limited to the tribe of Levi.
3. Transition: Among the tribes other than Judah, certain tribes had specific duties. Members of the tribe of Levi served as temple workers, and one strand of that tribe constituted the priesthood. Benjamin fulfilled a particular function because it provided the first king, though unfortunately a failure. Other tribes contributed to the military readiness of the nation.

B. COMMENTARY

1. The Tribe of Levi (6:1–81)
2. The Northern Tribes (7:1–40)
3. Benjamin and Saul (8:1–40)
4. The Return from Exile (9:1–44)

C. CONCLUSION: THE DRIVER'S LICENSE IS ONLY THE BEGINNING

VIII. ISSUES FOR DISCUSSION

1. What are some areas of church life (yours or the church in general) where one particular group of people seems to dominate?
2. How can we improve the way in which we show people that every believer, regardless of status, is a member of God's family?
3. In what ways can we encourage one another to use our differing gifts in ministry?

1 Chronicles 10:1–14

God's Judgment on Saul

I. INTRODUCTION
A Terrified Law Student

II. COMMENTARY
A verse-by-verse explanation of the chapter.

III. CONCLUSION
Sometimes Judgment Is Final

An overview of the principles and applications from the chapter.

IV. LIFE APPLICATION
Nothing Makes Life So Good as Almost Dying

Melding the chapter to life.

V. PRAYER
Tying the chapter to life with God.

VI. DEEPER DISCOVERIES
Historical, geographical, and grammatical enrichment of the commentary.

VII. TEACHING OUTLINE
Suggested step-by-step group study of the chapter.

VIII. ISSUES FOR DISCUSSION
Zeroing the chapter in on daily life.

"*T*he death of the soul takes place when God forsakes it, as the death of the body when the soul forsakes it."

Augustine

1 Chronicles 10:1–14

IN A NUTSHELL

*K*ing Saul, having been condemned by God for his disobedience, dies in a losing battle against the Philistines. In this tragic passage we see the inescapable truth that God judges our sinfulness, a truth that highlights the wonder of God's grace for us.

God's Judgment on Saul

I. INTRODUCTION

A Terrified Law Student

*M*artin Luther, the man who began the Protestant Reformation in the sixteenth century, started his serious religious life in a moment of terror. He was on his way along a forest road, heading back to the university where he was studying law, when a thunderstorm broke out and a lightning bolt nearly hit him. There he stood under a tree, overcome by dread, thinking that he might have died. In panic he raised his voice to the sky and vowed that he would become a monk (Bainton, 15–33).

To Luther the lightning was a warning, a sign from God that he could take his life at any time whenever it pleased him. Luther came to realize the reality of God's holiness and his own sinfulness and the utter incompatibility of the two. Becoming a monk seemed the best way of trying to avoid God's judgment, or at least to soften it.

Luther suffered another moment of terror when, as a newly ordained priest, he celebrated the mass for the first time. Again he was overwhelmed by the awareness of how impossible it is for a human being to stand in the presence of the righteous God. As he continued his life as a monk, he subjected himself to many austerities: flagellation, starvation, a pilgrimage on his knees, as well as the quest for some mystical experience that would alleviate his concerns. Nothing brought him the peace of mind he was looking for because he realized that no effort undertaken by a sinful human being could ever placate an angry God.

Finally, God brought Martin Luther to see the other half of this coin—his divine grace. Through studying the Book of Romans, the struggling monk became aware that, even though God is a holy and righteous judge, he has also given his Son, Jesus Christ, for us on the cross and is now imputing Christ's righteousness to those who come to him in faith. This recognition liberated Luther from his feelings of terror of God, and it would eventually lead him to bring a renewed understanding of the gospel to all Christendom.

The gospel begins with judgment. We all stand guilty before God in our sin. If there were no divine judgment, what would we be saved from? If God were not a pure and holy God who could not overlook sin, then what would make his grace so special? If we were not in our natural condition in a state of hostility toward God, then what need would there be for the atonement? So the Bible contains stories of God's love and grace as well as his judgment.

And so it is with Chronicles. In the introduction to the book, we claimed that Chronicles could be understood as the "gospel according to Ezra." If so, the chronicler picked a strange place to start. Having finally laid aside (for a time) his lists of genealogies, he launches into a narrative. But what a story it is! He begins to detail King Saul's death and the subsequent mistreatment of his corpse, a bleak way to get the plot going.

The chronicler is drawing a contrast between the disastrous reign of Saul and the subsequent successful reign of King David. But let us not forget that this contrast extends far deeper—to the difference between a life that culminates in God's judgment and a life that is crowned by God's grace.

II. COMMENTARY

God's Judgment on Saul

MAIN IDEA: *King Saul died a tragic death as judgment for his disobedience of God.*

A The Death of Saul (10:1–6)

SUPPORTING IDEA: *Saul died of his own hand as he was losing a crucial battle against the Philistines.*

10:1. This verse encapsulates the pathos of Saul's life. He had spent his kingship trying to rid Israel of her enemies, such as the Ammonites, Amalekites, and Philistines. There was a time when he had come close to achieving his goal and had established a unified and secure kingdom. With the help of his son Jonathan as well as David (both before and after their split), he had been able to keep the Philistines in check and confined to their towns south of Israel. But now all this was coming apart. The Philistines had managed to move their army up to the northern third of Israel, thereby circumventing Saul's defenses. A rout took place, and Saul's accomplishments were wiped out.

There was nothing new about the fact that **the Philistines fought against Israel**; there had been war with the Philistines off and on since the time of the judges. The new fact was that **the Israelites fled before them**. As we read in 1 Samuel 28:5, Saul had anticipated this defeat to such an extent that the once-intrepid warrior sought the advice of an occult practitioner. And so the Philistines drove the Israelite army from their position on Mount Gilboa. The

Israelite army was defeated; those who did not manage to escape were decimated. All that Saul had fought for was lost.

10:2. In contrast to more modern ways of warfare in which the leaders hold themselves aloof from battle, at the time it was expected that the king and his sons would take an active part in the fighting. They would not normally be right at the front of the line, but they would from time to time be actually engaged with the enemy. Thus, the Philistines were able to gain access to Saul and his sons: **Jonathan**, **Abinadab**, and **Malki-Shua**.

Of the three sons mentioned, Jonathan is best known, both as Saul's able battle leader (1 Sam. 14) and as David's close friend. Jonathan was willing to sacrifice his own claim to the throne to David, whom he knew to be called of the Lord (1 Sam. 20:14). We have no information on Abinadab (also called Ishvi in 1 Sam. 14:49) or on Malki-Shua other than that they were sons of Saul. Their deaths meant that there would be no dynasty of Saul on the throne since Saul's heirs had been exterminated. With their deaths, any continuity of Saul's line came to an abrupt end. (We will mention the ill-fated Ish-Bosheth below.)

10:3. Saul himself was not protected from the fighting. The Philistines grew closer and closer to where he was. Eventually he was hit by an arrow from the enemy's archers. The chronicler spares us the details of the injury, but it was a serious wound, since Saul expected that he would not be able to escape capture by the Philistines.

10:4. Saul accepted the inevitability of his defeat. This did not necessarily mean the inevitability of death, however, for there could be a fate worse than death. In his eyes there was good reason to request death at the hands of **his armor-bearer** rather than endure what might come later. He was afraid that **these uncircumcised fellows** would **come and abuse** him. There was far more to this threat than the danger of being killed by an uncircumcised man. The real calamity was the dishonor and humiliation that might be heaped on him by the Philistines.

Saul's request was understandable but not necessarily excusable. It was his attempt at a way out of a situation in which he should not have been to begin with. Because of his ongoing disobedience over the last years of his life, Saul had come to a point where he thought he had no good options left. So he asked his armor-bearer to deliver the final killing blow with his sword.

The lad was horrified at the idea. He was an armor-bearer, not a soldier. He had probably never killed anyone before, let alone his own king whom he was sworn to protect. When the staunch armor-bearer would not comply with his order, Saul impaled himself on his own sword.

10:5. The armor-bearer believed that his life was no longer worth anything after his master, the king, had taken his life. Perhaps he even felt that he had failed in his duties by not preventing Saul from killing himself. So he also **fell on his sword and died**.

We can contrast the young man's attitude with that of the Amalekite man mentioned in 2 Samuel 1:1–15. We know that the author of Samuel was aware of the facts of Saul's death since the account in 1 Samuel 31 is identical with that in our passage in Chronicles. But the Book of Samuel reports that an Amalekite man ran to David and claimed that he had, in fact, committed the mercy killing that the armor-bearer had refused. The Amalekite's assertion was false, but he thought David would praise him and reward him for his alleged action. But David had this man executed immediately. To kill the Lord's anointed, even as a supposed act of mercy, was a heinous thing to do.

10:6. The chronicler summarizes the devastation. He specifies first that Saul and his three sons died, and then he mentions more generally that the entire house of Saul was wiped out in the process.

In this verse we can clearly discern the intent of the chronicler in writing this story. Here we have one of the few points in this passage where the version in 1 Chronicles differs slightly from that in 1 Samuel. The contrast makes all the difference for understanding the chronicler's purpose. In 1 Samuel 31:6 we read, "So Saul and his three sons and his armor-bearer and all his men died together that same day." Note that the Samuel account enumerates the three sons, the armor-bearer, and all Saul's men. But the chronicler makes a much wider sweeping statement. He declares that **all his house died together**. The most obvious meaning of this phrase is that Saul's entire set of blood relatives together with any future lineage was eliminated.

We know that not everyone was eradicated. The chronicler himself had made reference just a few verses before to Esh-Baal (9:39), known also as Ish-Bosheth, and Merib-Baal (9:40), also called Mephibosheth. Ish-Bosheth would succeed Saul and govern most of the kingdom for a time until he was displaced by David (2 Sam. 2:8–5:3). Mephibosheth, Saul's grandson, would eventually come to live at David's palace (2 Sam. 9:1–12). And further, the chronicler himself has already reported on the continuation of Saul's line of descendants through Mephibosheth (1 Chr. 9:40–44).

So what could Ezra mean by writing that all Saul's house died? Simply this: God was finished with the house of Saul. There would be no further chances, no possibility of reinstatement. The time for Saul's house was over, done, concluded, finished. The fact that Ish-Bosheth may have attempted for a time to carry on Saul's lineage on the throne is totally irrelevant to the chronicler. God was through with Saul and his descendants, and that was the only pertinent truth for the chronicler.

Ⓑ The Treatment of Saul's Body (10:7–12)

SUPPORTING IDEA: *The Philistines desecrated Saul's corpse, but the people of Jabesh Gilead honored him.*

10:7. Once Saul's army had been driven from Mount Gilboa, the general flight continued into the valley. Not only soldiers but women and children as well ran ahead of the pursuing Philistine army as fast as they could. The second step in a successful military campaign, after defeating the enemy, is to hold his territory, and this is what the Philistines did on this second day. They **occupied** the Israelite villages, not in the sense of moving in and starting to live there but in the sense of placing soldiers in each of the villages and securing them for military purposes.

10:8. The third step in a military campaign is to "mop up." This means going over the conquered area and eliminating any pockets of resistance. This also meant that the soldiers would go from corpse to corpse to strip them of all valuable items: jewelry, armor, weapons, clothing, fasteners, as well as any personal belongings. This was a grisly business, sorting through the corpses as they were beginning to smell and fighting against scavengers in order to remove valuables. But this was the main way armies got paid in those days. Supply lines were usually poor or nonexistent. Wages, if any, would have been utterly undependable. Every soldier longed for generous booty to carry away from the battlefield.

As the Philistines were carrying out this gruesome task, what should they find but King Saul's body! It seems that they were surprised. Even if the archers knew they had injured the king on the previous day, they may not have realized that Saul was dead, and neither may the soldiers engaged in plundering. Suddenly the great trophies, the bodies of Saul and his sons, lay before them.

10:9–10. Saul had feared that the Philistines would abuse him if they caught him alive. They found him dead, but that did not stop them from dismembering his corpse and displaying their prize in triumph. They were following ancient customs. For example, after David killed Goliath, he displayed the giant's head in Jerusalem (1 Sam. 17:54), and his sword eventually wound up in the tabernacle at Nob (1 Sam. 21:9).

Still, our text conveys a particular brutality in the way the Philistines treated Saul's remains. After all, this was the king of the hated Israelites, someone who had inflicted many defeats on them. After they had removed his armor, they cut off his head and sent word throughout the territory that Saul had died. We read in 1 Samuel that the bodies of Saul and his sons were hung from the wall of the nearby town of Beth Shan (1 Sam. 31:10). The chronicler does not mention this fact, but instead he states that the Philistines mounted Saul's head in the temple of Dagon, their chief idol. There, as the supposed sign of Dagon's victory over the Israelites, the head of King Saul decorated the pagan house of worship.

The messengers who reported Saul's death were proclaiming their **news among their idols and their people**. Here we see firsthand the understanding of pagan deities by those who worshiped them. The false gods did not know what had happened unless a human messenger told them. Isaiah proclaimed of idols, "They know nothing, they understand nothing; their eyes are plastered over so they cannot see, and their minds closed so they cannot understand" (Isa. 44:18). And yet the idol worshipers felt compelled to go through the process of letting their deities know what had happened in the world.

10:11–12. Finding out how the Philistines had disgraced Saul's body, the **valiant men** of **Jabesh Gilead** rescued it along with the bodies of his sons and gave them proper burial honors. They buried the bones after burning the corpses (1 Sam. 31:12) and observed a seven-day fast as a memorial.

The inhabitants of Jabesh Gilead had good reason to be loyal to Saul. Located on the eastern side of the Jordan in the territory of the tribe of Gad, Jabesh had been the beneficiary of Saul's first military campaign (1 Sam. 11). The Ammonites had besieged the town and threatened the residents with cruelty and disgrace, but Saul, the newly anointed king, had rallied Israel and liberated the town.

C The Reason for Saul's Death (10:13–14)

SUPPORTING IDEA: *Saul lost his kingdom and died as judgment on his disobedience of God.*

10:13–14. Up until now, except for that phrase "all his house" in verse 6, the chronicler has not commented on the events that he is reporting. Now, however, the inspired writer gives us the reasons for Saul's fate: He was unfaithful to the Lord, he did not keep the word of the Lord, he consulted a medium for guidance, and he did not inquire of the Lord.

Saul was not what we would call an "evil" person. Was he troubled? Definitely. Ruthless? Absolutely. Self-willed? To be sure. But if we look at the total picture, Saul does not come across as a thoroughly corrupt king. Later on in Chronicles we will meet some kings whose actions and attitudes will curl our hair and set our teeth on edge. There will be kings who worshiped idols, practiced sorcery, and even killed their own babies. Saul did none of that.

But the degree of disobedience does not matter. For Saul to have placed himself outside the circle of obedience is all that counts. When God had Samuel install Saul as king, he expected the new monarch to rule as one who implemented his divine will. There was no room for a king who governed by his own desires. This passage represents a crucial moment in the history of Israel as they are shifting from the governance of tribes to having a king who would lead them and unify them in their identity as the chosen people of God.

With a king who felt free to question God's commands, the nation would never have been able to make the transition. Instead, the conditions during the period of the judges, which often verged on anarchy, would only have gotten worse, since a confused and divided people would have become a people united under confusion. Thus, it was not the extent of Saul's sins that mattered but the fact that he did not place his life under God as king.

We can assume that the chronicler expected his readers to have some knowledge of the story of Saul. The prophet Samuel had commanded Saul to wait until Samuel came to present a sacrifice to God before Saul's army went into battle. Saul had waited and waited, and then his soldiers started getting impatient and leaving. So Saul took it upon himself to conduct the sacrifice (1 Sam. 13:7–14). The king was not authorized to perform this act, and he was also disobedient by not waiting specifically for Samuel. Saul thought he could supplant God's orders with his own judgment; thus he was **unfaithful to the LORD**.

God, through Samuel, had commanded Saul to kill all Amalekites and their property, but he spared their King Agag as well as livestock that he supposedly planned to present as sacrifices to the Lord (1 Sam. 15:1–9). What was the great harm in this? Saul felt free to second-guess God and question God's specific orders, thus setting the precedent that the authority of the king of Israel could supersede the authority of God himself. In this way Saul **did not keep the word of the LORD**, and God would not permit this state of affairs to continue.

The further Saul drifted away from God, the more rebellious he became. Finally, he **even consulted a medium for guidance**. Deuteronomy 18:9–14 forbids all occult activities, and Saul himself had enforced this prohibition vigorously at one time. But just before the last battle with the Philistines, he made contact with the departed Samuel through a spirit medium (1 Sam. 28:7–25). By doing this the king committed two serious offenses: he consorted with the occult, and he took matters into his own hands rather than limiting himself to God's guidance. Thus, he also **did not inquire of the** LORD. Saul placed his personal discernment ahead of God's guidance.

So the kingdom would pass on. The monarchy would not come out of the tribe of Benjamin but out of Judah, and the king with the never-ending lineage would be David and not Saul. The chronicler, having dismissed Saul with this distressing account, is now ready to shift his attention to what will become a major focus—the rule of David over Israel. With the terse words, **the LORD . . . turned the kingdom over to David son of Jesse**, the chronicler expressed God's verdict.

The chronicler comes right out and says, **the LORD put him to death**, thereby leaving no doubt in anyone's mind why Saul's fate had befallen him. Sure, it was Saul's own sword held by his own hand on which he fell on Mount Gilboa, but it was God himself who brought about all these events. The Lord is not to be trifled with. He does not overlook sin, and he has the right to judge and to punish. If the gospel begins with judgment, then we have witnessed the first step in understanding the good news.

> **MAIN IDEA REVIEW:** *King Saul died a tragic death as judgment for his disobedience of God.*

III. CONCLUSION

Sometimes Judgment Is Final

As a college professor, I have to live with the fact that sometimes a student fails a course I am teaching. That is never a pleasant experience for me, but it is an unavoidable consequence of maintaining certain academic standards. One year a student failed a required course during the spring semester, and this kept him from graduating. He was very unhappy, so he went to see the dean to see if there was anything he could do to remedy the situation. "What are my options?" he asked.

"You don't have any," the dean replied. "You can take the course over next year, but you failed this year."

Nobody likes to hear or speak these words, but sometimes failure happens.

"What are my options?" seems to be the cardinal slogan for today. What else can I do? How can I undo what I have done? Is there some way I can achieve what I meant to do rather than what I did? Please show me a way of getting what I want without having to do what it takes to get there!

The story of Saul is a grave reminder that things do not always work that way. There came a point when God said, "Enough." God brought an end not only to Saul's life but also to his family's claim to the throne of Israel. Saul's options had run out.

American culture frequently portrays a silly idea about divine judgment. It often conveys the notion that when good people die they turn into angels. There is no biblical basis for such a belief since the Bible teaches that angels and humans are distinct kinds of beings (1 Pet. 1:12; Heb. 1:14; Rev. 22:8). Another part of this popular belief is that all it takes is one good deed for a person to make it to heaven. In God's universe this is not the way things are. God's forgiveness cannot be bought with the occasional good deed, not even with "daily acts of kindness" as performed so nobly by Boy Scouts all over the world. God wants to know if we are devoted to him, not holding back any areas of our lives from his lordship.

Martin Luther finally realized that being a monk and working on his own righteousness was not the way to get things right with God. He realized that there is another way, one that begins with God and comes to us by his grace alone. This is the true heart of the gospel, the good news of free salvation from God himself. The gospel may begin with judgment, but it does not end there. The grim truth of divine judgment prepares the way for the bright reality of God's salvation.

PRINCIPLES

- God is holy and pure and thus in a position of judge over us.
- Human beings are by nature sinful and liable to God's judgment.
- God's judgment can be final; we cannot count on unlimited "second" chances.
- We are not judged on the basis of specific acts that we may have committed but on whether our lives are submitted to God.
- The sinful actions that we perform are evidence of our rebellious attitude toward God.

APPLICATIONS

- Take a look at your own view of the seriousness of sin and compare it with God's view of sin (Gen. 6:5–8).
- Go to Gethsemane with Jesus (Luke 22:39–46) and follow him to Calvary. Observe sin's consequences in the body and spirit of Jesus who himself did not sin.

- Ask God to keep before you the seriousness of sin and the cost of forgiving sin as an antidote to the rationalizations we so easily make.

- Open all the rooms of your heart to God's Spirit and his Word so that he may indicate those parts that need to change.

IV. LIFE APPLICATION

Nothing Makes Life So Good as Almost Dying

Fyodor Dostoevsky, one of Russia's great novelists, was arrested by the tsar's police for supposedly plotting against the government. He was shipped to Siberia, where he was to be executed. Dostoevsky was already standing with the rifles pointed at him, expecting to hear the order to fire, when a last-second reprieve was issued. Instead of being shot, Dostoevsky was ordered to serve four years at hard labor. Although this imprisonment was a grueling time, having faced his own imminent death directly, he was glad to have his life back—and he took it as a gift from God.

Up to this time Dostoevsky had been a skeptic and a rebel. Now he realized that without God and his grace his life would be completely meaningless. This was a shift in attitude that became clear in his writings as well. When Dostoevsky was finally allowed to return home, his novels celebrated the individual who, against all intellectual fashions, maintains a simple faith in God. Having received his life back, he gave credit for it to the one who truly owned it—his Creator.

One of the reasons so many believers do not experience more joy in their salvation is that we are not appreciative of what we are saved from. Sin and judgment are taboo topics today. To speak of divine judgment is to appear "judgmental," and this invokes the specter of the ultimate contemporary offense—to be "intolerant." No one likes to be thought of as bigoted, so we shy away from the first truth of the gospel: that we all stand condemned by God for our sinfulness.

Recognizing our state of condemnation is vital for coming to terms with God's grace. This means (1) viewing sin with the seriousness that it deserves; (2) coming to God with no pretense about our own worthiness; (3) receiving our salvation as coming from God alone; and (4) walking with God in assurance of our salvation.

V. PRAYER

Lord Jesus, we look at the story of Saul and tremble. How hard your judgment appears to us! And yet we realize that you are a holy God and that your decrees are right. May we learn how serious it is to disobey you, and may this knowledge help us to see by contrast how undeserved and how magnificent your grace is to us. Amen.

VI. DEEPER DISCOVERIES

A. The Military Situation (10:1)

Deep in the bowels of the White House in Washington, D.C., is the "situation room" in which, during a war, the president and his advisors are continually updated on the latest military activities. On huge displays the commander in chief can see formations and positions as they develop and issue his orders as needed. Let us go into the "situation room" of the eleventh century B.C. and see what we can learn about Saul and the army of the Israelites.

We read in 1 Samuel 28:4 that the Israelites were camped at Gilboa, while the Philistines were at Shunem. These are locations in the eastern part of the Valley of Jezreel, about five miles apart (Walton, 318). The Valley of Jezreel is a relatively flat region nestled in between a number of larger mountains dividing Galilee from the rest of the country. It is in the northern part of the land, and Shunem is actually north of Gilboa.

This is a significant observation because Philistia lies south of Israel. In other words, the Philistines had sneaked around behind Saul and were attacking from the north, while their territory actually was located in the south. How did they get there? Presumably they marched their troops up the coastline to the western edge of the plain of Jezreel at Mount Carmel, moved east, and stationed themselves at Shunem, ready to swoop down on Saul and his smaller army.

This tactical positioning explains at least partially why Saul was so frightened about this battle (1 Sam. 28:5). With the Philistines' larger army staking out the plains and Saul's back against the mountains, the king was cut off and surrounded. Furthermore, if the Philistines could control Galilee, they would be in a position to take over Israel simply by cutting off all trade routes. It was "do or die" for Saul, and he was certain that it would come to the latter.

But here is the catch. By undertaking this campaign, the Philistines were putting themselves in a vulnerable position. They were placing their huge army in this northern area, cut off from contact with their own home bases.

All they could hope for was that they would maintain a clear line of communication and supplies along the coastal area. If they were attacked from the rear, it would be impossible for them to maintain their position in the Jezreel Valley. And this is precisely what happened. Even while the Philistines were enjoying a big victory at Mount Gilboa, David was organizing his forces in the south. The Philistines never were able to establish themselves in their conquered territory. Once David came to the throne not long thereafter, he dealt the Philistines a decisive defeat, making their victory over Saul short-lived and hollow.

But this leaves Saul in a truly tragic condition. We cannot say that Saul could have defeated the Philistines at Mount Gilboa. But the nation of Israel was not in such great danger of conquest by the Philistines as it may have appeared. In these difficult circumstances God already had a way for his people's release. If Saul had only learned to trust God totally!

B. The Philistines (10:1)

In the Bible the Philistines first appear in the person of Abimelech, king of Gerar, to whom Abraham pretended that Sarah was his sister (Gen. 20:1–18). From there they show up occasionally but not as an enemy nation. But when the Israelites conquered the promised land, they were not able to subdue the Philistines, who became an increasingly threatening presence. In the Book of Judges, the Philistines were counted among the oppressors of Israel and were barely held in check by several judges, such as Shamgar (Judg. 3:31) and Samson (Judg. 13–16), but continued in a position of superiority over Israel. This state of Philistine ascendancy still held true during the time of Saul, and it did not come to an end until David's reign.

Part of what made the Philistine's domination of Israel possible was their own early disastrous military campaign against Egypt. The Philistines attempted to invade Egypt from the north by land and sea and were crushed by Pharaoh Ramses III in 1179 B.C. Nevertheless, even though the Pharaoh had beaten the Philistines, he had taken enough losses himself to be willing to let the Philistines settle back in their coastland home and not to send his army after them. Thus, the Philistines, having been stymied in their attempted invasion of Egypt, were in a position to go after the tribes of Israel in the north without having to worry about outside interference. And it was during this time that they began to be Israel's biggest adversary.

The land of Philistia was not a single kingdom. Instead, it was a confederation of five kings who were lords of city-states: Ashkelon, Ekron, Gath, Ashdod, and Gaza. These five towns were located in the southwestern Mediterranean coastland, just south of the territory of Simeon.

We know little about the religion of the Philistines, and only three names of gods are associated with them: Dagon, Ashtoreth, and Baalzebub. Dagon may have been their main god; he was associated with the grain harvest. When the Philistines captured the ark of the covenant, they placed it in the temple of Dagon, only to discover that their idol fell on the ground before the ark. Ashtoreth was a goddess of fertility who was worshiped with slight variations in many mideastern cultures. Baalzebub, literally "god of the flies," was the god of the town of Ekron; his job may have been to ward off pestilence.

C. Did Saul Inquire of the Lord? (10:14)

In verse 14 we read that one of Saul's offenses was his failure to inquire of the Lord. Yet 1 Samuel 28:6 says, "He inquired of the LORD, but the LORD did not answer him by dreams or Urim or prophets." Did he or did he not seek guidance from God for the upcoming battle?

In order to answer this question, we need to understand what the verse in 1 Samuel is referring to. It mentions three methods of attempting to divine the will of God: dreams, Urim, and prophets. Saul apparently hoped that God would send him a dream, that he would speak through prophets (now that Samuel was dead), or that he could get a message through the Urim—the Hebrew device which apparently was used to confirm divine messages on a yes/no basis. In other words, what we are looking at here is a set of purely mechanical methods of trying to find out God's will—"perform the technique and God will send his directive."

We are not looking at genuine searching for God's will on Saul's part. He wanted to determine what God wanted on a simple input/output basis, but this is not the way to find God's will. Saul was missing genuine commitment to God that the Lord expected of him. To truly inquire of the Lord would have meant for Saul to make a total turnaround with his life and submit to God in all areas of his life, not to negotiate with the Lord for some information about the outcome of a particular ritual. Did Saul inquire of the Lord? In a purely mechanical sense of attempting divination, yes, but in a meaningful sense of really wanting to accept God's will for him, no.

VII. TEACHING OUTLINE

A. INTRODUCTION

1. Lead Story: A Terrified Law Student

2. Context: Up to this point Chronicles has been nothing but lists with just a few story lines interspersed. We have learned that these lists were important to the Jews of Ezra's day because they established continuity with the ancient people of God and his promises. Now the writer moves from establishing general lines of genealogy to discussing specific kings in order to show how God has worked consistently in the history of his chosen people. The next main subject of attention will be King David, but first we get a quick treatment of the death of King Saul.

3. Transition: King Saul is included in 1 Chronicles for negative purposes only, it seems. With his failure he provides a glaring background against which we can appreciate the success of David's reign. He also teaches a lesson about God's judgment on those who disobey the Lord.

B. COMMENTARY

1. The Death of Saul (10:1–6)

2. The Treatment of Saul's Body (10:7–12)

3. The Reason for Saul's Death (10:13–14)

C. CONCLUSION: SOMETIMES JUDGMENT IS FINAL

VIII. ISSUES FOR DISCUSSION

1. As you recall different parts of Saul's life, which ones show evidence of faith in God, and which ones do not? What is the reason for the difference?

2. Why does God judge human beings rather than just forgiving their sins?

3. Why is it hard to accept the idea of a holy and judging God? How can we learn to accept this biblical idea?

4. Is it possible to advocate the doctrine of the judgment of God in our culture? If so, how can we go about doing so?

5. Explore the ways in which the idea of the judgment of God is a necessary provision for understanding the grace of God.

1 Chronicles 11:1–12:40

The Reign of David: The First Camelot

I. **INTRODUCTION**
    King Arthur and the Round Table

II. **COMMENTARY**
    A verse-by-verse explanation of these chapters.

III. **CONCLUSION**
    King Christian and the Jews

    An overview of the principles and applications from these chapters.

IV. **LIFE APPLICATION**
    Lighting Up the Christmas Tree

    Melding these chapters to life.

V. **PRAYER**
    Tying these chapters to life with God.

VI. **DEEPER DISCOVERIES**
    Historical, geographical, and grammatical enrichment of the commentary.

VII. **TEACHING OUTLINE**
    Suggested step-by-step group study of these chapters.

VIII. **ISSUES FOR DISCUSSION**
    Zeroing these chapters in on daily life.

"*Can there be any greater evil than discord and distraction and plurality where unity ought to reign? or any greater good than the bond of unity?*"

Socrates

1 Chronicles 11:1–12:40

IN A NUTSHELL

The story shifts from the failed reign of Saul to the glorious reign of David. These chapters tell about David's new capital of Jerusalem, his heroes and military commanders, and the support that he received from all Israel. We not only receive the impression of strength and unity but even more so the insight that the strength is due to unity. In examining this scene, we are reminded of how much the church needs unity in Jesus Christ.

The Reign of David:
The First Camelot

I. INTRODUCTION

King Arthur and the Round Table

*A*n enduring part of mythology in the English-speaking world is the legend of Arthur Pendragon and Camelot. It is the story of a young king who ruled briefly over an idyllic realm, guided by Merlin, the magician. One aspect of the Arthur legend is the "round table," an assembly point for a council of warriors or knights. Arthur, as an idealistic young king, wanted to bring peace to his domain. He decided the only way to do so was to bring all his knights together on an equal basis and to let each of them have a voice in all decisions affecting the kingdom. So everyone would sit at a round table and would speak out as appropriate. No one person, including the king himself, would be above the law or the decisions of the council.

Arthur's strategy worked—but only for a time. The compliance by the knights in this council of the round table was motivated in part by Arthur's compelling personality. So for a few years everyone was happy to contribute, and the result was the golden age of Camelot. But then, for various reasons, Arthur no longer was able to hold the assembly together by his own charisma, and the ideal kingdom disintegrated. And as soon as the kingdom lost its unity, it also lost its strength and virtue. Peace and prosperity gave way to strife and lawlessness.

As we begin to examine the kingdom of David in this section, we are looking at the Old Testament's "Camelot." This, too, was a time of peace, prosperity, and virtue. Just as with Arthur's Camelot, these benefits came from the fact that there was unity in the kingdom. David was able to bring all Israel together under his rule, and all Israel flourished.

Was there more to the kingdom of David than David's heroic personality? If so, would subsequent generations be able to build on these principles? We will see in the rest of Chronicles that in the long run these questions received mixed answers. But there is no doubt that David's kingdom set the ideal standard and that he provided the people of Israel with the foundation for a truly long-term "Camelot" under God.

II. COMMENTARY

The Reign of David: The First Camelot

MAIN IDEA: *David earned the support of all Israel as king. This unity provided his kingdom with great strength.*

A David's Coronation (11:1–3)

SUPPORTING IDEA: *Representatives of the entire nation came to David in order to support him as king.*

11:1–3. By this time David had reigned as the king of Judah for more than seven years. His capital was **Hebron**, located squarely in the middle of Judah. Hebron was a city with a long and distinguished history. The patriarchs were buried here. This was the city that Caleb had claimed many years before as a reward for his faithfulness. After Saul's disastrous time on the throne, the tribe of Judah was not about to submit the rule of any other tribe's leader, so they made David their king. The other tribes were not ready to follow suit. But now they found themselves in serious need of leadership, and they turned to David.

The first statement the tribal representatives made established kinship with David: **We are your own flesh and blood**. Judah had held onto David precisely because he was of their tribe, while the other tribes had not been ready to accept him. But now they were willing to accept David as a relative in the extended sense of being a part of Israel. And, in a manner that must have sounded hollow even to them, they acknowledged that David had been their true leader all along.

Shortly after he killed Goliath, David became the most outstanding military commander in Israel, giving rise to the chant: "Saul has slain his thousands, and David his tens of thousands" (1 Sam. 18:7). Furthermore, David had been able to inflict significant losses on the Philistines. Still, the delegates ignored the fact that much of David's military prowess had been directed toward escaping from them as they—first as the army of Saul, then as the army of Ish-Bosheth—had attempted to capture him. Everyone knew that this entreaty really was a surrender.

The tribal leaders present at this council admitted that God himself had selected David to be their king. They made reference to the fact that he had received word from the Lord, and they phrased their acknowledgment in terms of David as the shepherd of his people, a description that would forever be associated with him. David had been the shepherd of his family's flock when Samuel's call first came to him (1 Sam. 16:13). And ever since then, the idea that David had been the shepherd of sheep but then had become the shepherd of Israel seemed to be an appropriate imagery.

Don't think of the **compact** that David made with the tribes at Hebron as a mutually acceptable service contract, as though the tribes were hiring David as their king. Even though they would have expected David to be faithful and considerate, the agreement would have been one-sided because it was essentially their acceptance of David's power over them. As Samuel had described to the people a generation earlier (1 Sam. 8:10–18), a king would be autocratic. Even though the tribes eventually would not tolerate abuse of power by the king (2 Chr. 10:16), at this point they abdicated their control over their own government.

After the formalities of verbal acknowledgment were concluded, the leaders of the tribes held an anointing ceremony for David. The king was a "messiah," someone who had been anointed by the Lord to hold his office. On many occasions (1 Sam. 24:6; 26:9) David had stated that Saul was God's anointed, and he had refused to harm him. God had already anointed David (1 Sam. 16:13), but this did not mean in David's eyes that he was allowed to replace Saul while Saul was still alive.

Ⓑ David's New Capital City (11:4–9)

SUPPORTING IDEA: *David established the city of Jerusalem as a new capital, thereby laying claim to a neutral site from which he could govern all Israel. Jerusalem was also a highly secure location from a military perspective.*

The fortified section of Jerusalem, called Jebus, had been a thorn in the side of the Israelites during the entire time they had lived in the holy land. Jerusalem was located in the mountains of Judea, right at the southern edge of the territory allocated to Benjamin. At Jerusalem, the settlement surrounding the city was highly vulnerable and had, in fact, been taken over by the tribe of Benjamin (1 Chr. 8:28). Already in the earliest years of the conquest under Joshua, the king of Jerusalem had been killed (Josh. 10:23–26). Nevertheless, the Jebusite fortress overlooking Jerusalem, the last stronghold of Canaanite power, had never been captured.

11:4–5. In a very brief, matter-of-fact account (for a few more details see 2 Sam. 5:6–10), the chronicler summarizes how David conquered the Jebusite citadel. Despite its occupants' taunts, David was able to take the fortification (possibly by climbing up the water channels; see 2 Sam. 5:8). The central point of significance for the chronicler was that David had captured **Zion, the City of David.** The verse makes it sound as though the location known as David's city had been there all along, and David merely claimed it for himself, and that is exactly the way the chronicler wanted us to read it. David took possession of what was already his.

11:6. David made the capture of Jerusalem the occasion for confirming the leadership of those reporting to him. There was no shortage of powerful warriors and their commanders among his troops. But there was one question that needed to be settled: Who would be in charge of them, and who would be the highest general reporting directly to the king? So David set up a contest. Whoever conquered the Jebusite fortress would become the highest commander of David's army.

Joab was a **son of Zeruiah**, David's half sister (see 1 Chr. 2:13–17; 2 Sam. 17:25). It is even possible that Zeruiah was a great deal older than David and that David and Joab may have grown up together in the same household. Joab had none of David's sensitivity and scruples; he seems to have lived in a "black-and-white" world. As far as Joab was concerned, whatever needed to be done should be done as soon as possible without any further reflection—but if something violated the law of God, it should not be done under any circumstances.

David would profit from Joab's pragmatic nature, even when he could not bring himself to endorse it. Joab had already served David faithfully in the civil war against Ish-Bosheth, but in the light of the recently established unity among the tribes, apparently David decided not to simply transfer the office of highest commander to Joab. Instead, he devised this test, which Joab passed, and so would continue at David's side as his general.

11:7–8. David moved his residence from Hebron to Jerusalem, which would forever hereafter be called the **City of David**. There were a lot of advantages connected with this move. For one thing it provided a fresh site as the capital of the united kingdom. Saul had ruled from Gibeah, his hometown located in his own tribal territory of Benjamin. Up to now David had lived in Hebron, which was centered in the land of Judah. Jerusalem, on the other hand, was nominally located in Benjamin but had not been fully conquered up to this point, and it straddled the boundary between Benjamin and Judah. So it was a good location for David to move to in declaring that he was king of all Israel and was not bound by any individual tribal commitment.

The second advantage of David's moving his capital city to Jerusalem was physical—the fact that Jerusalem was well fortified and highly defensible. After all, it took the Israelites more than four hundred years to take the Jebusite fortress, and even then it was not easy. So David now appropriated these advantages for himself; he had the fortifications rebuilt and—presumably on the principle that the person who was able to conquer the city also knew how to defend it against further conquests—enlisted Joab to oversee the restoration. The capital for the new "Camelot" was in place.

11:9. But let us not forget what made this "Camelot" possible and what set it apart from any human ambitions. The chronicler is quick to remind us that David's power was derived from the fact that **the LORD Almighty was with him**. David's power was ultimately given to him from the one who has all the power—the Lord.

The Great Warriors and Commanders (11:10–47)

SUPPORTING IDEA: *David's strength was enhanced by the large and diverse group of military heroes who supported him.*

The chronicler now presents us with a list of the warriors who comprised the core of David's army. This list includes some men who had achieved great exploits as individual fighters, while others distinguished themselves as field commanders. The list has essentially three parts: the "three," the "two" distinguished commanders, and the "thirty."

11:10–14. The first point we notice about the list of the "three" is that the chronicler gives us only two names: **Jashobeam** and **Eleazar**. The third name, that of Shammah, comes from the parallel passage in 2 Samuel 23. Jashobeam at one time killed three hundred people (presumably Philistines). Both Eleazar and Shammah won great victories while standing in fields—the first in a field of barley, the second in a field of lentils. These three men were the champions of David's kingdom. They had performed legendary deeds, and they served as David's special forces unit.

11:15–19. A particular incident illustrates the contribution of the "three." This was back during the time when David and his troops were living as outlaws, hiding from Saul in the wilderness. They were caught without an adequate water supply, and David sighed that he wished he could get some of the clean, fresh water from nearby Bethlehem. Soon, there stood his three heroes, grins all over their faces, presenting him with a skin of water that they had filled by sneaking into Bethlehem at the risk of their lives. How they must have anticipated the look on David's face while he thanked them and gulped down the water!

David was overcome with gratitude, but he could not bring himself to drink any of the water. This water, he declared, procured at the potential cost of people's lives, was too sacred just to gulp down to satisfy human thirst. So David poured it on the ground as an offering to God.

11:20–25. Next in the list are the two commanders, **Abishai the brother of Joab** and **Benaiah son of Jehoiada**, who are singled out for particular honor. Joab, David's chief commander, did not make any of these lists since he had been mentioned earlier. Abishai was one of David's older half nephews, and he supported David in the civil war against Ish-Bosheth. Later on we will find Abishai commanding one division in a decisive victory over the Ammonites (1 Chr. 19:11).

Benaiah's resume reads like that of a great hero of mythology. At one time he killed two Moabite champions; he also killed a lion all by himself by getting into a pit with it—while the pit was filled with snow. And then there was the Egyptian giant. He was not quite as tall as Goliath (1 Sam. 17:4), but like Goliath he carried an oversize spear that reminded everyone of a weaver's beam. Benaiah snatched the giant's own spear, reversed it on him, and defeated the giant single-handedly.

11:26–47. Several features stand out about the list of "thirty." There are forty-seven people mentioned here, not thirty. The parallel passage in 2 Samuel 23:24–39 gives thirty-seven names and has some additional differences. Clearly, this was a list of honor, which was not strictly delineated, rather than a list of fixed appointments. The very first name on this list reflects this fact since Asahel, the second brother of Joab, was dead by the time David became king. Asahel was killed by Ish-Bosheth's commander, Abner. He had been gone for about six years by the time David installed his forces as an official army. Nevertheless, thanks to his earlier efforts on behalf of David, he headed up this list.

As you scan the list, some of the names may strike you as familiar. A reader well acquainted with the story line of Chronicles may know that later on in the book there will be mention of an Elhanan who killed the brother of Goliath (1 Chr. 20:5). But this was Elhanan son of Jair, not the present Elhanan son of Dodo. There are several sets of brothers. Also, Joab's armor-bearer is mentioned. Although theoretically this position was that of a mere menial squire, Naharai the Berothite must have risen to prowess in his own right.

Apparently the sons of Hashem the Gizonite were known as a family. We do not learn how many of them there were or their individual names. Jonathan the son of Shagee the Hararite should not be confused with David's best friend Jonathan, the son of Saul. This Jonathan was the brother of the third member of the "three," Shammah, whose name was left out of our present account (but mentioned in 2 Sam. 23:11).

Three members of the "thirty" (at least) were of Gentile origins. Zelek the Ammonite is joined by Uriah the Hittite and Ithmah the Moabite. We do not know how any of these three men came to join David's army. Ammonites and Moabites carried a particular curse which specified they could not be assimilated into the people of Israel: "No Ammonite or Moabite or any of his descendants may enter the assembly of the LORD, even down to the tenth generation" (Deut. 23:3). Nevertheless, Zelek and Ithmah must have distinguished themselves by fighting for the one whose anointing was from the Lord.

Uriah the Hittite was the husband of Bathsheba, with whom David had an affair. In order to attempt to cover up his guilt when Bathsheba turned up pregnant, David had Uriah killed by having him abandoned in battle (2 Sam. 11). However, the chronicler again spares us the dark story. He makes no allusion to it here and skips it at the point where it would fit into the narrative (1 Chr. 20:1–2; cp. 2 Sam. 11:1–2). For Ezra, the personal failings of David are not as important as the ideal kingdom that he established.

Ⓓ Armed Bands That Came to Support David (12:1–22)

SUPPORTING IDEA: *Before David had become king, groups of supporters from various tribes rallied to his support.*

The chronicler does not observe chronological order. At least we are fastened to the time of David now, but within that time frame we are skipping back and forth. In the first part of this chapter, we return to the time before David was king, when he was still hiding from Saul and carrying out guerilla warfare. The emphasis in this passage is on diversity in tribal support; it was not just the men of Judah who supported David.

12:1–7. There was a group of elite fighters **from the tribe of Benjamin**. They had trained themselves to perform unusual skills in warfare, such as operating a bow or a slingshot with either hand, and the men whose names are listed here put their talents at David's disposal.

12:8–15. While David was at his headquarters in the wilderness of Engedi, during the most rainy and miserable month of the year, he was joined by a ferocious group of warriors from the tribe of Gad, situated across the Jordan River. They had crossed the river at a time when it was apparently considered suicide to try to do so, but also a time when Saul's troops would not have patrolled the banks of the river. These men came well-equipped with shields and spears, and they scared away everyone in the surrounding area.

12:16–18. On another occasion a further group of **men from** Benjamin and **Judah** showed up. **David** was suspicious that they might betray him to Saul, so he confronted them with that possibility. In response, Amasai spoke under the direct guidance of the Spirit. David accepted Amasai's testimonial and admitted him and his followers to his band.

Amasai is mentioned as one of the "thirty," but he is not included in the list in the previous chapter, thus supporting the idea that membership in this group was a flexible, honorary designation. Some people (Thompson, 124) speculate that Amasai might have been the same person as Amasa, the son of David's half sister Abigail. If so, he wound up leading Absalom's rebellion against David (2 Sam. 17:25; another negative episode left out of Chronicles).

12:19–22. There were warriors from as far away as the territory of Manasseh who signed up with David. At that point they thought David would fight alongside the Philistines against Saul. But as it turned out, the Philistines would not permit this out of fear that David would suddenly switch allegiance to Saul. These **men of Manasseh** came to David and stayed with him until David had a large army at his disposal. The chronicler says it was **like the army of God**, presumably thinking of the hundreds of thousands of men who fought under Moses and Joshua (Num. 1:46).

Ⓔ David's Coronation Feast (12:23–40)

SUPPORTING IDEA: *Large troops of soldiers from all the tribes came to recognize David as king and to celebrate his ascension to the throne.*

Once more the scene and time shift back to our starting point in 1 Chronicles 11:1 when the tribal representatives came to offer David the throne of all Israel. This time we get a few more details about this event: an enumeration of the soldiers from each tribe and a little description of the feast held in honor of David.

12:23–37. To be king was synonymous with being supreme commander of the army, so David's acclamation also involved the mustering of an army at his disposal. We do not get an exact number because for some tribes we are given the number of chiefs rather than the number of soldiers. Clearly, though, the army was huge. Just counting the soldiers without taking the officers into account totals up to 335,900 (though this number is still short of the total of 603,550 given for the Israelite army at the time of the conquest in Num. 1:46).

In verses 26–28, we discover that the tribe of Levi, though committed to religious duties, did not see itself as above participation in David's military conclave. The tribe of Benjamin had apparently been the last to hold out with support for David. At the last moment this tribe supplied a nominal representation—though their three thousand men were less than half of what every other tribe had mustered, with the exception of Levi.

Issachar in verse 32 illustrates the pragmatic attitude that may have guided many who supported this assembly. They were not idealistic supporters of David, let alone of Judah, but they knew that the time had come to join a federation that would be mutually advantageous to the entire nation. Both Zebulun and Dan, the two tribes left out of the genealogies, are mentioned with highest compliments in verses 33 and 35: **to help David with undivided loyalty** for one and **ready for battle** for the other.

12:38–40. When all the tribes came together at Hebron and the formalities had taken place, they settled in for a huge feast. They had come with their own supplies, which were probably meager. But people from all over the country sent food as a sign of support. A new king, acclaimed by all and anointed by God, was reason for **joy in Israel**.

The central point of this last section is not what was on the menu for the feast or how the ingredients were procured, but the statement in verse 38: **All the rest of the Israelites were also of one mind to make David king.** What happened here was not just the assembly of a huge army, and it most certainly was not just David preening himself in a display of power. It was a moment when the entire nation was of one mind.

> **MAIN IDEA REVIEW:** *David earned the support of all Israel as king. This unity provided his kingdom with great strength.*

III. CONCLUSION

King Christian and the Jews

The first phase of World War II in England was characterized by Germany's Blitzkrieg, its lightning-fast conquest of much of Europe. Denmark, under King Christian X, submitted to Germany in 1940 and maintained an uneasy coexistence with its new Nazi masters. However, the Nazis had plans to exterminate the Jews of all occupied countries. In 1943 it became apparent that Danish Jews were targeted for deportation to concentration camps.

Christian X and the Danish people could have made life easy on themselves by cooperating with the Germans and turning the Jews over to them, as other countries had done. Instead, the king refused to cooperate with this project, and the people of Denmark established underground railroads to smuggle Jews out of Denmark into Sweden. More than seven thousand Jews living in Denmark were saved.

"All for one, and one for all" was the slogan of Alexander Dumas's three musketeers. And it should be the slogan of the Christian church. Paul enjoins us: "Do nothing out of selfish ambition or vain conceit, but in humility consider others better than yourselves. Each of you should look not only to your own interests, but also to the interests of others" (Phil. 2:3–4). A true New Testament church is one in which all members place the welfare of the other members of the body of Christ ahead of their own.

Can you imagine what a church would look like if people took this approach? Rather than leaders trying to attract members into supporting their programs, their first question would be: "What can I do to support you?" Church members would not base their involvement on the question of what the church can do for them but on how they can discover the needs of other church members and minister to them.

This kind of unity is ultimately a supernatural thing. David's kingdom was strong because it was based on the guidance of the Lord. We need to allow the Holy Spirit to make us more like the body of Christ (Eph. 4:3–6).

PRINCIPLES

- The strength of an organization—a kingdom or a church—may be a direct reflection of the unity of its members.
- The unity of the members of a group depends on how much the individuals are more concerned for the needs of others in the group than their own.
- A group whose purpose is to represent God's presence on earth will endure only so long as it maintains its foundation in God.

APPLICATIONS

- On a scale of 1 to 10, evaluate the unity your church is currently experiencing. Let 1 and 10 be extreme disunity and unity, respectively.
- If your church is less than a 10, what changes in attitude and actions could move the church higher on the unity scale? How do these changes apply to you?
- What percentage of your church members view the church as just another human organization rather than the body of Christ? In which percentage are you?
- If all church members were exactly like you in attitude and behavior, how strong would the overall unity be?

IV. LIFE APPLICATION

Lighting Up the Christmas Tree

What if the tribe of Ephraim had decided not to be a part of David's kingdom? What if the Levites had held out and declared themselves the true leaders of Israel since they were the administrators of the nation's spiritual welfare? If this had happened, the kingdom of David as described in Chronicles would not have developed as it did. The blueprint of success for the kingdom required the cooperation of all the tribes.

This scenario is like the frustrating task of stringing lights on a Christmas tree. The problem is that not only do the individual lights tend to stop working with little provocation but when one of them does, they all do because they are wired in a series. Each light depends on all the other ones to continue working. When they stop giving out light, fifty (or more) individual lights have to be checked by exchanging them one after the other with a good one until the light that is causing the trouble is replaced.

Like Christmas tree lights wired in series, all the tribes came together under David—and the result was a glorious unified kingdom. In the body of Christ, we are the lights. As Paul declares in 1 Corinthians 12:25, God has arranged the church "so that there should be no division in the body, but that its parts should have equal concern for each other." When this picture becomes not just an ideal but a true representation of the church on earth, then God's plan will become fully actualized.

V. PRAYER

Lord Jesus, it is so easy for us to think in terms of ourselves: what we are expecting to get from you, from your church, and what we are doing that we expect to get credit for. Help us to reverse our thinking. Like the tribes of Israel willing to submit themselves to David, your anointed, give us the willingness to submit our interests and desires to you and to put the needs of your other children ahead of ours. Give us a unity of purpose that will result in your greater glory. Amen.

VI. DEEPER DISCOVERIES

A. David as Shepherd and Sheep (11:2)

When the tribes gathered for David's coronation, they asserted God's promise that David should be the shepherd of the children of Israel. Like a shepherd, he would rule them, lead them, and provide for them. But David was also accustomed to seeing himself in the opposite role—as the sheep. "The LORD is my shepherd" he proclaimed in the well-known psalm (Ps. 23:1). While he was a human shepherd to his people, David understood that he needed a divine shepherd to guide him. We can add that Christ came to be the shepherd for all of us (John 10:1–18).

B. The King of Jerusalem (11:4)

Ancient Jerusalem showed up not just in the Old Testament but in other documents as well. In the Bible it is first mentioned with the mysterious figure of Melchizedek, who is described as the "king of Salem" (an ancient name for Jerusalem) and a "priest of God Most High" (Gen. 14:18). Then later we read that, during the conquest under Joshua, King Adoni-Zedek of Jerusalem was vanquished and executed (Josh. 10:1–28).

But Jerusalem also comes up in the Amarna Tablets, which are correspondence from the Canaanite chiefs to the pharaoh in Egypt at roughly the time of the conquest and settlement. Many of these letters refer to the invasion by a group of people classed together as the "Habiru," no doubt a version of our word *Hebrew*. Here we run across a prince of Jerusalem known as Abdu-Heba. He was a schemer and manipulator (Pritchard, 268) who even made an alliance with his local enemies for the sake of a temporary victory against the "chief of the Habiru" (Pritchard, 269) but who later appealed to the pharaoh of Egypt for help against the Habiru.

Whether Abdu-Heba was the same person as Adoni-Zedek, or was his successor, his chief minister, or someone with a very different role altogether, cannot be pinpointed exactly. But those details should not obscure the fact that here we have eyewitness testimony coming right from the throne of Jerusalem at the time of Joshua and the conquest about the invasion of Palestine.

C. The Large Number of Soldiers in Hebron (12:24–37)

Many liberal scholars believe the number of warriors listed from each tribe coming to Hebron, totaling over three hundred thousand, is exaggerated. For example, Braun comments that the number is "an immense army for any time and seemingly out of the question for David's retinue at Hebron" (Braun, 170).

But why should this be so? Do we have different sources that give lesser numbers? As a matter of fact, we do not. Is it impossible, or even truly implausible, for there to have been that many people coming to David's coronation? There really is no good reason—other than a basic predisposition against large numbers—why that number should be unbelievable.

VII. TEACHING OUTLINE

A. INTRODUCTION

1. Lead Story: King Arthur and the Round Table
2. Context: In attempting to bring peace and prosperity to Camelot, King Arthur tried to establish unity among his warriors. Similarly, when David became king of Israel, he did so with the full support of all the tribes.
3. Transition: After Saul's death, David became king of Judah. Then a few years later, all the tribes came to make him king over the entire nation.

B. COMMENTARY

1. David's Coronation (11:1–3)
2. David's New Capital City (11:4–9)
3. The Great Warriors and Commanders (11:10–47)
4. Armed Bands That Came to Support David (12:1–22)
5. David's Coronation Feast (12:23–40)

C. CONCLUSION: KING CHRISTIAN AND THE JEWS

VIII. ISSUES FOR DISCUSSION

1. In what areas does the church need greater unity?
2. Where would a drive for unity within the church be unnecessary? Where might it be harmful because it could undermine the basics of Christian faith?
3. What are the potential benefits for the Christian church if it should develop greater unity?
4. What are some specific areas where people could subordinate some of their own interests to promote the welfare of other believers?

1 Chronicles 13:1–16:43

Bringing the Ark to Jerusalem

I. INTRODUCTION
The Interstellar Meteorite

II. COMMENTARY
A verse-by-verse explanation of these chapters.

III. CONCLUSION
No Superconductor for Holiness

An overview of the principles and applications from these chapters.

IV. LIFE APPLICATION
Trusting in a Holy God

Melding these chapters to life.

V. PRAYER
Tying these chapters to life with God.

VI. DEEPER DISCOVERIES
Historical, geographical, and grammatical enrichment of the commentary.

VII. TEACHING OUTLINE
Suggested step-by-step group study of these chapters.

VIII. ISSUES FOR DISCUSSION
Zeroing these chapters in on daily life.

Quote

"*A* true love to God must begin with a delight in his holiness, and not with a delight in any other attribute."

Jonathan   Edwards

1 Chronicles 13:1–16:43

IN A NUTSHELL

*K*ing David decided to bring the ark of the covenant to Jerusalem, but at first he did not respect the holiness of God as it was represented by this object, and a life was lost. When he esteemed the ark properly, the occasion turned into a great celebration, and God granted David continued success. A proper relationship with God must begin by recognizing God's holiness.

Bringing the Ark to Jerusalem

I. INTRODUCTION

An Interstellar Meteorite

*I*n the adventure novel *Ice Limit,* Douglas Preston and Lincoln Child take us on an expedition to the tip of South America—the rugged islands in the vicinity of Cape Horn. Scientists and engineers try to recover a huge meteorite spotted by an adventurer who lost his life in the process of locating it. The story includes the interpersonal dynamics within the company, armed conflict with a rogue destroyer commander, and insights into the engineering problems involved in trying to transport an object weighing twenty-five thousand tons. But the focus of attention is the huge rock itself and its properties.

This meteorite has qualities unknown for any elements currently on the periodic table. With a specific gravity of seventy-five (water sets the standard as "one"), the meteorite compacts more weight per volume than any object known. The most poignant property of this rock, however, is that virtually everybody who touches it immediately gets zapped by lightning discharges. All the resources available to the team have to come into play as they seek to excavate this meteorite, transfer it to a big ship, and take it to the United States.

If King David had read this novel, he would probably have nodded his head and told us that all this was old news to him. He was involved in a real-life instance of this dilemma when he set out to move the ark of the covenant to Jerusalem. On the one hand, the ark needed to be moved with great care so it would not be damaged in transit. On the other hand, David found out that anyone who touched the ark to hold it steady would be killed instantly. How do you move an object that seems too sacred to move?

Chapters 13–16 of 1 Chronicles describe David's efforts to move the ark to Jerusalem, and we will look at how both his technique and his thinking had to change in the process. David received success and blessings in his undertaking not because of the ark but because of the true God whose presence was signified by the ark. David came to understand the principle that holiness belongs to God and to him alone. The entire nation benefited from this insight.

II. COMMENTARY

Bringing the Ark to Jerusalem

> **MAIN IDEA:** *David needed to learn to respect God's holiness when he tried to transport the ark of the covenant to Jerusalem. When he did so, a joyous feast resulted. This story reminds us that God's holiness should be central in our thoughts of him.*

God had given specific directions to Moses at Mt. Sinai on how to construct the ark (Exod. 25). The ark was supposed to be a focal point of life and worship for the Israelites. It was to remind them of God's presence and his covenant with them. The ark was a rectangular box that contained three items: the stone tablets with the Ten Commandments (Exod. 40:20), a pot of manna (Exod. 16:33), and Aaron's rod, which had budded at one time (Num. 17:10; Heb. 9:4).

One of the most important features of the ark were the rings installed at the sides. A pair of poles, one on each side, was supposed to be permanently slipped through the rings so the ark could be carried by the designated Levites with the poles on their shoulders. This was the only legitimate mode of transportation for the ark.

When the Israelites were defeated by the Philistines at the beginning of Samuel's life and ministry (1 Sam. 4:1–2), they decided to take the ark into the next battle with them, thinking that they could compel the power of God to help them win (1 Sam. 4:3). But the Philistines defeated Israel again and captured the ark (1 Sam. 4:6–11). Eventually the ark wound up on the estate of a Jewish man named Abinadab (1 Sam. 6:21–7:1). This is where it stayed until David decided to bring it to Jerusalem.

A The Failed Attempt at Moving the Ark (13:1–14)

> **SUPPORTING IDEA:** *The first time David attempted to move the ark to Jerusalem, he did not observe the proper procedure for doing so and violated God's holiness.*

13:1. None of the events summarized above are included in Chronicles. Other than a brief mention in an earlier chapter that refers to the ark in the reign of David (1 Chr. 6:31), this is the first that we hear of it. Our story jumps right into the moment when David called a council to discuss the idea of bringing the ark to Jerusalem. He brought together the commanders of his divisions (thousands) and battalions (hundreds); just as the tribes' representatives at David's coronation had been soldiers, so this was also a military gathering.

13:2. David sought the approval of the people as well as the Lord's approval in order to carry out the project. He wished to include all people throughout the land, particularly the priests and Levites. From a purely human point of view, if he alienated the priesthood, he would not have the political clout he needed to be successful as king. In a less pragmatic light, those who had stewardship of the spiritual life of Israel were honored to be included in a major development such as moving the ark.

13:3–4. David gave an interesting rationale for moving the ark to Jerusalem. The idea was not—at least at this point—for it to be set up in a central location where everyone would have easy access to it; in fact, the traditional location in Shiloh might have been more favorable for that purpose. David wanted to be able to go to the ark himself on a regular basis so he could **inquire of it**, a practice that had been neglected while it was located in Kiriath Jearim. Apparently God used the ark at times to make his will known to the leaders of the people (see, e.g., Judg. 20:27–28). They would ask a question, and God would respond. David wanted to avail himself of this opportunity to walk more closely with God.

13:5–8. David appeared to give the transportation of the ark all the pomp and circumstance it deserved. He involved delegates from all Israel, from its southernmost border (the Shihor River in Egypt) to its northernmost extent (Lebo Hamath).

Kiriath Jearim was located about eight to nine miles from Jerusalem. Considering the hilly terrain, this would not have been an easy stroll for the crowd that assembled in this little town. Symbolically speaking, God was seated between the two cherubim with his foot resting on the top of the chest. The ark was **called by the Name**, that is by God's own holy name. It was not just a human implement.

The preparations for the move were thorough but ironic in retrospect. Out of respect for the ark, it was placed **on a new cart**, and the two men who took charge of guiding it—Uzzah and Ahio—were descendants of Abinadab (2 Sam. 6:3), the original owner of the plot where the ark had been kept. These two old-timers knew the area, knew the road, and knew where to be extra careful with their sacred cargo. King David recognized that it was God's ark, and he led a continuous musical celebration as the procession set out. Everyone was excited. If only David had taken the time to read the instructions.

13:9–14. Disaster struck when the oxen pulling the cart lost their footing. Uzzah reached out and attempted to steady the ark with his hand. But as soon as he gripped the ark he died, just as seventy people of Shemesh had died eighty years before him (1 Sam. 6:19). He had violated the sanctity of the ark.

The chronicler is careful to explain to us what happened. He tells us that **the LORD's anger burned against Uzzah, and he struck him down.** It was not the ark itself that caused Uzzah's death. The ark, sacred or not, was still just a physical object, and it did not contain spiritual power by itself. But there was a personal agent—God himself—who had declared the ark to be his own, and he brought judgment on the person who violated his decree. God reminded the people of his holiness—not the ark's—when he executed Uzzah.

David was angry. He had planned this fantastic day in God's honor, using the best new cart, experienced drivers, lots of music and chanting along the way—and God spoiled it all by zapping Uzzah. Maybe David was a little angry at Uzzah, too, but it seems more likely that most of his anger was directed at God. But God was not being arbitrary or capricious. He had given specific instructions on how to handle the ark. David had not read the instructions.

So the ark was abandoned for a while. It was left on the estate of a man known as Obed-Edom the Gittite. This man was a Levite gatekeeper (1 Chr. 15:18). The chronicler does not tell us anything about Obed-Edom's reaction to having this sacred box parked on his property. But it turned into something positive for him. During the three months that the ark was stored at Obed-Edom's residence, the Lord blessed him and his family.

B Gods of the Philistines Versus the God of David (14:1–17)

SUPPORTING IDEA: *In this chapter we see the contrast between the living God who supports David in all his undertakings and the useless wooden idols of the Philistines.*

The author of 2 Samuel gives us the story of the ark in its entirety right through its successful conclusion in Jerusalem. The chronicler, on the other hand, starts the story of the ark, then breaks it off just when it gets to the most exciting part in order to insert a report from the war department, and only then gets back to the ark.

One clear message of this chapter is that God continued to bless David, and that the episode with the ark did not mean that God would withdraw his favor. This chapter also refers to the idols of the Philistines that they took into battle but did not provide them with any help. We are struck by the contrast between the living God, who supported David, and the false gods of the Philistines that were weak and powerless.

14:1–2. From the point of view of human history, the time period of the unified kingdom, from Saul through Solomon, was a unique moment. It was a rare century of opportunity during which neither a Mesopotamian power nor Egypt were in control of Palestine. The Egyptians had defeated the Philistines, but they had used up too many resources in the process and thus were unable to establish themselves in Palestine. Now Egypt was coping with struggles of succession to the throne, while in Mesopotamia, the kingdoms of Babylon and Assyria were squabbling with each other for ascendancy. Consequently, the nations that occupied the Mediterranean coast—Phoenicia, Israel, Philistia—were free to spread themselves in unprecedented ways.

King Hiram of Tyre was a wily diplomat. We will find him at several places throughout Chronicles, negotiating with both David and Solomon to provide them with various benefits but ultimately strengthening his own position. At this point we see him simply reaching out to David in a gesture of royal fraternity; he sent David materials so the king could build himself a new palace. Hiram was probably not above calculating that once he got the king of Israel to develop a taste for his export products—cedar wood and skilled craftsmen—there might be additional business around the corner. For David this gesture was an endorsement that the Lord was establishing his kingdom.

14:3–7. The Lord blessed David by adding to his family as well. The list here repeats the information from 1 Chronicles 3:4–8, except that there is no direct reference to Bathsheba, the mother of the first four sons mentioned.

14:8–12. Now comes the account of two crucial battles with the Philistines. The emphasis is clearly on God's direction. David himself is not a particularly important part of the picture, though we can assume that he was as crafty and courageous as ever. Most importantly, David was obedient. He made sure that he had the Lord's directions, and then he followed them. What a contrast David's faithfulness presents to King Saul's second-guessing of God's commandments!

The Philistines had defeated Saul decisively at Mount Gilboa by the Jezreel Valley. Then, during the seven years when David was king of Judah only, they had free rein in the northern area of Israel. However, the territory they were controlling was basically divided into two parts: their own homeland along the coast south of Judah and the area throughout the northern tribes of Israel, with David's kingdom looming in between and getting stronger and stronger. Now David had been crowned king of all Israel, and he began to flex his muscles. The Philistines sought to put an end to this annoyance as soon as possible. If they could defeat David, the entire area of Palestine would once again be theirs.

The Philistines were planning an assault on David and were working their way toward Jerusalem. David's network of informants was functioning well. He found out where they were and launched a surprise attack when the Philistines advanced into the Valley of Rephaim, not too far from Jerusalem. But David was not about to do anything without consulting God first. The king asked if he should attack. The Lord not only told him that he should, but also that David would achieve victory. In giving credit to God for the victory, David compared it to a flood of water washing over the Philistines and sweeping them away.

The Philistines had brought their idols into battle with them, thinking the divine power of their gods would give them aid. But things went so badly for them that they wound up leaving these figurines lying around among the corpses of their fallen comrades. Idols are powerless, as the Old Testament prophets observed over and over again (Isa. 44:9; Jer. 10:5).

Another practice among ancient people was to collect the gods of their defeated enemies as booty. When they had captured the ark, the Philistines placed it in the temple of their god and hoped to gain benefits from it. Similarly, a common line of reasoning was that it would not hurt to keep a foreign idol. If it was powerless, it would not make any difference, and if it did have some power, you could always use it to augment your own gods' strength. But David did not follow this practice. Instead, he collected all the Philistines' idols and burned them. By this action he declared that only the living God, the Creator and Sustainer, is all-powerful.

14:13–17. The Philistines did not give up after this loss. They regrouped and tried once more, attacking by way of the same valley again. David again was well informed and contemplated the same strategy of another frontal attack. But he did not presume to know what God wanted him to do, so he consulted God again. The Lord gave him a different answer this time. He told David not to carry out a straightforward attack. Instead, he wanted David to circle around from the south, wait for a signal from God (a sound in the palm trees), and then surprise the Philistines from the rear.

When David carried out this plan, the Lord granted him victory over the Philistines. He wound up driving them north, far away from Judah. Even though the Philistine menace would not totally disappear (see 1 Chr. 18:1; 20:4; 2 Chr. 21:16; 26:6; 28:18), they would never again occupy the center of the stage as they had up to now. David was becoming known as a great and mighty king.

Success in Bringing the Ark to Jerusalem (15:1–29)

SUPPORTING IDEA: *When David followed the correct proce-dure for moving the ark of the covenant to Jerusalem, all went well, and the ark was relocated with much rejoicing.*

15:1. David had learned his lesson. Three months after the first attempt to move the ark, he had read the instructions and figured out why things had gone wrong. The problem was that the Levites had not carried the ark as God had commanded (15:2,13). David admitted that he had wanted the ark in Jerusalem in order to "inquire" of the Lord, but he realized that he had not inquired (15:13) how to get the ark there to begin with. This time he would do it right.

It appears that David let a little bit of human nature show through in his second set of preparations. He was committed to doing things right this time, but he also added more flair to the procedure—more songs, more music, more people, more excitement. But David didn't have to do it bigger and better; he just had to do it right!

This time David began by erecting a place for the ark to be deposited once it had been carried up the mountain. So he had a tent set up. In many ways this would rival the tabernacle, which was now situated at Gibeon. Theoreti-cally the new tent in Jerusalem had not replaced the old tent, and, as we will see below, David did not neglect the tabernacle either.

15:2–10. During the first attempt to move the ark, David had involved the Levites as participants. This time he did what he should have done the first time; he put the Levites in charge. They, and they alone, were allowed to transport the ark, and they should do so in the prescribed way by having the carrying poles for the ark rest on their shoulders. David called a council of Levites to give them instructions on the proper methods.

15:11–15. In addition to the descendants of Levi mentioned in the previ-ous verses, David now also included the two priests, **Zadok and Abiathar,** in his instructions. David informed the entire group without mincing any words about what their obligations were, and the priests and Levites complied. They went through the prescribed rituals of consecration (Exod. 29:1), lifted the ark by the carrying poles upon their shoulders, and got ready to start the pro-cession to Jerusalem.

15:16–24. Plenty of music was included as a part of the festivities. The three men previously mentioned—**Heman, Asaph,** and **Ethan** (1 Chr. 6:33–47)—were in charge and had an orchestra and choir at their disposal.

Kenaniah was considered **the head Levite**, and he had special responsibility for the choral portion of the production.

David also organized some of the other duties associated with the ark. Four men were designated as **doorkeepers** (security detail) **for the ark** once the tent was fully functional. These included **Obed-Edom**, the man on whose property the ark had rested for the last three months; he also played the harp in the procession to Jerusalem. Furthermore, there was a special detail of seven trumpeters who played in front of the ark.

15:25–29. This time everything went well, and they were able to take the ark from Obed-Edom's house to Jerusalem, where they celebrated with a sacrifice of **seven bulls and seven rams**. David was thrilled to have this procession take place, and his ecstasy increased as the ark approached Jerusalem. He was singing; he was dancing; he was in a state of rapture. Somewhere along the way the beautiful robe he had worn for the occasion came off, and David was prancing around in nothing more than a priestly loin cloth.

You may find it paradoxical that David did not get in trouble with God for this shameless display of his devotion. Didn't this behavior violate God's holiness even more than touching the ark? Obviously not, and the reason is that whatever David did was reflective of him and his worship of God, not of God himself, whereas the ark was supposed to represent God and his holiness. So David gave a demonstration of the contemporary worship of his day, and everyone, including God, approved.

Well, everyone approved except Michal, David's wife. Having been David's true love at one point, she now had accumulated many good reasons she did not appreciate David (see, e.g., 2 Sam. 3:15–16). David's all-too-public worship display was the last straw. The chronicler spares us the angry conversation recorded in 2 Samuel 6:20–23 and just lets it go with informing us that Michal **despised him in her heart**. Sometimes the moments of greatest spiritual triumph also carry the seeds of the deepest emotional defeat.

Ⓓ The Installation of the Ark (16:1–43)

SUPPORTING IDEA: *Once the ark was situated in Jerusalem, there was a great celebration, the highlight of which was a psalm David had written to commemorate the event.*

16:1–3. The ark was placed in the new tent, and immediately the priests performed the sacrifices. David presided over the ceremony and blessed the people at its conclusion (see Num. 6:22–27). Then there was a general distribution of food. Everyone in attendance received a loaf of bread, a date cake, and a raisin cake. These were not considered rations of staples but celebratory cuisine.

16:4–7. David continued to make sure that the musical side of worship was perpetually maintained. He put Asaph in charge and recruited a permanent orchestra. The responsibility for blowing trumpets before the ark was assigned to priests (see also 15:24). David marked the occasion by presenting Asaph with a psalm of thanksgiving. This composition drove home once again the point of emphasis for this entire section: the greatness of the true living God, who alone can act.

16:8–13. The psalm as David composed it is a unified whole, but parts of it have also been incorporated into other psalms. David's psalm has seven parts. It begins with an exhortation to praise God, then declares a reason for God's greatness, followed by another exhortation to praise, and so forth, making four exhortations and three declarations in all.

The first exhortation begins with the charge to **give thanks to the LORD**. The idea that the people should praise God recurs over the next few verses. But note that this is not an empty injunction. In contrast to many pagan activities of praise and worship, there is real content here: the praise of God refers back to real events, **what he has done** and **the wonders he has done**. It is not just the mindless accumulation of superlative attributes, but it is rooted in God's actions, not the least of which was the establishment of David's kingdom.

16:14–22. The first declaration focuses on God as the one who kept **his covenant**. Long ago he promised **Abraham** that his descendants would possess the whole land of Canaan, and now under David's reign this promise had been fulfilled.

16:23–24. The second exhortation tells the people to be a witness to God **among the nations**. Israel was now under the watchful eye of all its neighbors, and this was an opportunity for the people of God to demonstrate the reality of God to the Gentiles.

16:25–27. The second declaration emphasizes the point we have made throughout this section—the difference between the true and living God, to whom all glory is due, and the powerless idols of the pagan nations.

16:28–29. In the third exhortation to praise, the people are asked to ascribe to God the glory and worship that belongs to him.

16:30–33. The third and final declaration refers to the created order and how nature itself is prepared to glorify God in its own way.

16:34–36. Finally, the fourth exhortation, which closes the psalm, combines two ideas: to **give thanks** to God as well as to continue to **cry out** for salvation. Even as a period of strength and stability was beginning, the people, who were just coming out of a long and protracted series of wars, were conscious of how fragile any peace is. They were reminded to turn to God for true security.

16:37–43. David repeated his designation of Asaph as leader of the worship before the ark. Presumably, Abiathar stayed with the ark in Jerusalem as well, fulfilling the priestly role, but the emphasis now was on those who had been leading participants in the day's events. Obed-Edom, the gatekeeper turned harp player (1 Chr. 15:21), on whose property the ark had rested, oversaw the ministry in the tent with the help of sixty-eight colleagues.

But many of the Levites returned to the tabernacle in Gibeon. Zadok the priest, together with the two musicians Heman and Ethan (here referred to as Jeduthun), would continue a reinvigorated worship ministry in the old tent, which had been functioning without the ark for a long time anyway. This location would still be the site of the main offerings, including the central observance of the Day of Atonement. Still, Israel now had two main sanctuaries. It was clear from the beginning that this state of affairs could not last forever.

> **MAIN IDEA REVIEW:** *David needed to learn to respect God's holiness when he tried to transport the ark of the covenant to Jerusalem. When he did so, a joyous feast resulted. This story reminds us that God's holiness should be central in our thoughts of him.*

III. CONCLUSION

No Superconductor for Holiness

A Buddhist temple in Thailand usually has a steep pointed roof with many intricate decorations along the eaves. Inside, at the front, there is a large altar, typically crowded with many objects, including small statues and various offerings. Looming behind this altar is a statue of Buddha, who is sitting in a meditative position, usually with his hair coming together into a small flamelike spike on top of his head. This representation is intended to convey spiritual power and serenity, two important attributes of the Buddha in all Buddhist traditions.

But if you look closely at a statue of the Buddha, you may notice another unusual feature. In the Buddha's hands you will see thin ropes tied to the image and leading from the altar to other areas of the hall or, if there is more than one building in a temple complex, to the other houses. The purpose of these strings is to convey the spiritual blessings of Buddha to other places as well as to the worshipers who link themselves to these riggings. Divine power supposedly flows through these strings like electric current through wires.

The idea that spiritual benefits can be contained in objects and transferred to people is neither new nor unique. It is an aspect of all forms of idolatry. Thai Buddhists think they can convey Buddha's benefits by way of laundry rope; in many religions the idolatrous object gets carried around in processions.

The Bible teaches that all this is nonsense. Holiness cannot reside in material things, let alone be conveyed by them. There is no such thing as conducting spiritual power through physical "wires." You cannot transmit sacredness with physical conductors. Corporeal substances are not containers of holiness, and you cannot tap them for holiness as though you were milking sacredness from a holy cow.

In the Old Testament, the ark of the covenant was subject to a lot of misunderstanding along this line. On the one hand, the ark represented the presence of the Lord among the people of Israel. It was holy because it belonged to the Lord, and this sacredness was not to be abused. At the same time, it was not holy by itself as an object—the holiness belonged to God. He expected the Israelites to walk a fine line in this matter. They were to respect God's holiness as represented by the ark, but they were not to turn the ark into an idol.

As people with a sense of Christian love and duty, we may forgive other people for something they have done; after all, none of us is perfect. But God is perfect. He is holy, and when he reproves us for a sin, he does so as someone who stands totally apart from our sin-stained lives. He is so different from us that no words can possibly give us a clear understanding of his holiness. And yet he does forgive us. It is God's holiness that allows all his other attributes to take on their full meaning.

PRINCIPLES

- God is holy, and there are no persons or objects that are holy by their own nature.
- God sometimes designates certain objects, such as the ark of the covenant, as representative of his holiness to people.
- The objects that God has designated as representing his holiness must be treated with utmost respect.
- Our blessings do not depend on our association with certain objects but on our relationship with the living God.

APPLICATIONS

- Compare the views of and the ways of speaking of God in contemporary culture with God's revelation of himself during the effort to move the ark of the covenant back to Jerusalem.

- Consider this event in David's life in light of what happened to Ananias and Sapphira in the early church (Acts 5:1–11).

- Ask God for an appropriate sense of his holiness.

IV. LIFE APPLICATION

Trusting in a Holy God

The Old Testament code of holiness no longer applies to us under the New Testament. For example, we no longer divide foods into clean and unclean categories (Mark 7:18–19; Acts 10:15). But this does not mean that we no longer need to respect God's holiness. There is one event in the New Testament that may remind us of the incident with the ark in David's time.

In the Book of Acts, we have the tragic story of Ananias and Sapphira (Acts 5:1–10). Many early believers sold their plots of land and gave the proceeds to the church in order to support the poor. Ananias and Sapphira decided to join in. They sold a piece of land, set aside a sum of money for their own use, and brought the rest to Peter. Everyone thought the money they gave to the church was all the money they had received for the property. When Peter asked Ananias to confirm this supposition, he claimed that was all the money. Ananias died instantly, and a short while later, Sapphira repeated the same lie, and she also collapsed and died right on the spot. This couple was under no obligation to sell their land or to give all the proceeds to the church, but they should not have lied to God about it (Acts 5:4).

God's demonstrations of his holiness, which he sometimes underscores with severe punishment for those who disregard it, have one important aim: to remind us that he is, indeed, the one true God. He is the God who will not let people peek into his ark or let them lie about their commitment to him. But he is also the God who put all his power and glory at our disposal, first by bringing us undeserved salvation and second by providing for us as we walk through life. Only a holy God is a God worth trusting.

V. PRAYER

Lord Jesus, we come to you as the one who is always here with us, who walks with us every step of the way, and who allows us to come to you without formality or pretense. But sometimes we take this privilege for granted and forget that you are God and that you are holy. Forgive us our presumption, and help us to see you as the one to whom all glory and splendor belong so the miracle of your grace and mercy may become clearer to us. Amen.

VI. DEEPER DISCOVERIES

A. Hiram, King of Tyre (14:1)

Tyre was one of the Phoenician cities on the coast of the Mediterranean Sea just north of Israel. This city is frequently mentioned along with Sidon. In fact, Tyre was located right in the Mediterranean on a little island about half a mile from the mainland. From there it also established a mainland setting. So when the Bible refers to Tyre, it can refer either to the fortified city on the island or the settlement on the shore.

The Tyrians were Phoenicians, a race of seafarers and traders who made a name for themselves by establishing outposts all over the Mediterranean world. Good merchants are not of much use if they don't have a distinctive product to sell, and the Phoenicians excelled with their offerings to the world. They dealt in many fine and well-crafted goods, but their most outstanding merchandise was a dye that turned fabric a distinctive color that became known as purple ("Phoenician color"), ever since designated as the color of royalty.

The Phoenicians seem to have been heavily influenced by their Canaanite neighbors. They did not have a truly distinctive religion but worshiped an eclectic collection of Canaanite deities. King Hiram, when the occasion called for it, gave praise to the God of the Israelites (2 Chr. 2:11–12), though there is no reason to believe that he seriously worshiped the Lord. Eventually, the Phoenicians were the direct source for the spread of Baal worship into Israel when King Ahab married Jezebel, the daughter of the king of Sidon (1 Kgs. 16:31).

Hiram was one of the most successful Phoenician kings. He was able to establish Tyre as a powerful trading city as well as to fortify it against potential foreign invaders. He maximized his small kingdom's assets by exporting timber from the cedar forests of Lebanon and other natural resources and sending along craftsmen who knew how to work them. He found ready customers in both David and Solomon and managed to forge an alliance with them that profited both Israel and Tyre.

B. A Tale of Two High Priests (15:11)

It appears there were two people during David's reign who performed the office of high priest—Abiathar and Zadok. Abiathar was a close friend and associate of David, going back to his time in the wilderness (1 Sam. 22:20–23). Because his father, Ahimelech, had been the high priest, and since David was at least in part responsible for Ahimelech's death (1 Sam. 22:6–19), David made it a special point for Abiathar to accompany him and carry out priestly duties. Then, when David came to power, it was only natural that Abiathar should start to assume the office of high priest. However, before David had actually become king, Zadok had already been installed as high priest at the tabernacle.

Thus, there were two men who had a legitimate claim to the high priesthood. David accommodated them both by having Zadok continue to officiate at the tabernacle, while Abiathar was put in charge of the new tent for the ark in Jerusalem.

What must have been an uneasy relationship between the two men continued throughout David's reign. Both Zadok and Abiathar supported David during the revolt of Absalom (2 Sam. 15:24). But things came to a head when the question of who should succeed David arose. Zadok supported Solomon, while Abiathar cast his lot with Adonijah (1 Kgs. 1:7–27). Solomon inherited the throne, and he eventually deposed Abiathar and sent him into exile (1 Kgs. 2:26–27).

VII. TEACHING OUTLINE

A. INTRODUCTION

1. Lead Story: The Interstellar Meteorite
2. Context: In the novel *Ice Limit*, the characters have to move a meteorite of enormous weight that will kill anyone who touches it. King David, in establishing his reign in Jerusalem, sought to bring the ark of the covenant to his new capital, but it also turned out to be an object that was difficult to move.
3. Transition: David's first attempt to transport the ark of the covenant to Jerusalem turned into a disaster because David and his associates

did not respect the holiness of God. The second attempt, which followed the rules laid out by God, was successful.

B. COMMENTARY
1. The Failed Attempt at Moving the Ark (13:1–14)
2. Gods of the Philistines Versus the God of David (14:1–17)
3. Success in Bringing the Ark to Jerusalem (15:1–29)
4. Installation of the Ark (16:1–43)

C. CONCLUSION: NO SUPERCONDUCTOR FOR HOLINESS

VIII. ISSUES FOR DISCUSSION

1. Are there objects, places, or times Christians today might consider holy?
2. How can we learn to respect God's holiness in greater measure?
3. What can we do to appreciate the holiness of God without falling into the trap of transferring the concept of holiness to objects?

1 Chronicles 17:1–20:8

David's Undefeated Season

I. INTRODUCTION
An Undefeated Season

II. COMMENTARY
A verse-by-verse explanation of these chapters.

III. CONCLUSION
An (Almost) Undefeated Season

An overview of the principles and applications from these chapters.

IV. LIFE APPLICATION
Star Trek: Generations

Melding these chapters to life.

V. PRAYER
Tying these chapters to life with God.

VI. DEEPER DISCOVERIES
Historical, geographical, and grammatical enrichment of the commentary.

VII. TEACHING OUTLINE
Suggested step-by-step group study of these chapters.

VIII. ISSUES FOR DISCUSSION
Zeroing these chapters in on daily life.

"*The world has yet to see what God can do with one man wholly committed to him.*"

Henry Varley to a young, discouraged Dwight L. Moody

1 Chronicles 17:1–20:8

IN A NUTSHELL

Even though God put a stop to King David's plan to build a temple in Jerusalem, David rejoiced in the promise that God would always place his descendants on the throne. This promise was fulfilled with finality in Jesus Christ. God gave David many victories to establish domination over his land and to show that he rewarded those who came to him with unreserved trust.

David's Undefeated Season

I. INTRODUCTION

An Undefeated Season

*I*n January 1973, the Miami Dolphins of the National Football League completed an entire season without suffering a single loss. This meant that they won the fourteen games of the regular season of 1972, the divisional and conference play-off games, and the Super Bowl where they defeated the Washington Redskins, making seventeen games in all.

The Dolphins' flawless performance surprised most people. Many writers and announcers stated that this was the first time a professional team had achieved this goal, allowing us to think that sooner or later another team would match what the Dolphins had done. But no team has matched the Dolphins' achievement yet, and many experts say that—given the current structure of the league—it is virtually impossible for it to happen.

King David seems to have had an "undefeated season." In this section we will see how he was able to defeat enemy after enemy, even when the prospects looked bleak. There is no question that God had granted him success. All David's achievements were based on one premise: God made a promise to David, and he would keep it. We will see how this unmatched season played itself out, but we also need to prepare ourselves for the fact that it turned out to be a high point in the history of Israel that would never be matched again.

II. COMMENTARY

David's Undefeated Season

> **MAIN IDEA:** *As David and his generals trusted in the Lord, God provided them with victory over the surrounding nations.*

Many commentators caution us not to assume that the material here is in exact chronological sequence, that the chronicler was grouping his accounts thematically and not in the exact order in which they occurred. Obviously, some time had elapsed between the point where the previous account leaves off and this one picks up. Meanwhile David had made good use of the building material donated by Hiram, the enterprising king of Tyre, and for quite a while now the ark of the covenant had been resting in Jerusalem. We watch as David makes plans for a more permanent building for the ark, and how

God blesses him in response. Then the nature of this divine blessing is detailed by showing how David won victory after victory over Judah's enemies.

David's Desire to Build a Temple (17:1–27)

SUPPORTING IDEA: *Even though David was not allowed to build a temple, he rejoiced in the promise God made to him and his descendants.*

17:1–2. David had received free samples of building materials from King Hiram of Tyre. If Hiram had hoped that David would eventually come back for more materials, his plans worked out. The king of Israel had built himself a beautiful palace of cedar wood with all the amenities of his day, and now he wished to construct a temple as well. The ark had been staying in a tent in Jerusalem for a while now, with priests officiating at all the customary worship duties, over some of which Abiathar presided. Simultaneously the "real" tabernacle (with all the required implements except the ark) had still stood in Gibeon, where Zadok and his fellow priests also carried out the requirements of the law. Now David decided to unify the worship centers by building a single permanent temple in Jerusalem.

Nathan the prophet seems to have had ongoing access to David in his palace. His job was to provide direct counsel from the Lord, though at times he also had to come to pronounce judgment (1 Sam. 12). This particular story begins with a conversation between David and Nathan in which David expressed his dissatisfaction at having a splendid palace for himself, while the ark was resting in a tent. It was time, David believed, to build a real temple for the ark. Nathan replied with the confidence of an advisor to a king who knew that a pleasing answer would be the correct one. "Of course," Nathan said, "go ahead. You are a godly man, David, and surely this is the right thing to do."

17:3–15. But the next night Nathan received a different message from the Lord. God did not want David to build a temple, and Nathan had the duty of reporting what God had said to the king. We can break God's revelation to Nathan into three parts to help us understand it.

First, God conveyed to David the point that, whoever may have come up with the idea for building a temple, it was not the Lord. He had commanded the use of a portable tent, and he had never complained that he wanted better facilities. This almost humorous response to David displays for us God's reaction to some of the things that we try to do in order to please him; it is a natural human reaction to want to make our worship buildings and practices bigger, more ornate, and more of a display of our own efforts. But God said through his prophet, "Away with the noise of your songs! I will not listen to the music of your harps. But let justice roll on like a river, righteousness like a never-failing stream" (Amos 5:23–24). Striving after righteousness is not as exciting as a rousing "worship" performance, but if the first is not in place, the second is meaningless.

Second, God reminded David of all that he had done for him, taking him from shepherd boy to king over a mighty empire.

Third, God issued a promise to the king. David, who already had a house in the physical sense, would have a permanent "house" in the sense of being the first king of a never-ending dynasty. Even though David would not be allowed to build a temple, his son (Solomon, we learn later) would. Furthermore, his throne would be established **forever**. There would always be a descendant of David and Solomon on the throne of Israel.

17:16–27. David's reaction to God's response was surprising. We expect David to break out into protests, trying to make a case for why he should be allowed to build the temple. David was certainly not above complaining bitterly to the Lord about various issues (see Ps. 6:1–7). But not this time. David was overwhelmed by the love and generosity of God, and he expressed his thanks to the Lord in a beautiful prayer.

David's avowal focused on the aspect of the promise that there would be a permanent "house of David." Remember how David had seen Saul's house utterly decimated. David may have worried that the same fate might befall his own family. But with God's declaration that concern dissappeared because David knew he could count on God to be steadfast in his love toward him.

B Victories over Neighboring Kingdoms (18:1–17)

SUPPORTING IDEA: God blessed David by granting him victory over Israel's enemies.

This chapter recounts the victories of David over the various kingdoms in his vicinity, with the exception of Ammon, which will receive greater treatment in the next chapter. With these conquests David managed to establish a kingdom that spanned the entire area west of the Euphrates River to the Mediterranean Sea. Finally the full extent of the land, as it had originally been promised by God through Moses (Deut. 1:7), was attained.

18:1–6. Even though the Philistines had been defeated decisively within Israel (1 Chr. 14:11–16), David had not yet conquered the Philistines' own territory. This he now proceeded to do. The chronicler singles out David's victory over the city of Gath, hometown of David's old nemesis, Goliath. The victory over Moab, another thorn in Israel's flesh since the time of the exodus (Num. 25:1–2), is mentioned only in passing.

Hadadezer was king of Zobah, a part of the Aramean (Syrian) group of nations. His people lived in the area east of Damascus all the way to the Euphrates River. This is another instance of a minor country being able to assert itself while the Babylonians and Assyrians were focusing all their attention on each other. From what we read of the size of Hadadezer's army, particularly the seven thousand chariots, Hadadezer was quite powerful, although David's force was obviously even more powerful.

David's action of hamstringing thousands of horses may bother contemporary Western readers. Even in the context of the slaughter of many human beings, we may feel sad for the animals that got hurt. But for David this was arms control pure and simple. An army without horses could not be an effective enemy. When the western Arameans, who had their capital in Damascus, came to the aid of their eastern cousins, they were also defeated. David, to return to the imagery of our opening story, was enjoying an "undefeated season."

18:7–11. It is not clear why Hadadezer's officers carried gold shields into battle. Gold is a soft and heavy metal, and any armament made from it would have been impractical in combat. These shields must have been for show on the part of an upstart king who overestimated his own capabilities. They made a welcome addition to David's collection of war booty, as did a sizable amount of bronze. Furthermore, King Tou of Hamath (a northern Aramean kingdom) decided to forestall any Israelite invasion just by shipping the tribute without being defeated in a war first. He sent his son Hadoram in order to **congratulate him on his victory** and to present David with many articles in precious metals.

David did not add these treasures to his own wealth. Instead, he deposited them in the treasury of the Lord, just as the Israelites had been instructed to do during the conquest under Joshua. Everything should be destroyed except for articles of gold, silver, or bronze, which should go to the Lord (Josh. 6:18–19). Given the chaos prior to David's reign, the king probably had to revive the tabernacle treasury, into which he deposited all his war gains.

18:12–13. The chronicler writes about a military exploit made by Abishai. He was a brother of Joab, David's highest general and, thus, also a half nephew of David. In the next chapter we will see him as general of the Israelites, working with his brother to defeat the Ammonites. But here we hear about a time when he was carrying out a campaign on his own, routing a large army of Edomites in the vicinity of the Dead Sea. After achieving this victory, Abishai made sure that David would continue to have control of this territory by installing garrisons. Once more, the chronicler reminds us, David was in the middle of an "undefeated season."

18:14–17. We conclude with a quick overview of the leadership of the kingdom. Some of the names are familiar to us by now. These include Joab, who was commander of the army, and Zadok, one of the priests. Even though Abiathar would be around for a long time (1 Kgs. 2:26–27), the other priest mentioned was Abiathar's son, Ahimelech, named after his grandfather (1 Sam. 21:1). We also find the second of the two great commanders—Benaiah, the killer of an Egyptian giant—in charge of special troops (1 Chr. 11:22–25). Once the kingdom was established, perhaps Jehoshaphat, the recorder, and Shavsha, the secretary, were holding the real power because they provided the basis for all future administrative work.

Finally, the sons of David had various undefined positions of leadership. This description sounds as unhealthy as it turned out to be. If you are supposed to have power but have no job description to go with it, what do you do with all that alleged power? The chronicler does not go into the matter any further, but elsewhere we read of the disastrous consequences of this nonarrangement, which eventually came to a head with Absalom's rebellion (2 Sam. 13–22).

War with Ammon (19:1–20:3)

SUPPORTING IDEA: *The war with Ammon displays further how God granted David success, and it also highlights Joab's faith in God.*

The events described in this chapter probably occurred before David's campaigns in the previous chapter since the Aramean kings still had armies and were able to fight.

19:1–5. This is not the first or last time that a ruler engaged in self-destructive behavior that brought ruin to his nation (we will see more of it in the person of King Rehoboam in 2 Chr. 10). But perhaps Hanun's folly stands out for its pointlessness. **Nahash** had been **king** of Ammon for a long time. It was he who had first caused Saul to establish his authority as king with an attack on the town of Jabesh Gilead. This caused Saul to rally all Israel to come to the defense of the town (1 Sam. 11:1–11). Nahash was a mean, cruel person (1 Sam. 11:2), but—perhaps on the theory that "the enemy of my enemy is my friend"—he had shown kindness to David when David was on the run from Saul. When Nahash died and his son Hanun took the throne,

David sent a diplomatic mission to Hanun to convey his condolences to the new ruler.

When the Israelite delegation arrived at the Ammonite capital, the new king's advisors remembered the defeat at the hands of Saul's army a whole lot more than whatever sentiment there may have been between Nahash and David. They suspected that the Israelites were spies, sent to prepare for an attack by David's forces. The king bought into their suspicions.

What is amazing about this story is how King Hanun acted on these suspicions. One can think of numerous ways to deal with people suspected of being spies sent in ahead of an invasion. For example, one could kill them so they would not be able to file a report; one could pretend to honor them and send them back with false information; one could hold them hostage to forestall an enemy attack; and one would certainly pump them for information about the invading enemy's plans and position. King Hanun did not do any of these things. He just sent them back to David so they could report all their information if they really had been spies.

But first he went out of his way to humiliate them by shaving off their beards and cutting off their clothes to leave their private parts exposed. Then he drove them into the desert to trudge home in disgrace. David heard about the humiliation his personal ambassadors had suffered, and he was angry. He advised his men to remain secluded in the city of Jericho until their beards had grown back.

19:6–9. How do you make a bad situation worse? King Hanun found a way. As soon as he realized that the Israelites were offended at his behavior, he decided to forestall any punitive action by amassing a great army and setting out to attack Israel. Just to make sure that David would have no choice but to retaliate, he hired a combined army from several Aramean kingdoms. The two armies (the Ammonites and the Arameans) positioned themselves in such a way that an Israelite army would have to fight on two fronts at once. The fact that the Ammonites placed themselves with their backs to their city ensured that David's forces would not be able to encircle them from the back, while the Aramean forces would have the flexibility to offer them support.

In other words, the Ammonite soldiers would function as "bait." When the Israelites attacked them, the Arameans could swoop down and squeeze the Israelites between them and the Ammonites. David did the only thing he could do under the circumstances: he sent in Joab at the head of his army.

19:10–15. Joab, the general with the reputation of bringing off the impossible, abandoned all notions of subtlety in his counterattack. He divided his army into two parts, taking command of one division himself and placing his brother Abishai at the head of the other. Joab's troops faced the Arameans, who were the stronger army, while Abishai's soldiers faced the Ammonites. Joab made a deal with Abishai that if one of them got into trouble, he would call the other for help.

Before the battle broke out, Joab declared, **The LORD will do what is good in his sight**. Joab's decisions were direct and pragmatic and so was his faith in God. He did not presume that God would aid them, and he did not try to figure out some clever way in which God would bring about a victory. He was willing to leave it with God.

And God granted a great victory. First the Arameans lost courage and started to run. When the Ammonites realized their allies had abandoned them in the field, they also gave up and fled. Against the odds, Joab had won against this massive army. With the job accomplished, he returned to Jerusalem.

19:16–19. But the Arameans, having been brought into the war by the Ammonites, were not willing to accept defeat. They amassed another huge army with new support from further allies and began to march toward Israel again. This time David took matters into his own hands. He personally led the army and placed himself directly in the path of the Arameans. Once more the enemies took severe losses and finally resorted to flight. Eventually, they were willing to accept a peace treaty with David. From what the chronicler tells us, the reaction among the Arameans was, "Look at what those Ammonites got us into! We're never going to help them again."

20:1–3. Joab was out besieging Rabbah, a city of Amnon. Shortly thereafter David remained in Jerusalem, and it was during this time that the adulterous and murderous episode with Bathsheba occurred (2 Sam. 11:1–26). It is unlikely that Ezra would not have known about this story, nor should we think that he was deceitful for not including it. At this point he was not writing a character study of David. The chronicler was providing us with a blueprint for the ideal kingdom as it was set up under David. The fact that David committed some serious sins is certainly significant in the overall scheme; that is why God made sure it was included in 2 Samuel. To the chronicler, however, David's sin was not relevant to the purpose of his account.

It might seem strange to us that there was a **time when kings go off to war**. But a number of factors made a particular season optimal for warfare. Obviously, nobody would postpone defending themselves from an invasion or take some other emergency measures just because it wasn't the right month. But a good strategist setting out to war needed to observe the following rules.

He would want to avoid the rainy season so his troops would not bog down in mud. He should not have his troops in the field at a time when they would be scorched by the sun with little water to quench their thirst. But most importantly, he would need to make sure that his troops had food. This meant setting out at a time when the enemy's crops had just ripened. This meant the army, which would quickly exhaust whatever supplies it carried from home, could feed itself by raiding the fields in the enemy's territory. So there was a specific time that would work best for a general and his troops— late spring. This became known as **the time when kings go off to war**.

Joab once again was in command of the army as it besieged Rabbah, the Ammonite capital. David did not come to join him until the last phase of the assault (2 Sam. 12:27–29), just in time to clinch the victory and claim the booty. Among the captured treasures was a huge crown made of gold and adorned with jewels. This was the sign of authority for the king. David put on this crown to symbolize his dominance over the Ammonites, and then he designated the citizens of Rabbah for slave labor. How they must have regretted the day when they laughed at King Hunan's crude mistreatment of David's ambassadors! David, having finished his "undefeated season," returned to Jerusalem.

Victory over Three Giants (20:4–8)

> **SUPPORTING IDEA:** *The victory of three of David's men over Philistine giants added to David's glory.*

20:4–8. The Philistines had been conquered, but nothing stopped occasional instances of violent resistance. In this passage we meet three Philistine giants who led rebellions but who were killed by individual Israelites. The first flare-up was led by **Sippai**, who is called a **Rephaite**, a descendant of an ancient race of giants (Deut. 3:11). He was no match for **Sibbecai the Hushathite**, one of David's thirty mighty men (1 Chr. 11:29), who killed him and put down the rebellion.

The giant **Lahmi**, like his brother Goliath, went to war on behalf of **the Philistines**. He was killed by **Elhanan son of Jair**. Finally, there was more unrest **at Gath** again, this time led by a giant known for having **six fingers on each hand and six toes on each foot**. He also attempted to mimic Goliath by publicly taunting Israel, and he suffered the same fate. This time it was David's nephew Jonathan, the son of Shimea (1 Chr. 2:13), who brought him down. Thus, David, the giant killer himself, was surrounded and supported by giant killers. There seemed to be no limit to the power of David's kingdom.

> **MAIN IDEA REVIEW:** *As David and his generals trusted in the Lord, God gave them victory over the surrounding nations.*

III. CONCLUSION

An (Almost) Undefeated Season

In the 1950s, Taylor University basketball and football coach Don Odle agreed to become a part of a new kind of evangelistic ministry. He became the coach of a college basketball team that traveled to Asia, where they played against local teams before large crowds and then used the halftime breaks as an opportunity to share the gospel. This innovative missions team, known as Venture for Victory, became the model for many sports evangelism programs.

Odle's first team traveled to the Philippines and Taiwan in the summer of 1952. Then, beginning with the next year, the team added Japan and Korea to the schedule of ministry through athletics. In 1953 they played eighty-two games, of which they won eighty-one (Rousselow-Winquist and Winquist, 126). However, it would be wrong to classify the one loss as a defeat. Even though they did not win that particular athletic contest, they did accomplish their goal of witnessing for Christ that night. Venture for Victory may not have had an undefeated season in terms of final scores, but they did in terms of the spiritual mission, which was their real purpose.

King David, in cementing his empire, had an "undefeated season." From the Ammonites (1 Chr. 19) to the Zobahites (1 Chr. 18:3), he achieved victory over his enemies. His "undefeated season" is an important reminder that an omnipotent God is in charge of our lives and will bring us victory. Even if we lose our battles with our versions of the Philistines or Ammonites, if we are faithful to our calling from the Lord, just like Venture for Victory we will not be defeated.

PRINCIPLES

- A victorious life with God is not one in which we get everything we want.
- When God does give us victory over circumstances, we should acknowledge that he is the one in charge.
- When we experience defeat by the circumstances of life, we should realize that this need not defeat our spirit and put our trust in God.
- We need to remember where God has given us victories more important than any defeats.

APPLICATIONS

- Make an inventory of your blessings. Thank God for them. Acknowledge to others what God has done.
- Make an inventory of your losses. Ask for God's perspective on those losses.
- Meditate on Romans 8:28–29,37–39, and let its truths go deep into your heart.

IV. LIFE APPLICATION

Star Trek: Generations

What if Joab had decided to play it safe? He could have checked out the situation and reported back to David that the Ammonites and Arameans were too powerful to try to defeat for now, that surely they could afford to pay some tribute, and that in a worst case scenario Jerusalem would most likely be able to withstand a siege. Later on in Chronicles we will encounter this attitude by some kings, but neither Joab nor David fell prey to it.

Sometimes we do not give the Lord a chance to show what he can do. A few years ago when I was in a foreign country, I was talking to some young women who were thinking about coming to the United States and earning a college degree, something that was impossible for them in their own country. The big question was finances. They had the money to come and to pay for the first semester of their studies, but they were clueless about where the rest of the money would come from. We talked and prayed about the situation and agreed that, since it definitely seemed to be God's leading for them to do this, they should venture out, trusting the Lord to continue to supply for them.

As it turned out, they received sufficient support, and a few years later they graduated from Taylor University. But even if the Lord had closed the door on them after a short while, it still would not have been right for them to assume defeat and not step out on faith.

In the movie *Star Trek: Generations,* Captain Kirk, retired from his post on the starship *Enterprise,* had been absorbed into a state called the Nexus, an ideal existence in which everyone's wishes come true and there are no risks or dangers. A while later the new commander of the *Enterprise,* Captain Picard, found himself in a serious predicament that could result in the population of an entire planet being exterminated. When Picard, too, got swept up by the Nexus, he tried to recruit Kirk's assistance. At first Kirk refused, but then changed his mind after he got bored with the safety of the Nexus.

"I take it the odds are against us and the situation is grim," Kirk said.

Picard replied, "You could say that."

"Sounds like fun!"

And so they set off to save, if not the universe, then at least one planet.

Too many Christians expect to live in a Nexuslike state, where all their expectations are met and where nothing can ever go wrong. Then, when life does not turn out that way, they let themselves get defeated. Like Captain Kirk, the fact of the risk ought to spur us on to trust God and keep on fighting.

V. PRAYER

Lord Jesus, you have given us victory in all circumstances because you are our Lord and Savior. There is no one more trustworthy than you. And yet we find ourselves again and again focusing on everything but you, and we allow ourselves to suffer defeat in the process. Help us to look at you so we can partake of the victory that only you can give us. Amen.

VI. DEEPER DISCOVERIES

A. Where Is the King of Judah Now? (17:14)

There seems to be something wrong with God's promise that there would always be a descendant of David on the throne of Judah. After all, there had been no king of Judah from 587 B.C. on, except for the short-lived Hasmonean Kingdom, which lasted only about a hundred years (145–35 B.C. approximately), and those kings were from the tribe of Levi, not Judah. Did "forever" mean "about four hundred years"?

When God reveals something to us, whatever God meant to disclose to us must be true, but there is no guarantee that we will always grasp correctly just what God meant to reveal. That is the case in this instance. When God told David that there would be a descendant of his on the throne forever, David understood this promise as guaranteeing the succession of his dynasty in a physical, political kingdom. But since that turned out not to be the case, we need to look in another direction to see what God meant.

We do not need to look far. As a matter of fact, there is a descendant of the line of David (Matt. 1:1–7; Luke 3:23–38), who is the King, not just of a little plot of land surrounded by Egypt, Mesopotamia, and the Hittites, but of the entire universe (Phil. 2:9–11). His physical descent from David maintains the integrity of the promise. But much more importantly, the more exalted place that he has amplifies the richness of God's promise to David. That King with the everlasting kingdom is the Lord Jesus Christ (Rev. 11:15).

B. God's Sovereign Will (17:22)

God made Israel his own forever for no reason other than to make a name for himself. David, at the apex of his success, recognized this fact when he responded to God's promise of an eternal kingdom. There is no thought of God rewarding him for all his faithfulness while hiding in the desert or of Israel as a nation having earned God's favor. To the contrary, David's actions were far from pure, and the nation had failed every test that came its way. Still, God had chosen them as his people and had given David his throne purely out of his mercy.

This principle of divine electing love seems to go contrary to our human instincts. We want to take credit for whatever God gives us. It applies not only to God's choice of Israel but to our salvation as well. Surely God must have seen something within us that led him to want to save us. The contemporary desire for self-esteem may cause us to think that we also deserve God-esteem: Christ must have saved us because he thought we had such a high intrinsic worth. But the apostle Paul says, "It does not, therefore, depend on man's desire or effort, but on God's mercy" (Rom. 9:16). "He saved us, not because of righteous things we had done, but because of his mercy" (Titus 3:5).

If God were to elect people only if they are worthy of his salvation, no one would be saved. No human being can bring enough righteousness to the table to rate God's salvation. If that were possible, we would not need to be saved. It is precisely because we are incompetent and unworthy that God extends his free grace to us.

C. Giants in the Bible (20:4–8)

From time to time the Old Testament mentions races of giants. They were not so huge as to be totally incompatible with a basic human physiology, but they were definitely much larger than average human beings, and we cannot rule out that some of their biological attributes could have been different from ours in some details.

Goliath was nine feet tall (1 Sam. 17:4), but he may have been short compared to Og, the king of Bashan, whose bed was thirteen feet long and six feet wide (Deut. 3:11). Even if we allow for some overage on the size of the bed, there still would have been a lot of giant sleeping in that place each night.

There are three main groups of giants in the Old Testament, plus a number of individuals who are identified by their places of origin, such as the

Egyptian giant who was killed by Benaiah (1 Chr. 11:22–25). Goliath of Gath (the "Gittite") called himself a Philistine (1 Sam. 17:8), but he may also have been related to one of the larger groups.

The original race of giants were the Nephilim (Gen. 6:4). They were wiped out by the flood, but their genetic heritage may have been carried by Noah and his descendants (specifically Ham) as a recessive trait, which eventually came out again in certain Canaanite groups.

When the Israelite spies explored the promised land, they were frightened by the presence of the Anakites, who were descendants of the Nephilim (Num. 13:33). Intimidated by the spies' report, the people refused to enter the land. Only Joshua and Caleb believed that God could give them victory over the giants (Num. 14:6–9).

The third main group of giants were the Rephaites. King Og was the last pure Rephaite, but Philistines such as Sippai (1 Chr. 20:4) and the unnamed six-fingered giant in our story (1 Chr. 20:6; see also 2 Sam. 21:16) were able to trace their descent back to this ancient race.

In the biblical narratives giants serve one purpose. Although they seem to be physically superior to other human beings and carry menacing weapons, they inevitably fall before those men who may be smaller in stature but who trust in God. David said to Goliath, "You come against me with sword and spear and javelin, but I come against you in the name of the LORD Almighty" (1 Sam. 17:45).

VII. TEACHING OUTLINE

A. INTRODUCTION

1. Lead Story: An Undefeated Season

2. Context: Just as the Miami Dolphins had an undefeated season, culminating in a Super Bowl victory, so David had an "undefeated season," vanquishing all the surrounding nations and establishing his kingdom.

3. Transition: After God had denied David the opportunity to build a temple, God promised that David's descendants would always remain on the royal throne of Judah. Then God demonstrated how richly he was blessing David by granting him victory over all his enemies, including the Philistines, the Arameans, and the Ammonites.

B. COMMENTARY
1. David's Desire to Build a Temple (17:1–27)
2. Victories over Neighboring Kingdoms (18:1–17)
3. War with Ammon (19:1–20:3)
4. Victory over Three Giants (20:4–8)

C. CONCLUSION: AN (ALMOST) UNDEFEATED SEASON

VIII. ISSUES FOR DISCUSSION

1. What counts as a "victory" in a Christian's life?
2. What can legitimately be called a "defeat" in a Christian's life? What should we think of as only apparent "defeats"?
3. What are some specific things Christians can do to help them look beyond outward defeats to inner victories?
4. What are some specific things a church can do to help its members recognize victories in apparent defeats?

1 Chronicles 21:1–22:19

A Census and Its Mixed Results

1 Chronicles 21:1–22:19

Quote

"My point, little brother, is this: I expect more failure from you than you expect from yourself."

Brennan Manning

I N   A   N U T S H E L L

At the peak of his power, David overextended his God-given authority and took a census of the available fighting men in his kingdom. As a consequence, a plague came on all Israel. David's repentance averted the punishment and brought about the discovery of the location for the future temple.

A Census and Its Mixed Results

"Oops! There Goes My Testimony!"

*I*n the last chapter we mentioned Venture for Victory, the pioneering sports evangelism team. Beginning in 1952, this basketball team played games against local teams all over Asia and used their status as celebrities to share the gospel. Many people were saved.

However, while the power of Christ was on display, there were also moments of personal weakness. One night, player-coach Don Odle was whistled by the referee twice for moves Odle did not consider infractions. Already frustrated by injury and sickness on the team, he "in disgust threw the ball back over his shoulder unintentionally hitting the referee in the mouth. The force of the blow was great enough to ram the whistle against the man's teeth, breaking one. The crowd hissed Odle strongly, and he removed himself from the game in a state of absolute dejection" (Rousselow-Winquist and Winquist, 85).

Who would not feel utterly frustrated by such a personal failing? Here he was, the great basketball missionary who represented a new and different life in Christ to crowds of thousands each night, and then, in the heat of the game, he apparently nullified everything he stood for with one careless act of bad sportsmanship.

Who would not be stymied by such a breach of testimony? God would not. Late that night Odle was awakened by three local soldiers. His immediate thought was that he was about to be arrested for his accidental misdeed, but it turned out that what they wanted was for him to tell them about Jesus Christ. What a wonderful surprise! (Rousselow-Winquist and Winquist, 85).

King David might not have been surprised at either part of this story—neither the personal lapse nor the fact that God would continue his work despite a human being's failings. David had experienced not just one but many moments of sin and weakness. A person can scarcely think of a sin of which David was not guilty, whether it was murder and adultery or mistreating other people or overlooking his children's misbehavior. Still, God had made a promise to David, not because he deserved it, but purely out of his grace, and God would keep his word.

In these verses we will see a full display of the "gospel according to Ezra." The chronicler gives us a detailed account of one of David's sins, but then he also shows us how God forgave David and used David's sin to move ahead with his plan for his people.

II. COMMENTARY

A Census and Its Mixed Results

> **MAIN IDEA:** *David committed an act of disobedience by taking a census of the people. Even though he and the people were punished for this act, God used the occasion to lead David to the site of the temple that Solomon would build, and David began to make preparations for this project.*

A The Unlawful Census (21:1–7)

> **SUPPORTING IDEA:** *David asked Joab to carry out a census of all Israel and incurred God's punishment.*

21:1. Satan does not come up very often in the Bible as a whole—and very little in the Old Testament. Here, in one of his few appearances, we see him causing trouble for Israel by inciting David to take a census. The parallel passage in 2 Samuel 24 makes clear that Satan could not have done so if God had not permitted it.

There is no question that this census was wrong, but we may be puzzled about why it was wrong. After all, there had been a number of censuses in Israel (Num. 1:1–46; 26:1–51). We have run across several enumerations of troops supplied by various tribes in the course of 1 Chronicles, such as in 12:23–37. So what made this one bad?

First of all, this census was the outcome of the sin of pride by David. He was not counting the soldiers already in his army, supplied by the tribes, but he was setting out to count all men throughout Israel who might be available to serve in the army. In other words, he was being presumptuous in setting up for himself how large a reserve he could draw on if it should be necessary. There was no practical reason for doing this census. It was just a matter of David wanting to have an exact idea of how extensive his military resources were.

Second, this census violated several injunctions in the Old Testament. A broad count of this nature would not take into account the exemptions from military service that God had granted certain men, such as those who had recently become engaged, built a house, or planted a vineyard (Deut. 20:5–7). But most importantly, a census was supposed to be taken only of those men who were considered ritually clean according to the Old Testament law.

The rule stipulated that there should be a ceremony in which each man would donate a token of a half shekel into the temple treasury, thereby signifying that he was not in a state of defilement, and only then should he be counted (Exod. 30:11–16). Furthermore, the penalty of not abiding by this procedure was clear: the people would bring a plague on themselves. David's plan for his census did not include any of these provisions.

21:2–3. As we have already seen, Joab's faith in God was honest and direct. He was not a man of deep theological reflection, but he knew a major violation of God's law when he saw it. So when David instructed Joab to take charge of a census **from Beersheba to Dan**—that is, the entire land from south to north—at first Joab refused. By this time he had been through many deep waters with David, including wars against foreign powers and two civil wars (against Ish-Bosheth and Absalom). He asked David why he would want to do anything as stupid as to cause problems for the entire land with this unproductive measure because the census would not add a single warrior to the prospective pool of soldiers.

21:4–6. Nevertheless, when David did not relent from his order, Joab carried out the census. He did make two exceptions, however. He did not count the tribe of Levi because there was a specific prohibition against it (Num. 1:47–49), and he also did not include Benjamin, perhaps because Benjamin had experienced such a checkered history, having been devastated almost to the point of extinction at one time (Judg. 20:46) and then having been the last tribe to pledge loyalty to David (1 Chr. 12:29).

The total number of men counted, those **who could handle a sword**, was astounding: 1,100,000 individuals as a rounded approximation. Let us be clear again, though, that this was not the size of an existing army. This survey counted many men who might have been eligible for an exemption; it was strictly the number of those who could be conscripted by David without regard to the divine ordinances.

21:7. As Joab had feared, and as David should have known, the Lord punished Israel because of this census. Apparently a plague (the punishment prescribed in Exod. 30) must have broken out immediately. Why was the entire nation subjected to a penalty? The reason lies with the purpose of the law. The individual Israelites were supposed to declare their purity with the donation of a half shekel in order to be counted (Exod. 30:12–13). In the absence of this token, what David had accumulated was an army of ritually defiled people. Not only was David guilty of the moral violation of God's instructions about a census; he had also created a mass of people who were not clean in God's sight and so were liable to extermination by plague.

Sin is never purely private. The sin of the census turned into a national calamity. With the chronicler's purpose being to depict David's kingdom as an ideal, it is appropriate that he should zero in on the specific sin that affected the very fabric of the nation.

𝔹 David's Repentance (21:8–17)

SUPPORTING IDEA: *David had to confront the seriousness of his sin, but he repented.*

21:8. What had David been thinking? We will never know, but one thing is clear: David realized that he had done wrong and immediately asked God for forgiveness. However, it would not be this easy. Knowing the outcome of the story, we realize that God could have forgiven David immediately, but he used the occasion to teach David a lesson.

21:9–10. There were two important "seers" or prophets whose function was to declare the will of God to David. Both wound up having to confront the king because of a serious sin: Nathan in connection with David's adultery with Bathsheba (2 Sam. 11) and Gad, here, as a result of the census. But at least Gad did not have to convict David of his sin; he just had to pass judgment from God, and the Lord allowed David to choose the punishment from three options.

21:11–14. What a horrible set of alternatives David had to pick from! Plague, losing in battle, or famine—which was it to be? Obviously, there was no good choice among the three. David selected the plague. In contrast to famine, three months of plague would be over so much more quickly since wheat had been harvested already for that year (v. 20), and a famine would not begin for another year. Furthermore, the thought of having one of his enemies score a victory over him was unacceptable to David. He decided to go with the plague, the penalty that had been threatened in Exodus 30 for an unauthorized census. He was willing to accept a punishment that came straight from God but never one that came by way of people.

The plague was depicted as the work of the **sword of the LORD** wielded by **the angel of the LORD** (Num. 20:16; 2 Kgs. 19:35). Such a description does not rule out "natural" factors present as well, such as germs or viruses, but it does show that the disease would not have occurred at that place and at that time if it had not been sent by the Lord. The consequence of the epidemic was that seventy thousand people died.

21:15–17. But when the angel came to Jerusalem, which had apparently been spared so far, God called off the plague. The angel was positioned on Mount Moriah, north of David's palace at a place where the angel could see the entire city and where David could see the angel. At the time this location belonged to a Jebusite by the name of Araunah (also called Ornan), who used it as his threshing floor.

When David saw the angel, he was mortified. We don't know what this angel looked like, but he was obviously superhuman in appearance. He hovered over the ground, and he wielded a huge sword that he stretched toward Jerusalem—directly at David. The king, who could not have known that God had just called back the angel, summoned all his senior advisors. They held a public display of repentance and mourning.

In a moving prayer, David called on the Lord to take away the plague. He acknowledged his own responsibility and did not want the people, whom he called "sheep," to be punished any longer for something he had done.

The Altar on the Threshing Floor (21:18–22:1)

SUPPORTING IDEA: *David purchased the threshing floor where he had seen the angel and designated it as the site for the future temple.*

21:18–19. The angel was no longer using the sword, but neither did he leave; he still had work to do. He maintained his position with the sword still drawn and delivered another message that the seer Gad was supposed to pass on to David. God wanted David to build an altar on the very spot where the angel was standing. David, who would have been willing to do just about anything at that point, agreed.

21:20–21. Araunah had not planned on either celestial or royal visitors for that day. He was busy threshing when the angel appeared. His sons immediately fled, but for some reason Araunah remained in his place, maybe because his curiosity overcame any fright or perhaps because he was paralyzed with terror. But when David showed up, Araunah left the threshing area and bowed before the king.

21:22–25. Araunah, already befuddled by these events, had to listen to an astounding business proposition from David. The king wanted to purchase his land at full market value. Since Araunah was a Jebusite and not an Israelite, David could easily have invoked "eminent domain" and taken the land for minimal compensation, but instead he wanted to pay its true worth. David explained that he wanted to build an altar there to ward off the plague.

Araunah's reaction was that if David wanted to build an altar there, he was happy to give David everything he needed: the site, the meat, the wood, the grain—whatever was required for a sacrifice; it could all be the king's at no charge. But David would not accept the deal. It was not a matter of David not being willing to expropriate others' property or putting non-Israelites to work as slaves at other times (1 Chr. 20:2–3), but this situation was different. This time he was going to perform a sacrifice to the Lord as an expiation for his own guilt, and he did not want to do so if it cost him nothing. What would have been the point of a personal sacrifice if he were not sacrificing anything of his own?

So David paid Araunah the sum of six hundred shekels of gold and built the altar on that site. Apparently the price applied not only to the threshing floor and the oxen, which went for fifty silver shekels (2 Sam. 24:24), but for Auranah's entire estate.

21:26–27. David then built the altar and performed the sacrifice. Obviously, some time must have passed between David's initial visit and when everything was ready for the sacrifice. Other people such as priests were probably present by this time. And still the menacing angel loomed above the scene.

When David made the offerings, two things happened. God revealed his acceptance of David's sacrifice by sending fire down on the altar. And the angel sheathed his sword, and the threat disappeared.

21:28–22:1. Now that David had made sacrifices at this location and God had shown his acceptance of them, David designated this place as the official site for royal sacrifices. He still could not turn it into the central place of worship for all Israel. That designation still belonged to the tabernacle, which continued to be located at Gibeon, just as it had been throughout David's reign. The ark of the covenant was now in Jerusalem, and David had decided on a permanent place for his own sacrifices, but he could not just put the tabernacle out of commission. So David limited his religious activities to Jerusalem, and he declared that when the temple was built it would occupy the site of Araunah's threshing floor.

Ⓓ Preparations for the Temple (22:2–19)

SUPPORTING IDEA: *David set everything in motion to make sure that his son and successor Solomon would build the temple. He accumulated building materials and gave directions to Solomon and the elders of Israel.*

22:2–5. Short of actually building the temple, David left little undone in preparation for its assembly. He conscripted a large number of foreign residents as stonecutters to produce large building blocks. He also laid in a large stock of metal to be used in the construction of the temple. This included iron nails, a precious commodity.

David also acquired a large number of cedar logs, purchased from the opportunistic Phoenicians, who had first shown David the possibilities of cedar wood by giving him a free sample for his own house. The king stored up an immeasurable pile of logs. Finally, David, realizing the inexperience of his son Solomon, who would still have been a teenager at this time (Payne, 385), prepared a set of blueprints for the temple so it would be splendid enough to suit God and king.

22:6–16. David issued a formal charge to Solomon to build the temple. At this point we discover the reason God did not want David to build the temple. It was because David had **shed much blood** and **fought many wars**. The temple which signified God's dwelling place was not to be the final monument to the career of a great warrior but a house of peace that could bring the nations of the world together. The word *Solomon* is similar to the Hebrew word *shalom*, which means "peace." In fact, *Solomon* means "man of peace." During his reign, which would be the embodiment of peace, the temple would be built.

As David conveyed this charge to Solomon, he told him about the promise God had made earlier (1 Chr. 17:12)—that his throne would be established forever. However, he also exhorted Solomon to be sure to abide by God's law. And David gave Solomon a lengthy inventory of all the preparations he had already made for the temple.

22:17–19. David's charge to the elders of Judah was quick and to the point. He reminded them of all the blessings they had enjoyed as peace and prosperity had come to the land. He exhorted them to keep in mind that all of this was from the Lord and that they should be true to God. This meant that they should set out with the temple-building project when Solomon assumed the throne.

> **MAIN IDEA REVIEW:** *David committed an act of disobedience by taking a census of the people. Even though he and the people were punished for this act, God used the occasion to lead David to the site of the temple that Solomon would build, and David began to make preparations for this project.*

III. CONCLUSION

Sin Boldly!

One of the more controversial statements to come out of the Protestant Reformation was Martin Luther's advice to his younger colleague, Philip Melanchton, when he told him to "sin boldly." Taken out of context, Luther's statement seemed to encourage Melanchton to sin as much as he wanted to. It seems to line up with the attitude that was also falsely attributed to the apostle Paul that we could just "go on sinning so that grace may increase" (Rom. 6:1). But neither Paul nor Luther intended for people to sin willfully (Bainton, p. 175).

The bold attitude that Luther counseled addresses the question of how we deal with the fact that we have sinned. All of us sin. Before we are saved, we sin because we are living with fallen natures that cannot help but sin. After we are saved, we still find ourselves living as though we are subject to the same fallen natures. Sin we do, but what do we do about it? The problem for many Christians is that they have a hard time accepting their sins. They may rationalize, make excuses, or—as was the case for Melanchthon in this particular case—whine and let a preoccupation with their past sins paralyze their lives.

It is difficult to maintain a strong witness for God's grace and forgiveness if you are constantly in the throes of self-chastisement and repentance. It was to this attitude that Luther spoke: "Sin boldly," that is: "Own up to your sin, come to the cross, make things right with God and people, go on with your life, and stop dwelling on whatever you may have done in the past!"

Just as Satan tricked David into conducting the census, he also tries to trick us into focusing on our sins rather than our witness. Some Christians become so convinced of their unworthiness that they are afraid of uttering a word of testimony, lest they should make it appear that they are sinless. Others become preoccupied with their sin in another direction—by spending a lifetime putting on display some sin they may have committed early in their lives. The focus of their lives becomes their own actions rather than what Christ is doing in their lives.

I am grateful to the chronicler for bringing up only one of several serious problems in David's life, although we will read about many failed lives as we move on through Chronicles. But I am even more grateful to the chronicler for emphasizing the redemption that is an integral part of this story. We should not forget about the short glimpse we have received of Saul's ultimate condemnation. It is clear that David was not only subject to judgment, but that the judgment could have been even more serious than it turned out to be.

As we read this episode in Chronicles, we see that God had instructed the angel to desist from bringing the plague on Jerusalem even before David built the altar. And David, though he was inscrutably dense when he first carried out the census, finally came to his senses, owned up to his sin, and threw himself on God's mercy. And at that point God forgave David and allowed the king to take one step toward the goal of having Solomon build the temple.

The angel sheathed his sword and disappeared. Are we tempted to keep the mental image of a judgment angel in front of us at all times? God does not see us that way, so why should we?

PRINCIPLES

- It is an undeniable part of our existence that we sin.
- If we deny our sinfulness, we detract from the grace of God, which saves us as sinners, not as saints.
- When we sin, we need to experience reconciliation with God and other people and move on with our lives.
- We should not let our sins keep us from witnessing to God's grace.

APPLICATIONS

- Keep short accounts with God. When you're convicted of sin, confess it to God immediately and turn from it.
- Trust what God says about forgiveness (1 John 1:8–10).
- Meditate on the father's actions to the wayward son in Luke 15:20–24.

IV. LIFE APPLICATION

The Scraggy-Looking Sheep

In his insightful study of David, John Hercus imagines himself coming to visit David when he was still a shepherd boy. As the author begins to talk to the boy, one of the sheep nearby lifts its head from the grass it has been nibbling and trots over in an awkward, limping gait. It walks straight up to David, who strokes and caresses the scraggy-looking animal: "This is my favorite," he says simply (Hercus, *Out of the Miry Clay*, 129).

This imaginary scene encapsulates the story of David's life, who was shepherd to his flock and became shepherd to his people, while never ceasing to be the sheep of his own Shepherd, the Lord. Whatever right or wrong decisions David made, he never saw himself as anything but a scraggy-looking, awkward sheep that was loved beyond all bounds by God.

I do not understand David and his decision to do the census. After so many experiences with God, how could he perpetrate this power play, which was so obviously in violation of God's law? I do not know, and I do not understand it. But I do know that I can be just as much of a spiritual bonehead as David was in this story. Having been taught the same lesson many times does not keep me from forgetting it and making the same mistake again.

The question is, Am I willing to pick up and serve the Lord with the same enthusiasm afterwards as before? After having done this thing that brought death to seventy thousand people in his kingdom, why did David not abdicate the throne in disgrace? He did not because he knew that God did not want him to and that, furthermore, God had forgiven him and continued to have great plans for him. The consequence of this disaster was the first stage of the temple-building project. Having rebelled against God and lost (once again), David turned to serve God with greater enthusiasm than ever.

We should never be afraid to see ourselves as sinners; no amount of rationalizing can get us past that reality. It is precisely because we are sinners that we can experience God's grace and redemption. To return to our opening story: If Don Odle had been preaching the gospel of his own perfection, his testimony would have been irreparably damaged when he broke the referee's tooth. But since he preached the gospel of grace, that message was not stopped by this demonstration of his weakness. That is why the gospel is such good news: God forgives.

V. PRAYER

Lord Jesus, I am a sinner. The worst part is that, even as a Christian who is supposed to know all about sin and salvation, I still find myself trying to cover up my sinfulness to myself, other people, and even to you. Thank you that I am free to come to you and acknowledge how weak I am because I know that you accept me just as I am. Thank you that my sins have been atoned for on the cross where you died. Thank you that I am a forgiven sinner. Amen.

VI. DEEPER DISCOVERIES

A. Who Incited David to Take the Census? (21:1)

The account in 1 Chronicles states that it was Satan who incited David to undertake the census. But the parallel passage in 2 Samuel 24:1 states: "Again the anger of the LORD burned against Israel, and he [the Lord] incited David against them." So, who incited David—the Lord or Satan?

Even though we understand a number of passages in the Old Testament as referring to Satan, that insight is often retroactively based on certain New Testament passages. For example, most Christians agree that the serpent of Genesis 3 is Satan, but that fact is never stated in the Genesis passage. If we look at the Old Testament itself, we find that Satan is named in only three episodes: Job 1:6–2:7, Zechariah 3:1–2, and here in 1 Chronicles 21:1. In each of these passages, Satan appears as the adversary, not so much of God but of human beings. In Job and Zechariah he falsely accused Job and a high priest named Joshua, while in Chronicles he initiated trouble between David and God by goading David into the census.

Satan is an angel, and he has the privilege of appearing before God in the council of angels, but he uses this position to instigate problems for human beings in their relationship with God. It seems as though Satan's main opponent is the human race; it is not until later, through the interpretations we get from the New Testament, that we learn how much more Satan is the enemy of God himself.

Two key Old Testament passages (Isa. 14:3–15; Ezek. 28:11–19) teach us about Satan's rebellion against God and his subsequent condemnation. But the immediate context of these two passages is the judgment on the kings of Babylon and Tyre, respectively, and it would be daring to say of these passages that they are *about* Satan.

The New Testament uses these passages to clarify the nature of Satan, and this is how we know that this is their true intention. Revelation 8:10; 12:7–9; and 20:10 allude to the Isaiah and Ezekiel passages and apply them to Satan. What we see in each of the two Old Testament passages is a great and glorious ruler who thought he was greater than God and was hurled out of heaven and subjected to punishment. When we read the passages in Revelation and then go back to look at all the things that are being said about the rebellious kings, we realize that the kings were representations ("types") of Satan, and that ultimately only Satan could have epitomized such a high degree of enmity toward God.

The Old Testament passages keep us aware of the fact that Satan is not on a par with God. He is an angel, albeit a fallen one, and thus a creature with limited powers. Satan cannot do anything unless God permits him to do so as a part of his overall plan.

So in the case here in Chronicles, we should not think in terms of both God and Satan inciting David, if we mean by that expression that each did something independently of the other. But we can say that Satan was the more immediate inciter and that God permitted him to do so because God planned to use this occasion to teach his lessons to David and the people of Israel.

B. Low-Overhead Sacrifices (21:24)

David's statement to Araunah, as he rejected the offer of a free site and materials for the sacrifice, is both inspiring and potentially misleading. "I will not take for the LORD what is yours, or sacrifice a burnt offering that costs me nothing." As we have already pointed out, it would have been nonsense for David to perform a sacrifice to God to atone for his own sin if he used what somebody else placed at his disposal.

David's attitude may convict us of times when we have made things too easy on ourselves and served the Lord halfheartedly. I know church members who won't call someone in need because the call would be long distance and cost them thirty-five cents and congregations who cut their budget for outreach programs so they can install new carpeting. Christianity can become a religion of comfort and reassurance, with the desire to serve stretching no further than the bounds of our contentment. David's statement challenges this attitude. However, we should never fall into the trap of thinking that we can pay back God for his salvation or his blessings to us.

VII. TEACHING OUTLINE

A. INTRODUCTION

1. Lead Story: "Oops! There Goes My Testimony!"
2. Context: In the last chapter we saw David's "undefeated season," in which everything he did seemed to be successful. Now we see the opposite side of how David, riding the crest of his glory, wound up overstepping the law of God. He and the people had to suffer for his disobedience.
3. Transition: Don Odle, at the peak of his season as basketball evangelist, allowed his carelessness to reflect negatively on his testimony.

But God was not stymied by Odle's weakness and continued to use him as before. Similarly, when David was at the apex of his power, he betrayed his trust in God by conducting an illegal census. But God's forgiveness allowed David to go on and even make progress in preparing for the building of the temple.

B. COMMENTARY
1. The Unlawful Census (21:1–7)
2. David's Repentance (21:8–17)
3. The Altar on the Threshing Floor (21:18–22:1)
4. Preparations for the Temple (22:2–19)

C. CONCLUSION: SIN BOLDLY!

VIII. ISSUES FOR DISCUSSION

1. What factors lead us to commit sins that are self-destructive and avoidable?
2. Why is it so hard for us to admit we have sinned?
3. Is your church doing enough to help its members experience reconciliation with God and people after they have sinned?

1 Chronicles 23:1–29:30

Quote

"*I*n a family there must be order. If all the heirs strive for lordship, anarchy will reign in the family."

M a r t i n   L u t h e r

1 Chronicles 23:1–29:30

IN A NUTSHELL

*T*his lengthy section delineates the names and duties of those who held responsibilities during David's reign. The focus is on the temple, its priests, and attendants, though military leaders are also briefly mentioned. The section concludes with David issuing one final exhortation to build the temple.

Order in the Court

I. INTRODUCTION

Leadership by Design and by Default

About twenty years ago I saw a few installments of a documentary series that observed a group of people who had volunteered to live in the wilderness. They were expected to live pioneer-style with no modern amenities, drinking water from the river, eating what they could hunt and plant, living in huts that they would have to build themselves. The idea was that the film cameras would watch their every move, and researchers could use the results as a basis for further understanding of how humans react to stress.

As happens with "reality" television shows, after a time the people lost awareness of the cameras and simply went on with their work, and their interactions with one another became uninhibited. Two patterns emerged.

First, several people began to take on leadership roles. Before the group left, the researchers had arbitrarily designated leaders with no particular foundation for leadership, but these people were soon supplanted by those who took on dominating roles in a group due to their temperaments.

Second, the group split in half, and the newly emerged leaders functioned as advocates for their own constituencies. This split started after only a short time because of resentment between married and single participants. It took just a few weeks for a serious schism to develop, with each half accusing the other of not contributing to the welfare of the whole. The result was a group hampered in their mission by internal strife.

Whenever there is a group of people, there is a need for qualified leadership in order to maintain unity in the group. Letting people with strong personalities take charge may be counterproductive. King David was aware of this fact. He made sure that Solomon would inherit a kingdom in which order and cooperation were the norm. To this end he established subdivisions among his priests, temple workers, and military personnel.

In this passage Ezra (the chronicler) focuses on the temple and worship. This is the core around which the nation was supposed to be unified in David's time. As Ezra attempted to bring the nation back together again in his day, he made sure that everyone was familiar with the system that David had established.

II. COMMENTARY

Order in the Court

MAIN IDEA: *As David prepared the kingdom for Solomon to inherit, he instituted a number of divisions among those who worked in the temple and among his officials. His goal was that when Solomon became king, the kingdom would be orderly and peaceful and nothing would stand in the way of Solomon's building the temple.*

A The Levites (23:1–32)

SUPPORTING IDEA: *David divided the Levites into several large groups and assigned specific duties to them.*

23:1. We need to place all of what follows in the rest of 1 Chronicles into the context of David making preparations for Solomon's reign. David had neither temple nor tabernacle at his disposal. The temple had not yet been built, and the tabernacle still stood in Gibeon. So even though much of what he decreed could be implemented during his own time, it would not make sense until Solomon was king and the temple had been built.

The chronicler once again foregoes a lot of historical occurrences connected with the eventual coronation of Solomon. Later on we will outline some of them in order to get a clearer picture of the context (1 Kgs. 1–2). Suffice it to say for now that there may have been only five persons for whom the succession of Solomon to the throne was a settled matter: David, Solomon, Bathsheba, Nathan, and—perhaps—Zadok. But the Lord had selected Solomon, and the Lord's preference won out but not without serious strife and bloodshed. The chronicler simply tells us that David **made his son Solomon king over Israel**.

Even at that, note how the kingship at this point was something that simply passed from father to son. In contrast to Saul's earlier designation by lot and David's acclamation by representatives of the tribes, Solomon became king by descent from David. God's promise to David that the throne would be in his family forever was starting to be fulfilled.

23:2. Of course, the designation of succession could not have been private; it was done before a large assembly of leaders. The Levites are singled out, perhaps because of the power they may have held as a block of religious leaders but more likely because the chronicler wanted to focus on them in his delineation of their divisions and their duties.

23:3. Since David was counting those who had come forward in their role as Levites, there is no question here of a forbidden census as we encountered in chapter 21. It turns out that there were **thirty-eight thousand** members of the tribe of Levi over the age of thirty, the traditional age of eligibility for temple work, which then ended at age fifty (Num. 4:23). How do you put thirty-eight thousand Levites to work once there is only one sanctuary, there is no more need for the ark to be carried around, and the people are all settled into towns and villages? It took David's administrative genius not only to find duties for all of them but also to arrange things in such a way that the Levites would be a positive force in Israel.

23:4–6. In trying to impose order on this huge group of temple workers, David divided them along two lines: basic job description and descent. Four basic duties were assigned to the Levites: temple workers, officials, gatekeepers, and musicians.

The largest segment of personnel was assigned to work in the temple and to perform duties associated with the offering of sacrifices. Twenty-four thousand Levites received this certification. This group included not only priests but also those who would carry out many other chores, such as mixing flour for grain offerings, sharpening the knives, or sweeping the sanctuary. Later on we will see how David divided this large group into further subunits.

Six thousand Levites were assigned to serve as **officials and judges**. These men had the responsibility of inspecting prospective offerings, making sure the persons presenting them were not Gentiles, and keeping everything functioning according to the exact letter of the law. The job description of these officials extended beyond the temple to the country at large to assure that the people in their own towns and villages were sticking to the letter of the law as well.

Four thousand men were assigned security duties (gatekeepers), and four thousand were inducted into the musical ministry of the temple. There are no instructions about music associated with the tabernacle except some trumpet fanfares. But David, the musician whose whole life seems to have been accompanied by a soundtrack, understood the importance of music in worship, so he ordered it to be a permanent feature.

Genealogically, David reestablished the divisions of the Levites into their three main groups of descent: Gershon, Kohath, and Merari. The chronicler here reviews some of the information he has already given us in chapter 6 with a few additions.

23:7–23. Once again we receive an introductory survey of the genealogical derivations within the tribe of Levi. The listings here repeat some of the information in 1 Chronicles 6:1–30, but they also introduce some new names and relationships. Although this material is not exciting to us, for Ezra's original readership this may have been a crucial section because it specified not only who belonged in the various divisions of Levi but also exactly which duties and privileges were associated with their standing.

One of the sons of Gershon, Ladan, may also be called Libni (1 Chr. 6:17). The chronicler took the main branches of the Gershonites and separated them into families, which then served as the markers for grouping individuals into particular branches. There are two Shimeis in the list, one in verse 9 and one in verses 7 and 10. Since the Shimei of verse 9 is identified at the end of the verse as belonging to the line of Ladan, these are obviously two different individuals (Shimei could not have been among his own brother's descendants). Among the descendants of Ladan's brother Shimei are two men, Jeush and Beriah, who had so few offspring that they were counted as one family.

As the discussion switches to the descendants of Kohath, the division into Aaronite and non-Aaronite comes to the fore because only the offspring of Aaron were allowed to perform sacrifices. By contrast, the descendants of Moses received no special privileges, even though Moses was **the man of God**, the one person who may have had more direct communication with the Lord than any other in the Old Testament. However, even though the office of priesthood could be inherited, a relationship with God could not. So the non-Aaronite Kohathites, specifically Levites descended from Moses, served like any other Levite.

The descendants of Merari constitute the third branch of Levites. The chronicler notes that there was a convergence in the line of Merari's son Eleazar. When this man died without any male offspring, his line would have died out if it had not been for the fact that the sons of his brother (Kish) married Eleazar's daughters (their cousins).

23:24–32. The duties of the Levites were different now than they had been at the time of the exodus, when the law was first given. Many new obligations were associated with the more elaborate worship of God in the temple. David abolished any further assignments for the Levites in connection with carrying the ark of the covenant and the components of the tabernacle. The sanctuary had been moved little over the last few hundred years; and when it had, everyone had forgotten about the role the Levites were supposed to play in the process (1 Chr. 15:13). It is unlikely that anyone really thought of the ark as mobile any more. Nevertheless, David clarified that such an office would no longer exist. However, there were plenty of other jobs to be done.

At this point the official list of Levites was lowered from those who were thirty years old down to include those who were twenty and older. Even though some commentators have found this change puzzling, it seems a natural thing to do. The original roster was based on those who were old enough to perform services in the temple. But at this point we are looking at a theoretical division of the Levites for the sake of new duties in a temple that had not even been built yet. It makes sense that Levites in training would be included in the assignment of divisions and responsibilities.

The duties of the Levites included everything but actually officiating at the sacrifices. Their job was to get all the materials and tools ready and to make sure that everything was right. This allowed the priests to focus on the proper performance of worship services. The Levites were responsible for baking the bread, cleaning the temple, and ensuring that nothing used in the temple was ritually contaminated. They were also obligated to participate in community worship each morning and evening when the main sacrifice was brought and when special holiday services were held.

Ⓑ Divisions into Twenty-four Shifts (24:1–31)

SUPPORTING IDEA: *David established a set of twenty-four divisions among the priests, who would serve in shifts. The rest of the Levites followed suit with corresponding groupings.*

24:1–2. The chronicler reminds us of the history of Aaron's sons. His older sons Nadab and Abihu had been killed because they defiled the sanctuary (Lev. 10:1–2). Consequently Aaron's two younger sons, Eleazar and Ithamar, carried on the priesthood. So there were two lines of descent from Aaron—one through Eleazar, the other through Ithamar.

24:3–5. David sought the help of a distinguished representative of each of the two branches. Two men were functioning *de facto* as high priests during the time of David: **Zadok**, who came from the line of Eleazar, and Abiathar, who belonged to the Ithamar clan. **Ahimelech** was Abiathar's son, undoubtedly named after his grandfather, the high priest Ahimelech. Zadok and the younger Ahimelech conferred in order to sort through all eligible families and set up a reasonable apportionment of duties.

It turned out that there were about twice as many discernible families among Eleazar's descendants, so the final negotiations established a grouping by which there would be sixteen official sets of priests derived from Eleazar and eight from Ithamar. The actual assignments were then made **impartially** by drawing lots, so there could be no accusation of favoritism.

24:6–19. After the memberships in the twenty-four divisions were established, the results were officially recorded. Everything was done scrupulously to avoid any suggestions of bias. The end result was a list of twenty-four groupings and the order in which they would take their turns officiating in the temple.

These twenty-four divisions were not necessarily permanent, since the membership of some of them died out or was eliminated in war (Ezra 2:36–39; Neh. 12:1–7), but a number of them persisted right up to the time of Christ. Luke 1:5 tells us that Zechariah, the father of John the Baptist, belonged to the division of Abijah, mentioned here in verse 10.

24:20–31. When the priests had established their divisions, the rest of the Levites followed suit. They also set up twenty-four divisions to correspond to the shifts assigned to the descendants of Aaron. It is not easy to find exactly twenty-four sets in this passage. However, the chronicler tells us that **the families of the oldest brother were treated the same as those of the youngest**. We can take this as a clue to count two generations as separate branches.

Ⓒ Job Assignments for the Levites (25:1–26:32)

SUPPORTING IDEA: *David assigned divisions and responsibilities among the temple musicians, gatekeepers, financial staff, and officials-at-large of the Levites.*

25:1–31. Music was crucial in David's life. While a young shepherd, he was known as "a brave man and a warrior" (1 Sam. 16:18), but he first came to the court of King Saul because of his ability to play the harp. Although there is no record of David taking time out of his schedule as king to play the harp for relaxation, he did write numerous psalms. So it is not surprising that David integrated a musical dimension into worship, something that had not existed before.

The work of the musicians is described as "prophecy," and Heman is called a "seer." Clearly, the music was not included in order to create a "worship" mood or simply to express emotion toward God. It served as a way of conveying the commands of God. As we know from the Psalms, many ancient hymns of Israel contained historical and theological references. In Psalm 81, Asaph intertwined the story of Israel in the desert with exhortations to stay true to God. We also know that at times in the Old Testament, music was used to stimulate a prophet to speak God's message (2 Kgs. 3:15).

Asaph, Heman, and Jeduthun (also called Ethan) were responisble for the temple music. The number of their sons added up to twenty-four, thanks in particular to Heman, who supplied fourteen of them. Each son constituted a division, and since there were 288 musically qualified relatives in the combined clans, they were able to set up shifts of twelve artists each, listed in verses 9–31. These leaders had four thousand Levites whose talents they could draw on (23:5). The twenty-four divisions were under the direction of the man they were named for, but then each son reported to his father (Asaph, Heman, Jeduthun). This was one aspect of the temple service over which David was not going to give up control; the three main ministers of music remained under his supervision.

26:1–19. These verses contain a listing of the official gatekeepers for the future temple. The gatekeepers were the security guards. Their job was to enforce any necessary safety measures in case of local disturbances.

The list begins by making reference to the **Korahites**, the descendants of Korah, the Levite who claimed the rights of priesthood but was severely punished for it (Num. 16). Despite Korah's sin, his line of descent continued honorably (1 Chr. 6:22) and is represented with Meshelemiah's sons as commanders of divisions of guards. The Korahites were descended from the branch of Kohath, so the Asaph mentioned here was not the same as the Gershonite minister of music who was the subject of the last chapter.

There clearly was no attempt to try to make the numbers add up to twenty-four. The gatekeepers would not have been able to work in the same shifts as priests and Levites. Rather, they were assigned according to locations around the temple. Specific commanders were given responsibility for particular gates (26:13).

One familiar name in the group of gatekeepers is Obed-Edom. He was the man whose estate housed the ark of the covenant between the attempts to carry it up to Jerusalem (13:13–14). Even though he was a gatekeeper by trade, he joined the musicians with his harp on the second trip to Jerusalem (15:21). God blessed Obed-Edom by giving him a sizable clan, all of whom served in the temple.

In verse 10 we find a reference to Hosah, of the clan of Merari, who designated his son Shimri as firstborn. We do not know whether one of the other sons listed here was the actual firstborn, or if the firstborn might have been another son who for some reason became excluded from the family altogether.

In addition to the four gates identified by the cardinal directions, guards were detailed to the storehouse, the road leading up from the west, and the **Shalleketh Gate**. The last-named is the "dung" gate. The temple would have generated an enormous amount of refuse, and there had to be a place to discard it. But a guard also had to be stationed there, considering that the potential for mischief by anyone bringing discarded carcasses or entrails back into the temple would have been limitless. Even though the temple was not yet built, the guard was already active (9:17–27). With the location designated and occupied by the ark and many building materials, there would have been plenty of work for the security details.

26:20–28. Earlier in his reign David had included protection of the treasury among the duties of the gatekeepers (9:26). But now, as he started to promote the future temple, he created a separate department for this task. Whereas the gatekeepers in the previous section came from the clans of Kohath (Korah's clan) and Merari, now the clan of Gershon took pride of place. These Levites came specifically from Ladan, also called Libni. However, the clan of Kohath is also represented among the treasury agents. This time it was through the descendants of Moses' sons Gershom and Eliezer that they made a contribution to this effort.

A man named Shelomith received the job of taking care of all the plunder taken in battle that had been dedicated to the Lord. The list of donors to this fund was headed up by David, but there were also items going back to Samuel, Saul, the two generals Abner and Joab, as well as the military leaders of David's day. Shelomith demonstrated his business acumen by establishing an endowment for the eventual repair of the temple before it had even been built. On several occasions in 2 Chronicles, renovating the temple became a sign of revival for the king and the people.

26:29–32. One final duty was assigned to the Levites—to serve as "Levites at large." These men were called **officials** and **judges**. Their job was to enforce compliance with divine law throughout the land. They did such things as adjudicate in inheritance disputes, suppress idolatry, and make sure that all the food on the market fit the criteria of the dietary laws.

No geographical restriction was placed on the first such official, Kenaniah, but Hashabiah and his family were specifically designated for the western half of Israel. David had to do a little research before he finally settled on Jeriah to take charge of the eastern tribes. Only in David's last year—his fortieth—was this arrangement finally in place.

ⅅ Civil Order (27:1–34)

> **SUPPORTING IDEA:** *Just as David organized the duties of the Levites, he also structured government support in the military and administrative realms.*

27:1–15. David maintained a standing army, divided into twelve divisions of twenty-four thousand men, with each division serving one month a year during peace time. Trying to keep a larger army prepared would have been impractical. Who could feed over two hundred thousand soldiers every day year in and year out? Under David's plan, the soldiers could return to their home villages for eleven months of the year and participate in their family's vocation. David took great pains to organize this army, down to the level of battalions of one hundred men. This was quite a contrast to the early days of Saul's kingship, when raising an army meant calling people away from their fields and homes (1 Sam. 11:7–8). By this point in David's reign, a professional army was on duty at all times.

There were twelve divisions, each identified by the name of a great hero. The leaders of the divisions were included among the mighty men of chapter 11. Benaiah son of Jehoiada was one of the two great commanders (11:22–25). Asahel did not live to see David become king of Israel (2 Sam. 2:23), so he obviously never served in any capacity under this arrangement. But he was listed among the mighty men (1 Chr. 11:26), and the division was named in his honor with his son in command.

27:16–24. In case of war, the professional army, even in its full number of 288,000 soldiers, might not be sufficient. If there were an emergency, all the men of Israel might need to be called up, so David set up a commander for each tribe who would report directly to the king. Additionally, since the Levites were included in this list even though they were exempt from military service, it appears that these officers also functioned as tribal representatives for nonmilitary affairs.

This list does not mention all the tribes. Gad and Asher are missing, but we still have a list of twelve tribes because Ephraim and the two halves of Manasseh each get their own reference. In the notice for the tribe of Levi, we find Zadok, the high priest, representing the branch of Aaron, but "Aaron" was not a tribe in its own right.

Elihu, one of David's brothers, was the official representative for the tribe of Judah. He is not among the six brothers of David listed in 1 Chronicles 2:13–15. This has led some commentators to think that this is the same person as David's oldest brother Eliab. Alternatively, since 1 Samuel 16:10 states that David had seven brothers, Elihu may have been the seventh brother whose name was left out of the earlier list in Chronicles. He would have been older than David, but not by as much as Eliab.

The chronicler, having reported on the strength of the army, reminded his readers of the earlier unlawful census ordered by David. There would have been nothing wrong with counting the number of men presently in the army.

What was wrong with the census was counting all males theoretically available, particularly without paying the required ritual coins (Exod. 30:11–16).

The number derived from the census was not recorded in **the annals of King David**. This statement may sound surprising since a report, as recorded in 1 Chronicles 21:5, has come down to us. However, the Book of Chronicles is not the same thing as the "annals." The annals were the official records at David's court. These documents were not available at this point—or at least they have not yet been uncovered by archaeologists.

27:25–34. These verses list David's various administrators. All of these men made their mark in history by being a part of David's great empire, even if it was for something as minor as being in charge of the king's camels or donkeys. Obviously, the terms of service of these men would not have dovetailed precisely with the forty years of David's reign.

Toward the end of the list, we read of those who were more directly involved in David's government. There was an inner circle of David's friends and advisors (including his uncle Jonathan, heretofore not mentioned in any of the accounts). Ahithophel was well-known as a wise man; his reputation at one time was that of speaking virtually with the voice of God (2 Sam. 16:23). However, Ahithophel joined the rebellion of Absalom, who did not follow his advice, and Ahithophel eventually hanged himself (2 Sam. 17:23). Hushai the Arkite, on the other hand, never gave up on his friendship with David; he went over to Absalom as a spy in order to pass on information to David and to frustrate Ahithophel's advice (2 Sam. 17:14).

The chronicler does not mention Ahithophel's suicide, but he does refer to the fact that he **was succeeded** by two men. One of his successors was Jehoiada son of Benaiah (not to be confused with the living legend, Benaiah son of Jehoiada, last mentioned in 27:5), whom we cannot identify any further. The other later counselor was Abiathar, high priest alongside Zadok (15:11).

The list of David's advisors is rounded out with the great general Joab and an employee named Jehiel son of Hacmoni, whose job was to take **care of the king's sons**. These people were first-rate advisors in David's administration. The king surrounded himself with the best minds of his day. As we are led to consider David's kingdom as an ideal model, we find that subsequent kings did not follow David's pattern. At times they seemed to go out of their way to listen to the worst advisors available.

E David's Last Speech and the Investiture of Solomon (28:1–29:30)

SUPPORTING IDEA: *David closed his reign by passing all his preparations on to Solomon and exhorting the leaders to support the new king in the construction of the temple.*

28:1–8. David called a convocation of all his officials, consisting of the people mentioned in the last chapter along with all their subordinates. They would be responsible for the actual building of the temple, whether in coordinating the movement of building supplies through hostile territory, feeding the workers on the job, or issuing salaries to the master craftsmen. So David made sure they were on his side in the process.

The speech that David made was similar to what we have already read in 1 Chronicles 22:6–19. He recounted that, even though he wanted to build the temple, God would not permit him to do so because he had **shed blood.** However, Solomon carried the Lord's designation as the one who would build the temple and the one through whom David's perpetual kingdom would continue. David reminded the people that this promise carried with it the obligation for them to remain faithful to the Lord's commandments lest they should lose the land.

28:9–21. David faced Solomon and, still making a public speech, turned all his preparations over to his son and heir. The blueprints, the plans for the new decorations on the lid of the ark, the weight in gold or silver of all implements down to the last ceremonial fork—David had it all worked out, and he assigned it to Solomon to implement.

In his instructions to Solomon, David exhorted the new king to be devoted to the Lord and his commandments. The temple would be an expression of commitment to God, but building a temple could never be a substitute for obedience to God in all matters. David had received these plans from the Lord. They were not just his own creative ideas but granted to him by God's spirit. Thus, David's role parallels closely that of Moses, to whom God revealed the original plans for the tabernacle on Mount Sinai (Exod. 25). David also assured Solomon that even though this project was huge, he could rely on God to provide him with all he needed to see it through.

29:1–9. David turned toward the entire assembly and made a further appeal to them. Not only had he made a large share of his royal budget available for all the precious metals in the temple; he was now reaching into his personal wallet, so to speak, and donating another huge amount of gold and silver to the cause. Then he raised the question of who would follow him in his devotion to the Lord. Amid great rejoicing everyone contributed from their personal wealth, including valuable metals and precious stones. Jehiel, a Levite from the clan of Gershon, collected all the donations.

29:10–20. At the end of this offering ceremony, David prayed a public prayer, thanking God for all he had provided. In addition to praising the greatness of the Lord and interceding on behalf of Solomon and the people for faithfulness, David acknowledged the truth that, strictly speaking, they had made no donation to the Lord at all. After all, God owned everything. All human beings could do was to demonstrate their devotion to him with gifts, but ultimately they were only giving to God what already belonged to him. The entire assembly affirmed the prayer of David.

29:21–25. This great event culminated in Solomon's second coronation (the first one was mentioned in 1 Chr. 23:1). Amid enormous sacrifices and generous banqueting, this was a memorable occasion. The chronicler once again skips over the disagreeable episodes that led up to this occasion (1 Kgs. 1:1–2:10) because they are not relevant to his purpose, which is to demonstrate how the kingdom of David passed intact to Solomon, and how the temple functioned as the sign of investiture: whoever would be the next king would be the temple builder. Zadok, the high priest, officiated over these ceremonies. Solomon's coronation also signified Zadok's supremacy as priest and the elimination of Abiathar, his rival (1 Kgs. 2:35). This section closes with a general description of Solomon's splendor.

29:26–30. What a contrast there is between Saul's slaughter and dismemberment at the hands of the Philistines and David's peaceful death at Jerusalem! David's reign became the standard against which all others were measured. The **records of Samuel** may be a reference to our present Book of 2 Samuel, but we do not have books by Gad or Nathan.

At this point the curtain falls on Act 1. Even though Chronicles was not originally divided into two books, there is still an obvious break here. Having worked ourselves up from the earliest beginnings of humanity, as revealed in the opening genealogies, we have arrived at the ideal model for a kingdom that David had constructed under the Lord's guidance. Now that we have reached this point, what will happen to this glorious kingdom?

MAIN IDEA REVIEW: *As David prepared the kingdom for Solomon to inherit, he instituted a number of divisions among those who worked in the temple and among his officials. His goal was that when Solomon became king, the kingdom would be orderly and peaceful and nothing would stand in the way of Solomon's building the temple.*

III. CONCLUSION

Mission to Crete

When the apostle Paul was getting old, he took one last journey, visiting a number of churches he had started as well as some he had not visited before. In the latter group were the churches on the island of Crete. Paul had to leave before he finished what he had intended to do while there, so he left Titus in charge to bring his project to completion. The mission: to appoint elders (Titus 1:5).

What Paul realized was what David knew a thousand years earlier—that a firm structure is imperative for the people of God. In David's case, it was a matter of protecting an empire from enemies and establishing orderly temple worship. For Paul the issue was making sure that the teaching ministry of the church remained in the hands of those who were qualified to handle it (Titus 1:9) in order to protect the church from false teachings. In both situations the outcome was the same—to use orderly structures in the service of the Lord.

Just as God uses the talents and gifts of individuals, such as the ability to preach or sing, so God also intends for us to make the best use of various resources. Churches, missionary organizations, or Christian schools, for example, are accountable to God not only for how they use their staff as individuals but whether the group as a whole is glorifying God in the way it conducts its business. We read in 1 Corinthians 14:33 that "God is not a God of disorder but of peace."

David was obedient to God in how he conquered the land as well as how he administered his kingdom. This second part was less exciting, but it was just as important; otherwise the nation would fall into chaos, and the temple would never be built. In the same way, we need to make sure that our small segment of the body of Christ has a sound biblical structure.

PRINCIPLES

- God expects us to be responsible in the way we use structures to promote his work.
- God sometimes uses individuals by virtue of the offices they hold.

APPLICATIONS

- Take a look at your church. Are there places where lack of structure is undermining Christ's mission through your church?

- Have you ever seen church structures take on a life of their own so that the mission of the church is hindered by too much structure?
- Could your church become stronger if you delegated some of your tasks to others?
- Is planning a hindrance to spiritual effectiveness?

IV. LIFE APPLICATION

"You Were Lazy"

My father once told me about a preacher who decided to rely more on the Holy Spirit when he preached. He gave up his usual sermon preparation during the week and intended to step into the pulpit with an open heart and an open ear to listen to what the Holy Spirit inspired him to say. On the next Sunday, when it came time for the sermon, he entered the pulpit and he received a clear message from God: "You were lazy!"

Reliance on God is not the same thing as lack of preparation. No one knew better than David that nothing would ever come out right if it were not directed by God himself. There is no Bible character with greater awareness of his utter unworthiness in the sight of God and his total dependency on the Lord. And yet David did not allow this recognition to stop him from organizing his kingdom on all levels and making the most minute preparations for the future temple.

Jesus told us, "Do not worry about tomorrow, for tomorrow will worry about itself" (Matt. 6:34). But not worrying does not mean that we should gamble on the future or refuse to fulfill our responsibilities for other people. Paul stated in response to some Thessalonian Christians who had ceased working, "Such people we command and urge in the Lord Jesus Christ to settle down and earn the bread they eat" (2 Thess. 3:12). He also instructed the church at Ephesus through Timothy: "If anyone does not provide for his relatives, and especially for his immediate family, he has denied the faith and is worse than an unbeliever" (1 Tim. 5:8). King David has presented us with an example of how a person can trust God and yet make responsible provisions for those who are entrusted to us.

V. PRAYER

Lord Jesus, please let us learn from David's example so we will not substitute disorder for creativity, impetuousness for spontaneity, or lack of planning for conviction. Amen.

VI. DEEPER DISCOVERIES

Musical Instruments in the Bible (25:1)

Through the musical ministry of Asaph, Heman, and Jeduthun, we learned of some of the music instruments used in worship: harps, lyres, and cymbals. We also ran across trumpets and tambourines earlier, when the ark was being carried to Jerusalem (1 Chr. 13:8). Further Old Testament passages mention the flute (e.g., Ps. 150:4). Obviously, these instruments were different from the ones we use in worship today, and the translation from Hebrew to English involves a certain amount of extrapolation. Modern archaeology in Egypt and Mesopotamia has helped clarify some of the expressions, but there are still a number of mysteries—for example what playing a harp "according to *sheminith*" (1 Chr. 15:21) might be.

The harp and lyre are referred to separately although they belong to the same family of string instruments. It appears that ancient harps were larger than lyres, sometimes big enough to need positioning on the floor with a sound box on the bottom, just like modern harps (Millar, 2099). Some harps were compact enough to be carried. Lyres were smaller, more portable instruments, probably played on the shoulder.

Tambourines and cymbals were percussion instruments, just as they are today. Tambourines kept a beat, and cymbals may have served to augment the rhythm. Depending on their size and metal composition, cymbals could provide a great variety in the range of sounds. For example, the cymbals used in the procession of the ark to Jerusalem were made of bronze.

Several wind instruments are mentioned. Two instruments are called "trumpets" in our translations (Queen-Sutherland, 996). One is the "shofar," the ram's horn, which was blown not only in musical celebrations but also as a signal in battle and as the high point of the new year's service (Lev. 23:24). The other type of trumpet was made of metal, "thought to have a high, shrill tone" (Queen-Sutherland, 996). Also, there were several instruments that could be described as flutes, the most popular being a double-barreled reed instrument (Queen-Sutherland, 996).

One point becomes clear as we survey the use of music and instruments in the life of God's people during the Old Testament era: there was room for change and adaptation. Biblical music was never devoid of solid content. However, the form in which the music was presented was flexible, and new instruments were added as they were invented both inside and outside Israelite culture. The first two instruments mentioned in Scripture were those created by Jubal (Gen. 4:21)—the harp and the flute. By the time we get to David's era, there were many different instruments.

God said to unrighteous people through the prophet Amos: "Away with the noise of your songs! I will not listen to the music of your harps" (Amos 5:23). But to those who loved him he declared, "Let them praise his name with dancing and make music to him with tambourine and harp" (Ps. 149:3).

VII. TEACHING OUTLINE

A. INTRODUCTION

1. Lead Story: Leadership by Design and by Default
2. Context: Good leadership for any group is essential. Just as David was able to establish his kingdom, he also looked forward to the time when his son and successsor Solomon would build the temple. But a solid foundation of leadership was needed.
3. Transition: David accumulated a large stockpile of building materials for the new temple. He needed to make sure the personnel involved would be organized, so he set about dividing both the religious and the secular leaders into specific groups that would work in shifts.

B. COMMENTARY

1. The Levites (23:1–32)
2. Divisions into Twenty-four Shifts (24:1–31)
3. Job Assignments for the Levites (25:1–26:32)
4. Civil Order (27:1–34)
5. David's Last Speech and the Investiture of Solomon (28:1–29:30)

C. CONCLUSION: MISSION TO CRETE

VIII. ISSUES FOR DISCUSSION

1. What structures are essential for a church or Christian ministry group?
2. Can a church have too much structure? Too little?
3. How can we prepare for ministry while continuing to rely on the Lord?

2 Chronicles 1:1–17

Solomon Takes the Throne

I. INTRODUCTION
"If You Can Keep It"

II. COMMENTARY
A verse-by-verse explanation of the chapter.

III. CONCLUSION
Croesus, the Runner-up

An overview of the principles and applications from the chapter.

IV. LIFE APPLICATION
One State at a Time

Melding the chapter to life.

V. PRAYER
Tying the chapter to life with God.

VI. DEEPER DISCOVERIES
Historical, geographical, and grammatical enrichment of the commentary.

VII. TEACHING OUTLINE
Suggested step-by-step group study of the chapter.

VIII. ISSUES FOR DISCUSSION
Zeroing the chapter in on daily life.

Quote

"*Prudence considers the means of acquiring happiness,*

but wisdom considers the very object of happiness."

S t .   T h o m a s   A q u i n a s

2 Chronicles 1:1–17

I N   A   N U T S H E L L

When King Solomon came to the throne, he was faced with the daunting task of maintaining the great empire David had conquered and building a temple for God. When the Lord told Solomon that any one request of his would be fulfilled, the new king chose wisdom, which God granted, along with a long life and wealth.

Solomon Takes the Throne

I. INTRODUCTION

"If You Can Keep It"

*W*hen the founding fathers of the United States had finished their deliberation over the new constitution, a woman accosted Benjamin Franklin to ask him what kind of government they were going to have. His surly reply was, "A republic, madam—if you can keep it."

How do you keep a form of government? It takes constant attention and fine-tuning because there will always be pressure to move away from an ideal. Sinful human nature is bound to show itself by offering compromises that may seem more comfortable in the short run but become destructive in the long run.

How do you keep a nation? Solomon inherited David's empire, and he received the mandate to keep it united and flourishing. How do you do that when you are the king? It is one thing to build an empire; you do so by conquering your enemies. But once you have the empire in place, how do you hold it together? During times of war, when the empire is being established, people are willing to make sacrifices to support the cause. But during times of peace, everyone expects to eat, drink, and be entertained.

One way rulers have tried to maintain a stable nation is to brutalize their own people to keep them dedicated to their cause. In the twentieth century the world saw many revolutions around the world. What happened in many of these countries is that in the eyes of the new leaders, the revolution was never over. Decades after the actual revolution, a dictator would still be attempting to fire up his people in the cause of the "ongoing revolution," and not "participating" was considered treason. Solomon's own son, Rehoboam, stepped into that trap.

However, what kept Solomon's empire together were the many building projects. The nation that did not have great impetus to unite in war did come together to build a temple and various other projects of Solomon's devising. Everyone was able to participate in the prosperity engendered by Solomon's creative management style, which allowed trade and agriculture to flourish.

II. COMMENTARY

Solomon Takes the Throne

MAIN IDEA: *As Solomon began to reign over Israel, he asked God for wisdom, and the Lord answered his request and blessed him.*

A Solomon's Ascension (1:1–6)

SUPPORTING IDEA: *When Solomon became the undisputed ruler of Israel, he held a great worship ceremony at the tabernacle at Gibeon.*

1:1. The chronicler tells us that Solomon **established himself firmly** over David's kingdom. David declared Solomon as his successor, even to the point of having him crowned as king before he died. But still many people did not support Solomon as king. They threw their weight behind Adonijah, Solomon's older brother.

Solomon did not have the strongest claim on the throne in terms of birth order. He was the second son of David by Bathsheba (2 Sam. 12:24). This put him toward the bottom of the sequence (1 Chr. 3:1–9), even taking into account the fact that the first contenders had long been out of the running. Amnon, David's firstborn, had been killed by Absalom, the thirdborn, who then lost his life in his ill-fated revolt. The second son, known as Daniel or Kileab (2 Sam. 3:3), never was in the picture. This left Adonijah as the next eligible candidate. He had been born during the early part of David's reign, while the king resided in Hebron (1 Chr. 3:2), so Adonijah must have been in his late thirties. Perhaps he was tired of waiting for his turn to become king when David finally died.

Even before David's death, Adonijah attempted to outmaneuver Solomon. He lined up his supporters, including the general, Joab, and Abiathar, one of the two rival priests, and held a major sacrificial feast, followed by a huge banquet. Solomon had supporters in high places as well: David and Bathsheba, of course, but also the legendary hero Benaiah son of Jehoiada, the prophet Nathan, and Zadok, the other rival priest. As soon as they heard about what Adonijah was up to, while he and his supporters were still partying, they staged their own counteracclamation ceremony. At David's insistence, Solomon was anointed, rode on the royal mule, and took the throne. Those actions settled the matter, and Adonijah bowed before the new king after Solomon spared his life.

However, things did not remain that way. Shortly after David's death, Adonijah asked for Abishag, David's concubine, an act that would have been construed as attempting to usurp the throne, just as it had been many years before in the case of Absalom (2 Sam. 16:21). At that point Solomon ordered Benaiah to kill Adonijah. He also ordered the execution of Joab, and he fired Abiathar from the priesthood. The end result was that Solomon was the undisputed king with a firm grip on the land. But would he conduct himself properly in this office?

1:2–6. Solomon began his reign by making good decisions. He convened his first assembly, and all the people went to the tabernacle in Gibeon. Even though the ark of the covenant had been in Jerusalem for several decades now—and had not been with the tabernacle for a century—the tabernacle was still considered the highest place of worship. It still contained a bronze altar that went back to the time of Moses.

Not only was Solomon's appearance here an act of worship and dedication; it was also a gesture of respect for the place that he would overshadow with his extravagant construction. **A thousand burnt offerings** would have required quite a bit of space and time to be executed correctly.

B Solomon's Request and God's Response (1:7–13)

SUPPORTING IDEA: *When God gave Solomon a choice of one request, Solomon asked for wisdom rather than material benefits.*

1:7–10. Solomon spent the night in Gibeon, and that night God appeared to him in a dream (1 Kgs. 3:15). In this dream the Lord offered to grant Solomon a special benefit. What does a twenty-year-old king ask for? He could have asked for any number of things. As we know from later events, Solomon knew how to appreciate all the amenities that life could offer. At this time, however, we see him overcome with all his responsibilities. David's acclaimed council of advisors (1 Chr. 27:32–34) was dissolved, some of their departures having been caused by Solomon's own hand. The people might have been skeptical of whether this young king was up to the task. There had been only two kings before Solomon, and one of them, Saul, had made a mess of things.

Certainly, there was the promise of God, but would Solomon be able to conduct himself properly? Solomon needed one thing more than anything else—wisdom. This would enable him to be a competent king, so wisdom was what he begged for.

1:11–13. God was pleased with Solomon's request. The king could have asked for **wealth, riches or honor** or perhaps for his enemies to die or for a long life. But what he wanted more than anything else was wisdom so he could live up to the great responsibilities he faced. God told the young king that he would not only grant him what he had asked for but that he would also give him all the things that he had not asked for. Thus, Solomon became known for his great wisdom as well as his enormous wealth. He lived a long life, and his reign was characterized by abiding peace.

C Solomon's Wealth (1:14–17)

SUPPORTING IDEA: God demonstrated his endorsement of Solomon by providing him with enormous wealth.

1:14–17. As a display of how God bestowed on Solomon the material wealth he had promised, these verses contain the first of two lists enumerating some of Solomon's possessions. The other list is found in 2 Chronicles 9:13–28. Under the Solomonic economic boom, gold, silver, and cedar wood became common commodities in Jerusalem. Toward the end of his reign, Solomon's accumulation of wealth began to pose a burden for people who lived outside Judah (2 Chr. 10:3), but at the beginning it appears that everyone benefited from his policies. Much of the wealth of Solomon, the man of peace, was expressed in terms of military prowess. The horses referred to in these verses were not plow horses or riding horses, but they were designated for use in war.

Solomon owned a sizable collection of chariots, and his total of **fourteen hundred** is larger than most other chariot divisions mentioned previously (six hundred for Pharaoh in Exod. 14:7; nine hundred for Sisera of Hazor in Judg. 4:3), though according to Assyrian records, King Ahab later fielded two thousand chariots (Walton, 421). At one time the Philistines had lined up three thousand chariots (1 Sam. 13:5), but it does not appear that this strategy provided them with any tactical advantage after the intimidation factor had worn off (1 Sam. 14:20). Chariots were a hindrance, not an asset, in mountainous terrain.

More than owning a lot of chariots, which he would never use, Solomon was able to control the market in chariots. He bought horses and chariots from Egypt and Kue, which is probably a city in Asia Minor, at inflated prices (Walton, 421). Then the king sold them at the same confiscatory rates to the Hittites and the Arameans—the people whose chariot divisions David had disarmed a generation earlier.

Solomon's power was consolidated; the economy was booming; and there was peace in the land. It was time to build the temple.

MAIN IDEA REVIEW: As Solomon began to reign over Israel, he asked God for wisdom, and the Lord answered his request and blessed him.

III. CONCLUSION

Croesus, the Runner-up

History, aided by Greek mythology, tells us of another great ruler who had great wealth. Croesus was king of Lydia, whose capital was the city of Sardis during the sixth century B.C., roughly contemporary with Israel's exile in Babylon. According to the legend, Croesus had virtually unlimited wealth, which he loved to show off, and he also enjoyed surrounding himself with the wisest people of his day. But he lacked the most fundamental foundation for wisdom—the insight that material wealth will not provide a lasting foundation for happiness. One day Croesus talked with Solon, an extremely wise man. Croesus intimated that because of his wealth, he must be the happiest man in the world. But Solon replied that the happiest man in the world was some unknown commoner in Athens. He cautioned Croesus not to pass judgment on the happiness of a person until he knew how his life would turn out.

Sure enough, Croesus's own life did not end well. About this time King Cyrus of Persia was setting out to conquer Asia Minor, and Croesus thought he should stem the advance of the Persian army. But before heading off to fight Cyrus, Croesus consulted the oracle of Delphi, which told him that if he sent an army against the Persians, a great empire would be destroyed. So Croesus sent an army against the Persians, and before the war was done, his own great empire had been destroyed. He was not able to win against Cyrus, and his decision—reinforced by the oracle—backfired.

Unlike Croesus, Solomon knew he needed a stronger basis for a successful reign and a satisfying life than all the material benefits he could accumulate. He realized that, first of all, he needed wisdom from God, which could then function as a permanent measuring rod for all his other accomplishments.

The beginning of Solomon's reign calls us to focus precisely where Solomon himself focused: on receiving wisdom from God so we will not just spend a lifetime accumulating "stuff" but will please the Lord in all we do. James reminds us that "if any of you lacks wisdom, he should ask God, who gives generously to all without finding fault, and it will be given to him" (Jas. 1:5).

PRINCIPLES

- Wisdom is more important than wealth or material assets.

- To have wisdom means to live your life by the principles that God has revealed.
- To have wisdom also means to trust God, not yourself or others, when you must make difficult decisions.

APPLICATIONS

- If God came to you as he did Solomon and asked you what you most wanted, what would you say?
- Who are some people you have known who exhibited wisdom? What was it about them that showed they had wisdom?
- Tell God the tasks and responsibilities for which you need wisdom today.
- Meditate on God's willingness to give wisdom (Jas. 1:5–7).

IV. LIFE APPLICATION

One State at a Time

Last summer my wife and I picked up my mother-in-law in Michigan and drove to visit relatives in Florida. There were a number of routes we could have chosen to get there, but once we had settled on one, we needed to follow it in order to get to our destination. Our way to Florida led us through Ohio, Kentucky, Tennessee, and Georgia. Veering off to Illinois or Missouri would have impeded our progress.

There are some self-evident truths connected to this itinerary. For one thing, we could not have just skipped some of the states. In order to get to Florida, we had to drive through Georgia, but before we got to Georgia, we had to get to Tennessee, and so forth. The only way we could reach our final destination was to get to some intermediate points first. But on the other hand, simply driving to Georgia would not get us to Florida. If we reasoned that in order to get to Florida, we must get to Georgia, and so we drove to Georgia and stopped there, we never would have reached Florida. Many people do not wish to go through intermediate stages in order to achieve their final goals, or they stop at some preliminary stage and wonder why they never attained their ultimate objective.

Solomon realized that, even if the kingdom was guaranteed, he could fail if he did not govern well and wisely. In the same way, we should not shy away from having lofty and ambitious goals, but we should be prepared to travel a demanding road in order to get there. It would have been easy for Solomon to settle for second best. The king knew that external things would not be enough to make him a great ruler. What are you doing with your life? What are your goals? Are you settling for second best? Solomon could have, but he did not. There is no better way to begin a reexamination of our lives than to do as Solomon did—on our knees before the Lord.

V. PRAYER

Lord Jesus, we ask you for wisdom, just as Solomon did a long time ago. Apart from your wisdom and your guidance, we will never be able to make sense of our lives. We want to confess that we're a little leery of receiving too much wisdom because we're afraid we may have to change some things we are doing right now. So, Lord, please give us not only wisdom but also the strength to put your wisdom into practice. Amen.

VI. DEEPER DISCOVERIES

Solomon's Wisdom (1:10)

Solomon asked for a combination of wisdom and knowledge when God gave him the opportunity to make a request. Later on Solomon became as famous for his wisdom as for his wealth, astounding the queen of Sheba in both categories (2 Chr. 9:5–6).

Some of Solomon's wisdom has been left for us in written form—the books of Proverbs, Ecclesiastes, and the Song of Solomon in the Bible. Together with Job, these books constitute the "wisdom literature" of the Old Testament. These writings express thoughts about life and the meaning of human existence.

When we read through Solomon's wisdom books, we get a good picture of what the concept of wisdom must have meant to him when he requested it. One way of looking at it is with the following three points.

1. *Biblical wisdom reflects on life.* You can think without being wise, just by puzzling something out. You can have knowledge without being wise, just by accumulating a lot of information. You can even be virtuous without being wise, just by making the right decisions out of habit or a sense of obedience. But a wise person thinks about his actions and their consequences. He wonders about the meaning of what happens to him. And he tries to find connections between his life, his relationships with others, and his faith in God.

This side of wisdom challenges us not to take our lives for granted. Every day represents new opportunities for success, failure, and maybe a fresh start.

We do not need to do what we have always done or what others expect us to do. If we are wise, we will think about our choices.

2. *Biblical wisdom is practical.* This is a feature that biblical wisdom literature shares with many other ancient wisdom texts. They provide guidance on how to be successful in life, such as how to get along with a surly neighbor. But within biblical literature such practical advice constitutes more than a set of recipes on how to achieve certain things in life. The categories of sin and righteousness, rather than just pragmatic expediency, provide a greater sense of urgency to the counsel that the wisdom writers deliver.

In this aspect of wisdom, we see the need to incorporate our beliefs into our lives. As James reminds us, "Anyone who listens to the word but does not do what it says is like a man who looks at his face in a mirror and, after looking at himself, goes away and immediately forgets what he looks like" (Jas. 1:23–24).

3. *Biblical wisdom centers on God.* Solomon knew that he needed not just human wisdom, but the wisdom that only the Lord could provide. The king wrote later, "The fear of the LORD is the beginning of wisdom, and knowledge of the Holy One is understanding" (Prov. 9:10). This third dimension of wisdom reminds us that the one who created the world is the one who knows it best. True wisdom will always take God into account.

VII. TEACHING OUTLINE

A. INTRODUCTION

1. Lead Story: "If You Can Keep It"
2. Context: After David died, Solomon inherited the kingdom, but with it came the challenge to keep the empire intact and to be a worthy king. Just as Benjamin Franklin's famous words exhorted the American people to keep their country as a republic, so Solomon desired to rule over a nation that would be true to the promises of God.
3. Transition: Solomon found himself as the new king. He realized that he had not contributed to his own enthronement and consolidation of power. Where would he go from there? What Solomon needed more than anything else was confirmation from God himself.

B. COMMENTARY

1. Solomon's Ascension (1:1–6)
2. Solomon's Request and God's Response (1:7–13)
3. Solomon's Wealth (1:14–17)

C. CONCLUSION: CROESUS, THE RUNNER-UP

VIII. ISSUES FOR DISCUSSION

1. What is the role of wisdom in our society today? Do we value it in general? Do we value it in our leaders?
2. Is wisdom something that a church can teach? Do we need new programs or a rethinking of present programs in order to help people grow in wisdom?
3. Compile a list of men and women in the Bible with an eye toward which of them exhibited genuine wisdom.

2 Chronicles 2:1–5:1

Building the Temple

I. INTRODUCTION
Gilding the Sacred Lily

II. COMMENTARY
A verse-by-verse explanation of these chapters.

III. CONCLUSION
The Christmas Room

An overview of the principles and applications from these chapters.

IV. LIFE APPLICATION
From Temple to Closet

Melding these chapters to life.

V. PRAYER
Tying these chapters to life with God.

VI. DEEPER DISCOVERIES
Historical, geographical, and grammatical enrichment of the commentary.

VII. TEACHING OUTLINE
Suggested step-by-step group study of these chapters.

VIII. ISSUES FOR DISCUSSION
Zeroing these chapters in on daily life.

"God is holy and calls Israel to be a holy nation. The temple and its priesthood remind them of their vocation to holiness."

Stephen F. Noll

2 Chronicles 2:1–5:1

 I N A N U T S H E L L

Solomon had the temple built as a huge ornate structure. He used raw materials from Tyre, the talents of Phoenician craftsmen, and the forced labor of resident aliens to complete this project.

Building the Temple

I. INTRODUCTION

Gilding the Sacred Lily

*W*hen American evangelical Christians visit the Holy Land, they are often put off by the way in which most of the sites associated with the life of Jesus have been decorated. No site is so obscure, and no artifact so insignificant, that one should not build a church over it. And, oh, those churches! These churches are ornate, with crucifixes on the walls and incense in the air, and everything seems to breathe out the words: "Don't touch me; I am holy." Whether it be the garden of Gethsemane, the stable (cave) in Bethlehem, the remnants of Capernaum, or—most profoundly—Calvary and the empty tomb, they have all been swallowed up in the designs of ancient Catholic or Eastern Orthodox architecture.

Evangelicals tend to think that purity of design is the proper approach to a church building; functionality is the prime consideration, and even though a sanctuary may be made to look nice, architectural or decorative exuberance are suspect. Some churches over the last few years have allowed young people to hang colorful banners in their worship areas, but frequently these feel out of place and tacked on. This is a matter of what *feels* right to us in an artistic sense more than a moral or theological sense.

Other cultures take a different approach. For them it would be just as unthinkable to leave a sacred location bare as it would for us not to adorn someone we love. Parents who are proud of their children buy them nice clothes and make sure they are well-groomed when they go out in public. We would not think of showing off our children at a family reunion by having them appear with torn clothes or dirt smeared over their faces. Some Christian traditions see things in the same way: if a place is considered sacred, you make it as beautiful as you can.

This may be a large part of the motivation behind Solomon's extravagance as he began to build the temple. There may also have been a spirit of competitiveness with surrounding nations about who had the best temple, and no doubt we can see some personal pride as well. Still, the fundamental motivation appears to have been that God, the king of the universe, deserved a palace that put any human building to shame in its dimensions and beauty.

II. COMMENTARY

Building the Temple

MAIN IDEA: *Even though he knew that the temple could never contain God, Solomon spared no expense as he created a beautiful, impressive building.*

A Final Preparations (2:1–18)

SUPPORTING IDEA: *Solomon procured materials, artisans, and laborers to build the new temple.*

2:1–2. At the beginning of his fourth year as king, Solomon set out to begin the building project. David, his father, had originally been motivated to build a temple by the fact that he lived in a beautiful house, whereas God did not (1 Chr. 17:1). But Solomon's building plans included a new palace for himself as well as the temple.

Before construction could begin, Solomon needed to make sure there was a workforce that could do all the heavy manual labor. He did not turn to his own people but resorted to David's earlier method of taking a census to find out how many resident aliens were living in Israel at the time (2 Chr. 2:17–18). These were the men whom he forced to do the hard work of cutting stones and moving stones and logs to the temple site.

Of the 153,600 men who were registered, 70,000 went into the transport division, 87,000 were given stone-cutting duty, and the remainder received supervisory responsibilities. Obviously, the system worked because the temple was built. Solomon retained his policy of using foreigners as slave labor for most of his life (2 Chr. 8:7–9), although Israelites were also used on a limited basis (1 Kgs. 5:13–14). By the end of Solomon's reign, when building project followed building project, he apparently coerced Israelites into forced labor as well (2 Chr. 10:4).

2:3–10. When we read about David's preparations for the temple, we get the impression that he thought he had acquired more than enough building materials for the temple. Solomon thought otherwise. For his ambitious project he needed more of everything. We can infer either that David underestimated the amount of material needed or that Solomon's designs were much larger and ostentatious than what David had envisioned. The latter is more likely.

Solomon, as his father David had done, turned to Hiram, king of Tyre and permanent supplier of building materials to the kings of Israel. In a note to Hiram, Solomon explained exactly what his intentions were and how he could use Hiram's help.

The letter, as we have it in Chronicles, was more personal than most correspondence between royalty in ancient times. Solomon came right to the point, "Send me cedar logs." But then he referred to David's previous purchases of timber and went on to explain at greater length how he would use the logs.

Solomon told Hiram that he wanted to build a temple. In itself, this would have been nothing unusual. Everyone had temples, people placed statues of their gods in them, and Hiram was successful in the temple-construction business. However, Solomon wanted Hiram to understand that this temple was going to be different because it would not have the visible image of any deity.

A pagan would have asked an obvious question: If you don't have a statue of your god, why build a temple to him? After all, the point of having a temple was to have a place to house an image and to worship it. No image—no temple.

In order to forestall this misunderstanding, Solomon told Hiram—a Baal worshiper—exactly what would take place in the temple. He told him that the priests would burn **incense** to the Lord (Exod. 30:7–8). The **consecrated bread** would be set out every week (Lev. 24:5–9). Finally, there would be daily sacrifices as well as sacrifices for special occasions. Incense, food offerings, and sacrifices were things that Hiram could understand.

Solomon's next statement probably did not sound as audacious to Hiram as we might think. The king of Israel claimed that his God was superior to all other gods. This is the way people spoke of their gods in general. In the Ancient Near East, each nation had its own god. When there was conflict between people, the conflict would be between the gods as well. Whoever won the contest must have had the stronger god. Thus, people would generally tell everyone that their god was stronger than any other deity, and such aggressive theological claims could actually end up being settled in battle.

Solomon informed Hiram of a crucial point: God did not live in houses. It is unthinkable for God to be restricted to a building, particularly since he cannot be confined by **the heavens**. So the temple would be a place for worship and sacrifice, but it would not be the place where God actually lived.

Finally, Solomon asked Hiram to send a professional craftsman who could oversee all the artistic aspects of temple construction. Solomon would have known that a person had served as creative supervisor during the construction of the tabernacle under Moses (Exod. 31:1). Architectural design had not been a part of Hebrew culture, but the Phoenicians had the know-how to bring together the different elements that would go into the building of a truly outstanding temple. This man would have to be qualified to work with many metals and different yarns and fabrics (particularly Phoenicia's trademark purple), as well as to take charge of the many engravers who had already been recruited by David.

Further, Solomon also ordered another large shipment of lumber, if it is acceptable to refer to these woods (cedar, Lebanon pine, and—possibly—juniper) as "lumber." Solomon volunteered the services of his workers to contribute to the logging and shipping process, and he offered a handsome payment of several years' worth of grain, wine, and oil as compensation to the Phoenician men whom Hiram would put to work.

2:11–16. The chronicler breaks off the letter here and jumps right into King Hiram's reply. Hiram, the master diplomat, picked up exactly where Solomon had directed him and began with words of praise to God and Solomon; he even included David in this paean. The Baal worshiper Hiram expressed recognition of the Lord as **the God of Israel** and even echoed Solomon's reference to God as maker of **heaven and earth**. However, most of Hiram's admiration for God was reserved for the fact that he provided Israel with a king so liberally **endowed with intelligence and discernment**—in other words, someone who would contribute significantly to Hiram's gross revenue for the year.

Hiram had just the man for the job Solomon needed—Huram-Abi. This Huram met all the requirements imposed by Solomon's job description. He knew his metals, he had experience with fabrics, and he was qualified to supervise all the engravers. But Huram had a further feather in his cap. His **mother was from Dan**, so she was an Israelite who had married a man **from Tyre**. Thus Huram could communicate with the workers in Hebrew, and, most importantly, he understood the Hebrew religion.

Hiram was happy to accept the payment of wheat, barley, oil, and wine offered to him by Solomon. He asked for it up front so he could begin to feed his workers out of Solomon's pocket right from the start without incurring huge overhead expenses.

Hiram added one idea in order to make the process work better. Moving large objects to Jerusalem, which was located on top of a mountain, would not be easy, but Hiram thought of a labor-saving procedure. He would tie the lumber together in rafts and float them down along the Mediterranean seacoast to Joppa, thereby cutting the distance the logs would have to be carried on land by about two-thirds. Note how Hiram made the transportation of the logs from the coast to Jerusalem Solomon's responsibility.

2:17–18. The chronicler repeats the information of 2 Chronicles 2:2 with just a few more details to which we have already alluded.

B The Structures of the Temple (3:1–17)

SUPPORTING IDEA: *Solomon built the temple on a larger scale than the tabernacle, using the best materials and a lot of ornamentation.*

3:1–2. Solomon began this project officially on the second day of the second month in his fourth year as king. The site for the temple was the one to which God had directed his father David earlier—the threshing floor of Araunah on Mount Moriah. This was the same spot where Abraham had almost sacrificed his son Isaac (Gen. 22:2).

3:3–7. Everything that follows in the descriptions of the temple over the next two chapters combines two motivations. On the one hand, the account gives a detailed description of many of the features of the temple. On the other hand, it also emphasizes the splendor and cost of the project. We seem to move from architectural blueprint to an inventory of treasure and back.

Following the descriptions of the temple can be confusing if we lose sight of the fact that the word *temple* really does double duty. It can refer to the entire complex, including all the courts, but it can also refer to the actual building, which consisted of the holy place and the holy of holies. At times, when it is important to distinguish between these two elements, we will refer to the inner temple as the "temple proper." In 2 Chronicles 3, the "temple proper" is in view, and we receive information on four basic structural elements:

- the entry porch, or **portico** (3:4);
- the holy place, referred to as the **main hall** (3:5–7);
- **the Most Holy Place**, or holy of holies (3:8–14);
- the two pillars, **Jakin** and **Boaz**, placed just outside the entry door (3:15–17).

The description also includes three main decorations:
- the **cherubim** at the back wall of the most holy place (3:10–13);
- **the curtain** dividing the main hall from the most holy place (3:14);
- the decorations made of **pomegranates** on top of the pillars (3:16).

According to the dimensions the chronicler gives us—"old" cubits that were no longer in common use by Ezra's time—the building was prism shaped, sixty cubits long and twenty cubits wide (perhaps 105 feet by 35 feet; Payne, 393), not a very large building by itself. First Kings 6:2 tells us that the building was thirty cubits high, in which case it was taller than it was wide. The portico was an additional structure adjoining the front of the building as an entryway or porch, and it was as wide as the building itself. Inside, the building was laid over with gold and inscribed with decorations of cherubim.

3:8–14. The length of the temple was measured in thirds, with two-thirds going to the holy place and the last third designated as the holy of holies, which thus constituted a square of twenty cubits by twenty cubits. At the rear of this room were two sculpted cherubim, each with two outstretched wings five cubits long, so together the four wings covered the entire back wall. The most holy place was separated from the main hall by two doors that stood open (4:22), between which hung a curtain. Here the Phoenician fabric artists could display their skills, using all their special colors and techniques. This curtain was destroyed when the Babylonians razed the temple, but its later replacement was the curtain that tore when Jesus died on the cross (Matt. 27:51).

3:15–17. So far the plan of the temple proper was following the basic layout of the old tabernacle, but now, in a radical departure, Solomon added two pillars standing just outside the temple door. The top of the pillars, the capitals, were decorated with four sets of **interwoven chains**, from which dangled one hundred (artificial) pomegranates each, making four hundred pomegranates in all (4:13). Pomegranates were a Middle Eastern fruit, highly prized for making desserts or wine, and they were a part of the decorations for the high-priestly garment worn by Aaron (Exod. 28:33). Solomon gave the two pillars names. He called one **Jakin**, which may mean "he [i.e., the Lord] establishes," and the other one **Boaz**, which may mean "in him [i.e., in the Lord] is strength."

C The Temple Furnishings (4:1–5:1)

SUPPORTING IDEA: *Solomon provided the required furnishings as well as some innovative additions. In everything, he used precious materials and elaborate techniques.*

4:1. Most of the daily activity did not take place inside the temple, which was only entered twice a day to offer incense. All of the sacrifices and offerings were given outside in the main courtyard. All Israelite men had access to this courtyard. Here they presented animals for sacrifice, and the priests would perform the required rituals of inspection, slaughter, and burning. The base of the **altar** was a twenty-by-twenty cubit square—the same as the width of the building, and it was ten cubits tall.

4:2–6. The **Sea** was a huge washbasin. This bowl was half the width of the building in diameter and five cubits tall (i.e., approximately seven and one-half feet). In addition, it rested on a set of twelve outward-facing sculpted bulls, so there must have been steps to provide access for the priest. This large water container served as a wash station for the priests. The business of sacrificing animals would have been messy. The priests needed to scrub themselves constantly. In addition, both sides of the court were lined with **basins** to wash the sacrificial utensils.

4:7–11a. Joining the ten washbasins were **ten lampstands**. These were the seven-branched lights commanded by God for the tabernacle (Exod. 25:31–40). Further, Solomon added **ten tables** (Exod. 25:23–30) and **a hundred gold sprinkling bowls**. The sacrifice of animals involved the sprinkling of blood, usually against the four sides of the altar (e.g., Lev. 1:5; 3:8); this was the function of these bowls. The **courtyard of the priests** was a private area where priests prepared themselves for their duties. The **large court** was the area in which the routine activity took place.

It took many tools to perform all the work associated with making sacrifices. There were **pots**, which were used to remove ashes (Exod. 27:3) and to store the parts of animals that the priests could eat after a sacrifice (Lev. 6:28), **shovels** that the priests needed to clear the ashes from the altar, and more **sprinkling bowls**. Later on we also see references to meat forks (4:16), wick trimmers (4:22), and incense burners (4:22).

4:11b–18. The chronicler now reminds us of the master artist behind all these items—Huram-Abi, the man sent for this purpose by King Hiram. But there is no question that Huram worked under the careful supervision of Solomon in all aspects of this production. The material out of which they made the sculptures and implements was bronze, an alloy of copper and tin. Huram set up a work area outside Jerusalem in the Jordan Valley.

4:19–22. Solomon had put Huram in charge of all the bronze work associated with the rest of the temple, but the king reserved the gold work in the holy of holies for himself. Here were the items designated for use by the priests to carry out their daily, weekly, and annual rituals.

An altar (v. 19, see Exod. 30:1–10) stood in the holy place right in front of the entrance to the holy of holies. We should not confuse this altar with the one outside in the courtyard. No sacrifices were performed on this altar; it was supposed to be used twice a day for burning incense. The one exception to this rule was that on the annual Day of Atonement the high priest sprinkled the blood of a bull and a goat on this altar (Exod. 30:1–10; Lev. 16:18).

The tables inside the holy place were designated for **the bread of the Presence**, which was changed regularly to keep it fresh (Exod. 25:25–30). The **lamps** were kept burning all night long. It was the priest's duty to light the lamps each evening and douse them each morning while presenting the incense offering (Exod. 27:21; 30:7). This meant that they had to refill the oil and trim the wicks once a day.

While we are looking at the inventory of gold items in the temple, we learn of the two sets of **gold doors**, one from the holy place to the outside courtyard, the other connecting the holy place to the holy of holies. The latter set must have been for decorative purposes only since it was kept open at all times (2 Chr. 3:14).

5:1. Finally, after the temple and its furnishings were in place, Solomon moved in all **the things his father David had dedicated** to the Lord. These items were placed in the treasure chamber. Now everything was ready to bring in the ark and to dedicate the building to the Lord.

> **MAIN IDEA REVIEW:** *Even though he knew that the temple could never contain God, Solomon spared no expense in creating a beautiful, impressive building.*

III. CONCLUSION

The Christmas Room

When I was a child in Germany, we received presents on Christmas eve. On that entire day, the living room was off-limits to the children. Behind the door my parents were transforming the living room into the Christmas room. The most important thing they did, other than laying out the presents, was to set up and decorate the Christmas tree.

Then, in the evening after dark (and when we were a little older, after a Christmas eve vesper service at church), we children had to put on our best clothes and remain in our room for a few more minutes. Picture three boys sitting on wooden chairs, trying to contain their excitement. Suddenly we heard the sound we had been waiting for—the soft tinkle of a little bell on the Christmas tree. Immediately we jumped off our chairs, tripped over our feet in the hallway, and swooped into the living room.

I remember standing still, staring at the tree, overcome by its beauty. All the candles were lighted, their flickering flames reflected in shiny orbs. Silver birds were perching next to chocolate and jelly wreaths. The smells of pine, burning candles, sweets, and—of course—new toys saturated my feelings as well as my senses. My father, in his best dark suit, and my mother, in her nicest dress, stood by smiling. A few Christmas carols, a reading of the Christmas story from the Bible, the recitation of a poem by each of us boys, and a prayer—and the distribution of presents could finally begin. Even when someone turned on the electric lights, the room was not what it had been before. It had become a different place, no longer the living room but the Christmas room.

Over the next week or so, the room slowly changed back to its previous status as that part of our apartment in which we ate meals, held devotions, and listened to the radio. It would not become magically transformed for another year, when once again my parents would turn it into a different space.

In our contemporary industrialized society, there is not a lot of room for "sacred" space. No location is considered intrinsically different from others, and transformations, such as the one described above, are temporary. People construct church buildings and dedicate them to the Lord. But the church may eventually move out, and someone may turn the building into a store or maybe even a home. Even within our churches we often remind ourselves that, even though a sanctuary may be set apart for the worship of God, it is not holy in and of itself.

This attitude may keep us from appreciating the trouble to which Solomon went to make the temple a special place. Solomon understood that the temple was not a place in which God lived (2 Chr. 2:6). Still, the place he established was sacred. It was dedicated to the worship of God. Everything in it belonged to God, and a violation of its holiness was as serious as a violation of God himself.

We do not have a temple today (John 4:21; Heb. 9:11), and it would be wrong to try to turn our church sanctuaries into temples. The question is, What has taken its place? If there is no physical sacred space any more; is there something else that is sacred? The New Testament points to our very selves as believers in Christ. We are the temple of the Holy Spirit (1 Cor. 6:19) individually, and the church is the same temple collectively (1 Cor. 3:16). What an astounding insight! The same concept under which Solomon built the temple now applies to us: we are sacred because we as believers belong to God in a special sense.

PRINCIPLES

- God is holy, and those things that belong to him are holy.
- During Old Testament times, specific spaces were designated as holy because they belonged to God.

- The temple in Jerusalem emphasized the distinction between the normal space in which people lived on a day-to-day basis and the special space that was devoted to God alone.

APPLICATIONS

- Even though all times and spaces are God's, we come to recognize this increasingly by having special times and spaces dedicated to God.

- As you leave special times and spaces of devotion and worship, ask God to help you recognize that all of your life is his. Ask him to show you what that means today.

- Recall some times when you felt closest to God. What was the setting? What difference have those times of intimacy made in your life?

IV. LIFE APPLICATION

From Temple to Closet

At some special occasions I am often asked to give a public prayer. Afterward someone inevitably comes up and compliments me on it. "That was a very nice prayer." "Thank you," I reply, puzzled about what a "nice prayer" could possibly be.

To ancient Israelites, the central act of worship was the offering of sacrifices in the temple. These were public ceremonies, performed so any other Israelite could observe them. By the time of Jesus, some Pharisees had elevated personal devotions to a public display as well. They believed that in order for a prayer to be considered proper, people should assume certain bodily positions and show their piety to everyone. The Pharisees thought you could evaluate how pious a prayer was by looking at the external performance of the person who offered it.

Jesus turned this conception around. He forbade prayer as a public display of piety (Matt. 6:5–6). He taught that prayer should not be offered on the street corner, as some Pharisees were doing, but that we should pray in our private rooms behind closed doors. Our central way of relating to God is not through a public act but in a direct individual relationship with God.

V. PRAYER

Lord Jesus, in some ways we are envious of the Israelites of old. It would be so much easier to formalize our religion by going to a temple and doing our required sacrifices and then going home, having fulfilled our duty. But Lord, we realize how much better off we are. We have knowledge of what you have done on the cross, and so we have an assurance of salvation that the ancient Israelites were clueless about. Thank you for your grace that has made this possible. Amen.

VI. DEEPER DISCOVERIES

A. The Temple and the Tabernacle (3:1)

When the Israelites built the tabernacle after the exodus, they were acting in obedience to what God had commanded through Moses (Exod. 25:8–9). In fact, God not only told Moses that he should build a tabernacle, but he gave him specific instructions about its dimensions, materials, and decorations. Solomon did not violate any of God's ordinances, since the temple plans were revealed to David (1 Chr. 28:12) and to him (1 Kgs. 6:11), so it might be instructive to look at the similarities and differences between the tabernacle and the temple.

First, the tabernacle was a tent. It was designed to be taken down and put up again on a regular basis as the Israelites marched through the desert toward the promised land. Then, when they settled in the land after the conquest, it was not moved much, but it does appear in several different places at various times: in Shiloh during Samuel's boyhood (1 Sam. 1:3), at Nob during David's days as a fugitive (1 Sam. 21:1), and at Gibeon during David's kingship (1 Chr. 16:39). During all this time, the tabernacle was the highest place of worship, even after the ark was no longer a part of it. Here the main sacrifices were celebrated. However, the tabernacle was not considered to be the only legitimate location for sacrifices. For example, Samuel maintained an annual circuit by officiating at sacrifices throughout Israel (1 Sam. 7:15–17).

By contrast the temple was a permanent structure. Before the Israelites settled in Canaan, Moses declared that there would eventually be a permanent temple for worship. When this occurred, it would be the only place where it was permissible to make sacrifices (Deut 12:11–14). Any sacrifice outside the temple would be a violation of the law.

Structurally, the temple followed the same basic plan as the tabernacle, with the division into the holy place and the most holy place and the main altar out front in the courtyard. The differences were in size and number. The temple was approximately twice as large as the tabernacle. Solomon enlarged the size of the altar. The altar at the tabernacle was only three cubits tall, while the altar at the temple was ten cubits high. Solomon multiplied a number of the temple furnishings by ten, so that there were ten lampstands and ten tables in the court.

Solomon also augmented the original design of the tabernacle by setting up two courts—the larger outer court for all Israelites and the smaller inner court for the priests. And finally, Solomon left his mark on the structure of the temple with the two tall pillars, Jakin and Boaz, standing outside the temple entryway.

B. Types of Sacrifices (4:6)

There were several different kinds of sacrifices, involving different materials and different rituals. Here is a quick summary of the types of sacrifices, as they are enjoined in Leviticus:

- *Burnt offering* (Lev. 1:1–17). This sacrifice represented total devotion to the Lord. It consisted of burning an entire animal. The burnt offering was the most important offering in Israel, epitomizing the relationship between God and his people.

- *Grain offering* (Lev. 2:1–16). In this offering someone gave some cereal grain, either as flour or as a cake, which could be either baked or fried. One condition was that these cakes should not contain any yeast. By presenting a grain offering, a person acknowledged that the tithe of the entire harvest belonged to God.

- *Fellowship (or peace) offering* (Lev. 3:1–17). In this sacrifice the fat and inner organs, but not the entire animal, were burned. The rest of the animal became the featured entrée of a communal banquet. The fellowship offering represented peace with God.

- *Sin offering* (Lev. 4:1–5:13). This sacrifice was specifically established for anyone who might have unintentionally violated one of the laws of God, particularly those of ritual purity. The affected person had to confess his sin. The animal's unclean parts were burned. This time, the clean parts became dinner for the priests—unless it was a priest who had committed the sin, in which case they were discarded.

- *Guilt (or trespass) offering* (Lev. 5:14–6:7). The purpose of the guilt offering was to atone for violations of moral and legal laws and for intentional breaches of the ceremonial laws. Whereas the other animal sacrifices gave some leeway about which animal could be used, a ram was the only option for the guilt offering. Furthermore, if the occasion for the sacrifice was a crime, such as fraud or theft, the person who presented the sacrifice had to make full restitution to the victim, and pay another 20 percent for damages.

VII. TEACHING OUTLINE

A. INTRODUCTION
1. Lead Story: Gilding the Sacred Lily
2. Context: Contemporary evangelical Christians may be put off by the ornate and imposing nature of the temple that Solomon built. But we need to recognize that for him and his contemporaries, it was a way to celebrate how special God was to them.
3. Transition: When Solomon was firmly established as king, he began the process of building the temple. He set out to build a truly remarkable building.

B. COMMENTARY
1. Final Preparations (2:1–18)
2. The Structures of the Temple (3:1–17)
3. The Temple Furnishings (4:1–5:1)

C. CONCLUSION: THE CHRISTMAS ROOM

VIII. ISSUES FOR DISCUSSION

1. What places do people in our culture consider sacred today? How do they treat them?
2. How should we react to the different ways in which people may consider rooms or buildings sacred?
3. In what specific ways can Christians live according to the truth that they are the temple of God?

The Temple: God's Communications Hub

Quote

"*E*arnestly, tenderly, Jesus is calling, calling, O sinner,

come home!"

Will L. Thompson

2 Chronicles 5:2–7:22

IN A NUTSHELL

*W*hen the temple was finished, Solomon held a great dedication ceremony in which the ark of the covenant was installed and Solomon said a lengthy public prayer, to which God responded favorably. This prayer and God's answer teach us that God is always accessible to us.

The Temple: God's Communications Hub

I. INTRODUCTION

Finding My Way Back

Not too long ago I had the opportunity to be part of a conference in southern California. Feeling that it would be poor stewardship for me not to enjoy the beautiful, sunny weather, I left the conference sessions a little early to walk back to my hotel rather than ride back later in a van. I knew that the hotel was located two miles away, and I thought I knew exactly which way I was supposed to go in order to get there. With a steady pace of walking, I should get there within forty minutes.

After forty minutes I was not only not at the hotel; I was somewhere I had not seen before. Another twenty minutes at an accelerated pace did not help things any. A further ten minutes, and I realized that I was definitely not walking toward my hotel.

Fortunately, I was carrying my cell phone. Swallowing my pride, I called the hotel. The young lady at the hotel took my call, figured out where I was, and promised to send the hotel van to find me. Soon the van showed up and took me straight to the hotel. It was a blessing to have the resources of a cell phone and a hotel van at my fingertips.

Do you wish you had God at your fingertips? Well, you do. The Lord is always present and ready to hear your requests. Philippians 4:5 tells us that "the Lord is near!" For Solomon and his people, this truth was expressed through the presence of the new temple. The temple provided a focal point of access to God. It reminded the Israelites that whenever they were in need, if they turned to God, he would respond to them and forgive, heal, and restore.

In this section we see one of the highlights of the "gospel according to Ezra." In his grace God gave the people a temple as a visual reminder that they could always come to him with their needs. The apostle Paul stated several centuries later, "Do not be anxious about anything, but in everything, by prayer and petition, with thanksgiving, present your requests to God" (Phil. 4:6). The existence of the temple declared to the people in Old Testament times that this was a privilege they enjoyed.

II. COMMENTARY

The Temple: God's Communications Hub

MAIN IDEA: *God's special presence in the new temple demonstrated to all Israel that he would always be accessible to them in their time of need.*

A Installing the Ark of the Covenant (5:2–14)

SUPPORTING IDEA: *After a great celebration, the ark of the covenant was placed in the holy of holies, and God manifested his presence through a cloud.*

5:2–3. It took seven years for the temple to be constructed (1 Kgs. 6:38). When it was finally finished, an epic dedication ceremony was scheduled. A call went out to all Israelites in leadership positions to come to Jerusalem and be part of the ceremony in which the ark of the covenant would be moved into the temple. The date chosen for this celebration was a **festival in the seventh month**, when all Israelite men were expected to come to the temple anyway.

Actually, three festivals occurred in the seventh month: the feast of trumpets (Rosh Hashanah) on the first, the Day of Atonement (Yom Kippur) on the tenth, and the feast of tabernacles (or booths—Sukkoth) on the fifteenth. We learn later that the celebration finished on the twenty-third of the month (2 Chr. 7:10), so it was most likely in conjunction with the feast of booths that this celebration was held. By the time the temple was ready and open for regular services, it was the eighth month of the year (1 Kgs. 6:38).

The distance between Mount Zion and Mount Moriah is short, not more than a ten-minute walk. So the process of moving the ark was not as demanding as when it was first moved to Jerusalem. But this task received as much attention as when David moved the ark.

5:4–13a. Carrying the ark were **the Levites**. Also, one last time, they carried the tabernacle, the **Tent of Meeting**. The chronicler gives us no specific information on when the tabernacle was moved to Zion from Gibeon, but, obviously, there had been much opportunity to do so. One imagines that Solomon, in his excitement to accomplish his great temple-building mission, had kept the tabernacle ready to be moved. Once the tabernacle had entered the temple, it ceased its function; presumably the Levites stored its component parts in the treasury.

When Solomon led the procession with innumerable sacrifices along the way, these were the last sacrifices that could be legitimately performed outside the temple. From this point on, the only place in Israel where it was legal to perform sacrifices was on the altar within the temple court (Deut. 12:11–14).

Continuing to follow the law punctiliously, the Levites carried the ark into the holy of holies. They did not detach the poles (Exod. 25:15), but let them remain slotted through the rings on the ark. The poles were a little longer than the twenty feet allotted to the holy of holies, so they stuck out, bulging the curtain that separated the most holy place from the holy place. This constant reminder of the presence of the ark would be seen by all priests performing the daily service in the temple, even though they could not enter the inner chamber. Since by the time of Ezra this first temple had been destroyed and the ark had dissappeared, the phrase **they are still there today** must have come directly from one of the reports Ezra was using in recounting these events.

During the time that the ark had been mistreated (1 Sam. 5–6), its content had become depleted. Originally it contained three items: the tablets with the Ten Commandments, a jar of manna, and Aaron's stick that had blossomed (Heb. 9:4); now it was down to the **tablets**, which signified God's **covenant** with Israel more than anything else.

Once the ark was placed in the temple, the musicians took over. Led by the three master musicians—Asaph, Heman, and Jeduthun—the entire guild of musicians played their instruments and sang. A total of **120 priests** with their trumpets lent additional power and volume to the orchestra. Together they chanted the familiar refrain, **He is good; his love endures forever.** This was the same chorus that David and the musicians had sung when the ark was first moved to Jerusalem (1 Chr. 16:34,41), and which appears many times in the Psalms (e.g., Ps. 106:1).

5:13b–14. As the rejoicing reached its crescendo, a cloud filled the temple. This cloud was so dense that the priests could no longer see what they were doing, so they had to stop their activity. This cloud was a manifestation of the glory of God. This was not the first time that God had shown himself in this way. He had also done so when he gave Moses the Ten Commandments (Exod. 19:9) and as an indication of his presence in the holy of holies of the tabernacle (Lev. 16:2). The message was clear: God had taken possession of his new sanctuary.

![B] Solomon's Speech and Prayer (6:1–42)

SUPPORTING IDEA: *Solomon acknowledged God's work in providing the temple and implored God to answer prayers that were directed to him.*

6:1–3. Solomon took charge of the moment and began to speak. He acknowledged that God was present in the cloud, just as he had been in the past (Exod. 19:9). Then the king summarized his intention: he had built a permanent place for God. This was not a place to which God was permanently bound but a place where people could have access to him. Then Solomon said a blessing over the crowd and began his speech.

6:4–11. Much of Solomon's speech was familiar ground for his audience, just as it is for the contemporary reader of Chronicles. He rehearsed the account of how David wished to build a temple but was prevented from doing so by God himself, how God had allowed Solomon to come to the throne and to be the one to build the temple.

However, there were some significant sidebars to Solomon's speech as he laid out these familiar events. First of all, the reference that God had brought about this conclusion **with his hands** is striking, considering how much work had been done by people with their hands. Solomon realized that the human contributions meant nothing apart from God, who had directed these events.

Second, Solomon emphasized that the building of the temple was not only significant in itself, but it also set apart Jerusalem as the special city that housed the temple (Deut. 12:11). This was a fulfillment that had been long in coming. And third, the speech was centered on the idea of God's initiative. He was the one who had made the promise of a temple, who had chosen Jerusalem as the special city and Solomon as the ruler, and who had fulfilled his promise when Solomon was able to build the temple.

6:12–13. Now Solomon became dramatic. He had made himself a little stage, three cubits tall (about four and one-half feet), and he mounted it and assumed a kneeling posture with his hands spread out in the Old Testament gesture of prayer (Exod. 17:11). He signified that he was bowing humbly before God in prayer and that he was representing his entire nation before the throne of God.

6:14–17. In the first part of this prayer, Solomon reminded God of his faithfulness. God had fulfilled the promises he had given in a **covenant of love**. These promises were not something that a human being had extracted from him, but they were expressions of God's love right from the start. Now God had lived up to his pledge.

6:18–21. Solomon stated the truth that the temple in no way restricted God's presence. The king had understood this all along, as he had made the same point earlier to King Hiram at the beginning of the project (2 Chr. 2:6). Not everyone listening would have recognized that God was not limited. Idolatry was never too far around the corner. In fact, it is possible that there were some people in attendance at this assembly who worshiped at idolatrous shrines later on (1 Kgs. 12:28–33).

But Solomon was clear in his mind about the fact that God was not limited. He knew that God's dwelling place was in heaven—everywhere above and beyond the physical world. But Solomon also recognized that God had ordained that people should come to him through the facilities of the temple. So Solomon entreated God to listen to the prayers of everyone who prayed at the temple. In a sudden extension of this thought, Solomon begged God to respond to such prayers with his forgiveness.

6:22–39. In the central part of his prayer, Solomon mentioned specific situations in which someone might come to God by means of the temple and requested that God would answer such prayers favorably:

- to validate an oath that someone might swear on behalf of his innocence in a criminal case (6:22–23);
- to redeem the people if they were defeated by an enemy because of their sin (6:24–25);
- to bring relief in case of drought (6:26–27);
- to restore the land in case of an epidemic, a famine, or some other national disaster (6:28–31);
- to demonstrate his greatness to any foreigner who might come to Israel to learn about God (6:32–33);
- to support Israel in war when God sent them out on a mission (6:34–35);
- to redeem the people if they should repent after being brought into captivity because of their disobedience to God (6:36–39).

It is important in all these cases to recognize two assumptions. One is the central role that Solomon gave to the temple as the focal point of prayer. The other is the fact that these prayers were not just empty rituals; they were to be accompanied by repentance and resolve to become faithful to God from that point on.

6:40–42. Finally, Solomon repeated his request to God to respond to the prayers offered at the temple. He concluded his prayer with a poignant recitation, which is now also included among the Psalms (Ps. 132:8–10). The psalm as a whole, which may or may not have been written by David himself, describes David's burning desire to find a permanent place for the sanctuary and the promise by God that it would be David's son who would fulfill that desire. With the recitation of these lines of poetry, Solomon again acknowledged God's faithfulness and his own debt to God.

Ⓒ God's Answers to the People and to Solomon (7:1–22)

> **SUPPORTING IDEA:** *God once more revealed his presence and his glory to all the people, and then he gave Solomon reassurance.*

7:1–3. After Solomon finished his prayer, the people were in for another overwhelming demonstration of God's presence. This time it was not just the cloud of God's glory; fire came down from heaven and consumed the sacrifices on the altar. In the ancient manifestation of God's glory on Mount Sinai, there had been fire along with the cloud (Deut. 4:11; 5:22). Then, when Moses and Aaron dedicated the tabernacle, the same thing happened: a display of God's glory along with fire on the altar (Lev. 9:24). The divine fire had appeared another time when David had set up the altar on the threshing floor of Araunah (1 Chr. 21:26). With this fire God again declared that he was present among his people.

Once again the priests were prevented from carrying out their duties while the display lasted. The assembled crowd made the only response appropriate under these circumstances. They threw themselves on the ground and worshiped the Lord.

7:4–10. Now that it was clear that the Lord approved of the temple and everything was ready, the first sacrificial services could be conducted. And what sacrifices they were! Solomon offered a total of 22,000 cattle and 120,000 sheep. It would have been physically impossible to carry out all these sacrifices sequentially, so presumably there was some mass slaughter, and some sacrifices may even have been postponed after the animals were dedicated. The musicians continued to practice their craft, and the priests joined in with their trumpets.

People had come from as far south as the Wadi of Egypt and as far north as the city of Hamath, which is located in present-day Lebanon. But the celebration had to come to an end, and finally Solomon sent the people home. They adjourned with joy in their hearts and gratitude to God for what he had done.

7:11–16. It was some time later, after Solomon had finished building his own palace (1 Kgs. 7:1), that Solomon received a second visitation from the Lord (see 2 Chr. 1:7 for the first). At this point God gave him positive reassurances for himself and for the people, but he also issued a serious warning if they should forsake him.

God responded directly to the situations that Solomon had brought up in his prayer—times when there would be trouble and the people would come to God for aid and forgiveness. In such days of calamity, when the people turned to God, he would hear them and answer them out of his love and grace. God issued this promise specifically for [his] **people, who are called by [his] name**, the people of Israel. We know, however, that God's grace is not limited to Israel. For example, we read in the Book of Jonah that when the people of Nineveh repented, God relented in his punishment of them as well (Jon. 3:10).

God expected the people to **humble themselves and pray and seek [his] face and turn from their wicked ways**. There was nothing mechanical about God's acceptance of the people's repentance. Without a change of heart, prayers and sacrifices in the temple would be meaningless. This theme was proclaimed by the prophets continually. The Lord declared through Isaiah, "When you spread out your hands in prayer, I will hide my eyes from you; even if you offer many prayers, I will not listen" (Isa. 1:15a). God will accept honest repentance, but he will not listen to insincere prayers.

Whenever the people turned back to him, however, God would provide what they needed. He would not only grant forgiveness, but he would also remove the physical consequences of their sin. He would **heal their land** by turning back the plague or ending the drought, or whatever their affliction might be.

7:17–18. God also had words of assurance for Solomon personally. He repeated to him the promise he had given David—that he and his descendants would always have someone on the throne of Israel. However, in a manner stronger than before, he attached the warning that the blessings of the throne were contingent on Solomon's observance of the rules God had laid down.

7:19–22. At this point God warned that apostasy would have dire consequences. If the king or the people abandoned God's law or forsook him for idols, such actions would not go unnoticed. The people would lose the land and be carried off into exile. The temple—which was such a work of splendor at the moment—would be destroyed, and it would become an object of ridicule. People from other nations would laugh at it, and they would be aware of the lesson that the Israelites themselves had forgotten—that the Israelites had lost their building of glory and splendor because they had forsaken their God. Sadly, this warning to Solomon was a prophecy of exactly what would happen eventually.

MAIN IDEA REVIEW: *God's special presence in the new temple demonstrated to all Israel that he would always be accessible to them in their time of need.*

III. CONCLUSION

Stuck in Traffic with Jesus

In the 1960s controversial Episcopal priest Malcolm Boyd, who became known for a time as the "nightclub priest," turned a few heads with his antics, and evangelical Christians rightly rejected many of his practices. However, Boyd had a message to the world that was worth hearing—that Jesus was with him in every part of his life.

Malcolm Boyd's celebrated book was a collection of prayers entitled *Are You Running with Me, Jesus?* These prayers were not formal orations but chats that he imagined himself having with Jesus in the day-to-day occurrences of life. For example, he was talking to Jesus as he was having a bad day stuck in traffic, as he was reflecting on an exceptionally good day, or as he was pondering a person desperately in need of help. In all situations and under all circumstances, he was addressing Jesus, not disrespectfully, but as someone who was there with him, who knew of his joys and sorrows, and who understood his frustrations and doubts. Boyd helped us to see that prayer is conversation with God, to whom we have unlimited access.

In his prayer to God, Solomon was able to see beyond the rituals of incense and offerings. The king did not just request that God would pay attention to sacrifices made and worship ceremonies performed. Solomon entreated God to hear all prayers that were directed toward the temple. Such prayers could occur in a faraway land, where the people were exiled, just as much as in the temple court before the altar. In the final analysis it was not the temple rituals that made communication with God possible, but the temple represented the fact that the Israelites could communicate with God.

PRINCIPLES

- God provided the temple for the Israelites to express their relationship with him.
- God demonstrated to the people of Israel that he was in their midst.
- God revealed to the Israelites that they could have access to him if they turned to him in prayer and repentance.
- God has invited us to come to him whenever we are in need.

APPLICATIONS

- Recount some of the times in your life when you experienced the glory of God in an almost tangible way.
- Meditate on the fact that just as God chose Jerusalem and the temple for his dwelling in Israel, so he has chosen you and other believers as his dwelling place. As that truth takes hold in your heart, what difference does it make in how you live your life?
- Make a prayer journal in which you record daily some of the things you have told God and what you have asked him for. Keep track of how the Lord responds.
- Make an inventory of your normal daily activities. Then consider ways in which recognizing that Jesus is right there with you could affect your attitude and actions.

IV. LIFE APPLICATION

Access Denied

"Access Denied!" is the message every computer user dreads. It may come in different formulations, from the older, "Bad Command or File Name," to the more recent, "You are not authorized!" but the point is the same. You thought you were going to work with a particular file, but you were shut out of it. Perhaps it's your fault, perhaps the program's, perhaps something else is to blame. What caused it does not matter at the moment so much as the fact that you are looking at a barrier between you and the task you were going to perform. The reason many of us have gotten so used to our computers is that we want instant access to information or programs, and when we don't get it, we experience frustration.

"Access Denied!" is a message that God never displays. To be sure, we need to recognize that access to God takes place on his terms, not ours. God is not a

"Mr. Fix-it," on whom we can call whenever we have a predicament, only to send him home again after he has taken care of our problem. The Lord made sure that Solomon understood this, and we need to be aware of it as well, lest we think we can toy with God's forbearance. However, God is never far away from us. What he promised to Solomon is also true for us. There is no situation so dire, even if it is caused by our sin, that will keep God from hearing our prayers.

"Access Authorized" is what the temple represented in Solomon's day; it is the heart of the "gospel according to Ezra." Today we realize that access to God is made possible through the work of Jesus Christ. "Let us then approach the throne of grace with confidence, so that we may receive mercy and find grace to help us in our time of need" (Heb. 4:16).

V. PRAYER

Lord Jesus, as your disciples on earth once asked you, teach us to pray. Teach us not to make our prayers public displays of our piety or repetitions of empty words. Teach us to pray without ceasing. Teach us to pray, not as though we are making a long distance call over a bad line but in the knowledge that you are here with us, that you care about our needs, and that we will never be able to surprise you with anything we might say to you. Amen.

VI. DEEPER DISCOVERIES

A Call to Revival (7:14)

This verse has long been a favorite for Christians to claim as they pray for God to send revival. It reminds us of the mercy and grace of our Lord, while also exhorting us to come to God humbly and with a sense of repentance. Use of this verse has led to some excesses in its application, but we should not let those problems keep us from appreciating what it says to us.

Here are some misapplications of this verse. First, it should not be presented as a means of receiving salvation. God gives us our salvation apart from our works, not conditional on our humbling ourselves and turning from our wicked ways. Such changes are results of our salvation, not ways of achieving it. Second, 2 Chronicles 7:14 should not be considered a method of Christian growth. Although what is described may be a part of the total picture as we are transformed into the image of Christ, it is not by itself a formula on how to achieve maturity. And third, we ought not to apply this verse to a national entity today, except perhaps as we look forward to the future restoration of Israel (Rom. 11:26). This verse is addressed to the people who are called by God's name, and there is no country today that can lay claim to this title as Israel did at the time of Solomon.

However, we may apply this verse to the church today. We are God's chosen and redeemed people in this age, and we may claim this verse as God's offer of blessing to the body of Christ. If we seek to escape from congregational spiritual doldrums or to carry out a more dynamic ministry to our contemporaries, we may do well to ponder some of the stipulations in this verse.

1. *God works through humble people.* Particularly in response to the moral relativism that plagues our society today, it is easy for us to fall into a triumphalist attitude in which we make ourselves look superior to others. God does not want us to compromise the truth, just as he does not want us to lose sight of the fact that the truth is a gift, not our achievement.

2. *God works through people who pray.* Prayer is not a mechanical device to force God to do something against his will, but prayer is the way we stay in touch with him. It is our ongoing communication with him, and people who are close to God are people in whom others will see their Lord.

3. *God works through people who seek his face.* Too much of our activity as Christians is spent on achieving temporary, perishable goals, and not enough of our time is spent focusing on the Lord. Like Martha in the account of Jesus' visit (Luke 10:38–41), we may become so preoccupied with doing things for God that we no longer spend time with God. We should never lose sight of the fact that our relationship with Christ leads to works, not the other way around. The relationship comes first.

4. *God works through people who turn from their wicked ways.* Many churches do not deal with overt sin in their congregations, often at the level of leadership. I have heard of several cases where church members were committing adultery, and everyone looked the other way. It's true that a church is a collection of sinners, all of whom are saved by the grace of God. But this does not mean that we should be comfortable with sin. God wants his church to be a witness of his holiness, and that means to forsake all our "wicked ways."

VII. TEACHING OUTLINE

A. INTRODUCTION

1. Lead Story: Finding My Way Back
2. Context: It is a great convenience to have a cell phone handy in difficult situations, but it is even better to know that we always have

access to God. For Solomon and his contemporaries, the temple demonstrated that God was present among them and that he would listen to their prayers.

3. Transition: Solomon had finished building the temple, and now the time came for the official dedication. There were two big questions: Would God approve of his new sanctuary? Would he respond to those who came to him in the new temple?

B. COMMENTARY

1. Installing the Ark of the Covenant (5:2–14)
2. Solomon's Speech and Prayer (6:1–42)
3. God's Answers to the People and to Solomon (7:1–22)

C. CONCLUSION: STUCK IN TRAFFIC WITH JESUS

VIII. ISSUES FOR DISCUSSION

1. If you saw God's cloud of glory settle in your living room, what would this change in your life?
2. How can Christians remind one another of the fact that we have constant access to God?
3. Many Christian groups maintain an official prayer list. Unfortunately, such a list often does not do much more than keep track of hospital admissions. In a group discussion, brainstorm some ways in which Christians can become consistent in praying for one another's many needs, not just medical emergencies.

2 Chronicles 8:1–9:31

The Splendors of Solomon

I. INTRODUCTION
The Midas Touch

II. COMMENTARY
A verse-by-verse explanation of these chapters.

III. CONCLUSION
Potemkin Villages

An overview of the principles and applications from these chapters.

IV. LIFE APPLICATION
Running on Fumes

Melding these chapters to life.

V. PRAYER
Tying these chapters to life with God.

VI. DEEPER DISCOVERIES
Historical, geographical, and grammatical enrichment of the commentary.

VII. TEACHING OUTLINE
Suggested step-by-step group study of these chapters.

VIII. ISSUES FOR DISCUSSION
Zeroing these chapters in on daily life.

"*What* Solomon achieves comes as a direct

work of the Lord."

P a u l   R .   H o u s e

2 Chronicles 8:1–9:31

I N   A   N U T S H E L L

Once the temple was completed, Solomon lived a long time and had a successful reign. He accumulated enormous wealth, succeeded in his trade ventures, and astounded the visiting queen of Sheba with his riches and wisdom. Solomon clearly enjoyed the Lord's favor, although by the end of his life, his devotion to the Lord had become superficial. Yet the Lord continued to bless him.

The Splendors of Solomon

I. INTRODUCTION

The Midas Touch

A famous Greek myth tells about Midas, the king of Phrygia in ancient Asia Minor. Midas had great ambitions for wealth and power, and he believed that either one of the two could secure the other. He was able to do a favor to the Greek god of wine, Dionysius, by rescuing Silenus, a satyr of whom Dionysius was very fond. The opportunistic Midas decided to take advantage of the situation. When the god offered him one wish, he selected the ability to turn everything he touched into gold.

Midas imagined himself touching an object and turning it into gold at his command, but that's not the way it turned out. The wish had left out the part about the command, and so everything with which he came into contact was immediately transformed into the noblest of metals. For a little while this was fun for Midas, and he enjoyed turning lots of stuff into golden things. But the fun did not last.

There was no stopping the gold-making process. He sat on a chair and held a cushion, and both chair and pillow turned to gold. He grabbed a goblet of wine to refresh himself, and both goblet and wine turned to gold. He reached for some grapes, and they turned to gold. This was getting annoying.

Midas had an idea: he would just have his servants feed him. So he called them into his chamber and ordered them to bring him food and drink and insert it directly into his mouth. He opened wide, and the slaves started to pop in the delicious tidbits. But this did not work either. The instant the morsels came in contact with his tongue, they turned to gold. Now Midas realized that he had made an awful mistake, and he prevailed on Dionysius to undo his wish.

There can be such a thing as too much of a good thing. There can also be such a thing as getting used to a good thing and taking it for granted. Obviously, King Midas is an example of the first situation; King Solomon may be an example of the second.

As we come to the close of the life of Solomon in these two chapters, we learn about his accomplishmesnts in the thirty or so years after the completion of the temple. There is little to report other than the never-ending accumulation of assets. He did it without Midas's magic, and he avoided

Midas's ruin, but everything that Solomon touched turned to gold, literally and figuratively.

But Solomon turned into a hollow man. The portrait the chronicler creates of Solomon is that of an empty life. Solomon was blessed by God; he was rich and wise, but his zeal for the Lord seems to have peaked with the dedication of the temple. But here is the "gospel according to Ezra" for Solomon. In spite of Solomon's mistakes, God continued to grant him success because Solomon had built the temple and Solomon was the heir to the promise God had made to David.

II. COMMENTARY

Hollow Splendors

> **MAIN IDEA:** *God blessed Solomon with great wealth and wisdom, and the king continued his outward observance of his temple obligations.*

It is important for us not to read the content of 1 Kings into this section. There we learn of some serious sins that Solomon committed, even going so far as to commit idolatry himself (1 Kgs. 11:1–8). However, the chronicler does not include this fact in his account. Later on, Ezra the chronicler refers to the judgment that Ahijah had prophesied against Solomon (2 Chr. 10:15); this mention comes in connection with Rehoboam and should not be read back into chapters 8 and 9. If the chronicler had wanted to make use of Solomon's idolatry for this narrative, he undoubtedly would have done so.

A Solomon's Success (8:1–18)

> **SUPPORTING IDEA:** *Solomon enjoyed success in many endeavors and accumulated great wealth, as he continued to carry out his duties at the temple.*

8:1–6. Solomon undertook ambitious building projects during his entire life. It took him seven years to finish the temple and thirteen more to build his own palace (1 Kgs. 6:38–7:1), a complex of buildings. Then he took on numerous other construction ventures, some of them probably overlapping with the two major projects.

One project he took care of was a village renewal campaign for some towns in Galilee. Keep in mind that such "towns" would not have been much more than tiny aggregates of a few houses. In this case, there were twenty such municipalities, which Solomon had deeded to King Hiram of Tyre. These towns constituted a partial payment for the cedar wood and precious metals which Hiram had contributed to the temple building project (1 Kgs. 9:10–14). But when Hiram inspected these new additions to his domain, he discovered that they were eyesores and pronounced them worthless. He gave them back to Solomon, who fixed them up.

Despite his great army (or, perhaps, because of it), Solomon managed to stay out of military activities for most of his life. Here we read about a few exceptions. One was his capture of **Hamath Zobah**, a name that we should probably interpret as "Hamath, bordering on Zobah." Back when David had rolled off his string of victories over his neighbors, Tou, the king of Hamath, had submitted to David and agreed to pay tribute without a fight (1 Chr. 18:9–10). Now, maybe because Hamath was rebelling against Israel's domination, Solomon took this town forcibly.

Tadmor would have been the apple of any king's eye. Known in subsequent history as Palmyra, it was a desert oasis positioned about halfway along the main road between Damascus and Mesopotamia. Whoever controlled Tadmor was able to control the trade caravans along this route. Solomon took over this strategic spot and fortified it. He also reinforced certain storage facilities that he had established in Hamath. Thus, Solomon was able to dominate trade to the north and east.

Since Jerusalem is located on top of a mountain, an important aspect of its defense, right into the twentieth century, has been to control the road leading up to it. As recently as 1947, the British military attempted to isolate the Jewish population of Jerusalem by preventing any Jewish vehicles from traveling up the mountain. Solomon recognized the importance of fortifying not just the city but the way up to the city as well, so he built up two towns along the way: **Upper Beth Heron** and **Lower Beth Heron.**

Also on the list of fortifications was **Baalath**, whose location is not certain. Furthermore, Solomon built powerful defenses for all his towns and storage facilities. The phrase, **whatever he desired,** conveys to us Solomon's great resources and the peaceful conditions that made it possible for him to apply these funds.

8:7–10. During the temple-building project (2 Chr. 2:2,17–18), Solomon had begun the policy of conscripting aliens, or foreign residents of Judah, as slave labor to do all the hard work on his building projects, and he continued it. The Israelites were not put to use in the same way, but they were supervisors, soldiers, and commanders. This must have been Solomon's procedure for most of his reign, but toward the end of his life, he deviated from it. This caused the Israelites to rebel against his successor, Rehoboam (2 Chr. 10:4).

He did not enslave his fellow countrymen, but by the time of his death, he had imposed mandatory heavy labor on them.

8:11. Chronicles does not enumerate Solomon's many marriages (seven hundred according to 1 Kgs. 11:3) or the trouble they caused him by turning him away from the Lord. Many of these women were of foreign birth, and it was against the command of the Lord for Israelites to marry Gentiles (Deut. 7:3) because they would cause the apostasy of their husbands. This is exactly what happened with Solomon (1 Kgs. 11:6).

The chronicler highlights Solomon's commitment to the holiness of the ark of the covenant. The king built a separate palace for his wife, Pharaoh's daughter, outside the regular precincts of Jerusalem lest, as an idol worshiper, she might defile any places that had been in contact with the ark. Solomon may have practiced the obligations of the law, but his heart was no longer zealous for the Lord.

8:12–15. Solomon never missed any of the sacrifices he was supposed to bring, and he observed all the festivals as they came around monthly or annually. In light of what we know about Solomon, this is not surprising, but it is significant because it provides a contrast to what would happen over the next several hundred years. Sometimes no festivals were observed for a generation, and a new dedication to the Lord would take place in conjunction with a particular holiday. This is what happened during the celebration of Passover as a part of King Hezekiah's revival (2 Chr. 30:5). Solomon also was diligent in following David's plan for the different divisions of priests and Levites with their various shifts of duty.

8:16. This verse is important for understanding the point of what the chronicler is telling us. There is one reality that remains fundamental—that Solomon was the temple builder. Ultimately anything the king did can be tied back to the fact that he built the temple. Even though Solomon's life may have become shallow, and his observation of the law perfunctory, God continued to bless him because he was the temple builder and the bearer of God's covenant promise.

8:17–18. The cities of **Elath** and **Ezion Geber** were situated at the very tip of the Red Sea on the Gulf of Aqabah. This location has always served as an important opening for world trade out of Palestine. This has persisted into our day, though the opening of the Suez Canal in 1869 has made it less important. Until the canal provided a waterway directly from the Mediterranean Sea to the Red Sea, as close as these two bodies of water were geographically, there was no direct way for ships to connect from one to the other.

Thus, the only way a ship from the Mediterranean Sea could get to southern Asia was by sailing around the Cape of Good Hope at the tip of Africa, and it is a matter of conjecture about whether ships could have done so back then. Consequently, it was more efficient to maintain a port on the Red Sea. From there ships could sail to the southern parts of the Arabian Peninsula and pick up goods that had come by way of the trade routes from India, or they could even sail to India if they were willing to venture out from the Red Sea into the Indian Ocean.

Phoenicia, of course, was located on the Mediterranean Sea with no access to the Red Sea. But this fact did not stand in King Hiram's way of maintaining active sea trade with Arabia. With one of those contracts in which he specialized, Hiram managed to get into the Red Sea market with Solomon. Hiram would supply the ships and the officers; Solomon would supply the overhead, the laborers, and the seaport access at Ezion Geber. Solomon profited in the amount of 450 talents (or about 17 tons) of gold from the South Arabian kingdom of Ophir as the ships started to make regular runs down the Red Sea.

🅑 The Queen of Sheba (9:1–12)

SUPPORTING IDEA: *The visit from the queen of Sheba high-lighted all of Solomon's wisdom and splendor.*

9:1–4. During his reign Solomon received visits from many heads of state, but none has left the legendary aura of the visit from the mysterious queen of Sheba. "Sheba" most likely refers to the South Arabian kingdom of Saba, which was located in what is now Yemen. It was a transit station for trade from the eastern "horn" of Africa (Ethiopia) and western South Asia (India). Furthermore, Saba had its own industry that produced the highly desirable incense and myrrh (the items that the magi brought to Jesus, Matt. 2:11). This kingdom was able to profit significantly, and it had become wealthy and influential. Archaeologists are now unearthing splendid structures from Saba that may have existed during the time of Solomon.

Most scholars speculate that in coming to see Solomon, the queen may have wished to establish some trade arrangements because the maritime partnership between Solomon and Hiram may have impacted her balance sheets negatively. But most also agree that there must have been more to the visit than economic interests. The text does not mention any commercial intentions and specifies that she came to test the king **with hard questions**. This is also the assessment confirmed by Jesus when he said that the queen came "to listen to Solomon's wisdom" (Matt. 12:42; Luke 11:31).

Of course, she did not come empty-handed but brought many camel loads of spices along with gold and precious stones. If she had any intention of astounding the king with her fabulous presents, she was in for a surprise because the effect went the other way: **She was overwhelmed** by Solomon's wealth.

The queen observed the imposing temple rituals that Solomon performed. Most importantly, though, she found all the wisdom and knowledge that she had looked for in Solomon. We do not know what her questions were; obviously she had not traveled all that distance just to stump the king with clever riddles, but she must have wanted to discuss important issues of life and faith with Solomon. It is probably safe to assume that some of his answers to her are reflected in the books of Proverbs and Ecclesiastes.

9:5–8. When the queen of Sheba had verified for herself all the splendor of Solomon's life, she made a speech in which she praised him effusively. She mentioned that word of Solomon's greatness had made its way to her kingdom, but the reports did not even come close to the truth. More than anything else, she was impressed by Solomon's wisdom. Remember that the wisdom Solomon had sought, which was granted by God, was the wisdom necessary to govern the great empire he inherited (2 Chr. 1:10). So the queen saw Solomon's wisdom displayed not only in conversations with him but also in the way he conducted his affairs of state. Consequently, Solomon's wisdom translated into happiness for his people, as he upheld justice and righteousness.

The queen had also learned where the credit for Solomon's success should go—to God, who had established Solomon as king. It was God who had placed Solomon **on his throne**, and he had done so because of his delight in Solomon and his great love for Israel. The queen even realized that it was his—God's—throne. She witnessed the reality of God in the life of Solomon and the people of Israel. Solomon apparently did a good job of declaring the truths of God to her.

9:9–12. The king and the queen exchanged lavish presents. She gave him gold and jewels as well as Asian spices. In our day spices line our supermarket shelves and cosmetics are as easy to buy as vegetables. It is difficult for us to realize how valuable a little packet of cinnamon or a tiny jar of myrrh were in ancient times. Solomon gave the queen everything she requested along with so many additional items that she left with her camels loaded even more than when she had arrived.

The chronicler pauses to insert a quick progress report on how the trade partnership of Hiram and Solomon was coming along, and the news was good. Solomon's treasury was swelling with an influx of gold from Ophir along with valuable timber and precious stones. The wood went into steps for the temple and for Solomon's palace. The king also saw to it that the wood was used for musical instruments of high quality.

ⓒ Solomon's Wealth (9:13–28)

SUPPORTING IDEA: *The Lord blessed Solomon with great wealth, but the king engaged in activities that were contrary to God's standards for the ruler of Israel.*

9:13–14. The 666 talents of gold that Solomon reckoned as his annual income equaled about 25 tons. But he actually received even more as a result of trade and tribute.

9:15–16. Solomon came up with an ingenious method of storing his gold so it was accessible and could be put on display. He had his workmen form the gold into shields in two different sizes—two hundred large shields and three hundred medium shields—and hang them up in a building called the "Palace of the Forest of Lebanon" (1 Kgs. 7:2). This house was one of several structures that made up the elaborate complex of Solomon's palace.

9:17–19. King Solomon also put his creativity to work in the design of a new throne, which was tall enough to require six steps leading up to it. Obviously, one would not want the king to sit in such a tall chair with his feet dangling in the air, so there was a footrest for his use. The main motif for the decorations was lions, with twelve lions flanking the steps and one pair sharing the armrests with the king. Except for the ivory inlay, everything was covered with gold.

9:20. In fact, virtually everything in the palace was made of gold, including wine goblets and utensils. Solomon did not have anything made of silver because silver was not considered as valuable as gold at that time.

9:21. As mentioned already (2 Chr. 8:17–18; 9:10–11), Solomon and Hiram were partners in sea trade. Solomon had assumed ownership of the ships, which went out on three-year voyages. When the ships returned, they brought back not only gold, silver, and ivory but also exotic animals, such as apes and baboons (some translators say "peacocks"), for the amusement of the king and his guests.

9:22–24. Solomon had achieved a global reputation. Everyone had heard of his wealth and wisdom, and many heads of state visited his kingdom to learn from him. And everyone who stopped in to admire Solomon's treasury contributed to it with some high-priced gifts.

9:25. Solomon's wealth continued to be expressed in how many horses and chariots he owned. Furthermore, they were stationed at strategic locations throughout the country as well as in Jerusalem.

9:26. Just as had been true under David, the extension of the land in Solomon's time conformed to the boundaries promised to Israel by God through Moses (Deut. 11:24)—from the Euphrates River to Egypt.

9:27. In this verse the chronicler reiterates the statement of 2 Chronicles 9:20 on how common silver was during Solomon's reign. Silver was as plentiful as rocks, and cedar wood was as available as wood from **sycamore-fig trees**.

9:28. The concluding statement on Solomon's wealth states that his horses were **imported from Egypt**. This short and innocuous-sounding phrase packs a powerful commentary. If nothing else had caught the attention of the ancient readers of Chronicles, this statement would have stood out in their minds. Anyone familiar with the law would have remembered the instructions, given about four hundred years earlier for any future king of Israel: "The king, moreover, must not acquire great numbers of horses for himself or make the people return to Egypt to get more of them" (Deut. 17:16). Solomon's practice of importing horses from Egypt violated the Lord's command.

Furthermore, the same passage in Deuteronomy passes judgment on the rest of Solomon's activities as well: "He must not take many wives, or his heart will be led astray. He must not accumulate large amounts of silver and gold" (Deut. 17:17).

So Solomon, the man whose name was synonymous with the temple, sacrifices, and careful observance of all his worship obligations, was spending his life disobeying God by hoarding gold and silver, assembling unparalleled mounted and chariot divisions for his army, and marrying pagan women. The king had fallen into a chronic state of disobedience to God.

God let Solomon carry on. He had committed himself to maintaining Solomon on the throne, and he continued to bless him because he would not relent on his promise to David. But it would not be long before Solomon's provisions were eliminated.

D Solomon's Death Notice (9:29–31)

SUPPORTING IDEA: Solomon's obituary in Chronicles contains no words of praise.

9:29–31. When we compare the summary of Solomon's death with David's (1 Chr. 29:26–30), we notice many similarities, such as the length of his reign (forty years) and further sources of information about him. But there were no words of commendation as there were for David and would be for Asa (2 Chr. 16:14), Jehoshaphat (20:32), and Hezekiah (32:33). A number of kings were explicitly vilified in their obituaries, such as Rehoboam (12:14), Jehoram (21:20), and Ahaz (28:27), but Solomon was also spared that dishonor. In the end, the summary of his life was a glaring, eye-stabbing neutral.

> **MAIN IDEA REVIEW:** *God blessed Solomon with great wealth and wisdom, and the king continued his outward observance of his temple obligations.*

III. CONCLUSION

Potemkin Villages

When Catherine the Great was empress of Russia, her field marshall, Grigory Potemkin, led the military effort to capture the Crimean Peninsula, which then belonged to the Turkish Empire. In 1787 Catherine decided to take a grand tour of the newly annexed territory. By that time Potemkin had taken over as administrator of the area, so he took charge of mapping out the empress's itinerary and making arrangements for her accommodations. It was a matter of great importance to Potemkin that Catherine would be highly impressed by the area, though it actually was choked by poverty. He preferred that she not see the villages consisting mostly of shacks in various stages of collapse and decay.

Potemkin did not have time to rebuild entire villages, so he hired workmen to construct facades of nice, clean, well-built village huts along the route of Catherine's journey. As she was floating down the river in the royal barge gazing at the countryside that was now a part of her realm, she admired all the lovely, productive villages along the way. She had no idea that she was only looking at large wooden boards, behind which lay a poverty-stricken world. The phrase "Potemkin village" has come to mean any elaborate sham intended to cover up some embarrassment or incompetence.

Like a Potemkin village, the devotion that Solomon manifested was external. While making his reputation as the wisest man in the world, his own life was heading in the wrong direction. He built up a colossal treasury, put together the world's largest chariot corps, and set a record for numbers of wives and concubines. He finally succumbed to the ultimate betrayal of God by building and sacrificing to an idol. But even then, there is no reason to believe that he skipped his sacrifices to God on the day he worshiped the idol.

Solomon was not a hypocrite in the sense of deliberately deceiving people about how pious he was. He was faithful in his commitments, and the fact that he authored several books of the Bible as well as two psalms attests to this. But Solomon was never able to get his act together to the point where his life outside the temple was faithful to God.

Like Solomon, our lives may have turned into "Potemkin villages." We may have attained a comfort level in our Christian existence and may be experiencing a certain level of prosperity. We may convey to the outside world that we are living a solid life and setting a standard for others. Still, on the inside we may be holding back, reserving areas of our lives that we do not want God to take over. Perhaps Solomon's life can help us face up to where we fall short.

But God did not abandon Solomon. This is where the "gospel according to Ezra" becomes so important. For Ezra, this was a story of the life of a weak man who fell short of God's standard and yet who always experienced God's blessing. And this good news applies to us as well. Throughout history God has worked with flawed instruments.

PRINCIPLES

- God fulfills his promises of providing blessings for his people.
- God uses our words and actions as a witness to his work of grace and redemption.
- We may have a testimony that seems flawless but still have parts of our lives that are not submitted to God's will.
- God expects us to hold nothing back in our commitment to him.
- God may use us in his work while we are in the process of being transformed by him.

APPLICATIONS

- Think about people you have known whom God has blessed with material blessings. What are the various responses people have to God's material blessings?
- What is the difference between a blessing and a reward?
- Ask God to make you the kind of person through whom his wisdom can be shown to others.

IV. LIFE APPLICATION

Running on Fumes

Have you ever put 18.2 gallons of gasoline in a tank that you thought could hold only 18 gallons? You knew you were "running on fumes," but you didn't know how empty the tank really was. You thanked God for the miracle of letting you make it to the gas station.

Are you running on "fumes"? Is your spiritual tank empty? Congratulations, you find yourself in the company of the wealthiest and wisest man in ancient history! Here was a man who seemed to have it all together. But when we take a close look, we find that his life was so turned around that his success was due to the grace of God alone.

This was the "gospel according to Ezra" about Solomon, and it is also part of the good news for us. The Holy Spirit is in the business of transforming the lives of God's children, and he may deal with you severely while he is leading you to obedience. There is no room for playing games with God.

However, God deals with us as his children. It is precisely because of the relationship he has established with us by his own initiative that he places us in situations that demand our growth. Do not let Satan trick you into thinking that God has given up on you! "If we are faithless, he will remain faithful, for he cannot disown himself" (2 Tim. 2:13).

V. PRAYER

Lord Jesus, we come to you torn in two directions. We see Solomon's wisdom and riches, recognizing that they are your blessing to him, and we know that we will never own anything like that. We also see how shallow Solomon could be in his devotion to you, and here we see ourselves in a mirror. Lord, please remind us of your assurance that, even as we may be struggling in our faith, that you will not let go of us any more than you gave up on Solomon. Amen.

VI. DEEPER DISCOVERIES

A. The Queen of Sheba (9:1)

There are innumerable stories about the queen of Sheba. The Old Testament gives us just enough information to fuel the fires of imagination, and so this mysterious woman has been invoked by many people to endow themselves with a link to Solomon and the ancient kingdom of Israel, or simply to serve as a focal point for romantic stories.

Perhaps the best-known appropriation of the queen of Sheba has been in the country of Ethiopia, ancient Abyssinia. According to this tradition, the queen's name was Makeda, and Abyssinia was her home country. During her stay in Jerusalem, she had a liaison with King Solomon and found herself pregnant with Menelik, who turned out to be her only child. As an adult, Menelik paid a visit to Solomon; and when he left, he did so in the company of a group of Jewish men who contrived to take the ark of the covenant with them to Abyssinia.

Thus, according to this legend, from this time on the ark and the tablets of the Ten Commandments have been concealed in the ancient Ethiopian city of Axum. The kingdom of David and Solomon was now officially transferred to Abyssinia, the new Zion, and the throne of David actually continued to be passed on through the royal line of Menelik, Solomon's true heir. It did not come to an end until Haile Selassie, the 225th emperor in this succession, died in 1975.

Even though this story has served as the national saga of Ethiopia for a long time, there are some problems with it, not the least of which is the fact that the ark was still in Jerusalem during King Josiah's time (2 Chr. 35:3), three hundred years after Solomon's reign. Other traditional claims, such as locations for the kingdom of Sheba in Zimbabwe or Nigeria, can also be understood as a product of the natural instinct of people to find their own country as the centerpiece of an ancient legend.

The most credible theory is that Saba was an ancient kingdom in southern Arabia, roughly the territory occupied by modern Yemen. In fact, this theory enjoys some backing from archaeology as well as legend. There is a story preserved in the Qur'an, the holy book of Islam, referring to the queen of Sheba—located in southern Arabia—and her negotiations with Solomon, which finally resulted in her visit. Archaeological discoveries made from the 1980s on are demonstrating the existence of the ancient kingdom of Saba.

According to the Arabian tradition, the queen was named Bilqis or Balqis. She ruled over a powerful kingdom. The economic success of Saba in trade and in the incense industry produced a high culture with fortified cities that boasted multistoried houses, all of which have long since vanished in the sands of the desert. Archaeologists are currently unearthing the remains of a splendid capital city, for which the biggest points of attraction so far are a beautiful temple and an imposing throne room—structures worthy of someone with the reputation of the fabulous queen. And the date for these once-glorious edifices? The tenth century B.C.—exactly the time of Solomon.

B. Ancient Trade Routes and Israel (8:4)

By taking control of the territory on the outer edges of the empire, David and Solomon could claim ownership of the land to the full extent that God had promised. They were also able to exert great influence on nations around them by regulating trade and military routes.

The traditional name for the civilizations of the Ancient Middle East is the "fertile crescent," derived from the shape created by joining Mesopotamia and Egypt by way of Palestine. We now know that things were a lot more complex when this term was first coined. We are now aware of great cultures in Asia Minor and southern Arabia as well, so the "crescent" has become an X. At the center point of this X was the Mediterranean coastal area and the cultures that existed there.

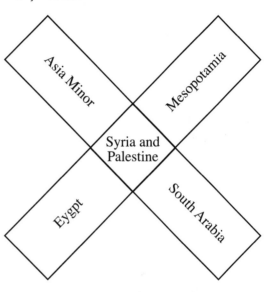

Kings needed roads for their armies. But perhaps even more importantly, roads were needed so traders could move their goods. Even a king at war wanted his commodities, particularly metals for armaments, so it was to everyone's benefit to maintain trade routes.

There were two north-south connections going through Solomon's empire. The first one was along the Mediterranean seacoast. Under the Romans, this highway became known as the *via maris*, the "way of the sea." The second road was on the eastern side of the Jordan River. Known as the "king's highway," this was the route along which the Israelites traveled when they went up from the desert to the place opposite Jericho where they crossed the Jordan River into Canaan (Num. 20:17).

Jerusalem stayed in communication with the rest of the world by means of a road leading up from Joppa. This was the way the lumber from Phoenicia was carried once the rafts had landed at this seaport, and Solomon went to great pains to maintain its security. It also connected with the *via maris*.

One of the most significant trade routes in Solomon's day was the road leading from Damascus to Mesopotamia. Later on, this highway became known as the "incense road" because the incense trade went up from south Arabia into Mesopotamia and from there over to the Mediterranean coastlands. Nevertheless, this thoroughfare was used for all types of trade between Syrio-Palestine and whoever the dominant power in Mesopotamia happened to be at the moment: Assyria, Babylon, or Persia. Solomon exercised control over Tadmor, a crucial station along this route, and, consequently, he could dictate his terms for transactions in international commerce (2 Chr. 1:17).

As soon as the Israelite empire fell apart, control over the trade routes was one of the first things to go. The king's highway and the incense road reverted to the control of other nations. In fact, Tadmor eventually became a power known as Palmyra. And sadly, the *via maris* became the expressway for Israel's enemies to enter their land.

VII. TEACHING OUTLINE

A. INTRODUCTION

1. Lead Story: The Midas Touch

2. Context: After building the temple and his palace, King Solomon continued to enlarge his wealth and influence. God was blessing Solomon, but the king's devotion to God was more external than heartfelt.

3. Transition: Just as the legendary King Midas turned everything he touched to gold, so King Solomon was able to succeed in all his projects. The greatest affirmation of his wisdom and wealth came when the queen of Sheba paid him a visit.

B. COMMENTARY

1. Solomon's Success (8:1–18)
2. The Queen of Sheba (9:1–12)
3. Solomon's Wealth (9:13–28)
4. Solomon's Death Notice (9:29–31)

C. CONCLUSION: POTEMKIN VILLAGES

VIII. ISSUES FOR DISCUSSION

1. To what extent should Christians understand their worldly success as a blessing from God? To what extent should they construe it as a reward for their devotion to the Lord?
2. How should Christians react when they find that someone who is outwardly devoted to the Lord is attempting to overcome a sin in his or her life? In what ways is Matthew 18:15–17 applicable?
3. The queen of Sheba learned some important lessons from Solomon by observing his court and his sacrifices. What are equivalent things people could see in our lives that would help them learn about the Lord?

2 Chronicles 10:1–12:16

Whoosh Goes the Empire!

Quote

"For all things were made out of nothing, and their being would again go into nothing except the Author of all things held it by the hand of governance."

G r e g o r y   t h e   G r e a t

2 Chronicles 10:1–12:16

I N   A   N U T S H E L L

Solomon's successor, his son Rehoboam, first lost most of the kingdom because of his poor decisions, and then he lost most of Solomon's treasures because of his unbelief. This story illustrates how much everything we are and have is dependent on God's will.

Whoosh Goes the Empire!

I. INTRODUCTION

Game Over!

$\mathcal{W}$hen I was a boy, the board game Monopoly was just as popular in Germany as it was in the United States, though the names of the streets were different, and the play currency was marks, not dollars. The German game, just like its American counterpart, consisted of the players acquiring real estate and attempting to build their wealth by charging their opponents rent as they landed on their property. Different streets had different values. Building houses, or even hotels, would increase the amount of rent you could collect from your opponent. My older brother and I played the game ferociously.

I remember one particular game when we had bought up all the properties and were adding buildings where we could. My brother had managed to take possession of the two most expensive streets (the dark blue fields corresponding to Park Place and Broadway in the American game) and had put up hotels on both. Landing on one or the other would drive me into bankruptcy. Luckily, I avoided them for several rounds.

Slowly the game moved along, with both of us circling the board, passing "go" and collecting salaries, paying rent and amassing rent in small amounts, neither of us gaining any serious financial ground. But then the inevitable happened, and I landed on a dark blue street. With one roll of the dice, I lost all my resources, and my brother won the game.

This was the reality Rehoboam had to deal with. He had inherited one of the most splendid kingdoms of his day. The borders were secure, the people were unified, the treasury was overflowing, and the army was well equipped. But it did not take Rehoboam long to lose all of that. He did not even make it through his coronation ceremony unscathed. Before Rehoboam had even officially become king, he had already lost most of his kingdom. Then, because of Rehoboam's failure to live according to God's commandments, God sent Pharaoh Shishak from Egypt with a mighty army, devastating the land, carrying off Solomon's treasures, and stopping just short of destroying Jerusalem and the temple. Whoosh! There went the empire!

II. COMMENTARY

Whoosh Goes the Empire!

MAIN IDEA: *Under the rule of Rehoboam, the kingdom of David and Solomon fell apart, both internally and externally. Without God's sustaining hand, the united kingdom was doomed.*

In these chapters we enter a new unit in Chronicles. After the history leading up to David, consisting mostly of genealogies, we had lengthy sections on the reigns of David and Solomon. Now we begin the fourth section, a history of the kings of Judah. No king gets as lengthy a treatment as David and Solomon did, and most of what follows, with a few exceptions, is in narrative style. There will be few lengthy lists.

Second Chronicles differs significantly from 1 and 2 Kings because it focuses specifically on the kings of the Southern Kingdom, Judah. Whereas 1 and 2 Kings alternate between the two kingdoms, in 2 Chronicles the northern kings of Israel appear only if they have direct relevance to a southern king, and there are a number of unexplained references to the Northern Kingdom. Presumably, the chronicler assumed that his readers already knew about the situations, so he did not include them in his narrative.

Remember that the chronicler's purpose was to demonstrate the continuity between the returned exiles living in Jerusalem and God's people in former days. The history of the northern tribes could not help with this purpose since they had long ago severed themselves from Jerusalem and the temple. But a survey of the southern kings, their struggles with God, and their relationship to the temple would provide the link that the people in Ezra's day needed in order to reconnect with God's plan.

A Rehoboam Squanders the Kingdom (10:1–19)

SUPPORTING IDEA: *Rehoboam made a bad decision that caused the northern tribes to secede from his kingdom.*

10:1–5. Rehoboam, forty-one years old (2 Chr. 12:13), was his father Solomon's designated successor, and theoretically this decision was a foregone conclusion. Only a ceremony of acclamation by representatives of all the tribes was needed to make it official. Rehoboam traveled to Shechem in Ephraim to take care of this detail.

But why hold the ceremony in Ephraim? Remember how the tribal representatives came to David in Hebron (1 Chr. 11:1). Solomon certainly did not travel a day's journey out of Jerusalem in order to become king (1 Kgs. 2:11).

The location of the proposed ceremony alerts us that something was amiss; the people of Israel were not going to take Rehoboam's rule for granted.

As soon as word of the impending ceremony reached Jeroboam, an opponent of Solomon who had served in Solomon's administration, he went to work on behalf of the people. A few years earlier the prophet Abijah had told Jeroboam that he would become king over the ten northern tribes. He then spent the rest of Solomon's reign in exile under Pharaoh Shishak. Clearly, he was a well-recognized figure, even while he was in exile (see 1 Kgs. 11:26–40). Otherwise, he would not have been called on to speak for the northern tribes, let alone have been offered the crown as soon as Rehoboam was rejected.

Jeroboam came to Rehoboam with a request on behalf of the Israelites who had been put to work by Solomon. Even though it was against Solomon's policy to make slaves of Israelites (2 Chr. 8:9), he had resorted to labor conscription by the end of his reign. So Jeroboam made what seemed to be an innocuous petition: "Please lighten up on the work! Solomon was extremely demanding. We're willing to go on working for you, but please cut down on the expectations."

Apparently everyone except Rehoboam understood that this simple request was much more than that: it was an ultimatum. Jeroboam made its fulfillment a condition of submitting to the new king. He asked Rehoboam to lighten the load, **and we will serve you.** For Rehoboam the question simply was on whose terms Rehoboam would be king: his or the people's. The idea that if he would not give in to the demand they might not want him to be king apparently did not occur to him. So, wanting to ponder the alternatives, Rehoboam called for a three-day recess and sought advice.

10:6–11. "Good advice is cheap," according to the proverb, but bad advice costs just as little up front, and often the quality control does not set in until it is too late. To his credit Rehoboam consulted as many people as he could about this request from the northern tribes.

Unfortunately he heeded the wrong people. The older corps of advisors, who had accrued years of experience under Solomon, recognized that this was an opportunity for Rehoboam to gain the favor of the people whom he was supposed to serve as king. If he made a gesture of accommodation now, the people would love him, and his position as king would be assured.

However, there was a second group of advisors—Rehoboam's own contemporaries, the playmates of his childhood days. These people were now a collection of minor functionaries in their forties who were anxious to make something of their lives. Their advice went in the opposite direction. Now was the time to crack down on any discontent, they told the king. There was no room for concessions; if the king showed weakness now, the demands would never end. With the cleverness typical of someone oblivious to the seriousness of a situation, they even made up a cute little saying for the king to recite. The new king's little finger would be as large in diameter as the old one's waist. He would appear as a giant compared to his father Solomon. He would make their yoke even heavier, and the punishment for not working would be scorpions—vicious whips with nails tied into the thongs.

10:12–14. When the three days had elapsed, the conclave reconvened with Jeroboam again serving as popular spokesman. Rehoboam decided to follow the advice of his young friends, and he made the obnoxious speech they had coached him into.

10:15. Just when we are ready to decry Rehoboam and the wrongheaded decision he made, the chronicler reminds us of an important fact. All of this was preordained. This was exactly the prophecy that Abijah had made to Jeroboam when he told Jeroboam that he would become king over the ten tribes. God had wanted this to happen because it was Solomon's punishment for his disobedience to God (1 Kgs. 11:13). Rehoboam was thickheaded, to be sure, but God used the king's stubbornness to bring about the consequence the Lord had ordained.

10:16–19. The outcome of this episode could not have been surprising to anyone but Rehoboam and his misguided friends. In an eerie way the chant taken up by the people echoed the acclamation of David seventy-three years earlier. Back then their forebears had said, "You are our own flesh and blood." Now they went in the opposite direction: **What share do we have in David, what part in Jesse's son?** In short, the house of David had no claim on the tribes of Israel, and they rejected his son's claim to rule over them. Not mentioned by the chronicler but assumed is the fact that before the people departed they made Jeroboam king over them (1 Kgs. 12:20). Only the tribe of Judah (and its affiliate Benjamin) remained loyal to Rehoboam.

Rehoboam was not willing to let things rest. He decided to force the people into submission, and he did so by sending after them the worst possible person for the job: the supervisor of forced labor, a man named Adoniram. The people, who had only expressed their discontentment verbally until now, had the chance to say it with rocks, and they did so forcefully. Adoniram lost his life, and Rehoboam, barely escaping with his, rushed back to the safety of Jerusalem.

𝔹 Rehoboam Settles In (11:1–23)

SUPPORTING IDEA: *After refraining from going to war with Israel, Rehoboam established the kingdom of Judah.*

11:1–4. Rehoboam's reaction was natural for any monarch who had just been snubbed by two-thirds of his people. He called up a large army, 180,000 strong, and made preparations to invade the north in order to reunite his kingdom. But this was not what God wanted. As we saw in the last chapter, these events were ultimately God's own doing. So the Lord sent another prophet, a man named Shemaiah, to command Rehoboam to turn back from his military campaign. Rehoboam obeyed, the army disbanded, and everyone went home, but the kingdom was permanently divided. From this point on, there would be two kingdoms. The northern kingdom was called Israel, and the southern kingdom went by the name of Judah.

The two kingdoms would never get back together again. In fact, an occasional military or marriage alliance was the closest the kingdoms would come to each other. Of the two, Israel was less stable, became more confirmed in idolatry, and was carried into exile earlier than Judah.

11:5–12. Adapting to the new situation, Rehoboam made sure that his new, smaller kingdom would be secure. He set about fortifying cities in a number of smaller towns in a perimeter around Jerusalem. Note that Gath, traditionally a Philistine city, was among the places mentioned. Most of these towns were not considered necessary for defense purposes during Solomon's reign. But now certain towns and cities found themselves on the edge of the kingdom or as strategic focal points in the new territory of Judah.

Rehoboam made sure that each of these towns was well prepared. Each received its contingency personnel, provisions, and a generously stocked armory. Thus, Rehoboam confirmed that he was solidly in control of the kingdom left to him.

11:13–17. Since the chronicler throughout his book wishes to remind us of the importance of the temple worship and the people responsible for it, he now emphasizes the faithfulness of the Levites in this time of national crisis. Jeroboam had turned the political issue into a religious one as well. Or, more accurately, he recognized the religious angle of the political question.

Jeroboam realized that if he wanted his new kingdom to survive, he had to endow it with its own religious centers. What good would it do to carve out impenetrable borders if the people crossed into Jerusalem three times a year to observe the festivals? Could he ever command the loyalty of his subjects if they could go to the temple any time they felt the need to sacrifice and be exposed to anti-Jeroboam propaganda? How would he maintain an independent realm if its religious backbone was supplied by a class of priests and Levites who were loyal to the temple in Jerusalem (1 Kgs. 12:25–33)?

So Jeroboam created his own new religion, modeled loosely after the worship of God, but with some major modifications. He established two new sanctuaries, conveniently located on the northern border (Dan) and close to the southern border (Bethel) of his kingdom, so that all Israelites would have easy access to religious sites without having to go to Jerusalem. He also insisted that his religion would not tax the people's intellect with the idea of some kind of invisible God hidden behind an impenetrable curtain. Jeroboam gave his grateful citizens gods they could see and touch, gods with a historical heritage. He made for them two golden calves, one for each location, reminding them perhaps of the ancient Israelite tradition of worshiping a golden calf (Exod. 32:1–6).

Joining these calves were goats, idols that may have looked like satyrs—creatures with horns and tails. In order to take away the incentive for a pilgrimage to Jerusalem, Jeroboam invented a new festival, designated for the fifteenth day of the eighth month, exactly one month after the Feast of Booths, when everyone would come to Bethel or Dan to celebrate.

Most importantly for the chronicler's purpose, Jeroboam dismissed the Levitical priesthood and replaced it with a corps of men who felt called to a religious vocation in service to calf and goat idols. These new priests would be loyal to the king and not clutter the heads of the people with ideas about the importance of Jerusalem and the temple.

Ezra, the chronicler, does not dwell on Jeroboam and his subsequent fate. It is obvious that Jeroboam's encounter with the prophet Abijah was not an event that focused the rest of his life on service to the Lord. Jeroboam must have seen this encounter as no more significant than a meeting with a religious crank. Although Abijah had spoken some words in support of Jeroboam, the king's national policy was to undermine the service of the true God.

Still, we read in 1 Kings 14:1–18 about how Jeroboam sent his wife to plead for help from Abijah, a prophet, when his son was seriously ill. The seer told her that God was judging Jeroboam for his flagrant provocations of the Lord. The child died before the queen made it home, just as the prophet predicted.

The chronicler, however, emphasizes how the Levites rallied to the support of Rehoboam. All over the Northern Kingdom they packed their belongings; said farewell to their homes, their lands, and their communities; and migrated to Jerusalem, where they could continue to practice their calling in service to God. Obviously, their cooperation was a great boost for Rehoboam's attempt to build a strong empire. However, the chronicler places a time limit on this state of affairs; it only lasted three years. After that, Rehoboam began to waver from the true faith as well.

11:18–23. Rehoboam's efforts to solidify his government also included regulating his family's standing in his kingdom. Solomon's errors notwithstanding, Rehoboam had multiple wives as well, although he limited himself to eighteen. Of these, two were considered the most important, and of those two, one was his favorite.

Rehoboam's second most favorite wife was Mahalath, a cousin with several bloodline connections. Her father was his uncle, Solomon's previously unmentioned brother Jerimoth. But also, her mother—Abihail—was the daughter of his grandfather David's brother Eliab. So Rehoboam married heavily into his own family, and three sons were the offspring of this union.

Administratively, Rehoboam made a wise decision with regard to his sons. He had probably learned from firsthand experience how frustrating it was to live in the palace as a prince, year in and year out, with nothing to do except wait to become king. So he gave each of his sons a position as district administrator of some part of his kingdom.

Ⓒ Rehoboam's Sin and Its Consequences (12:1–12)

SUPPORTING IDEA: *Rehoboam forsook the ways of the Lord, but Jerusalem was saved from annihilation when the king repented.*

12:1. Rehoboam, who had confronted the people earlier when they came to him with a legitimate request, showed no backbone in dealing with idolatry in the land. After just a few short years, everyone from the king on down began practicing idolatry, including the explicit sexual rituals of Canaanite religion (1 Kgs. 14:23–24). It was Rehoboam's duty to make sure that the nation remained true to God; instead, he not only tolerated idolatry; he practiced it himself.

12:2–4. The Bible sometimes compresses long stories into a few words, and this is certainly true here. First of all, we read that God punished the people by means of a military conquest **because they had been unfaithful to the LORD.** This event is presented as a natural outcome, the effect inevitably resulting from its cause. The people had violated God's law; therefore, punishment by foreign invasion was the result. God was faithful to his warnings, just as he was faithful to his promises.

Second, we see that Egypt was on the scene as an active participant in world politics again. David and Solomon's empire had been possible because the traditional superpowers of the times, Egypt and Mesopotamia, were preoccupied with matters closer to home. Now this arrangement changed. Egypt, under its new pharaoh Shishak, had been consolidated, and a new, stable dynasty was on the throne. Most likely, the pharaoh who had made a marriage alliance with Solomon was Shishak's predecessor (2 Chr. 8:11), whom Shishak deposed, since Shishak showed himself hostile to Jerusalem right from the start.

Third, what enormous calamity and devastation is packed into the expression **he captured the fortified cities of Judah**! We are forced to ask why Rehoboam's splendid fortifications did not hold back Shishak. What happened to Solomon's great building projects with walled cities and reinforced roads? Where was the army? What happened to the horses and the chariots? We are only a few years removed from Solomon's death, so his provisions should still have been in place. But against Shishak's enormous army, composed of troops from all over North Africa, they did not stand a chance. Shishak just came in and took it all. Game over.

12:5–8. Well, it was not quite over. There was one city left that Shishak had not taken—Jerusalem. However, it seemed only a matter of time before Jerusalem would fall before Shishak's unrelenting force. At this point, **the prophet Shemaiah**, the same one who had told Rehoboam to abandon any plans of invading the north, arranged for an audience with the king. His assignment was to ensure that Rehoboam understood exactly what was happening.

Shemaiah declared God's message in simple, straightforward terms: **You have abandoned me; therefore, I now abandon you to Shishak.** There was nothing ambiguous in that statement. Rehoboam's sin had resulted in his loss of everything. He had ruled at God's pleasure, and now the Lord was withdrawing his support.

Once again Ezra the chronicler shares with us the remarkable gospel around which his chronicle is built. The king and all his officials **humbled themselves**. They admitted that **the LORD is just**. Rehoboam and his company openly admitted their guilt. And God accepted their repentance. Jerusalem would not be destroyed.

Nevertheless, this reprieve did not mean that God would not use this situation to teach a serious lesson. Rehoboam was not just going to sit there unscathed after the rest of his kingdom had been trampled by Lybian boots and Egyptian chariot wheels. Rehoboam had to submit to the pharaoh; this humiliating act would have taken place as a gesture of self-effacement in which the king would pose as dirt beneath the pharaoh's feet. And then Rehoboam had to watch as the treasures of the temple were carried off to Egypt. The lesson was obvious: follow God and enjoy success as king or debase himself before a pagan tyrant.

12:9–12. Once again the Bible states in simple, compressed terms what was an incredible tragedy. Shishak allowed the temple to stand, but he carted off everything in the temple and the royal palace that was not permanently attached. Just a few chapters ago, we read about all the wealth that Solomon had accumulated and the treasures he had placed in the temple and his palace. Now Rehoboam had to bid them all good-bye. The golden bowls, cups, tongs, plates—everything was carted off. Even the large and medium-sized shields of gold, the centers of attraction in the palace of the cedars of Lebanon, were loaded up and sent south. The national treasury was emptied.

Rehoboam's reaction to the loss of the shields was poignant, although we need to remember that they had been a permanent decoration in the house he had grown up in. He replaced them with shields of bronze, which were far less valuable than the gold shields. Then he established a new set of security precautions. The new shields were kept in a safe place under the direct supervision of his soldiers and brought out to public view only to accompany the king when he went to the temple. As soon as the king's appearance with the shields was over, they would be placed under lock and key again. Maybe Rehoboam was giving himself and the people a visible reminder of how fleeting material wealth can be.

There was no question about the meaning of these events. Rehoboam had suffered punishment for his sins, but he had repented, and God had spared him the worst. As a matter of fact, the chronicler makes the cryptic observation that **there was some good in Judah.** In other words, not everyone had forsaken the Lord, and presumably many people had returned to him in the aftermath of the invasion.

Ⓓ Summary and Death Notice (12:13–16)

SUPPORTING IDEA: *In his final evaluation, Rehoboam receives some bad marks, but overall his reign is assessed in neutral terms.*

12:13–16. Just as we have seen with David and Solomon, and as we shall continue to see with the kings of Judah, the final evaluation for Rehoboam is packaged loosely with the standard obituary. This section mentions his age (forty-one) when he came to the throne and his total years of ruling as king (seventeen), which was far shorter than the tenure of either Saul, David, or Solomon. We learn that his mother's name was Naamah and that she was an Ammonite by birth, one of Solomon's many Gentile wives. Could it be that

Rehoboam's tendency toward idolatry, which manifested itself so early in his reign, was the result of influences from his mother long ago?

Rehoboam's report card comes out on the negative side: **He did evil because he had not set his heart on seeking the LORD.** We do not know anything about Rehoboam's religious life prior to his becoming king, although it seems a safe bet that he had received a good dose of divine truth along with Solomon's tolerant pluralism.

Finally, there is no way for us to verify how sincere Rehoboam was after his repentance due to Shishak's invasion. The upshot is that, quite possibly, the time span when Rehoboam was living according to God's law may have been just a few years at the beginning and end of his reign.

The political legacy of Rehoboam's reign was the permanent split between Israel and Judah. Rehoboam and his rival, Jeroboam, never ceased hostilities with each other, although God prevented them from invading each other's lands.

Finally, the specific references to Rehoboam's death are neutral. He died (**rested with his fathers**) and received the proper burial **in the City of David.** Even though this statement may sound quite innocuous, not every king who would die in the future would be permitted even this much recognition. Rehoboam's legacy was negative, leaving behind a divided kingdom, a depleted treasury, and a permissive attitude toward idolatry. Under some kings, things would get even worse, but some would undo Rehoboam's damage—for a time.

> **MAIN IDEA REVIEW:** Under the rule of Rehoboam, the kingdom of David and Solomon fell apart, both internally and externally. Without God's sustaining hand, the united kingdom was doomed.

III. CONCLUSION

The Trojan Horse

In her book *The March of Folly,* historian Barbara Tuchman wrote about people and governments who were so blinded by their desires that they perpetrated self-destructive policies or decisions. One of her first cases was the story of Rehoboam who alienated his own subjects needlessly and lost most of his kingdom in the process. Another example she used was the myth of the Trojan horse.

According to the story, there had been a siege of the ancient city of Troy by the combined Greek forces in order to liberate Helen of Troy. After ten years of tenacious fighting, the Greeks still had not attained their objective;

the Trojans were able to withstand their onslaughts. The gods of Greek mythology supposedly were taking sides in the conflict as well, but even they could not provoke a decisive blow.

Then the Greeks came up with a ruse that would gain with craftiness what had been impossible through power and weaponry. They made it appear as though they were giving up by loading their ships and moving them out of sight. However, they actually remained in hiding and built a huge wooden horse that was hollow on the inside. They crammed a number of Greek soldiers into this horse and set it on wheels. Then they placed it in front of the city gate of Troy and waited.

In the morning the Trojan guards opened the gate and saw this oversized horse parked in front of their gate. They notified the city fathers, who identified it as a gift that the Greeks had left as an offering to the gods. Eager Trojans rolled it into the city, and everyone began a party in its honor that lasted into the next night.

Finally the last person had placed the last garland on the horse's neck, proposed the last toast in celebration of its arrival, and made the last speech to point out how favored the Trojan people were to receive such a divine gift at the end of the siege. Then, after everyone had gone home, the warriors inside the horse let themselves out, unlocked the city gate, and admitted the Greek army, which wiped out the city of Troy.

What could have led the Trojans to make such a foolish mistake? Perhaps they got carried away in the moment of their apparent triumph over the Greeks and saw themselves as so invincible that they fell prey to this trick.

People do make decisions that destroy their lives, even when they should know better. Men and women give in to brief moments of temptation and wind up forfeiting their families for quick thrills that were not worth the price. Many people have lost their life's savings by investing all they had in a scheme that they knew was too good to be true. Neither Rehoboam nor the citizens of Troy stand alone.

However, there is a big difference between the episode of the Trojan horse and the history of Rehoboam. When the Trojans fell prey to the trick, they were all alone. No one, not even the gods, could help them. But Rehoboam's situation was different. His events were situated in a much deeper context—that of a God who acts decisively in history. Rehoboam did not just make a stupid decision when he repudiated Jeroboam and the people of the northern tribes; he was a part of God's larger plan. When he sponsored idolatry in his kingdom, he was not just pursuing poor domestic policy; he was violating his covenant obligations with God.

When Shishak of Egypt conquered the land, he did not just do so as a part of his attempt to become a great pharaoh; he was God's instrument sent to punish Rehoboam for his disobedience. And when Rehoboam repented, it was God who accepted his contrition and prevented Shishak from destroying Jerusalem. What Rehoboam did wrong, as well as what he did right, was a part of a history that lay ultimately not in his own hands but in God's.

What is the lesson we should learn from all this? One conclusion is that we should not engage in self-destructive actions, and we are not left to ourselves in this struggle. I don't need to stay up at night worrying about whether I might be doing something that is going to hurt me or my family. In his Word, God has given us principles to guide us along the way, and his Holy Spirit is present in our lives, leading us to implement these principles.

PRINCIPLES

- Human nature often leads us to take the short view of things and make decisions that will harm us in the long run.
- Sin will have negative consequences, not just on our eternal relationship with God, but on our human relationships as well.
- The Word of God is our guide to keep us from making self-destructive decisions.
- God is present within us to guide our minds and hearts as we make decisions.
- We can never overdraw the availability of forgiveness from the Lord.

APPLICATIONS

- Make a regular study of God's Word a part of your life.
- Look for the principles in God's Word by which you should make decisions about your life.
- Submit to the principles of God's Word as you live your life.
- Be alert for warning signs God may be sending to let you know you may be heading in the wrong direction.
- When you sin, turn quickly to God asking his forgiveness rather than living pridefully in the situation you may have created.

IV. LIFE APPLICATION

Short-Term Sacrifice—Long-Term Gain

On his Web site, gospel singer Danny Funderburk recounts the highlights of his career as well as some of the personal decisions he had to make along the way. Having received all the top awards possible as tenor for the Cathedral Quartet, including induction into the Southern Gospel Music Hall of Fame, he left that group in order to form a new quartet called Perfect Heart. Again he won many awards.

But Danny realized he had to make a difficult decision. Even though the opportunities as a gospel singer seemed unlimited, he needed to give up that life in order to be at home with his wife and children. As he tells it, "When I left Perfect Heart, I had my mind set on going home and being a good husband and father. After I stepped off that quartet bus in 1995, I honestly felt that I would probably never sing again."

Unlike countless other people, Christian and non-Christian, and certainly unlike King Rehoboam, Danny had become convinced that he needed to take a look at his life and forego more immediate goals for the more important obligations to his family.

As it turned out, God honored Danny's faithfulness by allowing him to continue doing the thing he loved so much. In Danny's own words, "God has a way of making things happen." Danny and his family found a way for him to pursue his passion for singing while not neglecting his family life. However, even if that had not happened and Danny had never performed again, we can be sure that his decision was not just the right one but one that the Lord would bless in the long run.

V. PRAYER

Lord Jesus, please give us rest. Help us to see our lives from the perspective you have provided for us in Scripture, not from our short-range view. Help us to make our decisions not based on our calculations but grounded in your design. And help us to recognize that when our lives are in tune with your leading, we can have the assurance that we are on the right track and that we can rest in your will rather than in our presumptions. Amen.

VI. DEEPER DISCOVERIES

Pharaoh Shishak (12:2)

Prior to the appearance of Shishak, the kingdom of Egypt did not seem to be a factor in the history of Israel, after they had settled in Palestine. Even though a number of pharaohs waged extensive campaigns in Syria and subdued Israel along the way, the Book of Judges does not mention these occasions, and they did not seem to have any long-term effects on Israel's governance. This silence on Egyptian invasions during this time period could not have been due to the fact that the exodus actually occurred at a later time, during the reign of Ramses II, as some scholars argue, because Judges does not mention the military excursions that occurred after Ramses's time either.

If we proceed with the date that the Bible helps us establish for the exodus (1 Kgs. 6:1; Judg. 11:26; Acts 13:20), the pharaoh during Moses' early life was Tutmoses III, who ruled for fifty years during the fifteenth century B.C. When he finally died, God told Moses, "Go back to Egypt, for all the men who wanted to kill you are dead" (Exod. 4:19), a statement that definitely included the pharaoh (Exod. 2:15). The new pharaoh was Amenhotep II, and he was probably the pharaoh of the exodus.

During much of early Old Testament times, Egypt had its own problems. Ramses II, despite his great achievements, suffered a major defeat at the hands of the Hittites. From time to time, an Egyptian army would sweep north to establish temporary control, but Egypt was not able to go much beyond the role of occasional bully in its relationship to Israel. These Egyptian invasions were not times of long-term affliction that merited reporting in the Book of Judges. Solomon even married the daughter of a weak and struggling pharaoh, Siamun of Tanis (Hoffmeier, 289).

Shishak, however, left a definite mark on biblical history. Known as Sheshonk I in Egyptian histories, he finally was able to bring some unity of structure and purpose to the Egyptian nation. This feat was paradoxical in two respects. First, Shishak was Libyan, not a native Egyptian, though this standing undoubtedly helped him create his multinational army. Second, Shishak was able to bring off the project of unifying his country at just about the same time Rehoboam allowed his to split apart.

Shishak took a part in Israel's history in several ways. He was the pharaoh who offered asylum to Jeroboam while he was biding his time waiting for Solomon's death. Then later he carried out his campaign to subjugate the lands along the Mediterranean Sea, which included Judah. His need to establish his empire even outstripped whatever positive feelings he may have had toward his ward, Jeroboam, because his troops carried out devastation in the Northern Kingdom as well. We know this because Shishak provided an inventory of all the towns he conquered during this operation (Pritchard, 187).

In the inscription in which Shishak tells the world about his accomplishments in this Palestinian campaign, he listed 150 cities that he crushed. In the biblical account, even though he forced the king to pay tribute and marched off with the royal treasury he did not besiege and destroy Jerusalem. And this account is also corroborated by Shishak's own record. When scholars studied the list of towns in Shishak's inventory, they soon realized that one city stuck out as missing—Jerusalem.

In the larger picture Shishak's adventure did not contribute to any permanent greatness for Egypt. Even though Egypt would be a player in world events again, it would be a long time before it would achieve dominance once more, and even that did not last long.

VII. TEACHING OUTLINE

A. INTRODUCTION

1. Lead Story: Game Over!

2. Context: Rehoboam became Solomon's successor to the throne of the united kingdom. It was up to him to hold it together and preserve the worship of God according to the law throughout the land.

3. Transition: Just as a person can land suddenly on an expensive property in the game of Monopoly and lose all his play money, it did not take Rehoboam long to squander his inheritance. His foolish decisions led the northern tribes of Israel to secede from the kingdom, and he also forfeited the wealth of what was left by giving in to idolatry.

B. COMMENTARY

1. Rehoboam Squanders the Kingdom (10:1–19)

2. Rehoboam Settles In (11:1–23)

3. Rehoboam's Sin and Its Consequences (12:1–12)

4. Summary and Death Notice (12:13–16)

C. CONCLUSION: THE TROJAN HORSE

VIII. ISSUES FOR DISCUSSION

1. Could Rehoboam have staved off the split of the kingdom?
2. What are some pressures that lead people to make self-destructive decisions? How can the church help prevent people from doing such things?
3. Did Rehoboam have too many advisors? What should be the role of other people's advice in our lives?
4. How does one choose the best advisors?

2 Chronicles 13:1–16:14

The Kingdom Survives

I. INTRODUCTION
The Ham, Please!

II. COMMENTARY
A verse-by-verse explanation of these chapters.

III. CONCLUSION
Straight Tiles on a Crooked Wall

An overview of the principles and applications from these chapters.

IV. LIFE APPLICATION
The Solo Part

Melding these chapters to life.

V. PRAYER
Tying these chapters to life with God.

VI. DEEPER DISCOVERIES
Historical, geographical, and grammatical enrichment of the commentary.

VII. TEACHING OUTLINE
Suggested step-by-step group study of these chapters.

VIII. ISSUES FOR DISCUSSION
Zeroing these chapters in on daily life.

Quote

"*S*in will take you farther than you want to go.

Slowly but wholly taking control;

Sin will leave you longer than you want to stay,

Sin will cost you far more than you want to pay."

Harold McWhorter, as sung
by the Cathedral Quartet

2 Chronicles 13:1–16:14

IN A NUTSHELL

*D*uring the reigns of Abijah and Asa, the Southern Kingdom of Judah remained powerful. Abijah put his trust in God and won a great victory over Jeroboam and the Northern Kingdom because he trusted God. Asa carried out extensive religious reform as well as winning a huge battle over the Cushites. However, toward the end of his life Asa started to waiver in his faith and received condemnation.

The Kingdom Survives

I. INTRODUCTION

The Ham, Please!

P. G. Wodehouse, celebrated British humorist, begins his delightful novel *Quick Service* by making one of his character's choice of breakfast food the event that sets the course for the rest of the plot. The seemingly innocuous decision made by Mrs. Chavender opens the door to the drama and hilarity of the next three hundred pages. It all begins when the young, officious Lord Holberton offers to serve her.

Lord Holberton inquires, "What can I get you, Mrs. Chavender? Eggs? Fish? Ham?"

Wodehouse, as narrator, explains, "If she had said 'Eggs,' nothing would have happened. Had she replied 'Fish,' the foundations of this little world would have remained unrocked."

"Ham," said Mrs. Chavender (Wodehouse, 7).

Tremendous consequences follow. Because Mrs. Chavender selects ham, the breakfast conversation takes a particular direction, which leads people to act in particular ways, which, in turn, brings about all the complications that make a Wodehouse novel so much fun but which eventually—because it remains a Wodehouse novel right to the end—brings everyone back together again in the best possible way.

Since all our actions are interconnected, whatever we do today will influence our lives tomorrow. This is not a particularly deep insight. If we decide for some reason not to eat today, we will be hungry tomorrow. If we pay the premiums of our auto insurance, we will be covered if we should have an accident. Nevertheless, sometimes these truisms go beyond the trivial. We may look back on what we did yesterday and recognize that a particular decision we made had an unforeseen impact on our lives, even though at the time the event seemed to have no importance at all.

It may seem almost as though some of our actions take on a life of their own. Once we have taken one step, we find ourselves on a new road, and, before we know it, we are heading for a destination we never suspected. Sometimes the impact is for good, but sometimes it is for ill. Sir Walter Scott talked about the "tangled web" that we weave as the result of a single deception;

however, lies are not the only missteps that may seem unimportant at the moment but carry us further and further into sin.

In this section we will look at two kings, Abijah and Asa, both of whom are portrayed in a positive light in Chronicles. We will see that Asa, all his zeal for the Lord notwithstanding, wound up making some decisions that opened the door for sin to make itself at home in his life.

II. COMMENTARY

The Kingdom Survives

> **MAIN IDEA:** *King Abijah and King Asa demonstrated trust in God, but King Asa showed that one wrong decision can lead to increasing alienation from the Lord.*

🄰 The Reign of Abijah (13:1–14:1)

> **SUPPORTING IDEA:** *Abijah won a miraculous victory over Jeroboam because he demonstrated trust in God.*

13:1–2a. Abijah's father, Rehoboam, was fifty-eight years old when he died. Abijah reigned for only three years before he died, and his son Asa was already old enough to take over as king in his own right. So we can picture Abijah as being in his late thirties when he took over the throne. He had been born in the glorious time of Solomon's reign, and, as a young adult, he had experienced the humiliation his father suffered when the kingdom split.

In what follows we see a marked contrast between the reports about Abijah in 1 Kings 15:1–8 and here in Chronicles. The account in 1 Kings issues Abijah a failing report card, indicating that he continued all the idolatry of which Rehoboam had been guilty. But once again the chronicler is looking in another direction. He does not mention the sins that 1 Kings depicts, but instead he focuses on one particular instant, when Abijah exemplified unreserved trust in God. Not only that, but—fitting right in with the chronicler's purpose—on that occasion Abijah also affirmed publicly the divine establishment of the Jerusalem temple and the Levitical priesthood. God rewarded his bold confession with a miraculous victory. Ezra the chronicler does not address the other matters in order to display Abijah's endorsement of the temple to his readers.

13:2b–3. There had been ongoing hostilities between Israel and Judah throughout Rehoboam's reign, but God had forbidden Rehoboam to invade the north (2 Chr. 11:4). This ban was no longer in force for Abijah, who deployed four hundred thousand soldiers in the hill country of Ephraim. This statement indicates they had penetrated into Israel already. Jeroboam managed to counter with an army twice that size, and the battle for the kingdom was ready to begin.

13:4–12. There are numerous accounts in ancient literature of kings or generals giving orations not just to their own troops but to the entire assembled multitude who are ready to start hostilities. In this case King Abijah was addressing his enemies, in particular King Jeroboam. His speech had three points: true kingship, true priesthood, and true faithfulness to God.

First, Abijah pointed out that Jeroboam's kingship was illegitimate. He accused Jeroboam of fomenting rebellion against the rightful king. Then he excused his father's bad decision by claiming that he had fallen in with the wrong crowd. According to his version of the events, the forty-one-year-old king had been a weak, inexperienced youngster who wanted to do the right thing, but he was pushed in the wrong direction by some **worthless scoundrels** who exploited him.

Regardless of his reconstruction of those events, Abijah was on target in stating that God had given the throne to the house of David permanently. A **covenant of salt** refers to an ancient practice among Near Eastern people. They sealed an agreement by consuming some salt or salted food together. Because of the preservative power of salt, the bond between these two parties would be considered permanently upheld. In the same way God had made a perpetual commitment to David's descendants.

Second, Abijah declared that Jeroboam had violated God's rules for the priesthood and that the true priesthood was the one established in Jerusalem. By this time Jeroboam had set up a simple system for recruiting people who wished to be priests at the shrines devoted to golden calves. A person would come forward with a bull and seven rams as an ordination fee, and he could then proceed to a prosperous career in the priesthood. Abijah tried to get the troops of Israel to think about what they were doing. Just a few years ago they had been busy driving out the authentic priesthood. Why should they now be fighting in support of a fake priesthood? They even carried the golden calves into battle with them, just like pagan armies marching into battle with their idols (1 Chr. 14:12).

The third point of Abijah's speech was to profess that the true worship of God was, indeed, being performed in the temple in Jerusalem. Here were the legitimate priests, the genuine sacrifices commanded by God, and the proper rituals for the table and the lampstands. And furthermore, Abijah affirmed, with the true priesthood blowing the battle trumpets, there was no question that God would defeat the army of the north. In short, Abijah counseled the army of Israel that, although they might be twice as large as that of Judah, their most prudent course of action was to put up their swords and go home.

13:13–21. The northern army did no such thing. Instead, they did not even pay attention to Abijah's speech. While the king of Judah was declaring God's will to them, they were sneaking around behind his army. When the soldiers of Judah realized they were surrounded, their only option was to fight for all they were worth. The priests blew the trumpet, the army took up the battle cry, and the combat began.

The north never had a chance. What Abijah had tried to tell them was that they were not just going against the army of Judah. **God routed Jeroboam and all Israel.** Because of Abijah's reliance on God, the cause had become God's and not just Abijah's. God used the army of Judah, of course, but he provided them with a triumph that defied the odds. The passage attributes the victory directly to the Lord.

The warriors of Israel fled, but the majority of them did not escape the blades of the southern army. Judah took control of the area around three towns in the southern region of Israel, most significantly Bethel, one of the two sites for golden calf worship. However, Abijah did not destroy this facility. Bethel eventually reverted to Israel's ownership, but regardless of which kingdom claimed the town, the golden calf shrine persisted through various political revolutions (2 Kgs. 10:29). Later on, as Baal worship became dominant in the kingdom of Israel, the veneration of the golden calves lost some significance.

But still the idolatrous sanctuary at Bethel remained in place even after Israel had ceased to exist as a kingdom. It was not destroyed until King Josiah of Judah carried out reforms (2 Kgs. 23:15–18) almost a hundred years after the fall of the Northern Kingdom.

For Jeroboam, this defeat was utterly demoralizing. He died in disgrace by God's own hand, while Abijah basked in glory for a time with fourteen wives and twenty-two sons. We get no further information on Abijah in Chronicles, and we know from 1 Kings that the expression of faith in God we saw here was the exception rather than the rule (1 Kgs. 15:3). Abijah's miraculous victory changed the terms of the *status quo* somewhat, but it did not abolish it.

13:22–14:1. The summary of Abijah's reign is brief, as befits a reign that lasted only three years. As usual, there are references to other sources of information on the king, this one to the writings of the prophet Iddo. Abijah was buried in the **City of David**, traditionally identified with Mount Zion, at a site that had become the official location for the royal tombs of Judah.

B Asa's Reforms and Success in Battle (14:2–15)

SUPPORTING IDEA: *King Asa began his reign with sweeping reforms, and God blessed him with a miraculous victory over an invading army.*

14:2–5. Two impressions arise as soon as Asa comes to the throne of Judah: reform and peace. There was peace for the first ten years of his reign, and this peace was directly related to his program of reform. In verse 3 we see that Asa purged the entire land of **foreign altars and the high places**, the shrines of idolatrous worship. The **Asherah poles** were particularly offensive implements that symbolized fertility rituals.

Verse 5 states that Asa also eliminated the **high places and incense altars**. These were places of worship dedicated to God which were no longer legitimate after the building of the temple (Deut. 12:8). Solomon himself had patronized them before the temple's completion and did not abolish them afterwards (1 Kgs. 3:2). Asa undertook a rigorous program to destroy all the places of false worship in Judah. Unfortunately, these sites would go back into business at the first opportunity.

Asa also issued a decree that all people should **seek the LORD and obey his laws**. It was not enough just to remove the sites of false worship. The people should observe the entire law, and many of them complied.

14:6–8. Like his predecessors Asa carried out extensive projects to defend his kingdom. The lengthy period of peace, made possible by the Lord, allowed him to rebuild the walls of the towns destroyed by Shishak. Remember that Abijah had ruled for only three years, so it had not been all that long since Shishak had defeated Rehoboam. Also, Asa retained a large army—300,000 men from Judah and 280,000 from Benjamin—to stand by in case of war. The soldiers were supplied with good weapons, an indication of Asa's standing in the world of foreign trade since he was able to acquire the necessary materials for these weapons.

14:9–15. After ten years of peace, Zerah the Cushite invaded Judah at the head of a large army. Historians are uncertain about the identity of this Zerah. Since he was from Cush, a traditional name for Ethiopia, he could not have been a new Egyptian pharaoh since the dynasty established by Shishak was Libyan. It is also very unlikely that there was a Cushite army totally independent of Egypt. So he must have been the chief general for the reigning pharaoh who was carrying out a campaign on behalf of his king—and perhaps also attempting to establish a power base for his own ambitions.

Zerah and his army marched up the road along the Mediterranean seacoast and reached **as far as Mareshah**, located southwest of Jerusalem. This put him practically at Asa's front door. Asa and his army managed to position themselves in the adjacent Valley of Zephathah. Once again, two armies were ready to begin combat.

Asa turned to the Lord for assistance. He expressed his reliance on God and reminded him that the king's army had come to fight Zerah in God's name. A defeat of Asa's army would be considered a defeat of God himself, and surely the Lord did not want that to happen. The victory would come directly from God.

Have you ever noticed how many times people pray fervently for something, and then, when the Lord grants it to them, they give themselves credit for all their planning, hard work, and skill? In this situation, the chronicler did not allow this to happen: **The LORD struck down the Cushites before Asa and Judah.** We get the impression that Asa and his army were merely spectators as God defeated the Cushite army.

Using the army of Judah as his arms and legs, the Lord drove the invaders back, and they were finally able to disengage at Gerar, a town on the southern border of Judah. Apparently Gerar had been Zerah's staging and supply area. Asa and his troops were able to collect a sizable amount of plunder. They demolished the town and its surrounding settlements and confiscated the livestock of the herdsmen, who had apparently been a part of the Cushites' supply train.

This was now the second major victory of a king of Judah who had expressed faith in God. One is reminded of David's "undefeated season" and Solomon's "Midas touch," both of which were also the work of God. In contrast, we can remind ourselves of Rehoboam's feeble attempts at fortification and his humiliation by Pharaoh Shishak. The lesson for any future action by a king of Judah was clear: stay true to God and rely on him alone, and his blessings will follow. But not even Asa remembered this lesson.

🌙 Asa's More Intensive Reforms (15:1–19)

SUPPORTING IDEA: *In response to a warning from the prophet Azariah, Asa carried out far-reaching reforms which were supported by the people.*

15:1–7. The prophet Azariah is another one of those men of God who make only a single appearance in the Bible. His admonition to Asa is the only time we hear about him, and yet he had a great effect on his contemporaries. Led by the spirit of God, he sought out Asa, perhaps still on the way back from the battle, and delivered his prophecy.

Azariah's message to the king was the same truth the Lord had just exemplified in his victory over Zerah. The prophet made clear that the Lord would continue to be on the side of the people as long as they continued to be true to him.

Azariah illustrated his point by making reference to the long period between the conquest and the establishment of David's kingdom. Until then, even though there was a priest officiating at the tabernacle, he did not teach the people, and, consequently, they lived **without the true God**, and **without the law**. The result had been an era of anarchy and lawlessness during which the Israelites had been easy prey for any foreign power. Azariah insisted that these bad times should be understood as judgment from God. However, the national situation should now be different since, with a central priesthood, everyone should be able to learn about God's demands and how to obey them.

Azariah's speech ended with a word of encouragement to Asa. The king was on the right track and should persevere; his efforts would not be in vain.

15:8. Heartened by Azariah's sermon, King Asa renewed his efforts at cleansing the land of idols. He scoured the land under his control, including some occupied territory in Ephraim, and destroyed all the idols he could find.

For the first time a king initiated a repair program for the temple. At this point the only part of the temple in need of restoration was the large altar, the main site for animal sacrifices. By this time the temple had been functioning for about sixty years. One would expect quite a bit of wear and tear, particularly on the altar where animals were slaughtered and burned.

15:9–15. The **fifteenth year of Asa's reign** would have been the fifth year after Zerah's failed invasion and Azariah's prophecy, so the king's purge of the land was already in full swing. But removing idols from the land would not change the fiber of the nation; that would take a full commitment by all the people to the law of God. So Asa called for an assembly of all his subjects so they could dedicate themselves to God.

The celebration began with animal sacrifices. Then the people **entered into a covenant**, renewing God's ancient covenant with his people. The law stated that idolatry was a capital offense (Exod. 22:20; Deut. 13:6–11). The only way Israel could be the people of God was by worshiping none other than the true God. Consequently, the assembled crowd took a double-edged vow. They committed themselves to the service of the Lord, and they pledged that they would execute anyone who worshiped false gods.

The oath that the people took on this occasion sounds brutal to our modern ears. What we need to remember is that this was the one, single, unique time when God took a particular nation and said of them, "These are my people." In that capacity Israel was under obligation to maintain this identity. This could be done only by eliminating idolatry and the people who were contaminating the nation with their worship of false gods.

The decision by Asa's people to abide by the law of God and to purge all idolaters was the cause of much rejoicing. A true spirit of revival broke out, and the Lord rewarded their renewed dedication to him. As they sought God, **he was found by them**; they perceived clear indications of his will. The result was **rest**, and they could live in peace and prosperity.

15:16–19. If the events recounted here are in strict chronological sequence, Asa saved one of his hardest jobs for last. His grandmother Maacah was committing idolatry. As the wife of Rehoboam, she may have encouraged his inclinations toward idolatry, and she may have done the same for Abijah. She held the influential position of "queen mother," so she probably served as a negative role model for the people of the land. Maacah was worshiping an Asherah pole, the Canaanite fertility symbol. Asa desecrated the object and burned it.

The chronicler comments on the full extent of Asa's devotion to the Lord, although he hedges slightly because Asa did not abolish the high places in the Northern Kingdom. Obviously, Asa did not have jurisdiction over most of Israel, so this comment must be directed specifically at some of the places Asa took over late in life and perhaps also at the opportunities Asa missed.

Even though the temple treasury had been cleaned out and handed to Shishak under Rehoboam, Abijah and Asa had been able to accumulate a sizable amount of wealth again because of their overwhelming military success. Asa, in keeping with David's practice (1 Chr. 18:11), dedicated the new treasures to the Lord and moved them into the temple. God honored Asa's zeal with a long reign marked by peace.

Ⓓ War with the North and a Fateful Alliance with Aram (16:1–10)

SUPPORTING IDEA: *When the king of Israel decided to invade Judah, King Asa did not trust God but made an alliance with the king of Syria instead.*

16:1. Jeroboam, the first ruler of the Northern Kingdom, was succeeded by his son Nadab, who reigned only two years before he was assassinated. His successor was Baasha, a man of greater ambition than ability. Baasha decided to undertake a military campaign against Judah. His first move was to amass an army and to blockade a main traffic artery between the two kingdoms. In addition to this barricade preventing Israelites from going to the temple in Jerusalem, it was also a "beachhead" for a future invasion of Judah.

16:2–6. At this point the story of King Asa goes sour. King Baasha had an alliance with King Ben-Hadad of Aram. Not that long ago Aram had been under the aegis of David and Solomon, but now it was a strong, independent nation once again. Ben-Hadad was happy to play both Hebrew states against each other. He had maintained a treaty with King Baasha of Israel, and undoubtedly Baasha was counting on his support.

Asa, however, persuaded Ben-Hadad to give up his treaty with the Northern Kingdom and agree to a new alliance with the Southern Kingdom. But it cost Asa the contents of the temple treasury, some personal wealth, his integrity, and his standing with God. Quite a price to pay!

From the human standpoint, Asa's diplomacy was successful. Judah stayed out of war. Ben-Hadad ransacked the towns of northern Israel while Baasha was focusing on the south, and thus was able to line his pockets even further without much effort. Baasha had to cease his blockade and rush home, leaving Asa the opportunity to move his troops in and steal Baasha's building materials. Everyone—except Baasha—was a winner.

But note what treasures Asa used to pay off Ben-Hadad. He emptied the temple treasury—the very items that he had dedicated to the Lord and placed in the temple as a sign of his piety. Now he was using God's treasure to bribe a pagan ruler to break a treaty.

16:7–9. Although his diplomatic success probably made Asa a popular ruler among his subjects, God was not happy with what he did. So the Lord sent a prophet named Hanani to confront the king about his shortcomings. Asa had made a serious mistake by relying on his alliance with Ben-Hadad, Hanani stated. By doing this, Asa had repudiated his reliance on the Lord.

Hanani reminded the king of how previously, when he had trusted God alone, God had routed Zerah's army, and that God was always ready to **strengthen those whose hearts are fully committed to him**. But Asa had given up on this divine support. In fact, Hanani told him, if Asa had continued to rely on God, he would have defeated not only Baasha and the Northern Kingdom but Ben-Hadad and the Arameans as well. He could have brought about a virtual restoration of David's empire. But instead, Hanani concluded, Asa would have to deal with war for the rest of his reign.

16:10. The king could have dismissed Hanani as a religious fanatic who was meddling in things he could not understand. He could have given Hanani the old line about "taking the matter under advisement." He could have thanked the prophet politely and sent him away. But he did none of those. Asa was cut to the quick by the prophet's words, and he had Hanani thrown into the dungeon.

Of course, Asa could also have done what other kings before him had done: he could have repented. David did so several times (2 Sam. 12:13; 1 Chr. 21:8), and even Rehoboam repented when confronted with his sin. But not Asa. This king, who had shown such zeal for the Lord, now let sin take control. The chronicler adds the cryptic note that **Asa brutally oppressed some of the people.** We do not know what kind of oppression this was, but it may have been persecution of those who took Hanani's side.

A disappointing character portrait now emerged as the once-so-devoted king turned into a tyrant toward some of his own subjects. Once Asa adopted an attitude of rebelling against God, he never got back on the right track again.

E Asa's Summary and Death Notice (16:11–14)

SUPPORTING IDEA: *Asa's life concluded with much human acclaim, but it was marred by his failure to return to God.*

16:11–12. Asa's rebellious attitude continued to the end of his life. He developed a disease in his feet, perhaps gout or gangrene from diabetes. But the king refused to go to the Lord with his affliction. Instead, he sought treatment **only from the physicians.** This statement is not intended to counsel people against seeking professional medical help, but it demonstrates how far Asa's trust in God had fallen.

16:13–14. In spite of this unhappy conclusion, Asa was a hero to the people of Judah. He had given them a new sense of unity and purpose. He had been at the head of the army that defeated Zerah. With a shrewd diplomatic maneuver, he had defeated Baasha. His reign was marked by peace. When Asa died after forty-one years on the throne, the people honored him with a special funeral ceremony.

MAIN IDEA REVIEW: *King Abijah and King Asa demonstrated trust in God, but King Asa showed that one wrong decision can lead to increasing alienation from the Lord.*

III. CONCLUSION

Straight Tiles on a Crooked Wall

As the owner of an old house, I find myself doing constant repairs. Last summer I took up a project that had needed doing for a number of years. The plastic enclosure for our tub and shower had seeped water into the wall to such an extent that the wall had to be repaired. I had to take down the old plastic covering and rip the moldy boards off the studs. Then I put up new boards, glued tiles to them, and applied the grout. Of course, such a quick description cannot possibly capture the true progress of an amateur's attempt at a project of this nature.

One problem I encountered was a crooked wall. Tiles are straight so they fit together well and create the impression of order and uniformity. Put those tiles on a crooked wall, however, and it is impossible to produce an orderly arrangement. No matter how you lay them out, sooner or later you have to get out the tile cutter and make some adjustments. With a little skill you may make your work look neat, but it will never be as straight as the ideal. One tile that does not fit right will throw the whole row out of line.

The placement of tiles illustrates the way our actions may shape our lives. One action out of line can influence all our subsequent actions. If we let things go, a wrong action can skew everything we do from that point on.

In previous chapters we have seen how David and Rehoboam responded with repentance when confronted with their sin. God accepted their contrition and gave them a chance to start over. Asa was a godly man, but when he did something wrong, he refused to repent. Consequently, his life ended on a bad note.

PRINCIPLES

- God rewards those who place their trust in him.
- At times all of us fall short of acting on our faith in God.
- When we do something wrong and ignore it, this may have negative influence on all our other actions, so that our lives become skewed.

APPLICATIONS

- Within the sphere of influence God has placed you, is he calling you to address idols of our culture that blind people to God's goodness and glory?
- Is there some specific sin in your life that you have not owned up to?
- Remember the victories God has given you. Take time to thank him and to acknowledge him as the source of that victory.
- Memorize 2 Chronicles 16:9a. Review the context in which it was spoken by Hanani. How does this principle speak to your present situation?

- Recall some of the times when you received godly rebukes. What were your reactions to these rebukes? Looking back on the rebukes and your reactions, what have you learned from them?

IV. LIFE APPLICATION

The Solo Part

My home church when I was in high school and college had a good choir. We had a knowledgeable director and many capable voices, including no shortage of soloists. Over the years, if we repeated a number with a solo part, the same person who had done the part before usually got to do it again.

One Sunday night the choir director did not follow his usual procedure. He selected a song for which Carolyn (not her real name) had supplied the soprano solo the last two times we had performed it. But this time he did not ask Carolyn to sing this part; instead, he turned it over to Veronica, a young lady who had just joined the church and the choir.

Carolyn's feelings were hurt. When the time came for the choir anthem during the evening service, she not only had to hear Veronica singing what she thought of as her very own part, but she even had to see the director smile at Veronica the way he had always smiled at her when she sang the part. It was more than she could take. Carolyn left the church.

As long as the church is composed of human beings, there will be misunderstandings, thoughtlessness, and even mean-spiritedness. There will be times when people are falsely accused of a sin, passed over for an office in the church, or left stuck cleaning the church kitchen all by themselves. These things happen. Our feelings do get hurt.

The question is, What do we do if our feelings have been hurt? Sometimes, when Christians are hurt, rather than attempting to resolve the situation, they welcome the anger to which they feel entitled, and they ask the anger to make itself at home in their lives. Soon the anger takes over. All the person's actions are colored by this one incident, and he or she may eventually lose all effectiveness in the kingdom of God.

King Asa is one example of such a chain of negative consequences. He grew angry, and the anger took over his life. Many of us have turned what was a legitimate anger into sinful anger by letting the anger define our lives. If there is something that needs to be resolved with others, let us do so swiftly before our lives become infected by sin and are closed off to God.

V. PRAYER

Lord Jesus, there are two directions we can go—that of Asa, who shut himself off from you more and more once he sinned, or that of David, who returned to you in repentance not just once but several times. Help us to choose the second direction, knowing that you are always willing to accept sinners who return to you. Amen.

VI. DEEPER DISCOVERIES

A. Size of Armies (13:3)

Many scholars have found the numbers associated with the armies in Chronicles quite challenging. Abijah commanded an army of 400,000, against whom Jeroboam sent an army of 800,000. At the end of the battle, the northern army had suffered 500,000 casualties. These are astounding numbers, eclipsing any other records of other ancient armies in both strength and number of casualties (Walton, 434).

The fact of the matter is that these numbers, though very large, are not impossible. Somebody has to hold the record for the largest number of soldiers in a military action, and presumably this may be it. As usual, considering how many times skepticism about biblical reports has been refuted by archeological evidence, the wisest course seems to be to accept the chronicler's numbers, even if they seem improbable to us.

One other legitimate option is to consider the possibility that we are looking at a matter of mistranslation or misinterpretation on our part. The chronicler was correct in what he reported, but we may not be understanding the terms correctly. Dillard mentions three options, though he does not consider any of them adequate:

1. The word *thousand* may refer to a standard military unit, whose actual head count might have been far fewer than a thousand soldiers.

2. The word *thousand* might be better translated as "commander," so an army of 400 "thousand" should be understood as an army with 400 commanders.

3. The word *thousand* is a deliberate exaggeration in order to demonstrate God's power and should not be understood as an actual number (Dillard, 106–07).

Of these three options, most conservative scholars tend to favor the first. However, given no direct evidence contrary to the chronicler's numbers, the most preferable option is to take the Bible's account at face value.

B. Asherah Poles (14:3)

Canaanite religion is not easy to put into a simple scheme. Many cultures that we lump together as "Canaanite" worshiped gods with the same names, but they adapted their religions to their specific needs and desires. Still, one trait that pervaded all of them was a strong emphasis on fertility and sexuality.

The oldest god of the Canaanites was called El. He was cast in the role of a sexually exploitative god. Together with his divine consort—his "wife" if you will—he was the father of seventy gods. The wife of El, and thus the mother of all of the seventy gods, was Asherah (sometimes referred to by the plural "Ashtaroth," not to be confused with another goddess named Ashtoreth). She was a goddess of sexuality, and her worship was supposed to produce fertility for crops and animals.

The precise nature of these "poles" that were an integral part of Asherah worship is not clear. Three options are commonly advanced. An Asherah pole may have been a natural tree, a plain wood column, or a wood column with an image of the deity. Whatever configuration the poles assumed, they were associated with fertility.

VII. TEACHING OUTLINE

A. INTRODUCTION
1. Lead Story: The Ham, Please!
2. Context: Rehoboam was succeeded by his son Abijah, who, in turn, passed on the throne of Judah to his son Asa. Both these kings were tested in their loyalty to God.
3. Transition: In the lead story, many future events were influenced by the fact that Mrs. Cavendish selected ham for her breakfast. One small decision affected the lives of a number of people. In this section of Chronicles, we see how King Asa's life of devotion to God was marred by a decision he made late in life that would have profound influence on his relationship with God.

B. COMMENTARY
1. The Reign of Abijah (13:1–14:1)
2. Asa's Reforms and Success in Battle (14:2–15)

3. Asa's More Intensive Reforms (15:1–19)
4. War with the North and a Fateful Alliance with Aram (16:1–10)
5. Asa's Summary and Death Notice (16:11–14)

C. CONCLUSION: STRAIGHT TILES ON A CROOKED WALL

VIII. ISSUES FOR DISCUSSION

1. How far should Christians go in expecting a miracle when they rely on God?
2. What could be an equivalent to Asa's zeal in eliminating idolatry for today's Christian?
3. Asa made a decision that seemed a masterful stroke based on a human perspective, yet it had disastrous consequences for his relationship with God. How can we correct our human deliberations with biblical principles without becoming otherworldly?
4. Contrast Asa's defensive reaction to being confronted with his sin with a biblically grounded way of dealing with sin in our lives.

2 Chronicles 17:1–21:3

Choose Your Friends Carefully!

"And why such separation? Because the unbeliever does not share the Christian's standards, sympathies, or goals."

Murray J. Harris

2 Chronicles 17:1–21:3

IN A NUTSHELL

Jehoshaphat was one of the godliest kings to occupy the throne of Judah. Yet he lacked wisdom when he made alliances with the Baal-worshiping kings of Israel.

Choose Your Friends Carefully!

I. INTRODUCTION

The Monkey and the Crocodile

A crocodile was resting in the river, hoping for some tasty prey for his next meal. Looking up, he saw a monkey in the trees and thought this might be his lunch. But the monkey also caught sight of the crocodile and began to throw scrumptious fruits from the tree to the crocodile. The crocodile loved these treats. When he came back the next day, the monkey had more fruit for him, and they started to meet every day and chat about this and that. All the while, though, the crocodile was thinking about how to capture the monkey so he could make a nutritious meal out of him.

Then one day the crocodile suggested to the monkey that he would take him across the river where there was even better fruit. The monkey climbed on the crocodile's back, ready to enjoy a free ride to the other shore. However, when they were in the deepest part of the river, the crocodile slowly began to sink, thinking to drown his rider and eat him.

When the monkey felt himself going down, he screamed, "What are you doing?"

"I'm going to eat you now," the crocodile replied. "And I'm going to start with your heart. That's the tastiest part."

"I always leave my heart in the top of the trees when I go out. But if you will take me back to the shore, I will get my heart for you to eat."

The crocodile believed the clever monkey, turned around, and deposited him on the original shore. The monkey climbed up a tree and enjoyed a hearty laugh at the crocodile's expense.

Crocodiles and monkeys just are not meant to be friends. In a folk tale such as this, they might be imagined to socialize together temporarily, but when you come right down to it, they are too different from each other to live in harmony. After all, what can possibly come from a friendship when one of the two has the basic biological impulse to make a meal of the other?

In our passage for this chapter, we see another attempt at an impossible friendship. King Jehoshaphat of Judah sought to maintain an alliance with King Ahab of Israel. There was only one problem: While Jehoshaphat was dedicated to the Lord, Ahab was a devout follower of Baal. Consequently, this relationship was bound to produce problems—for Jehoshaphat during his lifetime and for the kingdom of Judah in the aftermath.

II. COMMENTARY

Choose Your Friends Carefully!

MAIN IDEA: *Jehoshaphat was a godly king. However, he brought troubles upon himself and the kingdom by making alliances with the ungodly kings of the Northern Kingdom.*

A Jehoshaphat's Early Reign (17:1–19)

SUPPORTING IDEA: *When Jehoshaphat first came to the throne, he fortified his cities, promoted devotion to God, and strengthened his military.*

17:1–2. Jehoshaphat succeeded his father Asa as king of Judah. In fact, he may have carried the duties of king during Asa's last years when Asa was incapacitated by his foot ailment. We learn later on in Chronicles that Jehoshaphat was thirty-five years old at his coronation (2 Chr. 20:31). This would have made him just a young school child at the time of Asa's miraculous victory over the invading forces of Zerah. As we look at the information the chronicler gives us about Jehoshaphat, some weak spots show up, but we should never lose sight of the fact that he was one of the most righteous kings of Judah.

Jehoshaphat began his reign by fortifying certain strategic cities. These included towns that his father Asa had captured in the territory of the Northern Kingdom. In fact, the new king was clear in his mind about who his enemy was because he carried out these preparations **against Israel**.

17:3–6. The chronicler pays Jehoshaphat one of the highest compliments possible. He compares his commitment to God to that of King David, who represented the chronicler's ideal. Jehoshaphat's walk with God was above reproach. He did not worship **the Baals**, an expression that refers to all the Canaanite deities. Instead, he sought God's will for his life. As a result God blessed him with public acclaim that manifested itself in the presentation of many gifts. Like Solomon, Jehoshaphat accumulated a lot of treasure.

Jehoshaphat also renewed the program of eliminating pagan worship sites and high places from his kingdom. Specifically, he—like his father—went on a campaign to have the detestable Asherah poles removed throughout the land. Asa had already done this, but these lewd sites had popped up all over the country again, and Jehoshaphat set out to eradicate them.

17:7–9. But removing idolatrous objects does not necessarily turn people's hearts to God, let alone keep them there. In his day Asa had called together a great revival meeting in which everyone pledged to abide by God's law and, in fact, to kill anyone who did not. Whatever the tangible effects of that meeting may have been, they did not purge the land of idolatry for very long.

Jehoshaphat wanted to bring the law of God to the hearts and minds of his countrymen. He brought together a group of people knowledgeable in the law and designated them to travel throughout the towns of Judah and hold classes. Their one textbook was **the Book of the Law,** or the Pentateuch, the five books of Moses (Genesis through Deuteronomy). They instructed the people in how to worship God and how to follow his law.

Jehoshaphat had the insight to include some of his own officials, who presumably would have been from the tribes of Judah and Benjamin, as well as Levites and priests. This way, the groups would be able to speak with expertise on both the civil law and the sacrificial law. This teaching function had already been a part of David's division of labor among the Levites.

17:10–19. Jehoshaphat's reign resembled that of Solomon in many ways. Like Solomon, he received visitors from outside his own kingdom who brought presents. Who would have thought that the Philistines would send an embassy carrying silver and gold to the king of Judah? Also, the surrounding Arab tribes dropped by; they presented Jehoshaphat with a lavish gift of rams and goats.

As Jehoshaphat's wealth grew, so did his military strength. He fortified towns and built up an army. The total personnel count added up to 1,160,000 men. The divisions of this army were constituted by tribes, with three divisions coming from Judah and two from Benjamin. In keeping with the picture that we have of Jehoshaphat, he allowed himself to be guided in all respects by God. The military career of one of his generals, Amasiah, was in the **service of the LORD.** This is a description one might expect for a priest or a prophet.

Ⓑ Military Campaign Alongside Ahab (18:1–19:3)

SUPPORTING IDEA: *Jehoshaphat foolishly decided to fight a war with King Ahab of Israel as his ally and barely escaped with his life.*

18:1. The international situation had changed several times over the last few years. When we picked up the story of Asa, the Northern Kingdom under

Baasha had made an alliance with Aram. But Asa had bought off King Ben-Hadad of Aram, establishing his own alliance with him against Israel. The Arameans had been happy to take advantage of this new configuration and and had proceed to conquer some of the towns of northern Israel. However, by the time we get to Israel's King Ahab, we find him again allied with the Arameans against a larger and more fearful enemy, the Assyrians.

Together Israel and Aram held off Assyria at the battle of Qarqar (853 B.C.)—at least for the moment. However, once that battle had been fought, Ahab and Ben-Hadad clashed, and twice Israel repulsed attempts by Aram to conquer Samaria, Israel's new capital city (1 Kgs. 20:1–30). Then Ahab decided to take advantage of the situation and launch an attack of his own against Aram in order to take back the northern towns, particularly Ramoth-Gilead. He sought the help of Judah in this campaign.

Even before their joint military campaign, Jehoshaphat strengthened his alliance with Ahab with a marriage. He arranged for his son Jehoram to marry Athaliah, the daughter of Ahab and Jezebel. Athaliah came from solid Baal-worshiping stock. Her mother, Jezebel, had been a Phoenician princess. When she married Ahab (1 Kgs. 16:31), she insisted that Baal worship should be the only legitimate religion in Israel (1 Kgs. 19:10). There is no question that Athaliah was brought up to worship Baal.

It is a profound paradox that Jehoshaphat, who was so zealous for God, should marry his son off to this woman. Perhaps he saw himself as preparing the way for Jehoram to become the next Solomon, ruling over a kingdom united once again. In reality, the results would be horrendous.

18:2–4. Some time after he had confirmed his ties with Ahab, Jehoshaphat went to Samaria to pay a state visit. When he arrived, Ahab presented him with a proposal. Together their combined armies should have no trouble marching north and taking Ramoth-Gilead away from Aram again. Jehoshaphat, in a burst of fraternal affection, declared his brotherhood with Ahab and agreed to go to war alongside the northern army. Then Jehoshaphat said that, of course, they would first have to determine if this joint campaign was the will of God.

18:5–11. When Jehoshaphat requested a consultation with a prophet, what he got was four hundred prophets of Baal. Not only were they false prophets, but they were bad false prophets, putting on a show of "yes-saying" to the king's proposal. The leader of this mob of so-called prophets was Zedekiah, who decorated his head with a set of iron horns—the traditional symbol for Baal—and declared that it was God's will for Ahab to gore the Arameans.

18:12–27. Jehoshaphat saw through this charade. His question told the story: "Is there not a prophet of the LORD here?" "Well, yes," replied Ahab. "There is this Micaiah son of Imlah. But I don't like to call on him because he always says things that upset me."

By this time Jehoshaphat must have been fed up with the proceedings, but he made a common mistake: he thought he could get a Baal worshiper to think as a believer in God. Rather than telling Ahab, "This nonsense has gone far enough. I asked you to consult the Lord, and you trotted out this circus of Baal prophets, who dared to place God's name on their lips. Then, when I insist that we find a true prophet of the Lord, you tell me that you don't want to consult him because he disagrees with you. I think we can dispense with any more of this embarrassment." But Jehoshaphat did not say this. Instead he counseled Ahab, the confirmed opponent of the Lord and persecutor of God's prophets, "Oh no, you must not talk like that."

They brought out Micaiah. Just to make sure that Micaiah would not cause a scene before the assembled royalty, the messenger who had been designated to fetch him gave him instructions: "All the other prophets are agreeing with Ahab's plans to go to war. So you know what to say. Don't cause any trouble." Micaiah replied, "I will say whatever God tells me to say."

Still, when Micaiah first entered the area outside the city where the two kings were enthroned in all their splendor, he decided to play the game. "Go ahead," he told the two kings. "You will be victorious." But Ahab recognized Micaiah's insincerity. He did not want to hear his negative prophecies, but he certainly did not want to be played for a fool, so he charged the prophet to tell the truth.

Suddenly the scene was not funny any more as the gloomy prophecy rolled off Micaiah's lips. Israel would be scattered like sheep without a shepherd, he said, an obvious declaration that the king of Israel would be killed. Not only would this whole caper end in tragedy; it had already been planned by God. Micaiah informed the king that God had deliberately allowed a spirit to speak lies through the prophets of Baal in order to entice Ahab to ride off to his doom.

This was too much for Zedekiah, the prophet of Baal with the iron horns. He slapped Micaiah and gave a lame response: "Since you know all about this lying spirit, tell me: What route did the spirit go when it left me and gave you a false message?" Micaiah would not be turned aside into arguments about spirit possession. Instead, he came right back to the main point—the defeat of Israel. Zedekiah might scoff now, but he would know the truth when it was too late, on the day when he would have to fear for his life and hide **in an inner room**—an enclosed toilet.

Now the day was spoiled, and Ahab tried to put an end to it. "Cart this guy off to jail and keep him on a ration of bread and water until I come back from the battle." But Micaiah got in the last word, "If you return from the battle, then everyone will know that the Lord did not speak through me after all."

If Jehoshaphat said anything on either Micaiah's or the Lord's behalf, it was not recorded for us. Having insisted on consulting a true prophet of God, he ignored his advice and rode off to battle with his friend and ally, the Baal-worshiping Ahab, at his side.

18:28–34. The battle turned into a bizarre comedy of errors. Presumably trying to avert Micaiah's prophecy, Ahab got Jehoshaphat to agree to a deception. Jehoshaphat would keep on his royal battle outfit, while Ahab would disguise himself as a common soldier. Then all the attention would focus on the king of Judah while the king of Israel could go unnoticed. Jehoshaphat agreed to this scheme, perhaps because he knew his own death had not been predicted.

The plan worked. The Arameans, thinking that Jehoshaphat was Ahab, made a special point of trying to kill him. They had decided not to waste their arrows on just anyone because it was Ahab they were after, but God led the Arameans to recognize that the person in the royal outfit before them was not Ahab, so they backed off. It was Ahab they wanted.

However, Ahab's masquerade could not deceive God. An arrow from an Aramean soldier struck Ahab and penetrated his armor. In a gesture of defiance, Ahab had himself propped up in his chariot for the rest of the day, but the obstinate king died that night.

19:1–3. How disappointed Jehoshaphat must have felt as he rode back to Jerusalem, having barely escaped from this chaotic scene! But feelings of personal humiliation did not save him from getting a stern lecture from another prophet.

This time it was a seer named Jehu, the son of Asa's old nemesis Hanani (2 Chr. 16:7), who confronted him. Jehu scolded the king for his association with Ahab, whom he classified among the **wicked** and those **who hate the Lord**. Jehoshaphat's real enemy should have been Ahab, and it was unthinkable that Jehoshaphat was cooperating with him. Even though God was angry with Jehoshaphat, the Lord also took into consideration that the king's heart was still in the right place, as evidenced by his efforts to clear the country of idols. Severely chastened, the king went back to fighting for the Lord's cause within the boundaries of his own kingdom.

C Jehoshaphat's Further Reforms (19:4–11)

SUPPORTING IDEA: Jehoshaphat taught the people about God and established tribunals for judging matters of the law.

19:4. Jehoshaphat resumed his program of teaching the law throughout Judah. This time he went out personally and traveled the entire length of the country from the south (**Beersheba**) to the north (**the hill country of Ephraim**). Wherever he went, he spread word about the Lord and led people to follow God's will.

19:5–7. It makes no sense to teach everybody to obey divine law and then not to enforce it. Remember that there was more to the law than sacrifices and personal righteousness; it also included instructions for the people of God on how to function as a community. Jehoshaphat appointed magistrates to be posted around the kingdom and admonished them to keep in mind that they were accountable to God. There was no room for partiality in the Lord's standards of fairness (Deut. 16:18–20; Amos 2:6b–7a).

19:8–11. Jehoshaphat also set up a tribunal in Jerusalem—a supreme court staffed by ranking members among the priests and Levites. This panel would judge cases that could not be handled on the local level. Jehoshaphat charged this group to be meticulous in following God's rules. He placed Levites at their disposal for clerical matters and gave them access to the high priest and the head of the tribes to help them settle difficult cases.

D War with Nations East of the Jordan River (20:1–30)

SUPPORTING IDEA: When the land was threatened by a combined army of nations, the Lord granted Jehoshaphat a miraculous victory.

20:1–4. Some time later Jehoshaphat's faith and his program of teaching the people were put to the test. Like his two predecessors, he had to face a large army. By the time Jehoshaphat heard about the invasion, the enemies were already in the territory of Judah. The Moabites and Ammonites had made an alliance and had combined their forces with the Meunites in order to assault Judah. The Meunites were originally Ishmaelites who had associated themselves with the Edomites. This combined army crossed the Jordan River and took up a position in the wilderness west of the Dead Sea. This gave them a secure position from which to stage their march against Jerusalem.

King Jehoshaphat turned to the Lord and encouraged all the people to do the same. He declared a day of fasting as a part of a national convocation of prayer. The people responded enthusiastically, flocking to Jerusalem from all over the kingdom.

20:5–13. When the people had gathered, Jehoshaphat prayed publicly on the nation's behalf. This was not the prayer of someone who realized he needed to turn to God at the last moment, but the prayer of a person who was confident of having been in the will of God all along. After all, he was a king who had not noticed the invading army because he was so busy implementing God's law in the land.

Jehoshaphat began by confessing God's sovereignty. The Lord was Creator and sustainer of the world, and nothing would happen against his will. The king also acknowledged that the land the Hebrews were occupying was the gift of God, first promised to Abraham.

Jehoshaphat reminded the Lord of Solomon's prayer and God's promise in response. Solomon had built the temple and at the dedication ceremony had entreated God that, if in time of calamity people would pray in the temple, God would rescue them (2 Chr. 6:19–40). God had answered that he would come to their aid (2 Chr. 7:13–16). This was one of those critical situations.

Jehoshaphat pleaded his case with the Lord by pointing out the unfairness of this invasion by Ammon, Moab, and the Meunites. Skipping back over centuries of mutual hostilities, which had already flourished during the time of the judges (Judg. 3:12–30; 11:5–40), Jehoshaphat brought up Israel's original encounter with the Transjordanian nations during the time of the exodus (Exod. 2:1–23). At that point Israel marched through the territories of the lands of Edom, Ammon, and Moab without inflicting harm on them (Deut. 2:1–37). But now these ungrateful nations were paying back Israel's kindness to them with an invasion against God's people.

Jehoshaphat declared that he and his army could not defeat this enemy in their own strength. If they were going to get out of this spot, it would have to be God's doing. The king pleaded with God to rescue his people in this hour of trial.

Jehoshaphat prayed with the entire congregation of Judah behind him. This was not a case of the king alone praying as a representative of the people. The people, who had been taught by Jehoshaphat, were with him in heart and spirit. This was one of Israel's finest moments throughout the Chronicles. What a thrilling moment with the people united in Jerusalem before God under the leadership of a devoted king!

20:14–17. Jehoshaphat received an answer from God even before any fighting started. In the crowd was a Levite, Jahaziel, who could trace his ancestry back to Asaph, David's musician. He spoke up with a word directly from the Lord: **The battle is not yours, but God's.** Jehoshaphat was taken out of the picture. The prophet told him exactly where the invading army was, where Judah's army should take its position, and then just to watch because God would defeat the enemies.

20:18–21. The meeting that began as a hastily called prayer convocation of a kingdom in crisis turned into a praise service. Everyone bowed in a posture of worship; then a number of Levites began to sing praises to God. There was harmony because the chronicler points out that these Levites who joined in song included Kohathites (the priestly division that included the descendants of Aaron) and their ancient rivals, the Korahites (those Kohathites who were not descended from Aaron and thus could not be priests). On this day there was no arrogance or resentment; they all lifted their voices together in praise.

The same spirit of praise continued as Jehoshaphat and his army set out for the Judean desert the next morning. As the troops left Jerusalem, the king turned the military mission into a "singspiration." He reassured everyone of God's promise and appointed song leaders to lead the soldiers in praise choruses. Soon everyone joined in the familiar tune, **Give thanks to the LORD, for his love endures forever.** This anthem was associated with the occasions when David and then Solomon moved the ark of the covenant (1 Chr. 16:41; 2 Chr. 5:13). God was on the march again!

20:22–25. God was putting on a special display that Jehoshaphat and his men needed to watch. We are never told exactly how large the invading army was, but Jehoshaphat described it as "vast" (v. 12). The enemy army marched in separate detachments, apparently passing through the mountains by choosing several different valleys. As the Moabite and Ammonite divisions were moving along, they saw the Edomite contingent before them and did not recognize them. Here were these Ammonite and Moabite men, having been force-marched through the desert to catch the enemy off-guard as quickly as possible, burning for a battle at the earliest opportunity, and there, right before their eyes, were unfamiliar warriors—they must be the army of Judah.

The invaders drew their swords and began to massacre their allies from Mount Seir. How glorious the Ammonites and Moabites must have felt when they saw how easy it was for them to defeat their supposed enemy! Once this confusion got started, there was no stopping it. When the Ammonites and Moabites finished slaughtering the Edomites, they began fighting each other.

Nobody could tell friend from foe, so they fought each other indiscriminately until the entire invading army had annihilated itself.

By the time Jehoshaphat and his marching revival choir arrived on the scene, it was all over. There was nothing in front of them but devastation. Corpses were spread out for miles. For the victors, battlefields were mines of wealth. In this case the true victor was God since he had brought about the defeat of the invading army. But his people were entitled to the spoils, and they worked for three days, helping themselves to all they could carry away.

20:26–30. Finally, the men of Judah reassembled in the **Valley of Beracah**, the "Valley of Praise," also called later the "Valley of Jehoshaphat" (Joel 3:2). This place is identical to what is usually referred to as the Kidron Valley, which cuts between the eastern side of Jerusalem and the Mount of Olives.

One of the positive outcomes of this event was that Jehoshaphat gained standing in the international community. It was a common belief among the ancients that each nation had its own particular god. Word got out that you did not play games with the God that Jehoshaphat worshiped. Consequently, there were no further attempts at invasions of Judah. Jehoshaphat did engage in at least one more military adventure, a successful mission together with the new king of Israel, Jehoram (also called Joram) son of Ahab, and the king of Edom against the Moabites (2 Kgs. 3:4–27). But in the land itself there was peace, granted by God himself.

🅴 Summary, Further Alliances, and Death Notice (20:31–21:3)

SUPPORTING IDEA: *The final summary of Jehoshaphat's life is tarnished by references to his failure to complete the purification of his land and another alliance with the Northern Kingdom.*

20:31–34. Again, as we approach the last statements about Jehoshaphat, let us not forget that he was a righteous man who stood out among the mediocre and lukewarm rulers of Judah. For the twenty-five years that he governed from Jerusalem, he walked with the Lord. The chronicler compares him favorably to Asa, his father, but Jehoshaphat seems to shine even brighter because he did not turn cold and bitter as Asa did at the end of his life.

And yet the chronicler does not give Jehoshaphat perfect marks. At the end he did not achieve his goals. The high places still stood, and the people were not devoted to God. This last statement is particularly poignant since Jehoshaphat had made such a great effort to teach his subjects about God. Still, many of the citizens of Judah continued to practice idolatry. He brought into the family the daughter of Jezebel, the most notorious Baal worshiper and God hater in all Israel. He kept cooperating with the idolatrous Northern Kingdom. All of Jehoshaphat's sincere devotion notwithstanding, this message could not have been lost on the people who looked to him for leadership.

As always, the final summary includes references to further information about the king. This time it was Jehu son of Hanani, the prophet who had scolded him for his alliance with Ahab, who kept tabs on Jehoshaphat's life for public records.

20:35–37. Before we finish with Jehoshaphat, we hear of one more bad alliance that he made. One way in which he copied Solomon's programs was to get in the sea trade, just as Solomon had done with the assistance of Hiram of Tyre (2 Chr. 8:17–18). Like his role model, Jehoshaphat wanted to send ships from Ezion Geber to Ophir to bring back gold (1 Kgs. 22:48). In order to accomplish this, he established a partnership with Ahaziah, another son of Ahab, who was then king of Israel.

However, the Lord's opinion about Jehoshaphat's alliances with the Northern Kingdom had not changed. God sent another faithful prophet, Eliezer, to deliver the bad news to the king. Because Jehoshaphat had entered into this association with the evil king of Israel, he would lose everything he had put into this venture. True to this prediction, the enterprise failed miserably. A horrendous storm hit Ezion Geber, and all the ships were destroyed.

21:1–3. No further distinctive features are added to the report on Jehoshaphat's death and funeral. He was buried with his predecessors in the City of David, and his oldest son, Jehoram, became king. The chronicler does state that Jehoram became the successor, even though there were many other sons. Jehoram had functioned as heir apparent for all his life; it was he who had been married off to Athaliah, presumably in order to reunite the two kingdoms in true Solomonic style. He was the hope of bringing everyone together. And so Jehoshaphat's successful reign ended sadly with the promise of a fiasco as his legacy.

MAIN IDEA REVIEW: *Jehoshaphat was a godly king. However, he brought troubles upon himself and the kingdom by making alliances with the ungodly kings of the Northern Kingdom.*

III. CONCLUSION

Where Would They Build a Home Together?

The musical *Fiddler on the Roof* follows events in the Jewish section of a little Russian village in the nineteenth century through the eyes of Tevye, the milkman. Tevye is both pious and knowledgeable in Torah; he will quote the "good book" on every possible occasion, even to God himself—until he remembers that it was God who had written the book in the first place. Tevye leads his life by the rules and traditions of East European Orthodox Judaism.

A large part of the story is how Tevye's three daughters find their husbands and how he reacts to each one. All three push the bounds of what Tevye thought was acceptable. First Tzeitel, the oldest daughter, pledged her troth to a young and impoverished tailor, bypassing the traditional role of the matchmaker in arranging marriages. Tevye, though torn, reconciled himself to this breach; the tailor, after all, was observant of proper customs in all his other affairs. Then, Hodel, the middle daughter, fell in love with a revolutionary activist who wound up being exiled to Siberia. Still, he was Jewish, and Hodel promised to get married "under a canopy"—in a traditional Jewish ceremony—so Tevye could accept this marriage as well.

But things went too far for Tevye with Chava, the youngest daughter. She fell in love with a Gentile boy, and Tevye could not possibly approve of their union. To Chava's protestations that they loved each other, Tevye said, "A bird may love a fish, but where would they build a home together?"

Tevye's saying has relevance to the children of God, whether in the Old Testament or the New Testament, and their partnership with unbelievers. The apostle Paul said, "Do not be yoked together with unbelievers. For what do righteousness and wickedness have in common? Or what fellowship can light have with darkness?" (2 Cor. 6:14).

This verse is often applied to marriages between believers and unbelievers, and this is quite correct. But, of course, it speaks to any close relationship in which the believer runs the risk of violating principles contrary to his faith. It is not possible for a Christian to make common cause with a non-Christian on an intimate basis.

Let me add two points of clarification. First of all, by the time Paul wrote this, he had already made clear that a person who had become a Christian after he was married should not leave his nonbelieving spouse (1 Cor. 7:12–16). And furthermore, this injunction to be separate from unbelievers does not mean that we should not be "friends" with non-Christians; otherwise, how will we share the gospel with them?

But let us not make Jehoshaphat's mistake. He was a godly man in many respects, virtually flawless in the description that the chronicler gives. And yet, Jehoshaphat apparently never came to terms with how deep the divide was between himself and the house of Ahab.

My point is not to discourage anyone. Obviously, if a person is already in a situation of partnership with an unbeliever, and the non-Christian is becoming open toward things of the Lord and Scripture, this is a good thing, not because the person is increasingly becoming more Christian, but because he or she is learning and may eventually take the step of becoming a Christian. But until someone has truly come to Christ, we must recognize that there is a great divide between us. And, like Jehoshaphat, if we ignore this fact, we may find ourselves being drawn further away from our life with God.

PRINCIPLES

- God calls us to a life of obedience with him.
- It is not possible for believers to lead a godly life if they put themselves into relationships that compromise their faith.

APPLICATIONS

- When you seek godly counsel, don't just ask those who will say what you want to hear.
- Seek the friendship and company of people who will speak forthrightly and have your best interest at heart.
- When you seek God's direction, be prepared to obey when he shows you his will.
- Avoid relationships that will lead you to compromise what you believe.
- Ask God to strengthen you so that when you do his will, you will be able to withstand criticism.

IV. LIFE APPLICATION

The Continental Divide

The United States actually has two continental divides, one for the eastern half and one for the western half of the country. In each case it marks the boundary of which direction water will flow, either to the Atlantic Ocean or the Mississippi basin in the east, and either to the Pacific Ocean or the Mississippi basin in the west. Just think of it: on the top of the mountain ranges along which the divide runs, any drop of water—assuming that it is not evaporated or absorbed by a thirsty animal—must go in either one direction or the other. Each drop of water must go one way or the other, and it cannot do both.

There is such a thing as a spiritual continental divide. We are either on God's side or not. Jesus said, "He who is not with me is against me" (Matt. 12:30). Not everyone accepts the reality of this division. When I was a seminary student, for a time I managed a coffeehouse intended for an evangelistic ministry. The atmosphere was such that it also attracted a number of Christian teenagers who were looking for a safe and entertaining place to go on a Friday or a Saturday night. One young woman from a local church—call her Maggie—was starting to spend a lot of time with Gil, a non-Christian young man who came by frequently.

Wanting to make sure that Maggie was not getting into a bad situation, and not knowing whether she was sure of Gil's spiritual position, I asked her, "Are you aware that Gil is not a Christian?" I will never forget the look of piety that came over Maggie's face as she stated, "Oh, I don't divide people up that way: Christian or non-Christian, saved or unsaved. I don't believe in separating people like that."

According to the Bible, God makes a distinction between those who are his people and those who are not, but people like Maggie wish to include everyone among those who belong to God. Let me point out three reasons why, despite the charitable appearance, ignoring the spiritual continental divide is a harmful thing.

The Bible consistently affirms a distinction between those who are and are not God's people. Putting it bluntly, in our section in Chronicles, we see that it is not just the worship of Baal that is condemned but those who worship him as well.

To deny the fact that there are people who are not saved is theoretically to deny them a full chance at the gospel. Jesus said, "It is not the healthy who need a doctor, but the sick" (Matt. 9:12). He saved us because we needed to be saved.

There is a fundamental difference between Christians and non-Christians. Even though most of us have a lot of room for growth in our Christian lives, the essence of the Christian life is this: we have a new nature, and we are indwelt by the Holy Spirit who will bring out this new nature as he guides us to implement the principles of Scripture. The non-Christian does not, and—as little as some people want to hear this—it does show. In all the foibles surrounding Jehoshaphat's alliance with Ahab, one of the more poignant moments was Jehoshaphat's admonition of Ahab when he impugned Micaiah, "The king should not say that" (2 Chr. 18:7b). Ahab's problems were far more fundamental. The divide between those who belong to God and those who do not is more than cosmetic.

If you are looking for people who are spending their lives in service to others, alleviating suffering, providing health care, and sacrificing their own well-being in the process, chances are strong that you will find Christians in these roles. Christ really does make a difference.

V. PRAYER

Lord Jesus, thank you that by your love and grace we are allowed to be your children. Please help us never to act as though we deserve your salvation and never to take membership in your family for granted. Please help us also not to tarnish our standing by immersing ourselves in relationships that will dishonor you, but please help us to be witnesses through keeping ourselves pure. Amen.

VI. DEEPER DISCOVERIES

Is Idolatry Always Wrong? (17:3)

Not everyone is comfortable with the idea that idolatry is opposed to God. There is one passage in C. S. Lewis's last book of the Narnia Chronicles, *The Last Battle,* which contains a troubling scene. A man named Emeth, who had been serving the evil god Tash all his life, found himself redeemed by Aslan the lion, (a Christ figure) much to his surprise. Aslan told him that, while Emeth was serving Tash outwardly, he remained inwardly righteous, and so he was unwittingly serving Aslan. Worship of Tash was actually implicit worship of Aslan (Lewis, 165). Perhaps Lewis was saying that people who do not know Christ but serve idols can still have a relationship with God.

But Ezra's books of 1 and 2 Chronicles belie Lewis's Chronicles of Narnia on this issue. Worship of any idol, such as Baal, can never be construed as worship of the Lord, no matter how many good motives we may wish to read into the act. The service to an idol made by human hands, or, for that matter, the concept represented by the idol, was—and is—incompatible with the worship of God. There is only one thing to do with idols: abolish them.

Was Jehoshaphat using a rationalization such as Lewis's when he agreed to cooperate with Ahab? Even though he attempted to purge his own land of everything idolatrous, did he think that if Ahab focused on everything good about Baal worship, he would become an implicit worshiper of the Lord? It is hard to believe that Jehoshaphat could have gone that far in his thoughts, but then again, he did not save the prophet Micaiah from the dungeon, and he did go to war in spite of God's warning against it.

As you are reading these words, you may be attempting to honor two gods at once. You may think of yourself as mostly committed to Christ but not as totally closing the door on some other options. You could be saying that you are strong in your own faith but that you are not ready to say that no other religion leads to salvation.

The contemporary "open-minded" attitude toward other religions short-changes the wonder of the gospel. It is precisely because there are no other options that it is so amazing that God has provided one for us, beginning with his call of Israel as his own people and culminating when his Son died on the cross for our sins. God did not exclude other possible ways of salvation—there simply were none, and no new ones have come up since.

Think of it this way. You need to go to a city in the west to speak to the king who lives there. There are many roads before you, but most of them go in the wrong direction. Perhaps there are a few that start out going west, but if you walk on them for a short while, you will find that these, too, begin to bend, and pretty soon they are heading straight east as well. There simply is no road to take you where you have to go.

Then the king builds a new road, starting from his city, directly to where you are. This is the only road to take you to your destination, and this is the one you will take. The king did not declare the other roads to be wrong; he is not arbitrary or oppressive when he tells you that the other roads are wrong. They simply are wrong, just as they always have been.

There is nothing wrong with feeling challenged by the idea that there is only one way to God. Nobody likes the thought that there are people pursuing religions that will take them away from God rather than to him. Nevertheless, only if we are willing to recognize how lost human beings really are and that there is no way to find God except on his own explicit terms does the good news of the gospel really begin to shine.

VII. TEACHING OUTLINE

A. INTRODUCTION

1. Lead Story: The Monkey and the Crocodile
2. Context: Jehoshaphat inherited the throne from Asa and maintained his God-centered policies. But he, too, was not immune to mistakes.
3. Transition: By their very nature, monkeys and crocodiles cannot be true friends. King Jehoshaphat found out the risks in attempting to be friends with Ahab, who worshiped Baal.

B. COMMENTARY

1. Jehoshaphat's Early Reign (17:1–19)
2. Military Campaign Alongside Ahab (18:1–19:3)
3. Jehoshaphat's Further Reforms (19:4–11)
4. War with Nations East of the Jordan River (20:1–30)
5. Summary, Further Alliances, and Death Notice (20:31–21:3)

C. CONCLUSION: WHERE WOULD THEY BUILD A HOME TOGETHER?

VIII. ISSUES FOR DISCUSSION

1. In a Christian's relationship to non-Christians, what elements are fixed by Scripture, and which depend on the situation?
2. What steps might Christians take if they see a brother or sister getting into a potentially destructive relationship?
3. Why is it so important for Christians to insist on a separated identity to show the world that we are different from other people?

2 Chronicles 21:4–22:12

Implosion

I. INTRODUCTION
Here Comes the Flood!

II. COMMENTARY
A verse-by-verse explanation of these chapters.

III. CONCLUSION
Just a Few Grains of Rice

An overview of the principles and applications from these chapters.

IV. LIFE APPLICATION
Jackal in a Sack

Melding these chapters to life.

V. PRAYER
Tying these chapters to life with God.

VI. DEEPER DISCOVERIES
Historical, geographical, and grammatical enrichment of the commentary.

VII. TEACHING OUTLINE
Suggested step-by-step group study of these chapters.

VIII. ISSUES FOR DISCUSSION
Zeroing these chapters in on daily life.

Q u o t e

"*T*he Lord hands men over to the consequences of that which they have chosen for themselves."

A .   B e r k e l e y   M i k k e l s o n

2 Chronicles 21:4–22:12

I N   A   N U T S H E L L

*J*ehoram and Ahaziah were evil kings, worshiping idols and bringing ruin on the kingdom. When Ahaziah died, his grandmother Athaliah took the throne by force and wreaked even greater devastation.

Implosion

I. INTRODUCTION

Here Comes the Flood!

*H*ow much power should the ruler of any country have? Many countries, particularly democracies, state that whoever governs a country is accountable to his subjects. In most modern nations a representative body, such as a parliament or a congress, makes sure that no single individual's policies are beyond review. However, in Europe during the seventeenth and eighteenth centuries, a number of kingdoms bought into the idea of "enlightened despotism." This concept was based on the notion that to have one person at the top, who knows and understands what is best for the country, is preferable to the confusion and indecisiveness caused by spreading authority around.

The last few kings of France before the French Revolution ruled under this model. An obvious problem with such a system is that it also transforms one person's bad ideas into the irrevocable law of the land. Furthermore, for the person holding all the power, the distinction between the welfare of the land and his own personal welfare becomes blurred. This is what happened with the kings of France. Everyone has heard of Louis XIV and the splendid palaces he built for himself with funds from the public treasury.

King Louis XV continued the policies of his father. His personal splendor and enrichment were worth more to him than the faltering economy of the land. Together with his mistress he lived in luxury, not caring that his actions were taking France to the brink of disaster. When his administrators showed the king and his consort the financial consequences of his policies, his mistress responded, "Après moi le deluge" ("After me, the flood"). In other words, when they were gone, disaster might strike, and everything might collapse, but so what.

And sure enough disaster struck shortly after his death. The rule of his son, Louis XVI, and his queen, the celebrated Marie Antoinette, was brought to an end by the French Revolution, which culminated in the Reign of Terror. That, in turn, gave way to the barbarous regime of Napoleon. The flood had arrived.

In this section of Chronicles, we will see the flood come upon the kingdom of Judah. The first few kings of Jerusalem had some flaws, but they also had some abilities. But their policies, particularly those of Jehoshaphat, sowed the seeds for collapse. Jehoram and Ahaziah were idol worshipers as well as incapable kings. To make matters even worse, when Ahaziah died, his grandmother, the evil Athaliah, usurped the throne and set new standards of cruelty. The flood was covering the land.

II. COMMENTARY

Implosion

> **MAIN IDEA:** *The reigns of Jehoram and Ahaziah illustrate how sin often brings its own consequences.*

A The Reign of Jehoram (21:4–20)

> **SUPPORTING IDEA:** *Jehoram's reign was as disastrous in its outcome as he was short on devotion to the Lord.*

21:4–7. It's not easy to avoid confusion, but we must keep in mind that there was another Jehoram, son of Ahab and brother of Ahaziah, all of whom were kings of Israel. Our Jehoram is the son of Jehoshaphat and the father of another Ahaziah, all of whom were kings of Judah. The chronicler has nothing good to say about Jehoram. The first few verses of his brief description give a summary that tells the whole sordid story; what remains fills in some of the disasters that beset Judah because of its king's wicked policies. And what heinous disasters they were!

Fratricide was not unknown in the history of the Hebrew kings. We have already noted that Solomon executed his brother Adonijah (1 Kgs. 2:25), who was his rival for the throne. However, Jehoram killed all six of his brothers, not to mention other distinguished persons in the land, just to make sure there would be no challenge to his regime. Having thus alienated his own subjects, he began an eight-year rule under the domination of his in-laws in Israel, the house of Omri. Jehoram pursued the same practices and policies that were making Israel a disturbing place to live.

Still, even with Jehoram doing exactly what the kings of Israel were doing, he would not suffer the same consequences. The dynasty of Omri was about to suffer total extermination as punishment for their depravity. But Jehoram had one thing going for him: he was a descendant of the house of David. In spite of his disobedience to God, the Lord would not eliminate his entire family. It would be close, thanks to his own wife, but God had promised David that a descendant of Solomon's would always be on the throne (1 Chr. 17:14). This promise kept Jehoram's family from obliteration.

21:8–11. During Jehoshaphat's reign Edom had become subjugated to Judah again, as it had been during the reigns of David and Solomon. Now, as the kingdom began to fall apart, Edom was one of the first enemy nations to assert its authority. Recognizing a weak king in Jerusalem, it renounced its allegiance to him and reestablished its own monarchy. **So Jehoram went there**; his reaction when his will was thwarted was to send in a military unit to enforce his will. There is no record of any soul-searching or evaluation of different options by Jehoram in this situation. The king who celebrated his coronation by executing his brothers probably didn't spend a moment asking himself about any religious or political causes for Edom's rebellion. They were disobeying him; they needed to be punished.

So Jehoram called together his army, particularly his chariot units, and headed off to Edom. But the Edomites knew he was coming, and he had neither stealth nor overwhelming power at his disposal. The Edomites surrounded the army of Judah. It was because of a desperate sortie at night that Jehoram's punitive mission against Edom did not turn into his own massacre. The king and his officers barely escaped, and Edom stood independent and unpunished. Strike Edom off the list of tributary nations!

Around the same time the town of Libnah rebelled against Jehoram's rule. Libnah was located west of Jerusalem; it belonged geographically to Judah (Josh. 10:29–32; 12:15), and it had been designated as one of the cities of refuge. So it was not a foreign power. Some interpreters think it may have been located close to the Philistine city of Gath and may have become "Philistinized" in its culture and religion (Payne, 407). However, given the original nature of Libnah as a town under Levite control, and the reason the chronicler himself gives—**because Jehoram had forsaken the LORD**—it is more likely that Libnah was one municipality in Judah that got fed up with the king's idolatry.

Jehoram had not only built high places throughout Judah, but he had taken an active role in leading the people to betray God (i.e., **prostitute themselves**). Perhaps the citizens of Libnah united to take a stand against it.

21:12–15. Elijah the prophet had been Ahab and Jezebel's opponent in the Northern Kingdom. Now that Jehoram had bound himself closely to Israel and was following their ways, he also came under Elijah's judgment. Elijah made his presence known by sending a letter. This message may have been delivered to Jehoram after Elijah's departure from the world.

Elijah's letter first listed the charges against Jehoram: (1) not following the role models of Jehoshaphat, his father, and Asa, his grandfather; (2) leading the people of Judah and Jerusalem away from God and into idolatry; and (3) killing his own brothers. The second part of the letter detailed the punishment that Jehoram would undergo: (1) the destruction of his family and his personal property and (2) a horrible disease of the bowels.

The chronicler does not report any response by Jehoram to the letter, but this was the same thing as rejection of Elijah's message.

21:16–17. Not long ago Jehoshaphat had received visits from Philistines and Arabs, who had come to Jerusalem bearing tribute money (2 Chr. 17:11). Now they were back for Jehoram, but this time they were not bringing presents. Instead, they assaulted Jehoram's palace, appropriated its treasures, and killed his sons and wives. The chronicler mentions one exception to the devastation and implies another. The youngest son, Ahaziah, a teenager at the time, managed to escape. And one of Jehoram's wives, Athaliah, who had contributed most to the present calamity, went unscathed.

21:18–20. As foretold in Elijah's letter, Jehoram came down with an intestinal disorder. The chronicler tells us that **the LORD afflicted Jehoram**. Nobody was sad when Jehoram died. His death notice did not refer to any further sources of information about him, perhaps on the assumption that nobody wanted to know more about this miserable king. He was not even allowed to be buried in the same site as his predecessors.

Ⓑ The Reign of Ahaziah (22:1–9)

> **SUPPORTING IDEA:** *Ahaziah continued the evil practices of his father, but his reign was brief.*

22:1–4. If the people of Jerusalem had a choice about where to look for a new king, they did not avail themselves of the opportunity. There was only one eligible descendant of the house of David—Jehoram's youngest son Ahaziah—and he received their acclamation. This twenty-two-year-old, who had just recently become a father for the first time, decided to stick to the tried-and-failed methods of his father. Again, we can see the heavy hand of Athaliah at work. Ahaziah was the grandson of Ahab and Jezebel, and the northern royal family was all the family he had to relate to. They were willing to step in and guide him in the art of kingship—as well as the ways of false worship. The chronicler's assessment of Ahaziah is that **he did evil.**

22:5–6a. Ahaziah's uncle, Jehoram, son of Ahab and king of Israel, talked Ahaziah into going to war alongside him, once again to fight the Arameans at Ramoth Gilead. The players had changed from earlier events (2 Chr. 18:3), but it was still the same game. The Northern Kingdom had gone through a number of military engagements with Aram in addition to the ill-fated earlier battle for Ramoth Gilead. In some of these battles, they were miraculously preserved by God through the prophets Elijah and Elisha (1 Kgs. 20:1–43; 2 Kgs. 6:24–7:20). Now Ben-Hadad, king of Aram and Israel's foe, had been assassinated by Hazael, who became Ben-Hadad's successor. Jehoram of Israel felt the time was ripe to assert himself, particularly his claims to Ramoth Gilead. His nephew Ahaziah of Judah provided further troop strength.

This venture proved to be successful. However, Jehoram received an injury and had to seek refuge in the city of Jezreel to recuperate. Ahaziah withdrew as well.

22:6b–9. Considerate nephew that he was, Ahaziah went to see his ailing uncle in Jezreel. Unfortunately, he could not have timed this visit any worse. No sooner had he arrived than Jehu son of Nimshi came calling. And Jehu's intent was not to comfort the hurting king in his time of affliction. He came to kill the king and take the crown himself, because God had instructed him to do so.

As Jehoram of Israel and Ahaziah of Judah were enjoying their visit, they were interrupted by Jehu's arrival with his army. The chronicler does not give us the details we read in 2 Kings 9:1–26 of how Jehu was anointed by a prophet working for Elisha, how he and his chariot corps stormed Jezreel to catch everyone by surprise, and how he methodically executed anyone associated with the house of Ahab and Ahab's government. For Ezra the chronicler, the most important point is that Ahaziah and his princes were among the victims of Jehu's purge as well. Since Ahaziah and his retinue were inside the boundaries of Israel, Jehu did not need to invade the Southern Kingdom; he could carry out his mission right on his own soil.

Jehoram of Israel received an arrow in his back, but Ahaziah of Judah managed to escape. He got as far as Samaria, where Jehu's men wounded him. Continuing on the run, Ahaziah finally died of his injuries at Megiddo (2 Kgs. 9:27). Second Kings 9:28 clarifies for us the chronicler's brief statement on Ahaziah's funeral: Ahaziah's own men buried him, and the burial he received, out of respect for his godly grandfather, was among the royal tombs in Jerusalem.

The Coup by Athaliah (22:10–12)

SUPPORTING IDEA: *Athaliah did not have a legitimate claim to the throne.*

22:10–12. "The king is dead! Long live the king." But there was no king. There was not even a plausible candidate. Sure, there were Ahaziah's children, but they were toddlers. The youngest, little Joash, was barely a year old, and the former king's other children could not have been much older, considering that Ahaziah was only twenty-three years old at the most. Thus it looked as though the line of David, which had followed a straight descent as sons had succeeded their fathers, would have to diverge into some side branch. This was the first time the kingdom of Judah had faced this problem.

This was Athaliah's golden moment. After all, she was royalty herself—her father Ahab, was the king of Israel, and her mother Jezebel, was a princess of Sidon—and she had been influential in the government of her husband. Who else could come even close to her in terms of qualifications? Furthermore, in all fairness to Athaliah, we must recognize that she was in a quandary regardless of what she did. At this very moment, Jehu, the new king of Israel, was in the last phases of obliterating Athaliah's relatives—from her brother (Jehoram of Israel) on down.

As risky as it was for her to grasp the throne herself, it was almost certain that anyone else who became king of Judah would have been an isolated survivor of the savagery perpetrated by her husband (Jehoram of Judah) and would cooperate with Jehu in purging Ahab's line from the Southern Kingdom as well. Her only hope for survival lay in appropriating the kingdom for herself. Most commentators emphasize Athaliah's greed and lust for power, but we have to leave room for some fear on her part.

But let us not confuse understanding her motives with sympathy. Athaliah was ruthless in establishing herself as queen. She carried out her own purge of anyone who could be identified as associated with the house of David. She tried to wipe out all of them so no one could step forward with a legitimate claim to the throne. But she left out two crucial people—her step-daughter Jehosheba, and her grandchild, Ahaziah's infant son Joash. Perhaps Athaliah did not think there was any point in killing off the women of the clan, or Jehosheba may have enjoyed special protection as the wife of Jehoiada, the high priest. Maybe the self-acclaimed queen even felt some affection toward the daughter of her husband by another wife. Regardless of her motivation, Jehosheba was allowed to live. And Jehosheba spirited little Joash out of harm's way.

The chronicler does not give us any information about monarchs: length of reign, age of ascent, summary of accomplishments, not even the negative statements we saw for Jehoram. Athaliah was not a legitimate ruler in the chronicler's eyes. She was not a descendant of the house of David. As a confirmed devotee of Baal, she had no tie to the legitimate worship of God in the temple. She may have held the reins of the government for a time, but she had no right to the throne.

MAIN IDEA REVIEW: *The reigns of Jehoram and Ahaziah illustrate how sin often brings its own consequences.*

III. CONCLUSION

Just a Few Grains of Rice

A wise man invented the game of chess and presented it to a great king. The king was pleased with the gift and told the man that he could have anything he wanted for a reward. The wise man replied that all he wanted was one grain of rice. "Just one grain of rice?" the befuddled king asked.

"Well, OK," replied the wise man. "Let's just say that I'll ask you to cover the chess board with grains of rice. Please put just one grain in the first square, two in the second, four in the third, and so forth, doubling the number of grains in each successive square until all sixty-four squares are filled."

"Of course, my dear, fellow," the king replied. "We'll take care of that. You're certainly entitled to more than that, but I'm delighted to give you what you ask for." And he ordered his servants to bring a bag of rice.

But the bag was not enough. Halfway through the board, the thirty-second square alone would have had to hold more than two hundred million grains of rice. The total number of grains of rice required to complete the transaction would have been more than the number designated by 18 followed by 18 zeroes: 18,000,000,000,000,000,000. If the entire surface of the earth were a rice field, it would still only produce a fraction of that amount. This story has two possible endings: Either the king paid all he could and forfeited his kingdom, or he was outraged and had the wise man beheaded.

Like the king in this story, Jehoram of Judah did not see the end results of his actions before it was too late. He could have looked at the history of his predecessors. He certainly could have heeded Elijah's warning letter. Immersed in an impenetrable fog, he went his own way. And it was his way, not Athaliah's. She provided the means and opportunity for him to do wrong, but he was not born without the ability to say no; he clearly said no to his father, to his brothers, to Elijah, and to God. But he did not say no to the daughter of Jezebel. He must not have seen how catastrophic the consequences of his actions would be.

While Jehoram was busy filling the land with idols, his enemies started to chip away at the kingdom. Finally, the unthinkable happened, and the Philistines came into his palace, carted off his belongings, and executed his family. Then, with nothing left but a kingdom populated by subjects who despised him, he lost his health and died an excruciating death.

Jehoram is a warning to us. There comes a point when the flood will no longer hold back, when the grains of rice have multiplied beyond belief, when the outcome of actions that we thought we could cover up can no longer be contained or manipulated. The time to deal with them is now.

PRINCIPLES

- Sin, although primarily a breach in our relationship with God, will also have negative consequences in our relationships with others.
- The extent that sin has taken over our lives may not show up immediately but may eventually cause a sudden collapse.

APPLICATIONS

- Consider the sayings, "What goes round, comes round" or "You're gonna reap what you sow." How are these principles borne out in the reigns of Jehoram and Ahaziah?
- Imagine a debate between two people over whether people get all they deserve in this life. One argues yes. The other says no. What evidence could each person offer to support his position?
- What would you say to a person who told you he was about to do something that he knew was wrong, knowing that God is gracious and forgiving?

IV. LIFE APPLICATION

Jackal in a Sack

In August 1994, agents for the French government were in the Sudan making an arrest. Around three o'clock in the morning, they entered a house where a pudgy middle-aged man was recuperating from minor surgery. They surrounded his bed, held him down, and injected him with a sedative. Then they boarded a plane at a nearby airport with their prisoner's body wrapped in a sack and flew him to France. The agents did not unfasten the sack again until they were safely in France, at which point they could be sure that their prisoner was in their country's custody.

The person in question was Ilich Ramirez Sanchez, known around the world as Carlos the Jackal, one of the most notorious terrorists of the twentieth century. He was the mastermind behind numerous bombings, hijackings, and massacres, beginning with the murder of the Israeli Olympic team in Munich 1972 and ending with joint ventures alongside Osama bin Laden, the head of the Al-Qaida terrorist group. Known for his efficiency and ruthlessness as well as for his debonair "playboy" lifestyle, Carlos's *persona* grew larger than life. In addition to stories about him in the news, he even became a stock character in numerous works of fiction.

Carlos's primary occupation was selling death and destruction, but he was willing to adopt a façade of whatever philosophy might promote his business. Having started out as a Marxist terrorist, toward the end of his career he found it more suitable to call himself a Muslim.

But things eventually started to unravel for the revolutionary. As the Sudanese official who permitted Carlos's arrest grumbled:

> We welcomed him as a combatant, someone who fought . . . for noble causes. Now he's a hoodlum, his behavior is shameful. He drinks and goes out with women so much that I don't know if he's a Moslem. . . . We have no regrets. Because of his behavior, we are absolved from blame (Bellamy, Web site).

Carlos's life had disintegrated to such a point that he even earned the dislike of his immoral, murderous former employers. You cannot flaunt the laws of God and man consistently without sooner or later bringing harm to yourself. The person who justifies lying cannot trust anything anyone says to him; the person who says that human life is worthless is declaring his own life devoid of value; and the person who asserts that there is no standard of right and wrong other than one's personal power invites others to oppress him.

King Jehoram and his echoes, Ahaziah and Athaliah, are examples of this truth. Jehoram rejected all moorings with God and people, forsaking the worship of God and beginning his reign with an act of carnage. He had nothing to build his government on, and his life and kingdom wound up in shambles.

V. PRAYER

Lord Jesus, help us to take sin seriously in our lives. We have complete assurance of your grace and forgiveness, based on your shed blood on our behalf, but conviction does not give us a license to ignore sin. Help us to recognize that when it seems that a sin is advantageous to us, this is an illusion. Please bring us to greater trust in your revealed word and in the work of righteousness you are performing in our lives. Amen.

VI. DEEPER DISCOVERIES

The Arameans (22:5)

Who were the Arameans? Older Bible translations, such as the King James Version, use the term *Syria* instead of *Aram*. Those two words translate the same word in Hebrew. In general, the practice today is to think of "Syria" as referring to the geographic area, and Aram to the nation.

But there never was any single nation of "Aram" in the sense of one unified political entity. There were many Arams, or, more accurately, many kingdoms of Aram. For example, between 1 Chronicles 18:3–9 and 19:6, we can compile a list of five Aramean kingdoms: Aram Zobah, Aram Naharaim, Aram Maacah, Aram Damascus, and Aram Hamath. Although these small kingdoms frequently cooperated with one another, they never merged into one kingdom. In most of the passages in 2 Chronicles, the Aram referred to is the kingdom of Damascus.

But the bond among the various Aramean kingdoms was strong. They shared a common ethnic background—belonging to the descendants of Shem—as well as a mutual language, Aramean. According to the prophet Amos, the Arameans came to occupy their present territory with an exodus out of Kir, just as Israel had been led out of Egypt (Amos 9:7). Kir is another name for Mesopotamia. Amos also contains the prophecy that because of their sins Aram would eventually be brought back into captivity in Kir (Amos 1:5b), a prediction that was fulfilled when the Assyrians deported them.

Like their neighbors the Aramean kingdoms subscribed to their own assortment of Canaanite deities, with Baal occupying the highest position. The Arameans also shared a common devotion to their fierce storm god known as Hadad.

The various kingdoms of Aram battled and negotiated their way through the political realities of their day in competition with the other small nations—Ammon, Moab, Edom, Israel, Judah—attempting to survive. You were either oppressed or oppressing, and as long as you were oppressing, you could not be oppressed. Peaceful coexistence was not a viable concept; if nation A did not attempt to control nation B, nation B would attempt to control nation A. So Aram played its part in the ongoing shell game of ancient world affairs.

The kingdom of Damascus constantly readjusted itself in its relationship to Israel and Judah. Nothing was ever permanent; alliances and hostilities were ephemeral, depending on Aram's perceived advantage. Some scholars have questioned whether the accounts of the wars between Ahab and Ben-Hadad in Chronicles are historically accurate because Ahab also went to war alongside Ben-Hadad against Assyria (Pitard, 219). But this is expecting a consistency of the balance in world powers that cannot be found anywhere during this time. An account in which one ancient Middle Eastern nation with relatively limited power maintained a consistent policy over many decades would be far more suspect.

Even though the Arameans never became a superpower or left a unique cultural heritage, they did make one major contribution to history—their language. Aramaic became the language in which members of different nationalities communicated with one another. When Sennacherib of Assyria besieged Jerusalem, his officer yelled out their public taunts in Hebrew, the language of its residents. But the Jewish leaders asked him to speak in Aramaic since they knew that language, but the common people did not.

But by the time we get to the first century A.D., the time of Jesus, the language situation had reversed. When Jesus was calling out from the cross in Hebrew, the common people did not understand his cry—because now they knew only Aramaic (Matt. 27:46–49). Aramaic, initially a foreign language, had become the mother tongue for the Jews in Jesus' day.

VII. TEACHING OUTLINE

A. INTRODUCTION

1. Lead Story: Here Comes the Flood!

2. Context: Jehoshaphat, though a godly king, had made a marriage alliance with the house of Ahab, who were devoted to Baal worship. When Jehoshaphat died, his son Jehoram inherited the throne. Would he continue his father's policies of promoting obedience to God, or would he give in to the demands of his wife and his in-laws in favor of Baalism?

3. Transition: The phrase, "after me, the flood," has come to typify the attitude of King Louis XV of France, who expected his kingdom to collapse after his demise—an expectation that turned out to be accurate. Similarly, when Jehoshaphat died and Jehoram took over, the floodgates of Judah opened as Jehoshaphat's policy of friendship with Israel came home to roost.

B. COMMENTARY

1. The Reign of Jehoram (21:4–20)
2. The Reign of Ahaziah (22:1–9)
3. The Coup by Athaliah (22:10–12)

C. CONCLUSION: JUST A FEW GRAINS OF RICE

VIII. ISSUES FOR DISCUSSION

1. Will sin always cause harm in a person's life, or are there some sins that will only have negative consequences for a person at judgment day?
2. Is physical illness caused by sin? Always? Sometimes? Never? Take John 9:2–3 into account.
3. Ahaziah of Judah reaped judgment at the hand of Jehu because he "just happened" to be visiting Jehoram of Israel. To what extent does this event illustrate God's hand in history?

2 Chronicles 23:1–24:27

Lifelong Immaturity

| Q u o t e |

"True conversion will be demonstrated through subsequent events."

S t a n l e y   J .   G r e n z

2 Chronicles 23:1–24:27

I N   A   N U T S H E L L

The faithful high priest Jehoiada installed Joash on the throne of Judah. Joash pursued righteousness while Jehoiada was alive, but after Jehoiada's death he turned to evil.

Lifelong Immaturity

I. INTRODUCTION

Geronimo, Temporary Christian

"*G*eronimo!" To this day the very name of the famous Apache leader is synonymous with reckless abandon and daring. No one equaled his reputation for ruthlessness when he repeatedly escaped from a reservation and led bands of warriors against U.S. soldiers. Having experienced the slaughter of family members, Geronimo was ready to shed the blood of his enemies—and of anyone else who stood in his way.

However, at the end of his life, when Geronimo had given up his struggle and was trying to fit into life on the reservation, he turned to Christianity for a while. There were missionaries from the Reformed Church on the reservation, providing care and preaching the gospel. Even though Geronimo initially wanted nothing to do with them, eventually he was persuaded to attend services. Once there he started to study the "Jesus road" and recommend to everyone else that they do the same. Geronimo eventually had a conversion experience, was baptized, and joined the church.

However, Geronimo's time of church membership was short-lived. The "Christian interlude" (Debo, 434) soon yielded to his preference for drinking, gambling, and administering animistic healing practices, and the missionaries had no choice but to suspend his church membership.

How can a person seemingly belong to God for a time and then abandon the faith? The Bible has a sobering answer to this question: "For if they had belonged to us, they would have remained with us; but their going showed that none of them belonged to us" (1 John 2:19b). The person who, after having seemed to be thoroughly committed to Christ, turns against him and renounces him shows that he never truly belonged to Christ in the first place. This verse helps us understand a number of cases where an apparently righteous person makes a total turnaround away from God. One such person was King Joash.

II. COMMENTARY

Lifelong Immaturity

> **MAIN IDEA:** *King Joash pursued many policies in keeping with God's will as long as he was under the direct supervision of Jehoiada the priest, but as soon as Jehoiada died, Joash turned to evil.*

A The Overthrow of Athaliah (23:1–15)

> **SUPPORTING IDEA:** *Jehoiada the priest carried out a plot that removed Athaliah from the throne and installed Joash, the rightful heir, as king.*

23:1–3. Athaliah was the stepmother of Jehosheba (2 Chr. 22:11), who was married to Jehoiada, the high priest. Thus, she was Jehoiada's mother-in-law as well as Joash's grandmother. Jehoiada waited for the right moment. He probably knew he would have only one chance at a successful coup against Athaliah. If it failed, he and his supporters, not to mention Joash, would be executed.

Jehoiada first lined up support from all over the country of Judah. He recruited military leaders, **commanders of units of a hundred**, and Levites, so both the secular and religious sides were represented. The Levites would have responded well to an invitation to join a conspiracy that would result in the reestablishment of true worship. When enough people were on board, Jehoiada held a meeting in the one place in the entire kingdom that was safe: the temple of God. This was his place of work as the high priest. The Levites had a natural reason to be there. And Queen Athaliah did not make it a regular practice to worship God at the temple.

Jehoiada addressed his coconspirators with this premise: The throne of Judah belonged to the descendants of David, and the person entitled to this privilege was Joash, the son of the previous king, Ahaziah. This, Jehoiada reminded them, was God's promise.

23:4–7. No objective was more important than keeping the young king safe. Even if the plot should fail, as long as Joash stayed alive, all was not lost. But if Joash should get killed, there was no possibility of any second chance. So Jehoiada commanded all the people to set a heavy guard around the temple premises where the coronation would take place.

Jehoiada made use of the change in shifts for the Levites. As some of them were going off duty and some were coming on duty, there would be a massing of personnel which would not immediately arouse suspicion. But he did not have the present shift actually "clock out." They were consecrated already and could stay within the sacred precincts. The others were positioned in three details: one was deployed around the doors, one was set up to guard the main (**Foundation**) gate, and one was stationed right at the palace of the queen next to the temple.

No order could have been simpler than Jehoiada's directive to all these men—that anyone who tried to enter the temple would be killed. The Levites in the temple had the additional charge to protect the boy Joash by surrounding him with their weapons drawn.

23:8–11. The deployment went just as Jehoiada directed. With weapons in hand, the Levites secured the temple on the outside and the inside. Then Jehoiada proceeded with the coronation ceremony for Joash. The seven-year-old boy, having been kept in seclusion for his entire life, suddenly found himself surrounded by a horde of armed Levites in the middle of the sacred precinct.

Jehoiada placed a crown on the boy's head and **presented him with a copy of the covenant**. Although it is tempting to think that this was a scroll of the divine law, exhorting the new king to govern in godly fashion, it probably was something a little more prosaic. Jehoiada and his supporters had made a covenant specifically to make Joash king, and this was probably the covenant referred to. It was not so much a constitution as a coronation certificate.

Jehoiada and his sons carried out this coronation ceremony. The priests finished the ceremony by anointing Joash and proclaiming his kingship. "Long live the king!" they shouted. Now there was no need for secrecy. Everyone joined in the cheering. What had been a quiet rite carried out in secret turned into a noisy riot, loud enough to wake the neighbors.

23:12–15. Queen Athaliah heard the noise and rushed to the temple. After six years in power, she must have felt secure in her position. She had murdered all conceivable rivals; no one had come forward to challenge her. She may have felt by this time that she had lifelong tenure. What a shock when she stepped into the temple court! There was a little boy, standing next to one of the pillars at the entrance of the temple. And he was wearing a crown. And there was a crowd—a huge crowd—bowing before him and hailing him as the king. And there were officials and army officers and priests and Levites and hundreds of common people—all of them having a coronation party.

Athaliah screeched "Treason! Treason!" Only then did she attempt an escape to the palace. But this was exactly what Jehoiada wanted her to do. He had no intention of shedding any human blood within the temple, and he wanted to get to her before she had a chance to assemble guards around her. The priest's officers caught up with her outside the palace and executed her on the spot. The illegitimate ruler was dead, and the throne once again belonged to the family of David.

Ⓑ Reclaiming the Temple and the Throne (23:16–24:14)

SUPPORTING IDEA: *Jehoiada confirmed Joash's new rule with a recommitment to the worship of God, the proper installation of Joash, and a lengthy project of renovating the temple.*

23:16. There can be no doubt that the next several decades were the time of Jehoiada's kingship. He not only was the regent while Joash was just a boy; he also made decisions on Joash's behalf. In fact, he apparently was not able to teach Joash how to make proper decisions on his own. God allowed Jehoiada to live to the age of one hundred and thirty (2 Chr. 24:15). He was there for Joash for at least twenty-three years of his reign (2 Kgs. 12:6). When Jehoiada died, he received the full burial that belonged to a king (2 Chr. 24:16), an honor that would not be accorded to Joash himself (2 Chr. 24:25).

23:17. Before the coronation was over, Jehoiada reminded the crowd of the point of the effort. It was not just a matter of replacing one monarch with another; it was a matter of returning to obedience of the one true God. Consequently, he and the people agreed that they would be God's people. The Lord demanded their exclusive devotion.

The secret army that had turned into a coronation assembly now transformed into a mob that charged down to the temple of Baal, located in the Hinnom Valley, just below the city of David. They destroyed the building, the altars, the idols, and executed the high priest of Baal, Mattan.

23:18–19. While the crowd was decimating the temple of Baal, Jehoiada delegated responsibilities to the priests and Levites in conjunction with the temple of God. He reaffirmed the rules laid down by David for the offerings, the music, and the doorkeepers. Jehoiada reminded the guards at the doors to make sure no person who was not ritually clean entered the temple. During Athaliah's regime, Jehoiada had not been able to enforce this rule (2 Chr. 24:7).

23:20–21. All this time little King Joash had remained at the temple. But he had one more duty to perform—his official enthronement (1 Kgs. 1:30,35; 2:12). Jehoiada and his assistants led him in a parade from the temple to the palace, just vacated by Athaliah, and installed Joash on the throne. This last gesture was the final signal to the nation that Queen Athaliah, the ruthless tyrant, was gone.

24:1–3. When Joash was safely installed on the throne under Jehoiada's direction, the chronicler pauses to give us his usual summary for a king. Joash became king at age seven and was officially king for forty years, most of which were spent under the close supervision of Jehoiada. The priest Jehoiada took charge of Joash's life. He even selected his wives for him. Joash had plenty of offspring, so the line of David would continue.

24:4–7. King Joash decreed that the temple should be restored. By now the temple had stood well over one hundred years, and buildings do wear. Athaliah's sons had made off with some of the sacred temple implements and taken them into the temple of Baal. It was time to set things right in the temple.

Repairs cost money. Even if an ancient king were to use nothing but slave labor, the slaves needed to be fed and kept healthy. And work on the temple required skilled craftsmen and artists who had to be paid. Joash needed to raise funds for the renovation project, and he thought of a source.

When David was taking his illegitimate census, one of the requirements he forgot was that each Israelite was supposed to pay half a shekel as a sign of ritual purity, and the money was supposed to be designated for the upkeep of the tabernacle, now replaced by the temple (Exod. 30:11–16). Joash wanted those half shekels to use for the renovation of the temple. So he instructed the Levites to canvass all the towns of his kingdom and receive the necessary contributions **from all Israel**, referring here to the covenant name of God's people (obviously not the Northern Kingdom).

This policy, though not effective for Joash, was later revived and used successfully. In the Gospels we read that the temple tax collector came to Jesus in Capernaum, and Jesus made the required coin appear miraculously inside a fish (Matt. 17:24–27).

But the half shekels did not come in for Joash. The Levites did not cooperate, whether for reasons of conscience or indolence we do not know. For many years nothing was done on the project. So Joash had a talk with Jehoiada about the state of affairs, and they changed strategy.

24:8–12. Rather than having agents all over the kingdom collect a mandatory tax, the Levites let the people bring their contributions voluntarily. Joash directed that a large offering box should be placed at the entrance to the temple and that everyone who came to the temple should be reminded to pay their half shekel. This procedure was effective. The people kept filling the box, there was a strict accounting procedure for the proceeds, and all the money was allocated to its intended purpose—providing "paychecks" for the skilled workers involved in restoring the temple.

24:13–14. The workmen pursued their assignments with enthusiasm. Not only did they restore the building to its original condition, but they reinforced it at points that had shown weakness. It turned out that there was enough money to replace the sacred temple implements as well.

ℂ Joash Turns to Evil (24:15–27)

SUPPORTING IDEA: *As soon as Jehoiada died, Joash turned away from God and embraced idolatry.*

24:15–16. God had preserved Jehoiada for one hundred and thirty years, but finally his long life came to an end. He was closely related to the royal family; he was high priest, and he had led the country for several decades. So his funeral honored him as if he were a king, and he was buried in the tombs reserved for kings.

24:17–18. The people of Judah now had more than one hundred years to look back on and see a direct correlation between their worship of God resulting in times of peace and prosperity on the one hand and the worship of idols resulting in with war and decimation on the other. But no sooner had Jehoiada been placed in his tomb than the leaders of Judah approached Joash and persuaded him to abandon all that Jehoiada had stood for. With the king setting the example, they neglected the temple as well as the God who was worshiped in it. They transferred their loyalty to the idols that had been suppressed for more than twenty years. Out came the Baal statues, up popped the Asherah poles, and idol worship was once again in fashion.

24:19. God did not leave Joash or the people of Judah in the dark about what they were doing. In fact, there were **prophets** who proclaimed God's warning to them. But it was all to no avail. The king and his friends had made their choice.

24:20–22. In fact, Joash became so confirmed in his ways that he was willing to kill to try to suppress God's voice. His victim was a person named Zechariah. This priest and prophet was compelled by God to speak against the king. He confronted the people with the warning that God would not allow the king's policies to go unpunished; bad times would happen if the king and the people did not repent.

But neither the king nor the people repented. Instead, they conspired against Zechariah, and Joash himself gave the order that he should be executed. The carnage took place in the temple courtyard. Zechariah's dying words invoked strict retribution by God on Joash for his wickedness.

24:23–24. God's method of punishment for Joash was an invasion by the Arameans. As usual, the chronicler condenses a major event into a few short sentences. The army of Aram came and **invaded Judah and Jerusalem and killed all the leaders**. The chronicler does not even mention that a little earlier Joash had tried to buy off Hazael, the king of Aram, by sending him all the treasures of the temple and his palace (2 Kgs. 12:17–18). This policy worked for a short time, but it did not prevent the eventual invasion by Hazael and his conquest of Jerusalem.

The chronicler leaves us with no doubt about the significance of this event. Just as the people of God had been able to defeat enemies much stronger than they were because God came to their aid, so now the Arameans were able to overwhelm them with a smaller army because God used them to punish Judah for its sin and rebellion.

24:25–27. Joash himself died as a consequence of this defeat, though not gloriously in battle. Some people were upset with Joash for the execution of Zechariah and were looking for revenge against the king. As a result of the fight against the Arameans, Joash had been wounded and was lying on his cot recuperating. Two assassins killed him while he could not defend himself.

The chronicler gives us the names of the two assassins and links their ancestry to Ammonite and Moabite mothers, thereby demonstrating to us that, even in the case of a degenerate king, God would not permit the house of Judah to destroy itself. Other than that item, the obituary for Joash is perfunctory. There were further records about the restoration of the temple, and Joash was buried in the city of David at least, in the vicinity of the royal tombs (2 Kgs. 12:21) but not directly with the kings who preceded him. Not even in the location of his tomb would Joash be reconciled to Jehoiada, his benefactor, whom he had betrayed.

> **MAIN IDEA REVIEW:** *King Joash pursued many policies in keeping with God's will as long as he was under the direct supervision of Jehoiada the priest, but as soon as Jehoiada died, Joash turned to evil.*

III. CONCLUSION

Requiem for a Rosebush

For several years my wife and I attempted to grow plants in our front yard. We bought some rosebushes, dug little holes, inserted the plants, refilled the holes, applied the recommended amount of water, and hoped for the best. At first the little rosebushes showed great promise. But then, come

July or so, some started to wither, and no amount of water or fertilizer could rescue them. Another year, another dead rosebush.

The cause of this problem was not hard to find. When I dug the holes for the plants, I had encountered some "hard stuff." Finally we figured out that this was not just some scattered rocks. There was a solid layer of bricks just a few inches below the topsoil. I had cleared away enough dirt to insert the roots, but not enough for the roots to take hold and absorb all the nutrients the plants needed to survive over the long haul. The little rosebushes would get enough moisture to show adequate signs of life to raise our hopes. But once the scorching sun bore down on them, they would die.

Our attempts at rose gardening turned out to be exactly one of the four stages in Jesus' parable of the sower (Mark 4:1–20). He described four possible outcomes for seed that a farmer scattered over his field: (1) Some seeds would fall on the path where there was no soil. The birds would come by and swoop them up. (2) Some seeds would fall into shallow soil. They would give momentary signs of life, though with inadequate roots, the little plants would die. (3) Some seeds would fall into areas where there was sufficient soil for them to grow. However, weeds and thistles would grow in the same place and in the competition between plants, the weeds would win and the plants would die. (4) Finally, some seeds would fall into their intended place, where the soil was rich and the farmer protected them from weeds. These plants would thrive.

King Joash received decades of instruction from Jehoiada. The high priest told him exactly what to say and do, and it looked as if Joash was a godly man. But underneath the pious cover, the king had no personal bond to God or his law. Once Jehoiada was gone, the king demonstrated that outward piety does not automatically grow into inner righteousness.

PRINCIPLES

- Children and young Christians need to be taught the Bible and how to live according to its principles.

- The goal of Bible teaching is to produce Christians who become less dependent on the teaching of others and who learn to teach others themselves (2 Tim. 2:2).

- In our own strength we cannot guarantee that our work will have the results we hope for.

APPLICATIONS

- Do what you can to make sure that the lives of those entrusted to you—children or young Christians—will be grounded in solid teaching based on the Word of God.
- Prepare them for the time they will make their own decisions and will no longer be dependent on you for Christian guidance.
- Have confidence in God's Word, knowing that it is effective but also knowing that once you've communicated it, you don't control the outcome.

IV. LIFE APPLICATION

Turnabout Is Divine Grace

While on a trip abroad, my wife and I spent an evening with a wonderful Christian couple (let's call them David and Sarah). They were the parents of a young man (we'll call him Isaac) who would become a student at Taylor University when the next semester started. Early in the conversation, David and Sarah told us how proud they were of Isaac, specifically that he was a good student, a hard worker, and a strong and mature Christian. In fact, the pleased couple gave us a number of specific examples of how much Isaac was growing in his Christian faith.

I replied that such a testimonial was good to hear, that young people may not realize it, but parents never take the salvation of their children for granted. For a true Christian parent, when the many years of faithful teaching and prayer result in the commitment of their child or daughter to the Lord, it is always a miracle.

At that, David and Sarah started to chuckle. "In our case," they explained, "it was Isaac's many years of faithful teaching and prayer that resulted in our salvation." For the rest of the evening, they related to us how it was not until times of crisis in their personal lives that they came to trust the Lord, as their son had done several years before.

As we look at the story of Joash and compare it to the many different experiences that other people have, there are two factors we must keep in mind. There is the obligation that Christians have to provide a consistent Christian witness to anyone under our influence. This applies first to our children and grandchildren, but it also pertains to any situation in which we are given responsibility for the spiritual nurture of others. Our goal should never be just to give others Bible content and guidance but to enable them to become mature Christians in their own right.

However, as the story of David and Sarah illustrates, we should never forget about the supernatural work of God, the Holy Spirit, in our lives. We cannot achieve results; we can only be faithful in our calling. But God can produce mature and viable Christians.

V. PRAYER

Lord Jesus, how we would love to find a way of getting other people to become exactly what we want them to be! But we know that this is neither possible nor desirable. Help us to be faithful in teaching others about you through word and deed. Help us to let go where necessary so that others can learn to live in dependence on you, not on us. And help us to trust you to do what is right in a person's life, even if it does not meet our expectations. Amen.

VI. DEEPER DISCOVERIES

Zechariah's Tomb (24:22)

Zechariah, son of Jehoiada, though appearing briefly in this passage, became an important figure in ancient Judaism. He came to be regarded as a typical example of a martyr for righteousness, someone who spoke up for God and suffered the ultimate penalty for doing so. He said that even though Joash's tomb was deliberately kept obscure, visitors to Jerusalem today can still see the tomb of Zechariah (or at least a later restoration of it), situated prominently in the Kidron Valley on the eastern side of the temple. Zechariah's legacy outlasted that of the king who murdered him.

In confronting the Jewish leaders of his day with their hypocrisy, Jesus put a different twist on the story of Zechariah (Luke 11:47–51). Even though the religious establishment was outwardly devoted to God, they should not claim Zechariah for themselves but should assume the guilt for his death. Zechariah was killed because of unbelief, and it does not matter whether the unbelief comes in the form of idolatry or piety. The Pharisees, Jesus said, cannot escape their heritage as those who killed the prophets.

Jesus' rebuke of the Pharisees reminds us to examine our own attitudes. It is easy to condemn the evil King Joash and his faithlessness, but we also need to ask ourselves if perhaps we are attempting to silence the voice of God in our lives, not with murder but by hiding behind a shield of piety as the Pharisees did.

VII. TEACHING OUTLINE

A. INTRODUCTION

1. Lead Story: Geronimo, Temporary Christian
2. Context: Athaliah, daughter of Ahab and Jezebel, had usurped the throne of Judah and attempted to kill everyone who could conceivably have a claim to the kingship. But the infant Joash survived. When Joash was seven years old, the priest Jehoiada carried out a successful coup against Athaliah and installed Joash as king, with himself as his close advisor.
3. Transition: Geronimo, the fierce Apache leader, became a church member. But his subsequent life made clear that he had not truly experienced conversion and regeneration. Would the life of Joash show that he truly belonged to God?

B. COMMENTARY

1. The Overthrow of Athaliah (23:1–15)
2. Reclaiming the Temple and the Throne (23:16–24:14)
3. Joash Turns to Evil (24:15–27)

CONCLUSION: REQUIEM FOR A ROSEBUSH

VIII. ISSUES FOR DISCUSSION

1. What are the responsibilities of parents or guardians in the spiritual upbringing of their children?
2. Compare and contrast the situation of Jehoiada in relationship to Joash with the events related to Aaron (Lev. 10:1–5), Eli (1 Sam. 3:13), and Samuel (1 Sam. 8:1–3) and their sons.

2 Chronicles 25:1–28:27

Good, Bad, and Mediocre

Quote

"*I* am going to ask you to come with me in a study of some accounts written by none other than God Himself."

J o h n   H e r c u s

2 Chronicles 25:1–28:27

I N   A   N U T S H E L L

*T*he four kings in this section represent extremes in their obedience of God. Jotham was righteous, whereas Ahaz was the worst king of Judah yet. Amaziah was a godly king until he succumbed to the temptation of idolatry. Uzziah was also righteous, but he tried to take over the function of the priests and was punished with leprosy.

Good, Bad, and Mediocre

I. INTRODUCTION

Now You See It . . .

*F*or the last ten years or so, several professional sports leagues have made use of modern technology in attempting to settle disputed plays. Frequently the outcome of a play hinges on a split-second observation by an official. Take the case of an apparently fumbled ball in football. If a player carrying the ball lets go of it before being tackled, and the opposing team recovers it, possession of the ball goes to the opponent. But if the player releases the ball after his knee hits the ground, his team retains possession. Sometimes it is hard to tell which way it happened. What better way to settle the matter than to look at videotapes of the play?

But an unexpected twist may show up. Cameras do not always display objects in their proper relationship to one another. This is a feature that directors of action movies count on. As actors pretend to exchange blows with one another, they do not actually make physical contact, but the camera makes it appear as though they did. This optical deception also exists with instant replays in sports. What seemed like a clear-cut way to get a true picture sometimes brings up a whole new set of issues.

The four kings of Judah who are portrayed in this section displayed a similar kind of inconsistency. They occupied the same throne, had the same mandate from God, roughly the same resources, and yet they went in very different directions. Jotham was a righteous king; Ahaz was depraved; and Amaziah and Uzziah switched when least expected—one by losing his devotion, the other by an excess of it. The reader comes away confused.

But again, this is all a part of the "gospel according to Ezra." God is sovereign in all situations, not just the predictable cases. He honors faith and judges faithlessness. Let us look at what these camera angles on the kingdom of Judah reveal.

II. COMMENTARY

Good, Bad, and Mediocre

> **MAIN IDEA:** *The four kings of Judah in this section—Amaziah, Uzziah, Jotham, and Ahaz—represent four different ways in which people respond to God, some positive and some negative.*

A Amaziah, the King Who Should Have Known Better (25:1–28)

> **SUPPORTING IDEA:** *Amaziah was devoted to the Lord, and God gave him success. But then he lapsed into idolatry, and God withdrew his blessing.*

25:1–4. Amaziah's reign got off to a good start. He held to the law of God in both religious and societal matters. His mother **Jehoaddin** was a solid influence on him. After a succession of rulers who sought to establish themselves by means of bloody purges, Amaziah showed restraint in how he wielded the sword. In fact, he punished those responsible for the death of his father. Even though one could argue that Joash deserved execution, it was still wrong for someone to kill the Lord's anointed ruler, as David had recognized many years before when he had had the opportunity to kill Saul (1 Sam. 24:10).

Still, we receive a clue that all was not ideal in Amaziah's life. He was devoted to God, **but not wholeheartedly**. Somewhere underneath his outward compliance with the law, rebellion was brewing.

25:5–10. Amaziah's father, Joash, had suffered a humiliating defeat at the hands of the Arameans. Amaziah sought to reestablish a strong military that could withstand another invasion. He called up all available fighting men and was able to amass an army of three hundred thousand men from the tribes of Judah and Benjamin. Amaziah also decided to hire mercenaries from the Northern Kingdom who would assist him in any foreign conflicts. He dipped into the royal treasury for one hundred talents of silver (approximately 3.75 tons) in order to buy this manpower.

However, God did not approve of Amaziah's schemes. These mercenaries from the Northern Kingdom were forbidden. Once again God sent a prophet to convey a message to a king. The unnamed speaker declared to Amaziah that God would not allow the army of Judah to be successful if it included soldiers from the Northern Kingdom. They were banned from fighting for the Lord's causes.

Amaziah's reaction was, **What about the hundred talents I paid?** as if the money had any importance when it came to questions of obedience to God.

Of course, it did matter to the king, just as it continues to matter to people today. The prophet was able to bring some perspective to the situation. The king might lose this silver now, but compared to what God would provide if he followed the Lord's instructions, it was nothing.

Amaziah heeded the prophet and sent the northern soldiers back home. These men were incensed at the king's action. Perhaps they were looking for additional income in plunder and further wages; maybe they had hoped to indulge their lust for combat and adventure. For whatever reason, they headed home under a cloud of anger.

25:11–12. God gave Amaziah immediate confirmation that he had made the right decision. The king launched a military campaign against the Edomites and scored a decisive victory. Ten thousand Edomites were killed in battle, and another ten thousand were executed later.

25:13. However, just as Amaziah was asserting himself abroad, things were not going so well at home. The troops from Israel whom Amaziah had sent home had worked themselves into a frenzy and were rampaging throughout the country, destroying towns of Judah. God obviously knew what these "soldiers" were going to do, and Amaziah could have continued to rely on him, but the king let the situation get to him. He had just proved his power against the forces of the Edomites, and he would not put up with barbaric acts from these northern terrorists.

25:14–16. So Amaziah fortified himself spiritually as well as physically. Unfortunately, he brought home the gods of the Edomites and began to worship them. Under Ancient Near Eastern custom, when a country was defeated, its gods were defeated as well, and the victorious king would not normally start to worship a collection of losers. The only explanation is that Amaziah saw the Edomite gods and liked them. He adopted them as his own gods.

God once again sent a prophet. This seer pointed out to the king the obvious absurdity of worshiping gods, **which could not save their own people from your hand.** In other words, "You just defeated the people who were trusting these gods, and now you are trusting them yourself. This doesn't make sense."

But Amaziah was not to be turned from his idolatry by the prophet. He liked these gods, and he was not going to give up his new toys. So he pulled rank on the prophet: "Who are you to give me advice? If you don't stop this impertinence right now, I will have you killed." The prophet declared that just because Amaziah did not want to hear about the punishment did not mean it wouldn't happen.

25:17–19. Amaziah would not accept the idea that by his disobedience to God he had undermined the entire foundation of his kingdom. He continued to see himself as the great victor over the Edomites and thought it was time to take on Israel. Apparently he was convinced that he could defeat anyone with his army. He sent a personal challenge to King Jehoash of Israel (also called Joash), to meet him in battle.

But Jehoash did not think war with Judah was a good idea, and he declined the invitation. His refusal was less than diplomatic, however. Although he did not want to cross swords with Amaziah, he did take advantage of the opportunity to insult the king of Judah. Comparing himself to a cedar of Lebanon and Amaziah to a thistle that gets gobbled up by a wild animal, he told Amaziah to bridle his arrogance. A victory against Edom did not rule out the possibility of being defeated by Israel.

25:20–24. Amaziah was stubborn again. Just as he had not let the prophet of God turn him away from worshiping the gods of the Edomites, so he would not let the king of Israel keep him from going to war. Amaziah had closed his heart about the idols; God now closed his mind about this war so that Amaziah would receive his retribution.

Amaziah continued to provoke Jehoash of Israel until the northern king found it impossible to resist going to war. Jehoash launched a preemptive strike, and as both the prophet of God and the king of Israel had predicted, Judah took heavy losses. The soldiers of Judah fled, but Amaziah could not escape the hands of Jehoash, who captured him and paraded him back to Jerusalem. The cedar was putting the thistle back in its place (v. 18). Jehoash made sure that Amaziah would not indulge in any further military escapades for some time to come by razing a large section of the wall surrounding Jerusalem and taking away valuable articles from the temple. Then Jehoash took a few hostages and went home.

25:25–28. Amaziah outlived Jehoash by fifteen years and saw Israel under the long and stable reign of Jeroboam II. By contrast, Amaziah's own time on the throne was less than stable. His reversion to the evil ways of his father Joash, followed again by the same devastating consequences for the kingdom, generated a number of dissidents who decided that Amaziah, like his father, had to go. These men plotted against the king, but he managed to flee to the town of Lachish. There his enemies caught up with him and killed him. Amaziah fared somewhat better than Joash, though, since he was buried at the official royal site.

There had now been nine rulers of Judah (counting Athaliah). The last four of these had been assassinated, and the one before them had died of a disease sent upon him as punishment from God. Would the next king be able to break the chain?

B Uzziah, the King Who Got Above Himself (26:1–23)

SUPPORTING IDEA: *Uzziah served God, but when he attempted to take over the duties reserved for the priests, God punished him with leprosy.*

26:1–5. Do not let the many years given for Uzziah's reign make you think he had a long and effective rule; he actually spent much of this time in isolation, king of Judah in name only, while Jotham, his son, ruled as his co-regent. Uzziah's reign, like that of most of the kings we have looked at, turned out to be a story of what might have been, but he lost his effectiveness for reasons other than most of the previous monarchs, who succumbed to idolatry. Uzziah, the king who began his reign with great potential, ended his years as a lonely leper.

The initial information about Uzziah raises no red flags. He had popular support. Evidently not interested in suffering through any further succession disputes, **the people of Judah** declared him king. There would be neither debate nor bloodshed this time. In addition to being of royal descent, he came of good Jerusalem stock on his mother's side, and—like Amaziah in his earliest years—he obeyed the law of God. Uzziah had a mentor named Zechariah who provided him with guidance. Finally, we see at the outset that God blessed the king's obedience with success.

26:6–8. The king's success expressed itself in military victories. Remember that the Philistines, after almost a hundred years in submission to Judah after the time of David and Solomon, had reasserted themselves during the reign of Jehoram and had even gone so far as to invade Jerusalem and raid the temple (2 Chr. 21:16–17). Now Uzziah was able to turn the tables and subdue the Philistines along with their Arab allies. Furthermore, he also brought down the Ammonites again and required tribute of them.

26:9–10. Uzziah must have been the kind of king whom the people respected. He was powerful and commanding in his presence; yet visible everywhere so the people could see him at work on their behalf. The king built up protective fortifications in Jerusalem and around Judah; he sunk cisterns throughout the kingdom for the care of his livestock; and he created a royal agricultural workforce to look after his lands.

The statement that Uzziah **loved the soil** is a powerful testimony about Uzziah's faith. Among the Canaanites, the soil was the expression of the fertility goddesses (e.g., Asherah), who "demanded" worship through sexual celebrations. To "love the soil" in that context would have been to commit yourself to the horrifying claims of Baal and his consorts; there was no such thing as just loving the soil. But to Uzziah, who was committed to the Lord, the soil was a gift of the God who had created it for our benefit.

26:11–15. Uzziah was able to muster a large army. In fact, Uzziah's exceptional skill comes out in this context as well. He not only brought together a large assembly of people and called them his army, but he organized them and kept careful records of this fighting group of 307,000 warriors. Uzziah accumulated enough resources to outfit his men with weaponry: armor, shields, and helmets for defense, and spears, bows, and slingshots for offense. Finally, Uzziah erected catapults around the walls of Jerusalem.

26:16–20. And then Uzziah followed his predecessors by finding a way to spoil it all. At least he did not start to worship other gods. Still, it was in the context of worshiping God that Uzziah made a terrible mistake.

The right to perform sacrifices in the temple was reserved for the priests, the descendants of Aaron from the tribe of Levi. Early in the history of Israel, when Moses had first received the law from God, there had been an ugly incident when Korah, a Levite who was not of Aaron's clan, had attempted to usurp the high priest's prerogative and was severely punished for it (Num. 16:1–50). Ever since that event, even though the king might have been personally involved in the sacrifices (2 Chr. 7:7), only the priests were allowed to officiate or to burn incense. But Uzziah decided to perform some priestly functions himself.

What Uzziah did was not completely unknown in ancient cultures. Even though the great civilizations developed powerful professional priesthoods, they generally placed the king at the head of their ceremonial hierarchy, thereby amassing for themselves royal authority and putting on an outward display of unity before the people and the gods. Uzziah may have reasoned that if foreign kings could express their dedication to their false gods by performing worship rituals, why couldn't he come before God himself without a priestly intermediary?

The truth that Uzziah lost sight of was that genuine worship of God always begins with obedience to his commands and that sacrificial ceremonies are secondary in importance (Isa. 1:13). It was a sign of greater devotion to God *not* to assume the role of priest than to usurp it. But Uzziah had become blinded by his own success to the point that he authorized himself to enter the holy place of the temple in order to burn incense.

The Levites were aghast when the king entered the holy place. The high priest Azariah, along with eighty **courageous** colleagues, decided to confront the king. They followed Uzziah into the temple area and brought the proceedings to an abrupt halt. They proclaimed that the king was violating God's law by doing what only the descendants of Aaron were permitted to do.

Uzziah flew into a rage. These impudent priests had just interrupted their king as he was about to undertake the highest act of worship. But his outburst was suddenly cut short, replaced by a terrified silence.

The chronicler's terse statement, **leprosy broke out on his forehead**, tells the story, but it also leaves a puzzle. The priests saw the leprosy, but Uzziah did not. And yet, standing there with the incense burner in his hand, the king also recognized that he had contracted leprosy and immediately agreed to be escorted out of the temple. He had come to God in arrogance; he left his presence humiliated and stained by the disease that God had sent as punishment.

26:21–23. The end of this story is the end of Uzziah's story. Although he continued to be the king in name, he was insulated from his kingdom, excluded from the temple whose sacredness he had sought to violate, and shunned by his people. The affairs of the government he had worked so hard for were assigned to his son, Jotham. Uzziah did not even receive the standard honors at his funeral. As a leper he was buried in a field adjacent to the tombs of the kings. The chronicler mentions a further source of information about the king; this time it is Isaiah, the well-known prophet, whose life also crossed paths with all the following kings of Judah.

Ⓒ Jotham, the Righteous King (27:1–9)

SUPPORTING IDEA: Jotham was a righteous king, obedient to God and successful in his affairs.

27:1–2. Finally we come to a king who was thoroughly righteous. Jotham's life was characterized by the phrase, **he did what was right in the eyes of the LORD**, and there were no later incidents in which he departed from God's ways. He neither committed Uzziah's sin of entering the holy place of the temple nor slipped into idolatry as his earlier predecessors had done. But neither was Jotham a great reformer. In spite of his personal righteousness, he did not put a stop to the religious abuses throughout the kingdom, and his name is not associated with any renewal movement.

27:3–4. Like successful kings of Judah before him, Jotham elaborated on the fortifications of Jerusalem and various sites throughout the land. As we have witnessed so many times before, the real threat to the kingdom could not be turned back by bigger and stronger walls.

27:5–6. Once again, obedience to the Lord has military implications. Because Jotham **walked steadfastly before the LORD**, his power increased. Jotham was able to subdue the Ammonites and levy a large tribute on them.

But the chronicler stops his account with this short example. There were other wars (v. 7), but he does not tell us about them. Nor does he give us any more specific information on what Jotham's walk with the Lord was like. Presumably he was punctilious with his sacrifices, showed personal integrity, and dealt justly with his subjects, but the chronicler gives no details.

27:7–9. And so, one of the few success stories in Chronicles receives rather terse notice. Jotham died a young man at age forty-one after ruling Judah for sixteen years. He had done a good job, and he received appropriate honors at his funeral. Unfortunately, his last legacy to the people was his son Ahaz, who would open the gates of idolatry.

D Ahaz, the King Who Went from Bad to Worse (28:1–27)

> **SUPPORTING IDEA:** *Ahaz brought ruin on himself and the kingdom with his idolatry, and he increased his evil as he grew older.*

28:1. Jotham died and handed over the crown to his son Ahaz. In contrast to Uzziah, neither Jotham nor Ahaz are said to have received any official public acclamation as kings. They simply took over the throne as it was passed to them.

28:2–4. Ahaz found a way of committing every conceivable act of idolatry. He made idols, worshiped at the high places, engaged in nature-fertility worship, and—most hideous of all—even sacrificed some of his sons to Baal. He had no interest in worshiping God. His religion was Canaanite through and through.

28:5a. Abandonment of God inevitably led to abandonment by God. Once again the Arameans came as God's instrument of punishment, defeating Ahaz and carting away a group of men from Judah as hostages. A king's disobedience again brought defeat by an invading army.

28:5b–8. Not only did the Arameans serve as God's punishment for the sins of Judah; the army of Israel, the idolatrous Northern Kingdom, also defeated Judah. Pekah, the king of Israel, was far from a godly man himself, and he had his hands full dealing with the invasion by Assyria under Tiglath-Pileser (2 Kgs. 15:27–31). Still, he was able to take advantage of the weakened state of the Southern Kingdom under Ahaz, and he scored a decisive victory that resulted in a large number of captives being deported to Samaria.

28:9–11. What plans did the Northern Kingdom have for their captives from Judah? Presumably, they must have intended to use them in some way as slave labor to fortify against Assyria. But a prophet named Oded put a stop to any such notions. He met the returning army and declared to them that they were pushing their luck. God had used them to punish Judah, but they should not think that this gave them the license to do as they pleased. They were no more righteous than Judah, and—having already perpetrated a bloodbath—they were in danger of wearing out God's patience by stocking up on captives like this. The hostages had to go back to Judah!

28:12–15. The leaders of Israel listened. Three men in particular—Azariah, Berekiah, and Jehizkiah by name—took it on themselves to convey the divine warning to the officers of the army. Oded had instilled the fear of God in these men, and they were not inclined to risk God's discipline just as they were having to cope with Assyria. So they cooperated by sending the captives home, even attempting to minimize their suffering on the return trip by providing clothes, shoes, medicine, bread, and even donkeys for the weakest to ride on.

28:16–21. Meanwhile, things in Judah continued to deteriorate under Ahaz's guidance. The Edomites were back spreading destruction and carrying off prisoners, and even the Philistines were again making themselves at home in Judah. Ahaz was groping for a way out and decided that his solution was to buy protection from Tiglath-Pileser of Assyria. Taking a page out of the playbook of King Asa (2 Chr. 16:2), he took treasures out of the temple and presented them to the Assyrian monarch. However, he had only mixed success in that Tiglath-Pileser was happy to accept the donations but was not interested in protecting Judah. Nevertheless, Tiglath-Pileser did satisfy Ahaz by conquering Damascus, thereby eliminating the threat of Aram for the moment (2 Kgs. 16:7)—but this also established Assyria's presence right on Judah's doorstep.

28:22–23. Ahaz tried to circumvent his problems by redefining the situation in some way that he thought he could control. Baal and his associates had not been of much help to the king; a return to the worship of God was, of course, unthinkable to him. Even as confirmed an idolater as Ahaz would have found the gods of Assyria too repulsive to adopt. But the hybrid religion of Aram in Damascus, combining Canaanite deities with some of their own gods, seemed just right to the king of Judah.

In spite of Aram's obvious lack of success against Assyria and the fact that Ahaz had been able to hold off Aram himself at one point (2 Kgs. 16:5), Ahaz fantasized about the power of the Damascene gods, and he declared that from now on they would be his official objects of worship. In 2 Kings 16 we also read that Ahaz erected an exact replica of an altar from Damascus for daily use.

28:24–25. It was not just that Ahaz decided to practice and support idol worship. He wanted to supplant the worship of God. He shut the doors of the temple and promoted worship of false gods throughout his kingdom.

28:26–27. Unlike his ancestor Jehoram (2 Chr. 21:20), when Ahaz died he had his share of mourners, but there were enough influential people in Jerusalem to prevent him from being buried in the official royal tombs. This group of believers in the Lord may have included the prophet Isaiah as well as Ahaz's own son, Hezekiah.

> **MAIN IDEA REVIEW:** *The four kings of Judah in this section— Amaziah, Uzziah, Jotham, and Ahaz—represent four different ways in which people respond to God, some positive and some negative.*

III. CONCLUSION

God's Medical Log

John Hercus was an Australian ophthalmologist who, in addition to his lifelong work of healing people physically, also contributed to the spiritual health of many people through a ministry of Bible teaching. Dr. Hercus became well-known with his studies of Old Testament characters about whom he gained many insights through careful study and intuitive associations. In presenting his wisdom, Hercus frequently drew on his career as a medical doctor for a framework. He referred to the Bible as God's "casebook," a kind of medical log that records how God worked with different people to bring them from the sickness of sin to the health of a redeemed relationship with him.

To my knowledge Dr. Hercus never treated the stories of the four kings in this section. But we may increase our understanding of them with a little borrowing of his method. As medical laypersons, we may still know enough about the field to get some strong impressions of how the four kings would look as patients in a medical log.

For example, Ahaz was the man in denial who refused to acknowledge that he had a disease.

Amaziah represents the patient who will not follow through on his treatment. There is a danger that once the patient has received effective doses of his medication, he feels so good that he believes he no longer needs the treatment and stops taking his pills.

We can think of Uzziah as the patient who decides to take his therapy into his own hands. The doctors are doing an adequate job, but he can do even better. By his diagnosis and self-treatment, he did himself irreparable damage.

Finally, Jotham's imaginary medical case file does not contain anything dramatic. Blood pressure: 120 over 70; cholesterol: well under 200; blood sugar: right at 100; never a checkup missed, never a day without his multivitamin. But the physician notices that the family history of the patient is not all that good, and he realizes that Jotham's good laboratory results are not going to apply to the next generation. Jotham's reign as king was marked by righteousness and success, but he did not have a long-range effect on the kingdom.

How do we respond to God's "therapy" in our lives? Are we willing to admit that we are desperately ill? Are we willing to abide by his prescriptions, neither dropping some of what he has directed nor adding to it out of our own wisdom? Are we rejoicing in the spiritual health of being related to him by his grace and sharing this information with others?

PRINCIPLES

- People respond to the call of God in many unpredictable ways.
- Sometimes people do not acknowledge that they need God's help; sometimes they either drop his help after having tried it for a while; and sometimes they want God's help but try to take things into their own hands.
- A faithful walk with God is a sign of God's grace in a person's life.

APPLICATIONS

- Give thought to the phrase that summarizes Amaziah's life: "He did what was right in the eyes of the LORD, but not wholeheartedly" (2 Chr. 25:2). When people look back on your life, can they say that you did what was right in God's eyes and that you were wholehearted in doing so? If not, what changes could be implemented to make that an apt description of your life?
- Uzziah started well but did not finish well. What makes the difference between those who finish well and those who don't?
- What corrections, if any, do you need to make to finish well?
- Jotham walked steadfastly before the Lord. Who have you known in your own life who walked steadfastly before the Lord? What were they like?
- Ahaz was more influenced by the bad examples of neighboring kings than by the example of his father Jotham. What strategies

have you found effective in dealing with temptations to follow those who may be popular and fashionable but are clearly not walking in God's ways?

IV. LIFE APPLICATION

So Many Ways of Getting It Wrong!

Counterfeiters must find their criminal craft profitable enough to keep trying, but it certainly is a risky business. A genuine piece of American currency has to meet very specific standards. Some of these are next to impossible to reproduce without the resources of the government. Not only does the outward appearance have to conform to the correct patterns and colors in every intricate detail, but the paper used for currency is unique, and even the chemical composition of the inks used is reserved for this one purpose. People who are being trained to detect counterfeit money begin by learning the exact specifications for genuine bills; once they know exactly what the good ones are like, they will be able to detect the false bills. Counterfeiters get caught because there are just too many ways of getting it wrong.

When you look over the stories of the kings, you may begin to think that the same truth applies to them. It seems as though every king, from the well-intentioned ones to the evil-minded tyrants, found some new and different way of making mistakes and falling into sins that harmed not only himself but also his people. After reading about how both Amaziah and Uzziah dropped the ball, finally Jotham came along and seemed to get everything right. But the chronicler only gives him nine verses. Maybe he wanted to make sure we do not think that Jotham was the ideal king, seeming almost eager to launch into a longer description of Ahaz in all his depravity.

But if all the kings had been Jothams, there would have been no need for the Book of Chronicles. If everyone had been proper in their observance of their obligations toward God, there would have been no exile, and consequently no later return from the exile, and no need for Ezra to try to bring the people back together under God by reminding them of their history. But the kings were for the most part unlike Jotham. And even with Jotham's thorough devotion, he was not able to persuade the people to abandon their idols and return to God. Ezra has shown us from time to time what a good king should look like, but then he helps us to see the complexity of what is involved in being a righteous king by displaying more of the unrighteous ones because there are so many ways to "get it wrong."

So many ways of getting it wrong. Is that how you feel about your Christian life? Just when you think your walk with God has attained a certain level of consistency, do you find that you have botched it up in some way? Of course you do; this is what besets all of us fallen humans as we attempt to please God. It is just not possible. Not only are there too many ways of getting it wrong; there are too many times when we do get it wrong. But if this were not so, God went to a lot of trouble to rescue us for no good reason. It is not *in spite of* our failures that God provides forgiveness and help; it is precisely *because of* our failures that he does so.

When we read the stories of the fallen kings and all their sin, our reaction should not be, "We need to try harder so we won't wind up like this king." We should respond by recognizing that we are like this king already, but, Christ died on the cross for exactly this reason.

V. PRAYER

Lord Jesus, it seems as though the story of the kings and their sins is interminable. Help us to learn from their failures without becoming self-righteous or cynical. Help us to understand that you already know more about our sinfulness than we do but also that you are already more prepared to grant us your grace than we may be in seeking it at the moment. Help us not to despair over sin we see in our lives or the lives of others but to see any such sin as a signal to come to your cross once again. Amen.

VI. DEEPER DISCOVERIES

A. Leprosy (26:19)

Leprosy comes up often in the Bible. It was a major health concern in the law (Lev. 13–14), came up often in narratives (e.g., 2 Kgs. 7:3–11), and was a frequent object of Jesus' healing miracles (e.g., Mark 1:40–45). Even though people have been aware of leprosy's symptoms, the disease itself was not studied and understood until recently.

Leprosy is not a highly contagious disease. Children are the most vulnerable to catching it, and only people in a highly advanced stage become a great liability in passing it on. However, because of its serious nature and its horrifying effects, most cultures have dealt with leprous people severely; once the disease was diagnosed, the person was ostracized and forbidden all contact with others. The Old Testament laws were no exception. Today, although leprosy is still a potentially unpleasant disease, long-term treatment with antibiotics usually yields good results.

In biblical times lepers were not just considered sick; they were considered "unclean." They were not permitted to stand in God's presence in the temple, and anyone who touched them was defiled as well. When a man with leprosy came to Jesus, the Lord could have healed him by speaking a word. But in his compassion, he "reached out his hand and touched the man" (Mark 1:41) and healed him—an extraordinary action!

Our sins may cause us to feel like lepers in God's sight. But God is always ready to reach out his hand and give us his healing touch.

B. King Ahaz Versus God (28:2)

Few men in the Bible were as strongly opposed to God as King Ahaz of Judah. He would have nothing to do with God. He was aware of a possible invasion by the combined armies of Israel and Aram, and he even attempted to purchase the protection of Tiglath-Pileser of Assyria with the temple treasure. However, Ahaz had nothing to fear from either Israel or Aram. In the future Assyria would vanquish both of them. God's heart was bigger than Ahaz's, and he sent Isaiah to convey his divine reassurance to the apprehensive king (Isa. 7:1–17).

Isaiah conveyed to the king the reassurance that God would not allow a full-blown invasion by Israel and Aram to occur. "It will not take place, it will not happen" (Isa. 7:7). Not only that, but God bent over backward to demonstrate to Ahaz that he was secure and that he could rely on God. Ahaz could confirm what God had said with a sign. But Ahaz would have nothing to do with God. Wrapped in a mantle of false piety, he declined Isaiah's invitation. "I will not put the LORD to the test" (Isa. 7:12). Ahaz did not want any indication of the reality of God impinging on his confirmed unbelief.

Nevertheless, Ahaz's loss turned out to be everyone else's gain. Isaiah did not let the matter rest. If the king did not want to ask for a sign, God would still display his miraculous power for all the world to see. "The virgin will be with child and will give birth to a son, and will call him Immanuel" (Isa. 7:14). God's plan would not be stopped—not by Ahaz's lack of faith, not by Aram's and Israel's armies, not by the Assyrians, not even by the laws of nature, because he is sovereign over all that he created. Aram and Israel would be wiped out and—as the prophecy telescoped outward—the Messiah, the virgin-born Son of God (Matt. 1:23) would become king of God's people forever (Isa. 9:6–7).

VII. TEACHING OUTLINE

A. INTRODUCTION

1. Lead Story: Now You See It . . .
2. Context: Joash had departed from the throne and left a kingdom deeply mired in idolatry and unrest. The next four kings after him covered the spectrum of levels of devotion to God, ranging from one of the best to one of the worst.
3. Transition: Just as the replay camera at a sports event can give us many different angles of a specific play, so we are watching a number of ways in which kings of Judah attempted to govern their land—and got it wrong.

B. COMMENTARY

1. Amaziah, the King Who Should Have Known Better (25:1–28)
2. Uzziah, the King Who Got Above Himself (26:1–23)
3. Jotham, the Righteous King (27:1–9)
4. Ahaz, the King Who Went from Bad to Worse (28:1–27)

C. CONCLUSION: GOD'S MEDICAL LOG

VIII. ISSUES FOR DISCUSSION

1. What are some factors that lead people to shut themselves off from God, as Ahaz did?
2. Is there any explanation for why someone like Amaziah should suddenly embrace the Edomite gods?
3. Was Uzziah's decision to burn incense in the temple a sign of devotion, arrogance, or defiance?
4. Given Jotham's personal righteousness in the face of so much disobedience, why does he seem so bland to us?

2 Chronicles 29:1–32:33

True Reformation

Quote

"The kingdom of God is the reign of God, where His will is supreme, whether in the individual heart or in the community of his people in this life or in the life hereafter."

D a v i d   J .   E l l i s

2 Chronicles 29:1–32:33

I N   A   N U T S H E L L

Hezekiah carried out a thorough religious reform in Judah, which he tied to the observance of a great national Passover celebration. God protected him miraculously when the Assyrians attempted to conquer Jerusalem.

True Reformation

I. INTRODUCTION

Rethinking Space and Time

*I*f two spaceships were to collide with each other, both of them going at the speed of light, the total speed of the two vehicles in relationship to each other would not be twice the speed of light, as you might think, but would still only be the speed of light because nothing goes faster than the speed of light. If the sum of any two speeds were theoretically to exceed the speed of light, the total would still be just the speed of light—186,000 miles per second.

The speed of light as an absolute limit was a central part of the theory of relativity discovered by Albert Einstein. His ideas have caused people over the last one hundred years to rethink the nature of the universe. Rather than thinking of the cosmos as a great machine, we now have to think of it as being much more flexible and dynamic. The relationship of objects in space and time to each other can be paradoxical.

There are no spaceships moving at such astronomical speeds. But there are many things zipping at the speed of light—light "particles," for one. These considerations are not something that should make any difference to your planning a drive to New Hampshire for a family vacation. But for anyone considering the nature of the universe, it is something that requires a total rethinking of what things "out there" are really like.

A "paradigm shift," a radical reorientation of prevailing patterns of thought, was also brought about by Hezekiah with the Lord's help. While he was king, he not only applied laws that enforced the worship of God; he was also able to turn around people's minds and hearts, so that for a while there seemed to be a renaissance of the days of David and Solomon. This was eventually spoiled by the invasion of the Assyrians, but Hezekiah's faith in God preserved him and brought him back to prosperity.

II. COMMENTARY

True Reformation

> **MAIN IDEA:** *Hezekiah's unwavering devotion to God was rewarded with protection from Assyria and a prosperous reign.*

A Hezekiah's Temple Reclamation (29:1–36)

> **SUPPORTING IDEA:** *As soon as Hezekiah came to power, he reopened the temple and had the priests and Levites cleanse it for regular worship.*

29:1–2. Hezekiah came to the throne in his mid-twenties, energetic and full of ideals. The colloquial expression, a "take-charge kind of guy," definitely applied to him. Hezekiah may have had governing responsibilities before his father Ahaz's death. If so, the events related in these chapters came to pass once Hezekiah took control by himself.

The chronicler (Ezra) gives Hezekiah the highest possible praise by comparing his conduct to **his father David**. But there were many parallels between Hezekiah and Solomon as well.

29:3–11. Hezekiah had no sooner taken charge than he started to undo all the damage caused by his father Ahaz. King Ahaz had actually closed the doors of the temple and mandated idol worship throughout the kingdom. Hezekiah's first order was to open the temple again and renew the regular sacrifices. There was need for physical maintenance on the complex since it had been unused for a number of years. The temple had been defiled by pagan worship, and it needed to be cleansed ritually before being used for worship again.

Hezekiah's speech in which he instructed the priests and Levites to cleanse the temple was based on the dedication prayer Solomon had made about 250 years earlier (2 Chr. 6:14–42). Solomon had acknowledged the fact that disobedience to God would lead to national calamities, and he had asked the Lord to rescue the kingdom if the people returned to him, using the temple as their focal point of repentance. So Hezekiah stated that the present miserable state of the nation was because of God's punishment.

Hezekiah's plan had several dimensions that began with the reclamation of the temple. He commanded the Levites to first cleanse themselves and then begin to purify the temple. But Hezekiah also saw the need for a "paradigm shift," a fresh start for the kingdom. Representing the nation, he would commit himself to a new covenant. This began with the Levites resuming their duties, but it would also signal a fresh relationship between God and his people.

29:12–14. The Levites embraced the new project with enthusiasm. We find here the divisions of the tribe as it was first laid out in 1 Chronicles 6. Levi had three sons: Gershon, Merari, and Kohath. Only the descendants of Kohath through Aaron were eligible for the priesthood; everyone else drew various duties in support of the tabernacle and eventually the temple. Asaph (descended from Gershon), Heman (from Kohath), and Jeduthun (from Merari) were the chief musicians installed by David, and their positions were to be passed down to their descendants. Elizaphan had been a leader among the Kohathites (Num. 3:30), and his descendants had also preserved a separate identity (1 Chr. 15:8).

29:15–19. The work of decontaminating the temple proceeded at a steady pace over a period of two weeks. The Levites had to spend the first week on the external courtyard, the area that Ahaz had polluted with a pagan altar and idolatrous implements. They threw all tainted articles into the nearby Kidron Valley. When they were finished, they reported to King Hezekiah that everything had been purified and the temple was ready for use.

29:20–24. The rededication ceremony was a variation on the annual feast of atonement (Lev. 16:18) and the sin offering (Lev. 4), except that they used more animals than would normally be the case. The king participated in the observance by leading the people in laying his hands on the sacrificial victims, but, as required, only the priests did the actual sacrificing.

29:25–30. Just as David had instituted regular music as a part of temple rituals, so Hezekiah now revived the practice. The musicians, deployed in their assigned places, began their playing, and the official singers started their tunes the moment the king initiated the first sacrifice. Finally, the Lord was being worshiped again in Jerusalem. At the conclusion of the sacrifices, the king and everyone who had accompanied him fell on their knees in worship.

29:31–36. When the initial ceremony was over, Hezekiah invited others to come and bring their sacrifices. **Six hundred bulls and three thousand sheep and goats** were sacrificed. This caused a minor crisis. There were not enough priests to do all the hard work involved in sacrificing because a number of priests had not yet finished their personal ritual cleansing (Lev. 8:1–36). But there was a surplus of Levites since they **had been more conscientious in consecrating themselves than the priests had been.** They came to the priests' assistance by doing some of the hard labor.

The day was saved, and the entire crowd, led by Hezekiah, was jubilant not only because the temple sacrifices had been restored but also because of how quickly it had happened. A month ago Judah was mired in Ahaz's national idolatry; now God had used Hezekiah to bring the kingdom into a renewed relationship with the Lord.

Ⓑ The Great Passover (30:1–27)

SUPPORTING IDEA: *The next phase of Hezekiah's renewal policy was a national celebration of Passover that included representatives from both kingdoms.*

30:1–12. Hezekiah reached out to the people of the land and invited them to come to Jerusalem for a huge Passover celebration. He included the residents of the Northern Kingdom in this invitation.

Actually, the kingdom of Israel was no more. A few years earlier the capital city of Samaria had fallen to the Assyrians, and much of the population had been carried away into exile, to be replaced by Gentiles. There was no longer any king of Israel, but those people who remained and wished to identify with their Jewish roots could look to Hezekiah for leadership. From here until the end of Chronicles, the divided kingdom has given way to the single remaining kingdom of Judah, which gave itself a certain jurisdiction over the former kingdom of Israel.

Hezekiah appealed to the grief of the northern tribes in the aftermath of the Assyrian invasion and tried to get them to see that any undoing of their losses would be strictly contingent on a return to the Lord. As Hezekiah had done with his own people earlier, he attributed their suffering to their nation's disobedience to God and exhorted them to start worshiping **the God of Abraham, Isaac and Israel** in order to alleviate the calamity. If God's people would return to him in repentance, the Lord would hear them and bring them back to their land.

The response from the people of Judah was unified and unequivocal. But the north was a different story. The people who had brought ruin on themselves by forsaking God were not about to turn back to him, even when only a miracle from him could save them. They were so deeply entrenched in sin that they **scorned and ridiculed** Hezekiah's messengers. They would not acknowledge their responsibility for their hard times or God's way out of them. Still, a few men from the tribes of Asher, Manasseh, and Zebulun took the king up on this offer.

30:13–14. All this was happening just a few weeks after Ahaz had died and Hezekiah had assumed the throne, so nobody had a lot of notice for planning a visit to Jerusalem. But many people came. The pilgrims went through the city and got rid of the various fixtures of idol worship. The incense altars joined the pile of idol-worshiping equipment accumulating in the Kidron Valley.

30:15–22. Many of the people had not prepared themselves properly by going through the required purification ritual. That group even included priests, though they got on board quickly as the celebration progressed. But the common people presented a different picture. The people from the northern tribes—Ephraim, Manasseh, Issachar, and Zebulun—failed to make themselves clean in God's sight before beginning the Passover celebration. Some Levites slaughtered the lambs for those people and then gave it to them to eat while they were still impure.

Hezekiah prayed a prayer that was more of a reassurance than an entreaty to God. He relied on the goodness of God, assuming that the Lord would not discourage people from coming to him by enforcing rules that the people still had to learn. In contrast to other times when people were punished for violating God's holiness, these people were not acting out of an arrogant attitude.

30:23–27. When the standard seven days of Passover were over, everyone agreed to another week for the feast. People were still coming to participate, and still greater numbers of priests found their way home to the temple, underwent consecration, and performed sacrifices. The king supplied more sacrificial animals. Other important leaders followed suit and matched Hezekiah's gift of animals for offerings.

God was pleased with all that the people were doing; he heard their prayers and blessed in response. The king and his subjects had fulfilled the requirement to come to God, and God was fulfilling his promise not to abandon them.

Reforms in Judah and Israel (31:1–21)

SUPPORTING IDEA: *Hezekiah continued his reform by abolishing idols and establishing a system to support the priests and Levites in Jerusalem.*

31:1–2. When the people left Jerusalem, they did not go straight home. Instead, they went throughout the countryside and smashed idols and pagan altars. The people themselves were eliminating idolatry from north to south without being ordered to do so.

31:3–10. Having reinstated regular services at the temple, Hezekiah needed to establish a way for the personnel to be compensated for their services. The situation was radically different now than it was during the stable, unified kingdom under David and Solomon when priests were able to rely on their properties at home to provide their income. The king himself provided the standard offerings that needed to be made twice a day and on special occasions. He also made sure that the priests would not be cheated out of any portion of the offerings to which they were entitled (Lev. 6:14–18,26). But most importantly, Hezekiah brought back the law of the tithe (Lev. 27:30) so a regular income would flow into the temple. The people participated eagerly.

31:11–19. The next item of business for Hezekiah was to ensure that the assets would be treated responsibly. This meant distributing them to anyone eligible to receive them. First, he saw to it that storage rooms were set up in the temple for grain and vegetables. Then he designated people to oversee the distribution.

31:20–21. King Hezekiah was consistent in overseeing all the policies he established and unreserved in his commitment to God. The chronicler's terse statement gives us the result: **And so he prospered.** But Hezekiah would not be immune to hard times. His faith was about to be tested.

Ⓓ Sennacherib's Unsuccessful Invasion (32:1–21)

SUPPORTING IDEA: *When King Sennacherib of Assyria attempted to conquer Jerusalem, the king relied on God, and the Lord protected Hezekiah with a miracle.*

32:1. The Assyrians had conquered all the surrounding areas but had not yet taken Judah. King Ahaz had tried to buy Tiglath-Pileser's protection with temple treasures (2 Chr. 28:21), but he had been treated disdainfully by the Assyrian monarch, who took his treasures and gave him little in return. Hezekiah himself tried it when Sennacherib first showed his muscle (2 Kgs. 18:13–16), but it did him even less good than it did Ahaz. Assyria came with a vengeance and started to swallow up Judah.

32:2–5. Hezekiah understood that Jerusalem's survival depended on God's power (v. 8), but he did not let this assurance keep him from fortifying the city. He strengthened the walls and closed off the external access to the main water supply. In order for the inhabitants of Jerusalem to be supplied with water, he ordered the building of a tunnel that connected the upper springs with a lower basin (the Pool of Siloam, John 9:7). This tunnel is still visible today and is accessible to tourists. In addition to shoring up the walls of Jerusalem and controlling the water supply, Hezekiah also ordered a fresh supply of armaments.

32:6–8. Hezekiah gathered his military officers and gave them a brief pep rally. His message was: "Come on, men, God can do it!" They did not have to be afraid because God was with them.

32:9–19. There are three biblical accounts of this momentous occasion when Sennacherib attempted to conquer Jerusalem and eventually was defeated (here, and in 2 Kgs. 18:17–19:37 and Isa. 36:1–37:38). The report in 2 Chronicles is the shortest account, and we will focus on the elements that were most significant for the chronicler.

Part of the strategy for any army besieging a city was the propaganda war. The enemy army tried to get the people inside the city to rebel against their rulers and allow the invading army to march in and take over. Anything that could be used to demoralize the residents was fair game: insults, lies, false promises, flattery.

The spokesman for Sennacherib, who himself was not present, delivered his message in Hebrew so everyone could understand him: Could Judah count on God to come to their aid? The Assyrian herald accused Hezekiah of misleading his people and asking them to trust in a God whom he himself did not trust. Their God would fare no better than the gods of all the other countries who had opposed King Sennacherib.

32:20–21. The contest had been laid out: Sennacherib vs. the Lord. There is no question that Hezekiah's faith was being pushed to the edge, even though he had given such calm assurances to his men earlier. But God did come through. He annihilated the entire Assyrian army (185,000 men, 2 Kgs. 19:35). Exactly how this destruction happened is not stated.

Sennacherib had set the battle up as a competition between himself and God; the Lord had accepted the terms and had shown the Assyrian king that there was a limit to human power. Sennacherib had no choice but to collect his army and head back to Nineveh—where his own sons were even then plotting his assassination.

Ⓔ Hezekiah's Splendor (32:22–33)

SUPPORTING IDEA: *Though threatened by a serious illness, Hezekiah lived out the rest of his life in fame and splendor.*

32:22–23. Hezekiah realized the defeat of the Assyrians was not his victory but God's. But the rest of the world did not know that. For them, Hezekiah was the great king who had been able to hold off the Assyrians. So ambassadors came from surrounding nations, seeking to get on good terms with the king of Judah by bringing him splendid presents.

32:24–26. Hezekiah, who had distinguished himself up to now with such an exemplary life, started to slip in his attitude toward God. The Lord healed him miraculously of a fatal illness (see 2 Kgs. 20:1–11; Isa. 38:1–22), but Hezekiah became calloused in his response to God. Apparently, he started to take God's support for granted, and this resulted in God's displeasure. The king's public repentance, in which he included the entire nation, staved off any punishment for Hezekiah's generation.

32:27–30. Hezekiah also accrued great wealth: valuable metals and stones, agricultural products, livestock, and the buildings necessary to take care of it all. The chronicler also reminds us of Hezekiah's engineering feat—blocking off the Gihon springs and digging a water tunnel into Jerusalem.

32:31. Still Hezekiah was not perfect. This verse is probably intended to shed some light on the arrogant attitude mentioned in verse 25, because this event actually happened while Hezekiah was recovering from his illness (2 Kgs. 20:12). The king of Babylon sent some delegates to wish Hezekiah well on his recovery and to get firsthand information about miraculous events in Jerusalem. But Hezekiah turned the occasion into an opportunity to show off his wealth. Rather than giving God all the glory, he gave the Babylonians a grand tour of his facilities and showed them all his treasures. The prophet Isaiah condemned Hezekiah for this act and predicted Judah's eventual exile to Babylon (Isa. 39:1–8).

The chronicler does not mention these specifics, but his assessment is all the more sobering. God had set up this event as a test to see what Hezekiah really held **in his heart**. And though Ezra does not tell us in so many words how Hezekiah fared, it is clear, even from this cryptic summary, that he did not come out with a perfect score.

32:32–33. The report on Hezekiah's death is brief and no cause is given, though he was only fifty-four years old at the time. Among the sources to which the chronicler refers us for further information is the prophet Isaiah, for whom the death of Hezekiah also meant the end of his ministry at the court in Jerusalem. The king was buried with appropriate honors, and **all Judah and the people of Jerusalem honored him**.

> **MAIN IDEA REVIEW:** *Hezekiah's unwavering devotion to God was rewarded with protection from Assyria and a prosperous reign.*

III. CONCLUSION

A Tale of Three Teachers

Let us imagine three college teachers, each of whom intends to bring his students to a mature competence. Professor Sears has an exact plan of what he wants his students to know, and he spends all his time giving his students the required information. Professor Penney believes the students should be able to learn on their own. He gives his students massive projects to undertake and expects them to glean important principles and factual items in the process of doing them without his help. Finally, Professor Ward takes an approach halfway between the two. He attempts to provide his students with a firm grounding in his field, but he also expects them to apply the information in projects where they must work independently.

Professor Sears may have success getting his students to repeat to him all the content he has supplied, but he is not producing mature scholars. On the other hand, Professor Penney may get his students excited about working apart from his supervision, but they also are not going to become solid scholars in their areas because they will not have the necessary grounding in their field. Ideally, Professor Ward's students will become the best scholars because he is giving them the content as well as providing them with opportunities to grow on their own.

Hezekiah fell into the third category of effective teachers. He provided straightforward directives and was not afraid to enforce them. But he also got his subjects to become self-motivated in implementing the worship of God. Hezekiah's reign was good, even compared to the standard set by David and Solomon. He must have been subject to great pressure from people around him—those who had been supporters of his idolatrous father Ahaz, and those who would throw their weight behind his son Manasseh, whose evil outweighed that of Ahaz.

Hezekiah accomplished his reform because he was able to mobilize a broad cross-section of his people behind him. Everyone benefited from supporting the king's policies when God rewarded Judah by taking the Assyrians off their backs.

PRINCIPLES

- For a person to change, he must change on the inside, not just in the way he acts.
- An effective strategy of helping people grow in Christ is to provide them with opportunities to use their own judgment.

APPLICATIONS

- To Hezekiah, details were important. He began by opening the doors of the temple and repairing them. What is God prompting you to do as a next step in your service for him and others?

- Hezekiah knew he could do some things but not everything. He understood it was necessary to enlist others in bringing Judah back to God. Who in your circle of influence do you need to be enlisting to make your church one that honors Christ and is passionate about his purposes?
- Begin or continue the practice of bringing your problems before God. Place them before the Lord in tangible ways like Hezekiah did when he brought Sennecherib's letter into the temple.

IV. LIFE APPLICATION

That's Not Who We Are

A number of years ago, a television program portrayed the inroads of computer technology into the gambling industry. This was occurring right around the time when gambling was being legalized in a number of states. Many people were getting their first introduction to the wonders of the computer world and to the sordid environs of gambling casinos simultaneously. Now people could turn over their money to the casino by playing blackjack on a machine just as easily as sitting at a table. One segment of the television program focused on an elderly couple who were enjoying themselves. Apparently they could afford the money losses, and they explained that what they were doing was simply having fun.

However, the program closed with a brief update. The featured couple had later seen the videotape of themselves and were aghast at the sight. "That's not who we are," they decided as they viewed themselves stuffing the machines with money and squealing and groaning at their wins and losses. Even though they had rationalized their gambling habit while they were being filmed for the program, once they saw it, they decided to give up gambling.

"That's not who we are." Hezekiah convinced the people of Judah that they were not the people of Baal but the people of God. Once they caught this vision, they acted on it and carried out reform on their own initiative. The kingdom underwent a total shift in the process. The people of Judah rethought not only what they were doing but who they were. Hezekiah was able to restore the kingdom to prosperity and to survive the Assyrian invasion.

Who are you? Many Christians have not really come to terms with the fact that they are not just people who are supposed to act differently from non-Christians but that God has given them a new nature. As Christians we are not just Baal worshipers who have taken up the worship of God, but we are the Lord's own people.

V. PRAYER

Lord Jesus, please let us see that we no longer belong to ourselves, but we are yours. Give us the strength to act according to who we are. Amen.

VI. DEEPER DISCOVERIES

The Assyrians (32:1)

Assyria was the cruelest of all the empires of the ancient world. They did not set up a territory in order to incorporate it into a larger whole. Their goal was to squeeze as much tribute as possible out of their victims. If the captive nations did not comply quickly, they would inflict major damage on them. No one was better than the Assyrians at taking territories and intimidating anyone who stood in their way through acts of cruelty.

The original Assyrian territory was in northern Mesopotamia, and its history was closely intertwined with that of Babylonia. In fact, Assyrians came from the same ethnic stock as the Semitic Babylonians, spoke a similar language, and worshiped many of the same gods. One distinctive feature of their religion was devotion to the god Ashur.

The history of Assyria had for a long time been a constant back-and-forth oscillation with Babylon; sometimes one country had the upper hand, sometimes the other. During the biblical time of the Judges, an Assyrian king—Tiglath-Pileser I—expanded his territory all the way into Syria, but this accomplishment was short-lived because his successors had to pull back and deal with issues closer to home. This contributed to the era that made the large empire of David and Solomon possible.

Then, during the time of Asa and Jehoshaphat, King Ashurnasirpal II caught the bug to go conquering and reached all the way to Lebanon. His successor, Shalmaneser III, attempted to vanquish Aram but was not able to do so because of a strong coalition of Syrio-Palestinian kings, which included the short-lived alliance between Ahab of Israel and Ben-Hadad of Aram.

We have already met Tiglath-Pileser III, who conquered Aram and parts of Israel. He was the king to whom Ahaz submitted voluntarily. Next, Shalmaneser V conquered Samaria and brought the Northern Kingdom to its final end, but his successor, Sargon II, gave himself credit for taking Samaria as well, and it was he who deported the Israelites into exile and resettled the area with Gentiles. When he died, a coalition of vassals, led by Hezekiah of Jerusalem, rebelled against Sennacherib, the next Assyrian king.

In his own records, Sennacherib described himself as the hand of the god Ashur, sent to bring the world into submission to him. His messages to Jerusalem, in which he asserted that the gods of other nations, including the God of Judah, could not resist his power, fit in well with his accounts of his battles. Sennacherib hated Hezekiah. The Jewish king had the audacity to resist his might and even to hold as prisoner a puppet king whom Sennacherib had installed in the Philistine area. So the Assyrian king decided to carry out a large-scale campaign in which he would conquer the land of Judah and then capture Jerusalem.

But we know that Sennacherib never took Jerusalem. His defeat was confirmed by the Greek historian Herodotus, who blamed the death of the Assyrian soldiers on field mice that devastated their supplies.

VII. TEACHING OUTLINE

A. INTRODUCTION

1. Lead Story: Rethinking Space and Time

2. Context: Hezekiah wasted no time. As soon as he came to the throne, he began removing the idolatrous legacy of his father Ahaz from the temple, from Jerusalem, and from the country.

3. Transition: As the theory of relativity demonstrates, sometimes we have to rethink an idea from the bottom up and change our view entirely. Hezekiah was able to get the people of Judah and Israel to abandon idolatrous practices, to think of themselves as God's people, and to buy into the program to become a nation that worshiped the Lord.

B. COMMENTARY

1. Hezekiah's Temple Reclamation (29:1–36)

2. The Great Passover (30:1–27)

3. Reforms in Judah and Israel (31:1–21)

4. Sennacherib's Unsuccessful Invasion (32:1–21)

5. Hezekiah's Splendor (32:22–33)

C. CONCLUSION: A TALE OF THREE TEACHERS

VIII. ISSUES FOR DISCUSSION

1. What specific actions of Hezekiah made him an effective reformer?
2. What do we learn about God from the fact that he forgave the Israelites who participated in the Passover without being purified?
3. Imagine the siege of Jerusalem by Sennacherib from the point of view of the common people in Jerusalem. How would your experience differ from that of the king? How would it be the same?
4. Contrast Solomon's action of showing his treasure to the queen of Sheba (2 Chr. 9:3) with Hezekiah's action of showing his treasure to the king of Babylon.
5. What admonitions to Christians can we glean from Hezekiah's slip into pride and conceit late in his reign?

2 Chronicles 33:1–35:27

The Gospel in Full Flower

I. INTRODUCTION
Son of Sam in Heaven?

II. COMMENTARY
A verse-by-verse explanation of these chapters.

III. CONCLUSION
A Worm's Eye View

An overview of the principles and applications from these chapters.

IV. LIFE APPLICATION
The Turnaround of a Bible Scholar

Melding these chapters to life.

V. PRAYER
Tying these chapters to life with God.

VI. DEEPER DISCOVERIES
Historical, geographical, and grammatical enrichment of the commentary.

VII. TEACHING OUTLINE
Suggested step-by-step group study of these chapters.

VIII. ISSUES FOR DISCUSSION
Zeroing these chapters in on daily life.

| Q u o t e |

"*W*ould he devote that sacred head

for such a worm as I?"

I s a a c   W a t t s

2 Chronicles 33:1–35:27

I N   A   N U T S H E L L

*M*anasseh was a thoroughly evil king, yet he repented and experienced God's forgiveness. After the short, evil reign of Amon, Josiah implemented reforms that healed the land for a time. We see in both Manasseh and Josiah the full display of the "gospel according to Ezra."

The Gospel in Full Flower

I. INTRODUCTION

Son of Sam in Heaven?

*D*avid Berkowitz became infamous as a serial killer, taking the lives of six women and setting over a thousand fires before he was finally caught in 1977. Berkowitz gave himself the name "Son of Sam" based on his claim that a demon communicated with him through the dog of his neighbor, a man by the name of Sam. After his arrest, psychiatrists determined, however, that Berkowitz was legally sane. They could find no evidence that he actually believed that such alleged hallucinations were real. He was given a 365-year sentence.

According to Berkowitz's testimony, ten years into his prison term, he found Christ. As he states on his Web site:

> I was involved in the occult and I got burned. I became a cruel killer and threw away my life as well as destroyed the lives of others. Now I have discovered that Christ is my answer and my hope. He broke the chains of mental confusion and depression that had me bound. Today I have placed my life in His hands. I only wish I knew Jesus before all these crimes happened—they would not have happened ("Forgiven for Life" Web site).

Many people are happy to welcome Berkowitz as a redeemed brother, but others are not convinced. Part of the problem is that Berkowitz's story of what actually happened in 1976 has changed many times, and there is good reason to believe that some of the things he is claiming now—such as being part of a ring of similar criminals—are false. Furthermore, psychiatric evaluations continue to cast doubts on Berkowitz's sincerity in asserting spiritual matters. Some people go so far as to declare that, given what the "Son of Sam" has done, it is inconceivable that God would forgive him and allow him into heaven.

We should never go so far as to say that it is not possible for Berkowitz to be saved. We cannot put a limit on the amount of sin that God can forgive. There is no person so evil that he could not come to God in faith and be forgiven. Our prime example of this truth is King Manasseh. He may have been the worst king Judah ever had. But he repented and turned to God, and God accepted him. This is the "gospel according to Ezra" in full bloom.

II. COMMENTARY

The Gospel in Full Flower

MAIN IDEA: *Manasseh and Josiah give us two dimensions of the "gospel according to Ezra," one by repentance late in life, the other by bringing about reforms while still in his youth.*

A Manasseh: The King Who Repented (33:1–20)

SUPPORTING IDEA: *Manasseh was a wicked king, but when he repented, God forgave him.*

33:1–6. Manasseh became king at age twelve, leaving us with questions about why Hezekiah, dying when he was fifty-four years old, would not have had an older male heir. For the boy taking the throne, his young age and long reign—fifty-five years—provided opportunity for many years of mischief.

The account of Manasseh begins with a lengthy indictment and provides us with no explanation for the king's behavior. Did he have a deep-seated problem with his godly father? Were there other relatives who directed him away from God? All we are given is an itemized list of practices that reveal a king more devoted to perverted religion than even the best of kings was to the Lord.

Manasseh rebuilt the **high places** that Hezekiah had destroyed; made **altars to the Baals**; set up **Asherah poles**; bowed down to **the starry hosts**—the deities primarily of Babylon and Nineveh; placed pagan **altars** in the temple; **sacrificed his sons** to honor Baal; **practiced sorcery, divination and witchcraft**; and **consulted mediums and spiritists**.

When evil rides into town, the occult sits right behind it. This is true not only for idolatrous religions today as much as in Manasseh's times but also when religion per se is not strong in an evil society. No nation has had as rampant an epidemic of the occult as Germany under Hitler, who was enslaved to it himself. Life without God breeds fear, and people become inclined to resort to spiritualistic devices to try to control their own lives.

33:7–9. It was close to three hundred years now since Solomon had dedicated the temple. Who would have thought at the time that there would actually be a descendant of Solomon, one who benefited by God's long-term promises to the sons of David, who would install an idol in this temple? Solomon had recognized that no physical object could contain God, not even the temple (2 Chr. 6:18). Manasseh, on the other hand, erected a statue of a pagan god—presumably a version of Baal—right in the temple.

The chronicler reminds us that God had tied the Israelites' obligation to keep the law to their being able to stay in the promised land. God had first given them the country and then, about four hundred years later, the temple. If they desecrated the temple, their claim to the land would no longer be honored.

33:10. King Manasseh should have known how offensive his behavior was to God and that it would result in severe punishment. But even now God was giving him the opportunity to repent before the calamity set in. God's prophets (2 Kgs. 21:10) declared his certain destruction, but the king ignored them.

33:11. Then the calamity occurred. The Assyrian army captured Manasseh, **put a hook in his nose**, and brought him to Babylon in chains. These are all the explanations we get in the Bible; the Book of 2 Kings does not even mention Manasseh's capture, let alone his subsequent repentance and return.

The new king of Assyria was Esarhaddon, who smashed, tortured, and humiliated everyone who dared to stand in his way. Esarhaddon directed a large building program, and he thought of a novel way to get all his vassal states to transport the necessary building materials to Mesopotamia. Other emperors forced their vassal kings to supply slave labor, but Esarhaddon forced the kings themselves to serve as slavess. Would it not have been ironic if Manasseh had found himself chained to transport the statue of one of the deities that he had favored over God?

33:12–13. Manasseh, the king whose idolatry "out-Canaanited" the Canaanites, turned to God. It must have been God himself who opened Manasseh's mind and heart. In his childhood he may have heard his father Hezekiah recite Solomon's dedication prayer (2 Chr. 30:9), and we can imagine that the words suddenly started to burn in his mind. Manasseh, at the point of desperation, with an iron hook in his nose, being treated worse than an animal, repented. And the chronicler tells us that God heard him and allowed him to return to Jerusalem. Manasseh now had no doubt that the Lord was the one true God.

33:14–17. Manasseh reversed most of the evil he had perpetrated earlier. He abolished all the idols and altars, particularly the items with which he had desecrated the temple. He reinstituted regular temple sacrifices to the true God, and he also used his influence to get the people to stop worshiping idols. But he only achieved a compromise, since he was not able to stop the use of pagan altars altogether.

33:18–20. The chronicler's final summary of Manasseh directs us to some sources for further details, some of which are found in 2 Kings 21:10–15. When Manasseh died, he was not buried in the regular royal tombs but in his own palace.

B Amon: Short Reign of an Evil King (33:21–25)

SUPPORTING IDEA: *Amon revived Manasseh's idolatrous practices, but he was assassinated after only two years on the throne.*

33:21–25. Amon's reign was mercifully short. This may be the most positive comment we can make about him, although he had popular support. He brought Manasseh's earlier idol worship back into full vogue. It is hard to believe that he could have shown a lot of promise in any other respect, since his own **officials** set up a successful assassination conspiracy against him. Amon was the child of an occult-oppressed father, who was tortured and humiliated beyond imagining, and who later in life reversed himself on everything he had taught his children. This child, now barely out of his teens, must have been clueless about how to serve as king.

Once again the people did not let the murder of the Lord's anointed go unpunished. Then they did something that had not happened in quite a while: They themselves installed someone on the throne who would rule on the basis of popular acclaim as well as because of the right of inheritance (2 Chr. 26:1). But there was one problem: This new king was only an eight-year-old boy. Could he provide the leadership the kingdom needed?

The chronicler, eager to get past Amon, dispenses with an official death notice for him. In 2 Kings 21:26 we learn that he was also buried in the royal palace, not the official tombs.

C Josiah's Early Reforms (34:1–33)

SUPPORTING IDEA: *Josiah's program of abolishing idolatry and restoring the temple received a strong boost with the discovery of the Book of the Law.*

34:1–2. The chronicler tells us that Josiah turned out to be a good king. He followed the pattern set by David, **not turning aside to the right or to the left.** Josiah was not infallible as a ruler; in fact, a serious error in judgment wound up costing the king his life. But in the matter of central importance to Ezra—devotion to the Lord and dedication to his worship in the temple—Josiah was blameless.

34:3–7. Josiah, from early on, found his own way with the Lord. The first boyking, Joash, lived all his early life under the rigid directions of Jehoiada, the priest, and then abandoned God as soon as Jehoiada died. Josiah's situation was different. No single tutor seemed to be pushing him in a certain direction. Josiah must have had plenty of advisors, but this young king was capable of making up his own mind.

Josiah spent his early childhood in the household of the ungodly Amon, so it is safe to assume that idolatry was his first religion. Since he did not convert to the worship of God until he was sixteen years old, it is unlikely that he would have been installed initially as the puppet king of any "pro-God" party. In fact, no one may have been as disappointed about Josiah's eventual turn against idolatry than the people who had clamored for him to be king. When he did become a worshiper of the Lord, it was a slow process for him to learn everything involved. At the time the temple was in disrepair, and there were no copies of the law available. Josiah's first steps in the direction of serving the Lord must have been hesitant and uncertain.

At age twenty Josiah set out to purge the land of all idols. He went with his men as they traveled from place to place in Judah and Israel, destroying idols and executing the priests who served them. When he had finished this crusade, he returned to Jerusalem and started to focus on his own backyard—the long-neglected temple.

34:8–13. The temple had been shut down by Ahaz, purified by Hezekiah, desecrated and then reopened by Manasseh, neglected (or worse) by Amon, and relegated to a low status by Josiah. Now more than three hundred years old, it seemed to cry out for a thorough restoration, and Josiah was prepared to undertake the project. At age twenty-six, after serving as king for eighteen years, he appointed a committee to oversee the temple-renewal project.

The temple committee consulted with the high priest, Hilkiah, and turned the project treasury over to him. During all this time, the Levites had continued to collect the temple taxes, and quite a bit of revenue had accumulated. The funds were now used to pay the people who were to do the repair work and to buy raw materials. The Levites supervised the project.

34:14–18. The record-keeping and daily accounting pertaining to the temple could be handled by Levites, but there had to be some private office where the high priest could meet with people to counsel, pray, and plan. Apparently Hilkiah had not made much use of this space.

When the temple committee showed up and put Hilkiah in charge of the payroll, he suddenly had to use his office more efficiently. As he was rummaging around the stack of unused stuff, he found a scroll. When he picked it up and unrolled it, he recognized it as **the Book of the Law.** This was the law of God as revealed in the five books of Moses. Because of the curses mentioned later on (34:24), it is clear that it included at least the Book of Deuteronomy (Deut. 28:15–68). But the other four books (Genesis through Numbers) may have been on this scroll as well.

Hilkiah gave the book to Shaphan, the king's secretary, who was also a member of the temple committee, and told him what it was. Apparently the identity of the book did not mean much to Shaphan because he tacked its discovery on to the end of his next report to the king. He told Josiah that all the workers were being paid properly and then remembered, "Oh yes, Hilkiah has found this book." He began reading a few excerpts that he thought the king might find interesting.

34:19–21. Josiah's reaction was dramatic. The more he listened to the contents of the scroll, the more distraught he became. Every word of it sounded like a condemnation; very clearly this was not a book that the kingdom had lived by. Finally he jumped up, tore his robe to demonstrate how upset he was, and issued an order to five people—including Hilkiah, Shaphan, Shaphan's son, and two others, Abdon and Asaiah. They were to seek word directly from God on this situation because God must be very angry with his people.

34:22–28. Josiah was right: God was angry. The high priest and his colleagues found someone who could speak for God—Huldah the prophetess. She informed the delegation that the nation had invoked on itself the curses for breaking the law (Deut. 28:15–68). Judgment was inevitable.

But Huldah had words of hope for Josiah. God, the only one who could have known what was really in Josiah's heart, had revealed to her that the king's repentance was real, and he had shown her that the king would not be subject to the calamity that God would send. It would come some time after he died.

34:29–33. King Josiah called for a national service of renewal. He, along with all the men of importance and the people whom they represented, stood in the temple. Then the king himself read the book out loud. Such a public reading of the law was commanded in the book (Deut. 31:10–13). But since the scroll had been misplaced, no one had known about this requirement.

When Josiah had finished reading, he led the group in a ceremony to renew the covenant. He vowed to abide by the commandments of the law. Then he had all the people agree to the same. In attendance at this meeting was a young priest named Jeremiah (Jer. 1:1–3). How hollow this occasion must have seemed to him in later years as he lived through the ungodly reigns of subsequent kings!

Ⅾ The National Passover (35:1–19)

> **SUPPORTING IDEA:** *King Josiah and the people of the nation confirmed their rededication to the Lord with a Passover celebration that involved the entire country.*

35:1–9. As Hezekiah had done before him, Josiah used the celebration of a Passover to have the entire nation express their renewed devotion to the Lord. The chronicler tells us that this was the biggest Passover in the nation since the days of Samuel (35:18), exceeding that of Hezekiah in scope.

In order to bring off this celebration, the final touches needed to be put on the preparation of the temple. The chronicler has not mentioned the ark of the covenant since the days of Solomon (2 Chr. 8:11), but now it comes up again. Josiah ordered it to be placed back in the most holy place. With all the abuses of the temple over the last few generations, the ark had been carried to some other location, and there were Levites who had once more taken up the ancient tradition of bearing it on their shoulders. Josiah reassigned it to its permanent location in the temple.

Josiah reinstituted the specific shifts of duties as David had established them and gave each priest his specific job. He and his officials donated many animals to be sacrificed.

35:10–19. The Passover lamb was slaughtered, and the correct portions were burned or eaten. The heirs to Asaph, Heman, and Jeduthun provided the music. Even the temple security system functioned well because the gatekeepers were able to participate in the service without leaving their posts. These statements are a testimony to the way Josiah implemented the guidelines established by King David before the temple was built (1 Chr. 24–26).

Ⅾ Josiah's Death (35:20–27)

> **SUPPORTING IDEA:** *Josiah's reign comes to an end when he loses his life in a battle against Pharaoh Neco of Egypt.*

35:20–24a. In general Egypt was not a strong influence in Palestine during the time of the kingdom of Judah. But now this was changing. Assyria's power was waning, and Egypt was building up in its wake. In fact, Egypt and Assyria were about to embark on an alliance to defeat their common enemy, Babylon.

Babylon had been a longtime rival for power against Assyria. For the last century Assyria had held the upper hand, but now Babylon, under the powerful king Nabopolasar and his son and successor, Nebuchadnezzar, was vying for dominance. There seemed only one solution: let all Babylon's enemies unite and stop its imperial ambitions. This is exactly what Assyria and Egypt planned to do. They would meet near Carchemish and put Babylon in its place.

So Pharaoh Neco of Egypt and a huge army marched north up the *via maris*, the road along the Mediterranean Sea, in order to cut east across to Mesopotamia. The outcome of this battle would be crucial, and Neco had neither the time nor interest to pay any attention to Judah as he was passing through. But Josiah had plans of his own. Perhaps he thought Neco was just concealing his plans to attack Jerusalem. Perhaps he thought the Lord had provided him with an opportunity for a miraculous victory. Maybe he thought that he had an obligation to attack any Egyptian army.

Whatever his reasoning, Josiah deployed his own smaller army to block Neco's way. This encounter occurred on the plain of Megiddo, which is north and west of Jerusalem. It was clear that Neco did not pose any threat to Josiah, and he was not interested in Josiah's challenge. He was at a loss to understand why Josiah would want to spill blood in a foolish cause. He certainly did not wish to waste any time and effort on Judah when Babylon posed such a threat. He even went so far as to inform the king of Judah that God himself did not want him to get involved in this battle.

Still Josiah would not listen. He took Neco's unwillingness to fight personally, and he disguised himself as he went into battle. The king was hit by an arrow, and he died shortly after arriving back in Jerusalem.

35:24b–27. The people missed King Josiah. The group of official mourners was headed by Jeremiah, who wrote some official laments in Josiah's memory. The **Laments** referred to here are not our Book of Lamentations, also composed by Jeremiah. Josiah received full burial honors in the royal tombs.

> **MAIN IDEA REVIEW:** *Manasseh and Josiah give us two dimensions of the "gospel according to Ezra," one by repentance late in life, the other by bringing about reforms while still in his youth.*

III. CONCLUSION

A Worm's Eye View

Isaac Watts wrote a very powerful hymn, "At the Cross," one line of which I have used as the title for this section: "Alas and did my savior bleed, and did my sovereign die? / Would he devote that sacred head for such a worm as I?" But do not look for this verse to appear this way in most contemporary hymnbooks. The word *worm* has been changed in favor of some more diplomatic reference to oneself, such as "for sinners such as I." People do not like to think of themselves as worms.

Then again, if worms could think, perhaps they would not like to think of themselves as people. Worms do not have a sin nature; they are not consistently offending their Creator by acts of rebellion; and they do not live in a state of alienation from God. We humans have some problems that worms do not because we are sinful and in need of a redeemer.

Let us never think that God saved us because he saw something within us that was worth saving. He did not extend his grace to us because there was something intrinsically good within us that he did not wish to waste. It is precisely because we are not worth saving—in the sense of having any merit—that we need God's grace.

Manasseh and Josiah illustrate this point. Manasseh was corrupt in every conceivable area of his life, and yet God allowed him to repent when he was chained and tortured by the Assyrians. Josiah's life, by contrast, seems to have gone smoothly. Coming to the throne as a child, he gradually matured in his recognition and worship of God. The Lord also supplied the means for a greater commitment by the king.

The apostle Paul called himself the "worst" of sinners (1 Tim. 1:15). He understood a fact that Manasseh and Josiah also realized—that God's grace is magnificent only when we have come to terms with our unworthiness to receive it.

PRINCIPLES

- As fallen human beings, we have nothing within ourselves to merit God's love toward us.
- God's grace is always miraculous.
- Sometimes God's grace is demonstrated in a dramatic way, such as with Manasseh's repentance, while at other times we see his grace working slowly over an extended period of time, as in Josiah's life.

APPLICATIONS

- The case of Manasseh tests our understanding of grace. Review Manasseh's life and then read 2 Chronicles 33:19. How does Manasseh's humbling himself and his prayer to God make you feel? What do you learn about yourself as you meditate on this case? What new understanding of God does this yield?

- Think of the children within your sphere of influence. Think about what might happen if they turned their hearts to God at a tender age. Does God have a redemptive role for you to play in their lives now?

- In a recent sermon, Bible study, or time of devotion, has God spoken to your heart about repenting of an attitude or practice? Review the case of Josiah as an encouragement to turn to God now.

- Review the circumstances of Josiah's death (2 Chr. 35:20–26). Is stubbornness a character flaw or a virtue? We sometimes say that we are resolute and decisive but other people are stubborn. What is God's Word saying to us about this human characteristic in this passage?

IV. LIFE APPLICATION

The Turnaround of a Bible Scholar

Eta Linnemann is a scholar of great achievement, but her early work took the methods of liberal criticism one step further than her teacher, Rudolf Bultmann. Other scholars had supposedly shown that the four Gospels are a collection of various fictitious fragments pasted together to serve the needs of the early church, but they had believed that at least the narratives of Christ's death and resurrection had integrity. To the great acclaim of some scholarly circles, Linnemann advocated the view that the crucifixion story could not be believed either. Her scholarship provided underpinning for contemporary unbelief.

Many years later we find this very same Eta Linnemann doing missionary work in Indonesia. A new set of publications in which she asserts the full authority of God's divine Word have followed. The woman who had impressed liberal scholars is now putting her academic skills at the disposal of the Lord. She has found that with her earlier methods of dismembering the Word of God on the basis of human judgment, she was also cutting herself off from God's declaration of salvation in Christ. Eta Linnemann has found Christ as her Savior, and she is now proclaiming the message of the gospel with every tool at her disposal.

Eta Linnemman's salvation was a miracle. So was Manasseh's; so was Josiah's. And so is ours. Why did Manasseh come to salvation whereas King Saul, the first king of Israel, did not? Saul's condemnation was just and earned because he refused to repent. In Manasseh we see how God can save those who turn to him.

V. PRAYER

Lord Jesus, we spend a lifetime giving evidence of our sinful state. Yet you came and died for us, called us to yourself, and let us experience your saving grace as we came to you in simple trust. Help us not to look within ourselves for what you might have thought worth saving, nor rationalize in others why they were worthy of your grace or deserving of their condemned state. Let us see that your grace is an expression of your undeserved love. Amen.

VI. DEEPER DISCOVERIES

A. Manasseh's Repentance and God's Salvation (33:13)

Let's be clear about something that applies to Manasseh as well as the other godly kings of Judah. Do not think that the king's salvation turned him into a perfect person. We know that he was humiliated, that he repented, and that once he got back to Jerusalem, he started to worship the Lord. But God had heard Manasseh's prayer a long time before he got back to Jerusalem. Similarly, Josiah and his associates had only just discovered the Book of the Law and had a long way to go in its implementation when Huldah prophesied God's mercy on the king.

Just as God does not save us because of what we are, he also does not save us on the basis of what we may become. God saves us so we will demonstrate his glory and righteousness in the world. But our changed lives as Christians are not the grounds for our salvation any more than our previous lives as non-Christians could have been.

Some people think that "grace" is necessary to help us do the works that will get us saved. But this idea is no more correct than the notion that we can be saved without God's grace. As Paul states in Titus 3:5, "He saved us, not because of righteous things we had done, but because of his mercy." Our works are never a factor in determining whether we will be saved.

B. Huldah the Prophetess (34:22)

The prophetess Huldah was one of a few female seers in the Old Testament. Moses' sister Miriam was called a "prophetess" (Exod. 15:20), and she was considered one of the persons in charge of the exodus (Mic. 6:4). In Judges 4:4 we read that Deborah was "leading Israel" in her time. One other person, Noadiah, is mentioned by name as a prophetess, but she was an evil person who opposed Nehemiah's project of rebuilding Jerusalem (Neh. 6:14).

Also, perhaps whimsically, Isaiah referred to his wife as the prophetess, though she was not associated with any prophetic activity (Isa. 8:3).

When we turn to the New Testament, we find a few more women with that title. There was a prophetess named Anna in the temple at the time of Jesus' dedication (Luke 2:36), and an unnamed false prophetess was misleading the church at Thyatira (Rev. 2:20). We also do not have the names of the four daughters of Philip who were prophetesses (Acts 21:9).

VII. TEACHING OUTLINE

A. INTRODUCTION

1. Lead Story: Son of Sam in Heaven?
2. Context: Hezekiah had been a righteous king. But when he died, the question was up in the air once again: Would his successors follow the Lord or worship idols?
3. Transition: Is David Berkowitz saved? We cannot say, but stories like his push us to the limits in trying to understand how radical God's grace can be. We see God's grace in action in marvelous ways in the lives of Manasseh and Josiah.

B. COMMENTARY

1. Manasseh: the King Who Repented (33:1–20)
2. Amon: Short Reign of an Evil King (33:21–25)
3. Josiah's Early Reforms (34:1–33)
4. The National Passover (35:1–19)
5. Josiah's Death (35:20–27)

C. CONCLUSION: A WORM'S EYE VIEW

VIII. ISSUES FOR DISCUSSION

1. What are some biblical principles on the question of judging whether a person is a true believer? How legitimate is it even to ask the question?
2. Christians have been known to show two extreme reactions when some famous person confesses to faith in Christ: to question the reality of the conversion or to celebrate the conversion without raising any reservations. Are there potential problems with either reaction?

2 Chronicles 36:1–23

The Door Remains Open

I. INTRODUCTION
The Plane That Returned

II. COMMENTARY
A verse-by-verse explanation of the chapter.

III. CONCLUSION
Patching Up the Foundation

An overview of the principles and applications from the chapter.

IV. LIFE APPLICATION
Unexpected Opportunity

Melding the chapter to life.

V. PRAYER
Tying the chapter to life with God.

VI. DEEPER DISCOVERIES
Historical, geographical, and grammatical enrichment of the commentary.

VII. TEACHING OUTLINE
Suggested step-by-step group study of the chapter.

VIII. ISSUES FOR DISCUSSION
Zeroing the chapter in on daily life.

"*C*hrist is there, standing at the door."

L e o n   M o r r i s

2 Chronicles 36:1–23

I N   A   N U T S H E L L

*T*he last four kings of Judah exceeded their lack of devotion to God only by their incompetence as rulers. The first one, Jehoahaz, was taken hostage by Egypt; the other three were a part of successive deportations by Babylon. The books of 1 and 2 Chronicles conclude by stating that after the Babylonian exile, King Cyrus of Persia allowed the Jews to return to Jerusalem.

The Door Remains Open

I. INTRODUCTION

The Plane That Returned

*Y*ears ago, before the current security restrictions on air travel, a college student named Kathy had intended to fly to a conference, but she was late in getting to the airport. In fact, by the time she got to the boarding gate, the plane had already taken off. Disappointed, she turned around, trying to see what other arrangements she could make, when an airline employee told her the airplane was coming back.

Sure enough, her plane was turning around. It landed, Kathy was able to board, the plane took off again, and Kathy was able to get to the conference. Everyone was laughing—though half seriously—at the idea that perhaps God made a plane turn around in the air just to pick up Kathy. Obviously, there were other reasons the plane needed to return to the airport, but that does not change the fact that, when Kathy needed the transportation, God provided it.

In the last chapter of Chronicles, the plane takes off. With the thunder of a supersonic jet, it takes to the air and speeds off to the horizon. Or, to refer to the actual reality, the kingdom of Judah gets obliterated. In a series of devastating conquests, Jerusalem, the temple, even the king are swept away for good. Judah receives its punishment for centuries of disobedience.

And yet the plane returns. Second Chronicles ends on a note of hope. The exile does not last forever. After about seventy years, Cyrus, king of Persia, allows the Jews to return to Jerusalem, where God's plan of salvation moves on.

II. COMMENTARY

The Door Remains Open

MAIN IDEA: *Even though the kingdom of Judah received its due punishment by means of foreign conquest and exile, God provided the hope of a fresh start when King Cyrus of Persia decreed that the Jewish exiles could return home.*

This last chapter of 2 Chronicles takes us on a rapid overview of the last four kings of Judah. More details are found in 2 Kings 23:31–25:29 as well as throughout the Book of Jeremiah. The prophet's ministry overlapped with these times. In broad outline we see four kings, none of them faithful to God, caught between Egypt and Babylon. Politically, the key to these last events is that God had chosen Babylon as his tool of divine punishment for his people and that the kings of Judah had an obligation not to fight the Babylonians but to submit to them.

But the kings did not accept their fate and repeatedly rebelled against Babylon by making alliances with Egypt. As a result, things went from bad to worse, and three times Nebuchadnezzar took Jerusalem, each time inflicting greater damage and taking more people into exile.

🅐 Jehoahaz, Short-Term King (36:1–3)

> **SUPPORTING IDEA:** *Almost as soon as Jehoahaz becomes king, he is carried off to Egypt as a hostage.*

36:1–3. Pharaoh Neco, having dealt with King Josiah on his way to the battle of Carchemish, was in a foul mood when he passed by Judah on his way home to Egypt. The Egyptian and Assyrian armies had suffered a serious defeat. He now had the opportunity to vent his rage on Jerusalem, and he did so. The people had just placed Jehoahaz, son of Josiah, on the throne, and he was the perfect target for Neco's anger. Neco captured Jehoahaz and made him a hostage, keeping the lid on any further ideas that a future king of Judah might get to play spoiler in world affairs. Neco also received a large tribute from Judah. We read in 2 Kings 23:32 that Jehoahaz was in the process of becoming an evil king, so the kingdom probably did not suffer greatly from his dethronement. Jehoahaz died while in exile, and there is no information about his funeral.

🅑 Jehoiakim, Evil King (36:4–8)

> **SUPPORTING IDEA:** *Jehoiakim was evil and rebellious, and he was taken away to Babylon under the first deportation by Nebuchadnezzar.*

36:4. Before leaving Jerusalem with Jehoahaz in tow, Neco installed a king of his own choosing on the throne of Judah. He selected Eliakim, who was actually Jehoahaz's older brother, though from a different mother (2 Kgs. 23:36). Neco changed Eliakim's name to Jehoiakim. This was not a radical change because both versions of the name meant "God raises up," but the latter used the specific term *Yahweh* instead of the more generic *El* (Payne, 419). Perhaps the pharaoh wanted an instant association of his vassals with the religion they observed.

36:5. Jehoiakim seemed to think he was above any law, and he played every situation for what he perceived to be even a momentary advantage. Jehoiakim callously burned Jeremiah's scroll piece by piece when he did not like what it said (Jer. 36:10–26).

36:6–7. Jehoiakim did not remain Egypt's vassal for long. Nebuchadnezzar of Babylon asserted his power and inflicted a sizable annual tribute on him. At first the king of Judah complied—but only by squeezing the necessary funds from his own subjects (2 Kgs. 23:35) rather than turning to his own treasury. However, when Jehoiakim decided not to cooperate with Babylon any longer, Nebuchadnezzar emptied Jehoiakim's treasury and carried the king into exile along with some of the finest youths of Jerusalem, including Daniel (Dan. 1:1–3). Apparently Jehoiakim's exile was temporary, and he was permitted to serve out his short reign (2 Kgs. 24:6).

36:8. Jehoiakim did receive a death notice from the chronicler, though it was not a flattering one. We read that we can find out more about Jehoiakim's evil in further places. Once again neither a funeral nor the location of his burial is mentioned.

Ⓒ Jehoiachin, Short-Term King (36:9–10)

SUPPORTING IDEA: *Jehoiachin's short reign was also marked by evil, leading to further punishment.*

36:9. Jehoiachin ruled for only three months and ten days—those ten days putting him ahead by that much over his uncle, Jehoahaz. Taking the throne as a teenager, he made sufficient use of his short reign to earn him the label of **evil in the eyes of the LORD.**

36:10. We are not given much information about Jehoiachin. But it is clear that he, like his father, rebelled against Nebuchadnezzar and the Babylonian overlords. This time it resulted in a serious siege of Jerusalem. When Nebuchadnezzar left Jerusalem this time, it was after he had emptied the temple of its treasures and had chained together a large number of exiles, including the king himself, who would spend the rest of his life in Babylon. Many of the people who were carried away wound up doing hard slave labor on excavation projects (Ezek. 1:1–3). Among these exiles was the prophet Ezekiel, who followed the subsequent events from afar (Ezek. 33:21). Jerusalem had not been destroyed with finality, and the temple still stood when this group of people departed for exile.

D Zedekiah, the Last King (36:11–21)

SUPPORTING IDEA: *Zedekiah, the last king of Judah, reaped all the punishment he deserved and that the nation had accrued during its existence.*

36:11–13. When Neco of Egypt had removed Jehoahaz from the throne, he had crowned his brother Jehoiakim in his stead. Now that Nebuchadnezzar had deported Jehoiachin, the king of Babylon in turn designated yet another brother of Jehoahaz and Jehoiakim to be the next king. Thus, Zedekiah was the third son of Josiah to become king.

Zedekiah turned out to be as bad as his brothers and his nephew. He supported idolatry, and he did not listen to Jeremiah's word from the Lord. He got the idea that he could get out from under Babylon's thumb by seeking an alliance with Egypt. This notion made little sense politically, but it was also wrong in other respects. For one thing, God wanted Judah to accept domination by Babylon at this point, and Jeremiah made this fact clear to the king (Jer. 38:17–18).

36:14. Zedekiah's poor judgment took the whole nation down with him. Things were bad to begin with, but in the eleven years after this twenty-one year old took the helm, the kingdom went further and further down in corruption. The chronicler specifies **the leaders of the priests** as among those who went along with Zedekiah, and the fact that **the temple of the LORD** was defiled.

36:15–16. The chronicler reminds us that nothing of what was happening was occurring without warning. Whenever a king made a bad decision, a prophet would appear, telling him exactly what God thought about his actions. But repentance was in short supply. The kings of Judah **mocked God's messengers** and **despised his words**. Finally, **there was no remedy**. It was too late for the nation to escape God's punishment.

36:17–19. God's display of his wrath was triggered by Zedekiah's rebellion. Nebuchadnezzar came and obliterated Jerusalem, this time finishing the job that he had done only partially on the other two occasions. Many people were massacred, a number of them **in the sanctuary** of the temple. Did they think that the Lord would give them miraculous protection in his temple as they huddled between the idols? Nebuchadnezzar carried off whatever treasure was. He demolished the walls of Jerusalem and burned the temple.

36:20. Almost everyone was marched off to Babylon. Jeremiah tells us that a few people escaped exile, but they wound up bringing further difficulties on themselves (Jer. 44:15–23). In Babylon, the Jews would live as slaves, longing for their homeland (see Ps. 137:1).

36:21. In the meantime, the land **enjoyed its sabbath rests**. The law of God had specified that every seventh year should be a sabbath year (Lev. 25:1–22). During the seventh year the Israelites were to abstain from all agricultural activity. But the Israelites had not observed the sabbath year in a long time, and so the seventy-year period of the exile would be its enforced implementation. The length of seventy years had been predicted by Jeremiah several times (Jer. 25:9–12; 27:6–8; 29:10). This length is derived not from the final destruction of Jerusalem but from the second deportation, the one that occurred when Jehoiachin was king.

Zedekiah's reign ended tragically. When Jerusalem was about to crack under the Babylonian siege, Zedekiah, his family, and his royal entourage took flight, but Nebuchadnezzar's men captured them quickly. Zedekiah had to watch as the Babylonian soldiers executed his sons. Then the soldiers blinded the king so his sons' dying moments would be the last visual images he would carry in his head. He was then dragged off to Babylon along with the other exiles. With this act of cruelty, Nebuchadnezzar had spent his anger, and Zedekiah died in Babylon as a king without a kingdom.

🄴 Cyrus's Decree to Return (36:22–23)

SUPPORTING IDEA: *Chronicles ends on a note of hope. The exile comes to an end, and, thanks to the decree of Cyrus of Persia, the nation can rebuild.*

36:22–23. Cyrus the Great, king of Peresia, was a great conqueror, an expert at defeating his enemies and acquiring territories. But more than any of his predecessors, he knew how to bond an empire together. Cyrus attempted to weld his empire together by allowing vassal states to maintain as much of their own culture as possible while absorbing them into a rigorous political grid. Cyrus implemented the policy of respecting all religions and enabling each group of people to worship their own gods. In short, he ruled by inspiring the loyalty of the nations he had conquered.

Cyrus claimed that he had a directive from God to supply him with a new temple. We should not take this statement to imply that he actually believed in the God of the Bible. He was simply treating the Lord as he was treating all other gods—following what he believed to be his instructions from Marduk. "May all the gods whom I have resettled in their sacred cities ask daily Bel and Nebo [two other Babylonian gods] for a long life for me and may they recommend me to him [Marduk]" (Pritchard, 208).

From the point of view of the people of God, Cyrus's pagan notions fitted into God's own plan. The Lord had predicted through Jeremiah that the exile would last seventy years. After this length of time, Cyrus took over and issued his order to rebuild the temple, thereby allowing the people to return home. It was not leniency to the Jews that motivated Cyrus to send them home; it was his desire to make sure that the God whom the Jews worshiped would be happy.

And so they returned. The slate was not blank, but the mistakes on it had been erased, and the nation could begin again. Once again they had the opportunity to build a community under the Lord. It would not be easy, but there would be many stories from the past to draw on. The people would need to know about their heritage and about the successes and failures of previous generations.

One leader during the long process of restoration was Ezra. He tried to get the people to understand how important it was to return to their roots, to appreciate that God had chosen them, and that God had provided the temple and the priesthood so they could worship the one true God. It occurred to Ezra that he should lay it all out in a book. He spent a lot of time collecting as much material as he could find on the history of his people. Then he wrote it all down in the books of Chronicles.

MAIN IDEA REVIEW: *Even though the kingdom of Judah received its due punishment by means of foreign conquest and exile, God provided the hope of a fresh start when King Cyrus of Persia decreed that the Jewish exiles could return home.*

III. CONCLUSION

Patching Up the Foundation

There comes a point in the life of an old, crumbling house when a patch job no longer works and the only way to preserve it is to rebuild the foundation. The house needs to be propped up on jacks while the foundation is replaced with new materials.

To apply this analogy, Israel's return from the exile would only be a temporary patch on a wall that needed replacement. It would not mark the end of their problems. There were roughly four hundred years of turbulent history between the time when Ezra wrote Chronicles and when the biblical story picks up again with the coming of Christ. There continued to be times of suffering inflicted on the people of God from the outside as well as periods when they waned in their loyalty to him. Ezra's efforts were successful to some extent, but only temporarily so.

God knew all along, of course, that Israel's problems needed a greater solution—the coming of the Messiah. And Israel represents for us in the microcosm of one nation what is true of all humanity: each of us stands in need of total transformation by God.

So was the restoration after seventy years of exile just a waste of time? Did it not just postpone the inevitable need for God to do something far more radical? Again, we may respond by pointing out that postponement can be valuable in itself. Yes, the Lord would eventually bring this phase of his demonstration to an end, and he would start to work with Gentiles and Jews on the same basis (Eph. 2:11–18), but for the moment he would allow Israel to come to him as a national and political unit. Maybe, given a fresh start, the chance to rebuild the temple, and the removal of any pressure to fall into idolatry, they could become fully obedient to the Lord. The outcome of this opportunity takes us past the pages of Chronicles, but we see in Ezra, Nehemiah, and Malachi that the results continued to be disappointing.

Nevertheless, the decree by Cyrus represented the truth that God would not let go of history. God had shown his sovereignty in judgment, but he would also display his sovereignty in grace once again. The Lord is not done with his work until he has declared it finished, and that will not be until the end of time. God, not Nebuchadnezzar, will declare when it is all over.

PRINCIPLES

- God is a God of grace and mercy, but he will also issue judgment.
- Not accepting God's discipline may be just as sinful as the sin that brought on the discipline.
- Even when we are going through times of discipline, this does not mean that God has withdrawn his offer of salvation or fellowship from us.

APPLICATIONS

- Read Psalm 119:67,71. Are there hardships in your life which these verses illuminate?
- Read Romans 5:3–5 in several translations. What kind of progression can trials lead us through when taken in the right spirit?
- Imagine how Simon Peter's view of the future and his own future changed just after his denial of Christ (Luke 22:54–62). Roll the

calendar forward only fifty days and watch Peter preaching before a huge crowd in Jerusalem (Acts 2:38–42). Does it look like he was finished?

- Is there a failure in your life that has led you to conclude that you're finished or that has virtually rendered you ineffective in God's kingdom? Take a second look at what God did with Judah seventy years after the exile. Take a good look at Simon Peter the morning of Jesus' arrest and then the morning of Pentecost. What does God delight in doing?

IV. LIFE APPLICATION

Unexpected Opportunity

Bob had wanted to be a missionary when he was young, but the Lord closed the doors through some minor health problems. His desire had been to serve the Lord among Muslims in the Arab world. But instead he and his wife settled into a successful ministry of pastoring in the United States. For the last fifteen years or so of his career, Bob worked for a mission board, though still strictly stateside as a recruiter. Then the organization sent him on a trip into a Muslim country to visit various workers in their locations.

While spending one evening at the house of some local Christians, Bob and his hosts were praying for the salvation of one specific young man (call him Rahman) with whom the local believers had shared the gospel several times. At that very moment Rahman entered, and he and Bob got into a lengthy conversation. God gave Bob just the right words to say. Rahman let down all his defenses and received Jesus Christ as his Savior that night. In the years since this evening, Rahman has grown in the faith and has been able to be a part of the support for other new Christians in that country.

For Bob, this event was an overwhelming joy. As a pastor, he had been used by the Lord to lead others to salvation many times, but he had always dreamed of doing evangelism in the Muslim world. Now—utterly unexpectedly—God had given recognition to Bob's faithfulness by granting him this surprise. Bob's story is a reminder that God may provide us with blessings "out of the blue" at a time when we are least expecting them.

Who would have thought that Cyrus would allow the Jews to return home so they could build a temple to God? How is it possible that this pagan king not only encouraged but insisted on the reinstitution of the worship of God? It was Cyrus's paganism (his belief that Marduk wanted him to make all gods happy) that triggered the edict for the Jews to return and rebuild the temple.

Cyrus's edict encourages us to remember that God may surprise us, often in dark situations, when we don't see a way out.

V. PRAYER

Lord Jesus, there is no question of our guilt before you, and that punishment of us is as justified as punishment for the kingdom of Judah. We thank you that, just as you allowed your people to return from exile, your grace is never far away from us. Amen.

VI. DEEPER DISCOVERIES

A. The Babylonians (36:6)

To say that Babylon was important to biblical history would be an understatement. But the kingdom that we associate with that name was actually very short-lived. As God declared to Habakkuk, he raised up Babylon as his agent of punishment, but it, in turn, would also be punished (Hab. 1:6; 2:8).

The first Babylonian kingdom succeeded Sumeria, which had been the dominant culture in southern Mesopotamia since the fourth millennium B.C. The Sumerians had a very advanced culture; they invented cuneiform writing, produced a system of mathematics based on the number sixty (rather than ten), and applied their mathematical insights to discoveries in geometry and astronomy. The Babylonians, though coming from a different background, adopted and transmitted much of Sumerian culture; in fact, our current practice of dividing the day into twenty-four hours consisting of sixty minutes each goes back to this ancient way of doing things. The best known king of ancient Babylon was Hammurabi, who in the eighteenth century B.C. created a famous code of law.

But Hammurabi's kingdom did not endure, and for about a thousand years kings and dynasties of various ethnic origins claimed the throne of Babylon. When the kings of Assyria created their empire, they went to great lengths to make themselves out as sovereigns of Babylon as well. It was Nebuchadnezzar's father, Nabopolassar, who finally reasserted an autonomous Babylonian kingdom.

Babylon shared many features with other ancient cultures. They worshiped numerous gods in the forms of idols, and they believed that specific gods were particularly at home in certain places or with certain people. In contrast to the Canaanite deities, which were preoccupied with virility and fertility, the Babylonians propagated the Sumerian tradition of focusing on celestial phenomena, such as the sun, moon, and stars, as gods. For example, the residents of Ur, the place from which Abraham came, were devoted to the moon god. Marduk, the highest god of the Babylonians, was originally only the main god for the city of Babylon. But he grew in stature along with Babylon's influence until he was considered the most powerful of all deities.

VII. TEACHING OUTLINE

A. INTRODUCTION

1. Lead Story: The Plane That Returned
2. Context: Josiah had a good reign, but he allowed it to be cut short by his foolhardy venture against Pharaoh Neco. He placed his kingdom right into the whirling propeller blades of three kingdoms—Assyria, Babylon, and Egypt—that were vying for world domination. His sons would reap the harvest of his foolish action and create their own problems with consistent disobedience to God.
3. Transition: Kathy certainly did not expect the plane to return to the airport and let her board, but it did. In the same way, one would not have expected Cyrus to release the Jews as soon as he came to power, but he did. Sometimes God extends his hand to us at the most surprising moments.

B. COMMENTARY

1. Jehoahaz, Short-Term King (36:1–3)
2. Jehoiakim, Evil King (36:4–8)
3. Jehoiachin, Short-Term King (36:9–10)
4. Zedekiah, the Last King (36:11–21)
5. Cyrus's Decree to Return (36:22–23)

C. CONCLUSION: PATCHING UP THE FOUNDATION

VIII. ISSUES FOR DISCUSSION

1. Was Nebuchadnezzar's sole reason for existence that he could serve as God's instrument of punishment?
2. Consider the idea that the kingdom of Judah had to submit to a foreign power. How does this differ from God's expectations of his peo-

ple earlier in history? How could they be sure that this was God's will for them?

3. What is the difference between *hope* and *optimism*? How do the two concepts apply in the context of Cyrus's decree to release the Jews?

Glossary

ark of the covenant—The chest containing the tablets of the Ten Commandments, kept in the holy of holies in the tabernacle and temple

Aram—A collection of various kingdoms located west of Mesopotamia, such as the kingdom of Damascus

Baal—Highest god of Canaanite religion; frequently associated with human sacrifice

Canaanites—Occupants of Palestine prior to the Israelite conquest and of the surrounding area, known for their sexually charged religious practices

Edomites—Descendants of Esau, living on the eastern side of the Jordan River in the vicinity of the Dead Sea, used synonymously with Mount Seir

Ephraim—(1) Younger son of Joseph, who became dominant, father of the tribe that bears his name; (2) the leading tribe of the Northern Kingdom, whose name is frequently used to represent the Northern Kingdom of Israel

idol—A physical object, usually in the shape of a person or an animal, thought to represent a god and to be indwelt by the deity

Israel—(1) The covenant name for Jacob, son of Isaac, father of the twelve sons who gave rise to the twelve tribes; (2) the name for all the people of God, usually used synonymously with the Hebrews, possibly also the Jews; (3) the ten tribes who became the Northern Kingdom, sometimes referred to as Ephraim

Judah—(1) Son of Jacob, founder of the tribe with his name; (2) the Southern Kingdom comprised of the tribes of Benjamin and Judah, whose capital was Jerusalem

Levite—A member of the tribe of Levi, designated by tribal heritage to serve the Lord in the context of the temple or the tabernacle; only a small group of Levites—the descendants of Aaron—could serve as priests

monotheism—The belief that there is only one God, as taught in the Bible

Philistines—People who settled in the southern part of Palestine (the region that still bears their name), enemies of Saul and David. After thorough subjugation, the Philistines gained power during the time of Ahaziah.

polytheism—The belief that there are many gods that should be worshiped

Glossary

priest—Someone who was professionally engaged in performing rituals that mediated between people and God; in the Old Testament, a descendant of Aaron who was permitted to perform sacrifices in the temple

prophet—A person who directly conveyed God's message to people, sometimes predicting future events, but more frequently communicating messages of judgment, used interchangeably with "seer" and "man of God"

Samaria—Capital city of the Northern Kingdom of Israel; destroyed by the Assyrians, it gave its name to the Gentiles ("Samaritans") imported into the region by Assyria

Sheba—Ancient kingdom in the southern part of the Arabian peninsula; it flourished during the time of Solomon; its queen visited Solomon

tabernacle—A tent, the designated place of worship in the Old Testament until the construction of the temple

temple—A fixed structure used for worship; in the Old Testament, the building in Jerusalem designated as the only legitimate place to offer sacrifices to God once it was built

Bibliography

Sources for Bible Exposition

Archer, Gleason. *Encyclopedia of Bible Difficulties.* Grand Rapids, Mich.: Zondervan Publishing House, 1982.

————. *A Survey of Old Testament Introduction.* Chicago: Moody Press, 1964.

Beecher, Willis J. "Chronicles." In *The International Standard Bible Encyclopedia.* Vol. 1. James Orr, ed. Grand Rapids, Mich.: Eerdmans, 1956.

Bennett, W. H. *An Exposition of the Books of Chronicles.* Minneapolis, Minn.: reprint 1983 (orig. 1908).

Bimson, John J., ed. *Baker Encyclopedia of Bible Places.* Grand Rapids, Mich.: Baker Book House, 1995.

Braun, Roddy. *1 Chronicles.* Word Biblical Commentary. Vol. 14. Waco, Tex.: Word Books, 1986.

Browning, Daniel C., Jr. "Assyria, History and Religion of." In *Holman Bible Dictionary.* Trent C. Butler, ed. Nashville, Tenn.: Holman, 1991.

Butler, Trent C., ed. *Holman Bible Dictionary.* Nashville, Tenn.: Holman Bible Publishers, 1991.

Coggins, R. J. *The First and Second Books of the Chronicles.* New York: Cambridge University Press, 1976.

Corduan, Winfried. *Shepherd's Notes: 1, 2 Chronicles.* Nashville, Tenn.: Broadman & Holman, 1998.

Crockett, William Day. *A Harmony of the Books of Samuel, Kings, and Chronicles.* Grand Rapids, Mich.: Baker, 1956.

Curtis, Edward Lewis, and Albert Alonzo Madsen, *The Book of Chronicles.* International Critical Commentary. Vol. 10. New York: Scribner's, 1910.

Dillard, Raymond D. *2 Chronicles.* Word Biblical Commentary. Vol. 15. Waco, Tex.: Word Books, 1987.

Easton, Burton Scott. "Zoroastrianism." In *The International Standard Bible Encyclopedia.* Vol. 4. James Orr, ed. Grand Rapids, Mich.: Eerdmans, 1956.

Easton, M. G. *Easton's Bible Dictionary.* Oak Harbor, Wash.: Logos Research Systems, Inc., 1997.

Gwaltney, William C., Jr. "Assyrians." In *Peoples of the Old Testament World.* Alfred Hoerth, Gerald L. Mattingly, and Edwin Yamauchi, eds. Grand Rapids, Mich.: Baker, 1994.

Bibliography

Henry, Matthew, *Matthew Henry's Concise Commentary on the Bible.* Oak Harbor, Wash.: Logos Research Systems, Inc., 1997.

Hercus, John. *God Is God: Samson and Other Case Histories from the Book of Judges.* London: Hodder and Stoughton, 1971.

————. *More Pages from God's Case-Book.* Downers Grove, Ill.: InterVarsity Press, 1965.

————. *Out of the Miry Clay.* Downers Grove, Ill.: InterVarsity Press, 1967.

————. *Pages from God's Case-Book.* Downers Grove, Ill.: InterVarsity Press, 1963.

Hoerth, Alfred, Gerald L. Mattingly, and Edwin Yamauchi, eds. *Peoples of the Old Testament World.* Grand Rapids, Mich.: Baker, 1994.

Hoffmeier, James K. "Egyptians." In *Peoples of the Old Testament World.* Alfred Hoerth, Gerald L. Mattingly, and Edwin Yamauchi, eds. Grand Rapids, Mich.: Baker, 1994.

Hoglund, Kenneth G. "Edomites." In *Peoples of the Old Testament World.* Alfred Hoerth, Gerald L. Mattingly, and Edwin Yamauchi, eds. Grand Rapids, Mich.: Baker, 1994.

Hooker, Paul K. *First and Second Chronicles.* Louisville, Ky.: Westminster John Knox Press, 2001.

House, Paul R. *Old Testament Theology.* Downers Grove, Ill.: InterVarsity Press, 1998.

Howard, David M. "Philistines." In *Peoples of the Old Testament World.* Alfred Hoerth, Gerald L. Mattingly, and Edwin Yamauchi, eds. Grand Rapids, Mich.: Baker, 1994.

Hunt, Harry. "Wisdom and Wise Men." In *Holman Bible Dictionary.* Trent C. Butler, ed. Nashville, Tenn.: Holman, 1991.

Hurlbut, Jesse Lyman. *A Bible Atlas.* New York: Rand McNally, 1910.

Japhet, Sara. *I and II Chronicles.* Old Testament Library. Louisville, Ky.: Westminster John Knox, 1993.

Millar, James. "Music." In *The International Standard Bible Encyclopedia.* Vol. 3. James Orr, ed. Grand Rapids, Mich.: Eerdmans, 1956.

Myers, Jacob M. *1 Chronicles. 2 Chronicles.* Anchor Bible. Garden City, N.Y.: Doubleday, 1965.

Payne, J. Barton. *I and II Chronicles.* In The Wycliffe Bible Commentary. Charles F. Pfeiffer and Everett F. Harrison, eds. Chicago: Moody Press, 1962.

Pitard, Wayne T. "Arameans." In *Peoples of the Old Testament World.* Alfred Hoerth, Gerald L. Mattingly, and Edwin Yamauchi, eds. Grand Rapids, Mich.: Baker, 1994.

Pritchard, James B., ed. *The Ancient Near East: An Anthology of Texts and Pictures.* Princeton, N.J.: Princeton University Press, 1958.

Purkiser, W. T. *Exploring the Old Testament.* Kansas City: Beacon Hill Press, 1955.

Queen-Sutherland, Kandy. "Music, Instruments, Dancing." In *Holman Bible Dictionary.* Trent C. Butler, ed. Nashville, Tenn.: Holman Bible Publishers, 1991.

Selman, Martin. *1 Chronicles. 2 Chronicles.* Downers Grove, Ill.: InterVarsity Press, 1994.

Thiele, Edwin R. *Mysterious Numbers of the Hebrew Kings.* Chicago: University of Chicago Press, 1955.

Thompson, J. A. *1, 2 Chronicles.* The New American Commentary. Nashville, Tenn.: Broadman & Holman, 1994.

Tisdall, W. St. Clair. "Persian Religion." In *The International Standard Bible Encyclopedia.* Vol. 4. James Orr, ed. Grand Rapids, Mich.: Eerdmans, 1956.

Tobias, Hugh. "Hiram." In *Holman Bible Dictionary.* Trent C. Butler, ed. Nashville, Tenn.: Holman Bible Publishers, 1991.

Unger, Merrill F., ed. *Unger's Bible Dictionary.* Chicago: Moody Press, 1966.

Walton, John H., Victor H. Matthews, and Mark W. Chavalas. *The IVP Bible Background Commentary: The Old Testament.* Downers Grove, Ill.: InterVarsity Press, 2000.

Ward, William A. "Phoenicians." In *Peoples of the Old Testament World.* Alfred Hoerth, Gerald L. Mattingly, and Edwin Yamauchi, eds. Grand Rapids, Mich.: Baker, 1994.

Wilcock, Michael. *1 and 2 Chronicles.* In New Bible Commentary: 21st Century Edition. D. A. Carson, R. T. France, J. A. Motyer, and G. J. Wenham, eds. Downers Grove, Ill.: InterVarsity Press, 1994.

_____. *The Message of Chronicles: One Church, One Faith, One Lord.* Downers Grove, Ill.: InterVarsity Press, 1987.

Wilson, Charles R. *First Chronicles. Second Chronicles.* In Wesleyan Bible Commentary. Vol. 2. Charles Carter, ed. Grand Rapids, Mich.: Eerdmans, 1967.

Yamauchi, Edwin. "Persians." In *Peoples of the Old Testament World.* Alfred Hoerth, Gerald L. Mattingly, and Edwin Yamauchi, eds. Grand Rapids, Mich.: Baker, 1994.

Sources for Enrichment and Illustrative Materials

Bainton, Roland H. *Here I Stand: A Life of Martin Luther.* Nashville, Tenn.: Abingdon Press, 1950.

Barth, Heinrich. *Travels and Discoveries in North and Central Africa: Being a Journal of an Expedition Undertaken Under the Auspices of H.R.M.'s Government in the Years 1849–1855.* London: Cass, reprinted 1965.

Bellamy, Patrick. "Carlos the Jackal: Trail of Terror" URL: http://www.geocities.com/kokalo69/carlos/carlos.html

Berkowitz, David. "Forgiven for Life!" Official Web page of David Berkowitz. URL: http://www.forgivenforlife.com/1a-testimony.html

Boyce, Mary. *Zoroastrians: Their Religious Beliefs and Practices.* London: Routledge & Kegan Paul, 1979.

Boyd, Malcolm. *Are You Running with Me, Jesus? Prayers.* New York: Holt, Rinehart, Winston, 1965.

Brand, Paul and Philip Yancey. *Pain: The Gift Nobody Wants.* Grand Rapids, Mich.: Zondervan, 1993.

Debo, Angie. *Geronimo: The Man, His Time, His Place.* Norman, Okla.: University of Oklahoma Press, 1976.

de Ramirez, Lori Langer. "Jataka Tales from India and Nepal." URL: http://www.columbia.edu/~ljl17/jatakas.html

Funderburk, Danny. "Biography." URL: http://www.dannyfunderburk.com/

Graham, Franklin, *Rebel with a Cause.* Nashville, Tenn.: Thomas Nelson, 1997.

Haley, Alex. *Roots: The Saga of an American Family.* New York: Dell, 1975.

Internet Movie Database. URL: http://www.imdb.com

Lewis, C. S. *The Last Battle.* In The Chronicles of Narnia. New York: Collier, 1956.

"Linen." *Webster's Interactive Encyclopedia.* Cambridge, Mass.: The Learning Company, 1996.

Linnemann, Eta. *Historical Criticism of the Bible: Methodology or Ideology.* Robert W. Yarbrough, trans. Grand Rapids, Mich.: Kregel, 2001.

Parada, Carlos. "Croesus: Between Myth and History." Greek Mythology Link. URL: http://homepage.mac.com/cparada/GML/Croesus.html

Preston, Douglas, and Lincoln Child. *The Ice Limit.* New York: Time Warner Books, 2000.

Ringenberg, William C. *Taylor University: The First 150 Years.* Grand Rapids, Mich.: Eerdmans, 1996.

Rousselow, Jessica L., and Alan H. Winquist, *God's Ordinary People: No Ordinary Heritage.* Upland, Ind.: Taylor University Press, 1996.

Rousselow-Winquist, Jessica L., and Alan H. Winquist. *Coach Odle's Full-Court Press*. Upland, Ind.: Taylor University Press, 2001.

Schweitzer, Albert. *Out of My Life and Thought: An Autobiography*. Baltimore, Md.: Johns Hopkins, 1998.

Suplee, Curt. *Everyday Science Explained*. Washington, D.C.: National Geographic Society, 1996.

Tuchman, Barbara W. *The March of Folly: From Troy to Vietnam*. New York: Ballantine Books, 1992.

Wilkinson, Bruce H. *The Prayer of Jabez: Breaking Through to the Blessed Life*. Sisters, Oreg.: Multnomah, 2000.

Wodehouse, P. G. *Quick Service*. New York: Doubleday, Doran & Co., 1940.